The Signifying Animal

ADVANCES IN SEMIOTICS
General Editor, Thomas A. Sebeok

THE
SIGNIFYING ANIMAL

The Grammar of Language and Experience

Edited by
Irmengard Rauch and Gerald F. Carr

Indiana University Press ~ *Bloomington*

"What Is a Language?" originally appeared in *Psycholinguistic Research: Past, Present, and Future,* edited by Doris Aaronson and Robert Rieber, © 1979 by Lawrence Erlbaum Associates. "Semantics and Pragmatics of Sentence Connectives in Natural Language" originally appeared in *Speech Act Theory and Pragmatics,* edited by Ferenc Kiefer and John Searle, © 1980 by D. Reidel Publishing Company.

Library of Congress Cataloging in Publication Data
Main entry under title:
The Signifying animal.
(Advances in semiotics)
Proceedings of a conference held June 28–30, 1978,
on the University of Illinois at Urbana-Champaign campus.
Includes bibliographies and index.
1. Semiotics—Congresses. 2. Language and languages—Congresses.
3. Linguistics—Congresses.
I. Rauch, Irmengard. II. Carr, Gerald F. III. Series.
P99.S494 401'.41 79-3624
ISBN 0-253-18496-7 1 2 3 4 5 84 83 82 81 80

Contents

CONTRIBUTORS

William P. Alston	University of Illinois
Raimo Anttila	University of California, Los Angeles
John N. Deely	Loras College
William Orr Dingwall	University of Maryland
Paul Ekman	University of California, San Francisco
Robert B. Lees	Tel-Aviv University
David McNeill	University of Chicago
Charles E. Osgood	University of Illinois
Roland Posner	Technische Universität, Berlin
Joseph Ransdell	Texas Tech University
Irmengard Rauch	University of California, Berkeley
David Savan	University of Toronto
Rulon S. Wells	Yale University

PREFACE

The papers contained in this volume represent in essence the proceedings of the conference on The Signifying Animal: The Grammar of Man's Language and of His Experiences, held from 28 to 30 June 1978 on the University of Illinois at Urbana-Champaign campus. The final paper is an additional contribution which speaks to the closing topic of the conference. The lead paper, "What Is Signifying?" although not presented at the conference, incorporates much of the rationale for the meeting, its central themes, and the immediate and ultimate goals as they were outlined to the National Endowment for the Humanities in seeking that agency's support. The conference organizers are grateful to the endowment for their generous support, which enabled them to assemble an international spectrum of scholars in the fields of linguistics, semiotics, philosophy, anthropology, and psychology.

Many individuals contributed to the success of the conference, particularly Thomas A. Sebeok. His advice during planning and his presentation, "A Semiotic Canter from Clever Hans to Signing Apes" (recently published as chapter 5 of *The Sign and Its Masters* [Austin: University of Texas Press, 1979]) bear witness to his enduring commitment to the discipline of semiotics and to the humane sciences in general.

Morton W. Weir, then Vice Chancellor for Academic Affairs at the University of Illinois, opened the conference. Several eminent University of Illinois faculty served as chairmen of the various sessions: Charles E. Caton of Philosophy, Robert B. Lees (Tel-Aviv) formerly of the Department of Linguistics, Frederic K. Lehman of Anthropology, and Howard S. Maclay of Communications Research. To them and in particular to Braj B. Kachru, Head of the Department of Linguistics and Director of the 1978 Linguistic Institute of the Linguistic Society of America, who chaired the opening session and gave unstintingly of his advice in the organization stages of the conference, we express our gratitude.

We further acknowledge the kind help of George Godfrey and G. Trevor Tunnicliff in providing an excellent sound system and recordings of the proceedings. The assistance of Lynne Bils, Barbara Greim, Warren Hapke, Wayne Harbert, Jürgen Högl, Michael Phillips,

Josephine Wilcock, Barbara Woodward, and Donna Zych will ever be highly valued. Finally we thank the University of Illinois, especially the George A. Miller Committee, the School of Humanities, the School of Social Sciences, the Departments of Anthropology, Linguistics, and Philosophy, as well as the Division of English as a Second Language for joining the sponsorship of the conference on The Signifying Animal.

What Is Signifying?

IRMENGARD RAUCH

I

From 28 to 30 June 1978 approximately two hundred persons, representing eighty-five institutions of higher learning and fifteen nations around the world, convened at the University of Illinois in Urbana-Champaign in order to bring into open and direct association the disciplines of semiotics and linguistics. The locus for this gathering of interested scholars and students was particularly felicitous, since the 1978 Linguistic Society of America Summer Institute was in session at Illinois in that period. Indisputably, the time for such a conference was ripe, in view of what appear to be the ever fading borders of certain allied humane sciences, in particular those of philosophy and linguistics, psychology and linguistics, and anthropology and linguistics, and, in turn, their probing research into the realms of the natural sciences.

Why then was semiotics chosen as a "cover" term for those sciences which were regarded as being juxtaposed to linguistics? That is, Why was this meeting not simply conceived as one concentrating on linguistics and its related sciences? The answer to this question is not a simple one. It resides within the very nature of the two disciplines of semiotics and linguistics, both in their noncontroversial characteristics and in their vigorously disputed properties. Linguistics in its tendency to be reductionistic ardently strives to contain its interests within the bounds of *language*, even at a time when the very definition of language is becoming increasingly elusive. Semiotics in its expansionistic tendencies claims, nevertheless, a unified object—the sign—whose better understanding is progressively strengthening the scientific underpinnings of this discipline. An alleged tug-of-war ensues then between these two disciplines, with the premier sign system *language* in the middle. But is this tug-of-war real?

1

A bond between contemporary semiotics and modern linguistics was assured by their common rebirth out of structuralism and indeed was determined by the inalienable position of language within semiotics. Charles Sanders Peirce, master of synthesis that he was, equated language with man, man with the sign, the sign with thought, and thus thought with man. Goudge interprets Peirce's equations as suggestive of the conclusion "that the major factor in the development of mind has been language. To the use of words and allied signs the human spirit owes its evolution" (1950:233). For Peirce the evolution of the human spirit is correlative to man's biological development; Goudge explains that "rational thought is held to have arisen in the course of the human animal's struggle to escape from a state of doubt and re-establish stable belief. Certain procedures of thinking prove themselves efficacious in this struggle, are repeated until they become fixed habits, and are eventually formulated by the logician as the principles of inference" (1950:128). Peirce underscores the fact that man's ability to hypothesize is instinctive, a product of nature, comparable to the instinct of any species of animal for feeding and breeding. Thus man as "The Signifying Animal" portrays in a few words the heart of Peircean phenomenology underlying semiotics. It shows language to be integral to thought, thought to man, and man to nature—elements welded into a framework eminently appropriate as a construct for effecting cross-fertilization between linguistics and its sister disciplines.

Many linguists and semioticians would be startled to learn that in 1978 Noam Chomsky, called "the greatest theoretical linguist of our time" by Bar-Hillel (1970:214), wrote that "the philosopher to whom I feel closest and whom I'm almost paraphrasing is Charles Sanders Peirce" (Chomsky 1979:71). However, Chomsky's turn to Peirce can only surprise those unaware of the history of the independent, parallel, complementary, and mutual developments in linguistic method and in semiotic method. If we suppose recent semiotic history to begin with Peirce and with Ferdinand de Saussure, we can perhaps uncover some of the seeds of the seeming tug-of-war between linguistics and semiotics with the reawakening of semiotics in the nineteenth and early twentieth centuries. Saussure was first and foremost interested in defining the linguistic sign, and he saw the understanding of it as the key to unraveling all other semiological systems, while Peirce did not base his sign system on any particular modality. Subsequently, linguistic literature is filled with references to the primacy of linguistics in semiotics, such as the claim by Leonard Bloomfield, another linguistic leader of the century, "Linguistics is the chief contributor to semiotic" (1939:55).

Not only was the association of linguistics with semiotics culti-vated, but the indispensable presence of language in life was stressed, with the understanding of language as the object of linguistics. By im-plication, the verbal language of humans within the life of humans was thus stressed. As is to be expected then, from another spokesman of this century's linguistic heritage, Edward Sapir, we hear, "Every cul-tural pattern and every single act of social behavior involve human communication in an explicit or implicit sense. . . . Language is the communication process par excellence in every known society . . ." (1931[1958]:104–105).

The central position of language was advocated in nonlinguistic circles as well. Claude Lévi-Strauss, in formulating a concept of society with an integrated theory of communication consisting of the exchange of messages, of goods, and of mates, observed that "language comes into play at all levels" (1963:83), while Julia Kristeva wrote that "the *major constraint* affecting any social practice lies in the fact that it sig-nifies, i.e., that it is articulated *like* a language" (1975:47).

It is likely that this increasing momentum to viewing language within semiotics as an analog to language within linguistics has exacer-bated the tug-of-war between the two disciplines. On the semiotic side there result widespread speculation and doubt about the existence of a unified method; and linguistics, for its part, is concerned that a grad-ual erosion of precision and rigor in its approach may take place. This bewildering state of semiotic and linguistic affairs prompted another of the twentieth century's giants, claimed rightfully by both disciplines, Thomas A. Sebeok, to say: "The subject matter of linguistics, as we all 'know,' is communication consisting of verbal messages and the under-girding verbal code enabling them. By contrast, the concept of non-verbal communication is one of the most ill defined in all of semiotics" (1977:1065).

II

The declaration of Sebeok confining linguistics, although not lin-guists, to verbal language, and, in turn, laying bare the indeterminate state of nonverbal communication represents a sobering moment in this history which we have been describing. It brings to a sudden halt the territorial struggle between semiotics and linguistics, for the striking clarity of Sebeok's conviction provokes researchers on both sides to reassess their positions. The researchers who convened to address the grammar of language and experience at the conference on The Sig-nifying Animal were essentially confronted with the task of answering the singular question, What is signifying? that is, What does it mean to signify and what sort of agent does the signifying?

To address this question, the working plan of the meeting was constructed around six particular topics. The opening session focused directly on the problem of the nature of language. Charles E. Osgood, in "What Is a Language?" aims to answer, "How would one identify something as *a language* if he encountered what *might* be one in an obviously nonhuman species? . . . for that matter, is the natural signing of deaf-mutes a language? The game of chess? And what about the 'language' of music or art?" (p. 9). These questions posed by Osgood indicate the leitmotiv of the conference. Osgood for his part undertakes to consider them by proposing a definition of language. Indeed, he hypothesizes a definition of language consisting of six criteria general enough for measuring communication in several species; assesses various animals for possession of language; and concludes a total no for the clam, a partial yes for the bird and the dog, and a solid yes for the bee and the ape. Ten additional characteristics, five structural and five functional, are minimally necessary for a language to cross the threshold into being a strictly human language. Besides these sixteen universal features, Osgood postulates a set of five nondefining traits of human language, without which a language would still be considered human but nevertheless "rather strange" (p. 27).

William Orr Dingwall, in "Human Communicative Behavior: A Biological Model," deals a further blow to traditional definitions of language. In studying communicative behavior as a biological function, Dingwall concludes that "the determination whether one communicates in a human manner cannot be made in absolute terms; rather, some gradient measure must be employed" (p. 78), and he designs six biologically based features against which he measures nonhuman and human primates and normal and abnormal humans, both adults and children. Significantly then, the two linguists Osgood and Dingwall approach a Peircean semiotics in extending the domain of language possibilities to include nonhuman species.

The second conference topic considered the language act, which, by consisting of an organism that produces an expression in order to refer by the expression to something, correlates to the *semiotic act*, comprising an interpretant, a sign, and an object, that, in turn, correlate to the triad pragmatics, syntax, and semantics, respectively. The reformulation of the definition of language is particularly conducive to constructing linguistic descriptions pragmatistically; indeed this was clearly demonstrated by the fact that papers presenting linguistic data around the second topic turned to pragmatics. Thus, Roland Posner, in explaining the "Semantics and Pragmatics of Sentence Connectives in

Natural Language," shows, on the basis of primarily English examples, the indispensable role played by larger linguistic context and by extra-linguistic context.

It would seem that the so-called linguistic sentence, that is, a sentence descriptively self-sufficient within its own immediate confines, is dead—not a minor matter in the history of modern linguistic method. In fact, the conceptual dependence of semantics on pragmatics is understood so clearly by William P. Alston in "The Bridge between Semantics and Pragmatics" that he states it in the form of a "Use Principle," followed by the identification of the meaning of a sentence in terms of his postulated "Illocutionary-Act-Potential Thesis". The pragmatic turn in linguistics certainly mirrors, albeit still somewhat dimly, the semiotic attitude toward words and sentences which is grounded in Peircean pragmatism—a tradition in the light of which Carnap proclaims: *"pragmatics is the basis for all of linguistics"* (1959:13).

Appropriately, the third topic considered by the conference went to the core of Peirce's method of observing all phenomena, of which language of course is one, namely, Firstness, Secondness, Thirdness—the all-pervasive categories in his cognitive procedure. For Peirce "the entire universe . . . is . . . composed exclusively of signs" (*CP*5.448n) whose "most fundamental division" (*CP*2.275) is effected by the trichotomy icon, index, symbol, correlating to his phenomenological categories, respectively. The icon, the index, and the symbol correlate back to the sign, the object, and the interpretant, respectively, since they are obviously a First, a Second, and a Third, in that order. Peirce's elegant superstructure is elucidated by Joseph Ransdell in his comparison of "Semiotic and Linguistics." Ransdell understands the essence of signs, and therefore words, to reside basically not in their use, but in their using, that is, *in their doing*, and he shows how the life of a sign or a word is ultimately explicated by the icon/index/symbol distinction.

In discussing the category "Thirdness and Linguistics," Rulon S. Wells highlights additional properties of language, specifically its creative aspects and its constraining aspects, to which he finds an analog in art. Both the rules of language and the rules of art are Thirds, but they differ from the rules of nature, which are also Thirds, in that the latter are laws rather than rules, in a strict sense. The distinction between rule and law is vital to the axiomatic method by which the interpretation of signs takes place—a topic which fittingly formed part of the final session (see below). The present session served well to underscore the trichotomous epistemological nature of Peirce's model in distinction to the strongly dichotomous model of Saussure.

The fourth conference topic exploited another contrast between the linguistically based and the philosophically based nineteenth-twentieth century traditions of semiotics, namely, a semiotics particular to human language and its immediate modalities, and a semiotics general to all communication, the former indicative of the Saussurean convention, the latter of the Peircean. Accordingly, the fourth topic sought out the *language-inlay* in nonverbal communication. John N. Deely, in a stunning reverse approach to the topic, opens with "The Nonverbal Inlay in Linguistic Communication." Deely posits a prelinguistic zoo-semiotic level of experience common to both man and higher anthropoids, a level of experience which can yield postlinguistic sociocultural institutions only by passing through a language layer. Thus, while the philosopher Deely is magnifying the crucial role of language, he is simultaneously presenting the nongeneral view of language, which would equate it with linguistics.

All the more stunning then, in contrast, is the paper of the linguist Robert B. Lees, "Language and the Genetic Code," which entertains the analog of the language of the mind to the language of the cell. In maintaining that "the mind arose and evolved in parallel fashion, aided by the invention of an internal representation system, language, in much the same way that biological evolution was aided by the invention of the genetic code" (p. 218), Lees echoes Peirce's understanding of the evolution of the human mind (see sect. I above). With Peirce, Lees might fittingly conclude: "It is somehow more than a mere figure of speech to say that nature fecundates the man with ideas which, when those ideas grow up, will resemble their father, Nature" (*CP*5.592).

The strong analog of language to biology continued into the fifth topic of the conference, which expanded the *language-inlay* to *language-likeness* in all of animate existence. Paul Ekman, in designing a system to describe "Facial Signals," suggests the possibility that facial actions as conversational signals derive their specific role from their biological function. Whereas raising the brows enlarges the visual field, lowering them diminishes it. As he observes: "It seems consistent for a movement which increases vision to be employed in greetings, exclamations, and question marks, and for a movement which decreases vision to be employed in calls-for-information, and in emphasis marks and question marks where there is some uncertainty or difficulty" (p. 237). Differing from Ekman, who considers conversational facial actions with speech and without speech, David McNeill concentrates on the interlacing of motor action with speech. In "Iconic Relationships between Language and Motor Action," McNeill implies that the long-disregarded symbiosis of language and motor action is of such an extent that the universal grammar of language is adapted according to that relationship. Obviously, this contention introduces a further parameter in the definition of language, and McNeill holds that confirmation of his theory depends on the thorough investigation of the affinity between language and thought.

The closing topic, language at the crossroads of linguistics and semiotics, elicited papers which exploit Peirce's theory of how we reason, how we introduce new ideas. The conference has finally come full circle in the "cover" discipline, semiotics, proceeding from the nature of language through the tools of semiotic to the nature of thought, which interlocks again with language (see sect. I above). For Peirce, the mind is commensurate with cognition through the laws of inference; it is equal to the continual interpretation of signs and, therefore, "all thought whatsoever is a sign, and is mostly of the nature of language" (Peirce 1955:258). It is for the theory of inference, specifically abduction, that the Peircean model finds an advocate in the linguist Chomsky (see sect. I above). Strikingly, Saussurean semiotic tradition takes a turn toward formalized language in the history of linguistics through the application of Peircean abduction to linguistic problems. While David Savan in his paper "Abduction and Semiotics" chose an Old Czech sound change as data for elucidating the subtleties of the three types of reasoning, Raimo Anttila in "Language and the Semiotics of Perception" applies the Peircean categories Firstness, Secondness, and Thirdness, which have correlates in abduction, induction, and deduction, respectively, to general linguistic concepts such as phoneme, morpheme, and allophonic variation. With regard to allophonic variation, Anttila asks "Why would such a disturbing agent be the rule in the languages of the world?" (p. 275). He answers that language perception, to which abduction is integral, feeds upon variation, and that "[t]hrough this variation, phonemes absorb signals of individuals, emotional states, geographical regions, and social strata" (p. 276). The final paper of this volume, "Between Linguistics and Semiotics: Paralanguage," has been added to the conference collection as an example of phonological variation signaling geographical region. Such variation is not unusual for linguistics; what is unusual is the fact that this paper uncovers a unique type of verbal communication, that of a dead language whose primary characteristic lies in the twilight zone between linguistics and semiotics.

The tug-of-war between linguistics and semiotics (see sect. I above) appears negligible, perhaps only a mirage, after one has viewed the amalgam of autonomous but dependent disciplines which emerge from the papers of the conference on The Signifying Animal: The Grammar of Man's Language and of His Experiences. That these two humane sciences, as demonstrated in this conference, have the ability to harness, albeit to varying degrees, a common object, is all the more remarkable in view of the fact that the common object, communication, represents, in Sebeok's words, "the capacity . . . that distinguishes living beings from inanimate substances" (1978:20). To signify then, is ultimately to be alive.

REFERENCES

Bar-Hillel, Y. 1970. *Aspects of language*. Jerusalem: Magnes Press, Hebrew University.

Bloomfield, L. 1939. *Linguistic aspects of science*. International encyclopedia of unified science, vol. 1, no. 4. Chicago: University of Chicago Press.

Carnap, R. 1959. *Introduction to semantics*. Cambridge: Harvard University Press.

Chomsky, N. 1979. *Language and responsibility*. J. Viertel, trans. New York: Pantheon.

Goudge, T. A. 1950. *The thought of C. S. Peirce*. New York: Dover.

Kristeva, J. 1975. The system and the speaking subject. In *The tell-tale sign: a survey of semiotics*, T. A. Sebeok, ed., 47–55. Lisse: Peter de Ridder Press.

Lévi-Strauss, C. 1963. *Structural anthropology*. C. Jacobson and B. G. Schoepf, trans. New York: Basic Books.

Peirce, C. S. 1931–58. *Collected papers of Charles Sanders Peirce*. Vols. 1–6, C. Hartshorne and P. Weiss, eds.; vols. 7–8, A. W. Burks, ed. Cambridge: Harvard University Press.

————. 1955. *Philosophical writings of Peirce*. J. Buchler, ed. New York: Dover.

Sapir, E. 1931. Communication. In *Selected writings of Edward Sapir in language, culture and personality*, D. G. Mandelbaum, ed., 104–9. Berkeley: University of California Press, 1958. (Reprinted from *Encyclopedia of the social sciences*, vol. 4, 78–81. New York: Macmillan, 1931.)

Sebeok, T. A. 1977. Zoosemiotic components of human communication. In *How animals communicate*, T. A. Sebeok, ed., 1055–77. Bloomington: Indiana University Press.

————. 1978. "Talking" with animals: zoosemiotics explained. *Animals*, December 1978, pp. 20–23, 36.

TOPIC **I** *Defining Language*

What Is a Language?

CHARLES E. OSGOOD

What is a language? You may well be wondering why I ask this question when everyone *knows* what a language is—it's what you're expressing and I'm comprehending, you say. Let's change the question's form a bit: How would one identify something as *a language* if he encountered what *might* be one in an obviously nonhuman species—for example, flowing kaleidoscopic color patterns on the bulbous bodies of octopus-like creatures who land in a spaceship right in one's own backyard? And, for that matter, is the natural signing of deaf-mutes a language? The game of chess? And what about the "language" of music or art? Or suppose that pale, eyeless midgets were discovered in extended caverns far below the present floors of the Mammoth Cave—emitting very high-frequency pipings from their rounded mouths and apparently listening with their enormous, rotatable ears. How might one decide whether or not these cave midgets have an identifiably *humanoid language?* Only if one can say what defines a language in general and defines a human language in particular can he go on to offer possible answers to some other, very important, questions: Do certain nonhuman animals "have" a language? What is common to prelinguistic cognizing and linguistic sentencing? When does a developing child "have" a language? How may languages have developed in the human species? Answers to all these questions, of course, would have relevance to the basic issue of universals and uniqueness in human communication.

Reprinted from *Psycholinguistic Research: Implications and Applications*, edited by Doris Aaronson and Robert W. Rieber, © 1979 by Lawrence Erlbaum Associates, Inc.

I. DEFINING CHARACTERISTICS
OF LANGUAGE GENERALLY

If anything is to be called "a language," it must satisfy the following criteria: It must (1) involve identifiably different and nonrandomly recurrent physical forms in some communication channel, (2) these forms being producible by the same organisms that receive them, their use (3) resulting in nonrandom dependencies between the forms and the behaviors of the organisms that employ them, (4) following nonrandom rules of reference to events in other channels and (5) nonrandom rules of combination with other forms in the same channel, with (6) the users capable of producing indefinitely long and potentially infinite numbers of novel combinations that satisfy the first five criteria.[1] Now, with our Octopian visitors (from the planetary system of the nearest star, Arcturus, as was later discovered) particularly in mind, I will elaborate a bit on these criteria for something being "a language" in general.

1. The Nonrandom Recurrency Criterion: *Production of identifiably different and nonrandomly recurrent physical forms in some communication channel.* A few years ago there was quite a flurry of excitement over apparently nonrandom, recurrent signals being received over interstellar radio receivers—was it something unusual in sunspot activity or, possibly, communication attempts from some distant form of intelligent life? (As I recall, the decision was in favor of sunspots!) As far as ordinary communication is concerned, humans have opted for the vocal-auditory channel (for reasons that will be considered a bit later), but there are many other possible channels that we *are* aware of, because we have also these sensory modalities (light-visual, pressure, tactile and chemical-odor, at which dogs seem particularly adept), and many others that we are *not* aware of (e.g., radiant wavelengths above or below the visible-to-humans range)—and what about ESP? The only critical thing is that such signals be combined in nonrandom ways to produce energy *forms* that are identifiably different (using special equipment if necessary) and are themselves nonrandom in distribution in time and/or space. Note that there is no requirement that the forms be discretely digital (as is generally the case for human languages); they could be continuously analogic in nature.

Back in our own backyard, having recovered from the shock, and being convinced that our octopus-like visitors intend us no harm, we note that as one Octopian pirouettes slowly, with its whole bulbous body flowing with multicolored visual forms, the other stands "silently" neutral gray—only to begin displaying and turning when the first has become "silent." We begin to think that this *may* be some form of communication—not merely displays of emotional states as in the "blushing" of the chameleon.

2. The Reciprocality Criterion: *These forms being producible by the same organisms that receive them.* It is difficult to imagine a human society in which, say, women were the only ones who could produce language (but not comprehend it, even from other women) and men could only comprehend language (but not produce it). For one thing, knowing what we do about the intimate interactions between comprehending and expressing in the development of language in children, one would be hard put to account for the development of such a system. But what about communication between species? Yucca plants and Yucca moths certainly interact for their common survival, but one would hardly call this communication; the "language of flowers" is only a euphemism—we humans can't smell back! But what about mule drivers and their mules? There is no question but that there is communication here, even though the mule can only "kick" back when ornery, but obviously the same organisms are not both producing and receiving the same forms—indicating clearly that communication is not the same as language. Noting that some of the flowing visual forms produced by Octopian A are reproduced in apparent "response" by Octopian B, always along with some uninterpretable contextual variations—and observing this systematically later with color movie films—we become convinced that this may, indeed, be some kind of language.

3. The Pragmatic Criterion: *Use of these forms resulting in nonrandom dependencies between the forms and the behaviors of the organisms that employ them.* This criterion applies most testably to the recipients of messages (behaving in appropriately differential fashion to signals received), but also to the initiators of messages (displaying a nonrandom tendency to communicate about entities and events that are proximal in other channels—see criterion 4 below). This is really the criterion that there *is* communication going on. Except for obviously representational art and music—and for purely affective reactions —this criterion would seem to rule out anything other than euphemistic use of phrases like "the language of art" or "the language of music." There is no doubt that bright dogs (like my poodle, Pierre!) develop a large repertoire of appropriate behaviors dependent upon the verbal commands of their masters (e.g., fetching his bone rather than his ball when requested "go getcha *bone*").

Note, however, that there is no implication here that pragmatic dependencies must be acquired through experience (learning), although this is clearly the case for human languages. In the language of the bees, when the observing bees in the hive fly the distance and direction signaled by the returned dancing bees, this satisfies the pragmatic criterion

—albeit on an innate, "wired-in" basis. What, then, about communication between a human master and a completely "wired-in" *computer* servant? I would argue that this meets the pragmatic criterion (see Winograd, 1972, for a nice example)—but obviously not others (particularly criterion 6, combinatorial productivity). And what about our Octopian friends? Satisfaction of this criterion would be indicated by, for example, a certain color pattern in Octopian A being conditionally dependent upon the presence in front of their spaceship of some complicated scanning device and, when accompanied by various contextual color patterns, by behaviors with respect to this device (shifting its orientation, taking it back into the ship) on the part of Octopian B.

4. The Semantic Criterion: *Use of these forms following nonrandom rules of reference to events in other channels.* This criterion implies that for anything to be a language it must function so as to *symbolize* (represent for the organism) the non-necessarily-*here* and not-necessarily-*now*. Although such representing relations are clearly acquired via learning by humans, the language of the bees again tells us that this is not necessarily the case—their dance, upon returning to the hive, does symbolize the not-here (source of nectar) and the not-now (to be found at some indicated flying time in the near future) on a purely innate basis. This criterion is clearly *not* met by the game of chess (where the pieces, despite their names and their moves, bear no symbolizing relation to anything other than themselves) *or* by the "game" of mathematics (where the symbols are deliberately abstract and bear no necessary relations to anything in the real world, but by virtue of this property are *potentially* relatable to any set of real-world entities). Even in humans, semantic relations are not necessarily arbitrary: there is *onomatopoeia* (the name of a thing or event being based on its characteristic sound, e.g., *cuckoo, cough, hiss, slap* and *wheeze* in English) and there is *phonetic symbolism* (in my classes I like to ask the male students which blind date they would prefer, Miss *Pim*, Miss *Bowloaf*, or Miss *Lavelle*, and then to describe her probable appearance).

Forms in a language can also be *iconic*—witness much of the natural signing of the deaf as well as the gestural accompaniments by ordinary speakers (e.g., in describing my "blind dates" above)—and *this*, we come to infer, might well be the case, at least in part, for our Octopians: we noted that, on the first appearance of Pierre the poodle in our yard, there was a silvery blob followed by a rising line on Octopian A (possibly a question?—"what on earth [sic!] is that?") answered by a nondescript wobbly fuzz figuring near the bottom of Octopian B's bulbous body (possibly meaning, "I haven't the foggiest idea!"). Later, after we demonstrated feeding doggie biscuits to Pierre, taken from a box (for which one Octopian extended a multiple "fingered" tentacle in request—which needless to say we honored), the appearance of Pierre would produce exchanges of silvery blobs, plus some angular pattern, and one Octopian would slip into the ship and reappear with the box of doggie biscuits. And still later they would "call for" an absent Pierre with his "blob" (and that rising line pattern)—and Pierre in turn quickly learned to come to beg the Octopians for biscuits!

5. The Syntactic Criterion: *Use of these forms following nonrandom rules of combination with other forms in the same channel.* As will be seen, all human languages may be characterized as being *hierarchical* in structure (analyzable in terms of units-within-units); they are also organized *temporally on a "left-to-right" basis*—that is, from prior to subsequent forms at all levels—as a necessary consequence of their utilization of the vocal-auditory channel. But these by no means must be defining characteristics of language in general, and one wonders to what extent space could be substituted for time in the organization of messages by organisms using other channels. Presumably there would be some limit—for example, we might discover (although the "how" of this is not as obvious as with the preceding criteria) that the Octopians "flash" the equivalents of whole paragraphs on their N "panels" as they rotate in the process of communicating, the within-paragraph information being spatially represented—"sentences" thus being an unessential carving up of the information flow (I might note that whole paragraphs, consisting of a single sentence, multiply conjoined and embedded, are not exactly a rarity in, particularly, scholarly writing!). The diverse recursive devices (e.g., as in center-embedded sentencings like *the man the girl the teacher likes married plays poker*) might be entirely unnecessary in a spatially organized language like Octopian.

And yet *some* structuring, representing what is "natural" in sentencing based on prelinguistic cognizing experience—for Octopian "squidsters" just as for human youngsters—might be expected for all organismic languages. For humans, the two basic types of simple cognition appear to be Action and Stative Relations (and both in SVO order), the former highlighting the typically $^+$Animate Actor as subject as against the typically $^-$Animate (or at least relatively passive) Recipient as object and the latter highlighting the $^+$Salient Figure as subject against the $^-$Salient Ground as object—thus *Pierre chased the ball* and *the ball was on the grass* as simple Action and Stative cognitions respectively.[2]

After having mastered some of the pragmatics and semantics of Octopian, we might study our video-tapes with such Naturalness Principles in mind. For examples: are the visual patterns centered on a "panel" (e.g., the silvery "Pierre" blob) characteristically representations of the more animate and/or figural entities, and the other blobs with which they are diversely linked radially by angular lines (verb phrases?) characteristically the less animate and/or figural? Is there some spatial ordering discernible for several sets of "conjoined" radial patterns involving same or different centered "topics," and does this ordering typically fit our human notions of naturalness in ordering?

6. The Combinatorial Productivity Criterion: *The users of the forms being capable of producing indefinitely long and potentially infinite numbers of novel combinations that satisfy the first five criteria.* At any particular time, synchronically, this novelty in human language lies in the combining and not in what is combined; thus, my statements about the Octopians' linguistic behaviors, although entirely novel as wholes (I presume), utilized thoroughly familiar lexemes (criterion 4) and constructions (criterion 5) in contemporary American English. However, it must be admitted that anyone who has done an analysis of the semantics and syntactics of telephone conversations comes away rather unimpressed with the combinatorial productivity of ordinary speakers using ordinary language. Of course over time, diachronically, human languages do display adaptive changes by both expanding the lexicon (criterion 4) and by changing the rules (criterion 5). Presumably, any organismic language would display such adaptivity—either via evolution over very long periods (for languages with innately based semantics and syntax, like that of the bees) or via learning over relatively short periods, dependent upon changing environmental conditions (for languages with individually acquired semantics and syntax, as happens with human cultures and languages in contact).

Testing for the presence of this combinatorial productivity (criterion 6) in another language—particularly a very strange one like Octopian—would undoubtedly be most difficult. Although nearly all of the communicative exchanges among the Octopians, and between them and ourselves, would seem novel in whole or in part *to us*, that would be no proof that they were not elaborately stereotyped patterns, analogous to most human telephone conversations. Only after we had mastered *their* language to the point where *we* could compose Octopian statements of indubitable novelty for them (and see if they comprehended them) and ask questions requiring indubitably novel answers (and see if they could produce them), could we determine if they had this crucial capability. And—horror of horrors!—we might discover that they did *not*, that they were entirely "programmed" like computers, and in fact were *robots* sent out by the real Arcturians, whatever they might be like. However, one thing this little experiment by Arcturians would have demonstrated is this: if two species each have a language by these criteria, then either directly (or mediately, via appropriate equipment) they should be able to communicate to some extent with each other; the extent and direction would depend on the amount and balance of intelligence, that organism with the lower channel capacity determining the limit on communication (the dog in effect setting limits for the master).

A. DO ANY OTHER, NONHUMAN, ANIMALS HAVE A LANGUAGE?

One can trace a continuum of levels of interorganismic communication: from *proximal interactions* (contacting, mating, mothering, fighting and . . . consuming!), though *distal SIGNAL sending and receiving* (unintentional odors such as the bitch in heat, mating calls, baboon warning and food-supply noises), through *distal SIGN sending and receiving* (intentional expression of affect, like growls, tail waggings, postural and facial expressions designed to influence the behavior of the receiver), to *SYMBOL creating and interpreting* (the food-supply dance of the bees, "play" in dogs and other higher animals, referential gesturings by chimps and humans). For any given species, we can ask, *does its intraspecies communication satisfy the six criteria for something to be a language?* Take the *clam*—which, if anything, seems to have specialized *away* from communication in its evolution: because, as far as I know, there is no evidence for clam-to-clam non-random recurrence of signals in any channel (criterion 1)—and, given the limited motility and reactive capacity ("neck" retracting, shell clamping, and . . . ?), it seems likely that communication would be limited to chemical broadcasts at most (unless the clam has been fooling us and specializes in the development of ESP!). If criterion 1 is not satisfied, of course, then none of the others (reciprocality, pragmatics, semantics, syntax, or combinatorial productivity) can be met. The answer to whether this species has a language is, in a clam shell, no! So let's move along up the evolutionary tree.

a. The Bee. Briefly (necessarily),[3] the bee communicates three species-significant things: *showing its pass-badge* (a scent pouch that is opened on entering the hive and, if the scent is wrong—execution); *location of a nectar supply* (the well-known "dance," whose angle with respect to the sun indictaes direction, whose number of turns per unit time indicates distance, and whose number of abdomen wags indicates quality of the supply); *location of a new "home"* (a kind of "election" in which, when local supplies have dwindled, that returning bee which gets the crowd at home to follow his dance—usually the one that has found the richest load, has had to fly the shortest distance back, and hence is the most energetic—ends up with the whole hive flying off to his new location). Because the dance forms are obviously nonrandom, because any worker bee functions equivalently as sender or receiver, because behaviors of both are nonrandomly dependent upon the messages, and because the forms have nonrandom rules of reference (to the not-here and not-now nectar locations), criteria 1–4 appear to be clearly met. As far as syntactic criterion 5 is concerned, because the messages involve three types of forms (direction, distance, and quality indicating) that must be combined in certain nonrandom ways, this would seem to be met. But what about criterion 6, the combinatorial-productivity criterion? For any given bee "speaker" or bee "listener," a given combination of direction, distance, and quality indicators must often be novel, yet communication is successful. So we conclude that, within very narrow limits of what can be communicated, "the language of the bee" is not a euphemism—and, most remarkably, it is entirely innate ("wired in").

b. The Bird. The varied calls of the many subspecies of birds (which must be acquired, particularly during an early "imprinting" stage) are sufficient evidence for satisfying criterion 1 (nonrandom recurrency of forms), and the back-and-forth callings that awaken us so pleasantly in the early mornings of spring are evidence for satisfaction of criterion 2 (reciprocality). In the bird-to-bird communication of crows, for example, their "alarm" and "assemble" calls are evidence for at least rudimentary pragmatics and semantics (criteria 3 and 4)—and there are even crow "dialects" (taped *alarm* calls of American crows have been shown to produce *assembling* on the part of French crows!)—but these are essentially absent in bird-to-man communication. Given criteria 1 and 2, plus use of the vocal-auditory channel, one can teach some birds (e.g., parrots, parakeets, myna birds) to talk "human" in limited ways, but these appear to be purely imitative, sensory and motor integrations—meaningless, without expressing representational significances and intentions. I well remember in the early 1950s a research assistant of O. Hobart Mowrer spending many months and thousands of trials trying to get a talkative myna bird to say something like "wanna-eat" and "wanna-drink" (both in its imitative vocabulary) *differentially* for seeds vs. water, when made hungry vs. thirsty and shown the appropriate reinforcers—with never a significant shift from pure chance performance. So the bird appears to be strong on criteria 1 and 2 and weak on 3 and 4, with both 5 (syntax) and 6 (combinatorial productivity) totally lacking—talking birds repeat phrases as wholes, never piecing together parts of different phrases to make new combinations.

c. The Dog. This species might almost be said to have developed "writing" before "talking," because it seems to depend more on persistent (odor) than evanescent (visual or auditory) *denotative* signs—everytime I return to the house, my Pierre has to lift up and sniff my hand, just to make *sure* it's me! However, in dog-to-dog (as well as dog-to-human) communication, connotative meanings (primitive affective Evaluation, Potency and Activity, also found to be universal in human languages—see Osgood, May, and Miron, 1975) are richly displayed and reacted to in gestural-vision and vocal-auditory channels, the dog's tail being a particularly expressive organ: up vs. down signaling the Pleasantness, rigid vs. limp, the Forcefulness, and moving vs. stationary, the Liveliness of the animal's affective states. Dogs can acquire extensive repertoires of differential significances for human-produced signs through training, either formal (for hunting or circus performance) or informal (as pets), and this definitely satisfies both pragmatic (3) and semantic (4) criteria. Thus, in contrast with the bird, the dog is weak on criteria 1 and 2 (dependent on what I call the Integrational Level of behavior) but strong on 3 and 4 (dependent on the representational level). But, like the bird, the dog does not satisfy 5 (syntax) and at best only minimally meets 6 (combinatorial productivity)—and that only in comprehending (e.g., behaving appropriately to the pivot phrase "pick up" plus a new object name like "your leash").

d. The Ape. I use this term to refer to nonhuman, but close-to-human primates—rather than the *chimp*—because others have been shown to have similar capabilities (e.g., recently the gorilla). I will also concentrate on the Gardners' Washoe (R. A. Gardner & B. T. Gardner, 1969; B. T. Gardner & R. A. Gardner, 1975) rather than the Premacks' Sarah (D. Premack, 1971; A. J. Premack & D. Premack, 1972). The laboratory research with Sarah (comprehending sentence-like vertical sequences of plastic symbols and behaving appropriately; producing plastic sentence-like sequences of her own and being differentially reinforced) demonstrates the astonishingly complex cognitive capacity of a chimpanzee: ability to signal the "sameness" or "difference" of object pairs, that symbol X is or is not "the name of" various presented real objects (bananas, apples, etc.), responding appropriately to "clause" pairs conjoined by an "if–then" symbol (e.g., SARAH TAKE APPLE ("if–then") MARY GIVE CHOCOLATE SARAH / MARY NO GIVE CHOCOLATE SARAH), and so forth. However, whether this represents comprehension and production of *sentences* or "simply" complex, differentially reinforced reactions remains obscure (usually only a single set of alternative responses was required on any given problem). And although there is ample evidence for semantics and pragmatics, there is little for syntax or combinatorial productivity.[4] In any case, Sarah's would be a highly arbitrary *written* "language" rather than the gestural–vocal one natural for the chimpanzee.

Prior to the Gardners' work with Washoe, several psychologists (e.g. the Kelloggs' Gua and the Hayes' Viki) had also brought up an infant chimpanzee in their home as they would a child of their own, but the only attempts at "language" seemed to be to teach the ape to talk human—and they failed miserably (Viki ended up with about four imperfectly produced simple words like "papa" and "cup"). Given the lack of hemispheric dominance in nonhuman primates, which is critical for voluntary control over the medially located speech apparatus, this failure was not at all surprising. The decision to bring a chimp up in a human environment, *but with constant exposure to the natural sign language of the deaf-mute*, was long overdue, and one of the most exciting developments in decades resulted.[5] Facial, manual and postural gesturings, along with strong tendencies to imitate, are characteristic of chimps in their natural state, and Washoe took readily to signing, imitating her human companions in the context of meaningful everyday events (with their motivating and reinforcing properties) and babbling away manually on her own (with her companions "shaping" her signs into the human-proper forms). And I understand that Washoe is now in a colony of chimps at Norman, Oklahoma, busily communicating with others just acquiring . . . the language?

So now let's check Washoe's communicative performance (as reported in R. A. Gardner & B. T. Gardner, 1969) against our criteria of something being "a language." Criterion 1 (nonrandom recurrency of forms) is obviously met by the differential use (by age 4) of some 80 gestural signs. Criterion 2 (reciprocality, both sending and receiving) is obviously met—first with humans "at the other end" but more recently with other chimps. Criterion 3 (pragmatics) is satisfied by such evidence as her making the "toothbrush" sign "in a peremptory fashion when its appearance at the end of a meal was delayed," by her signing "open" at the door of a room she was leaving, and so forth *ad infinitum*. There is also no question about satisfying criterion 4 (semantics): her spontaneous "naming" of toothbrushes, with "no obvious motive other than communication"; her learning to sign "dog," mainly to those in picture books, but then signing it spontaneously to the sound of an unseen dog barking outside; her signing "key" not only to keys being presently used to open locks but also to "not-here" keys needed to unlock locks! And there is also no question but that criterion 6 (combinatorial productivity) is satisfied: the Gardners report that as soon as Washoe had a vocabulary of a dozen or so signs (including verbs like "open" and "go," nouns like "key" and "flower," the pronouns "you" and "me," and adverbials (?) like "please," "more," and "hurry") she spontaneously began combining them in sequences like "open flower" (open gate to flower garden), "go sweet" (to be taken to raspberry bush), and "you me out" (you take me outdoors); she also displays the "pivot/open-class" productivity familiar in child language development (e.g., "please sweet drink," "please key," "hurry out," and "please hurry sweet drink").

But what about criterion 5 (syntax)? This has been the focus of most questioning of Washoe's "having a language," and in early critiques both Bronowski and Bellugi (1970, p. 672) and McNeill (1970, p. 55) stress the fact that Washoe's "utterances" display no constraints on "word" order, her signings seemingly having free ordering (e.g., "up please" or "please up," "open key" or "key open"). However, in an equally early commentary, Roger Brown (1970, pp. 224–230) makes several very significant points:

1. that Washoe's linguistic performances should be compared with those of a 3- or 4-year-old *deaf-mute child* rather than with normal children of this age;

2. that just as normal children already control several prosodic patterns when they begin to produce combinations (e.g., the falling pitch of declaratives, the rising pitch of interrogatives), so do the deaf—*and quite spontaneously* (according to the Gardners) *Washoe*—hold for a perceptibly longer period the last sign of a sequence to indicate a question; and

3. that just as in human language development, Washoe displayed a gradual increase over time in the sign length of her "utterances"—two common before three and three common before four—and Brown asks reasonably, "why should this be so if the sign combinations are not constructions [p. 225]?"

Perhaps most significantly, Brown (1970) observes that "there is little or no communication pressure on either children or Washoe to use the right word order for the meanings they intend [p. 229]" when language is being used in contexts that are *perceptually unambiguous* to both producer and receiver—which is the case in much of early child language and in just about all of Washoe's signings (and it should be noted that, although Washoe's companions "corrected" the signings of particular lexical items, they apparently did not "correct" for sign orderings, as do most adult companions of young human children).

Relevant here is an actual experiment with Washoe (B. T. Gardner & R. A. Gardner, 1975) designed to get at evidence for recognition of "sentence constituents" in her communications. In English, answers to *wh*-questions require identification of the relevant NP constituent; given the sentence *Roger put the key on the table*, for example, the question *Who did it?* specifies the subject NP (Roger), the question *What was put somewhere?* specifies the object NP (key), and the question *Where was something put?* specifies the NP-head of the locative phrase. The Gardners were able to demonstrate not only that Washoe's replies (including single-sign) to such *wh*-questions were significantly contingent with the correct NP constituents (at the .00001 level) but also that her 84% correct NP inclusion in replies was supe-

rior to the performance of normal children of corresponding linguistic
age! It is also interesting that David McNeill, in a recent paper (1974),
now concludes that the chimpanzee (Washoe data, primarily) *does*
meet criterion 5, ". . . spontaneously adopting an apparently novel form
of syntax based on social relationships (such as addressee and nonaddressee)." Generalizing, it appears that, whereas human language is designed for humans to talk *about* people and things, natural chimp "language" is designed for chimps to talk *to* other chimps (or people, in
Washoe's case).

II. DEFINING CHARACTERISTICS
OF HUMAN LANGUAGES

Human languages must, of course, satisfy all the criteria for *anything* to be called a language—thus having nonrandom recurrent signals
in some channel, producible by the same organisms that receive them,
which display nonrandom pragmatic, semantic, and syntactic dependencies that are combinatorially productive—but there are additional
delimiting criteria that must be met if something is to be called a natural
human language. These additional defining characteristics can be categorized (at least superficially) as either *structural* or *functional*.

A. STRUCTURAL CHARACTERISTICS OF HUMAN LANGUAGES

For something that is a language to be called a *human* language, it
must have the following structural characteristics: it must (7) involve
use of the vocal–auditory channel, and thus (8) nondirectional transmission but directional reception and (9) evanescence in time of the
forms in the channel, these characteristics requiring (10) integration
over time of the information derived from the physical forms, but also
(11) providing prompt feedback to the sender of his own messages.
All of these structural characteristics are direct, combined functions
of the physical nature of sound and the biological nature of the human organism.

7. The Vocal-Auditory Channel Criterion: *All natural human languages use vocalization for production and audition for reception.* This,
of course, refers to the primary communication system for humans,
there being many other derived systems—the most general being writing
(a more lasting gestural-visual sort of channel) but also drum signals,
smoke signals, and Morse code. It should be noted that the vocalic response system is both relatively "lightweight" (in terms of energy required, as compared, say, with locomotion) and minimally interfering
with other ongoing activities (like toolmaking, hunting, and fighting)
—properties we shall find relevant to the question of the origin of human languages.

8. Nondirectional Transmission, Directional Reception: *In human languages, speaking is broadcast and hearing is selective.* Broadcast transmission is simply a function of the manner of propagation of sound waves—in all directions and, conveniently, around corners (an advantage lacking in visual Octopian, by the way); selective reception is simply a function of the fact that we have a head between our ears, this interaural distance yielding phase differences for sound waves originating in all directions except along the medial line, and hence providing cues for direction of the source. This channel characteristic may well have had significant influence upon the social structures of primitive human groups—Mr. "Big-mouth" being heard by all "Little-mouths" at once, but the "Little-mouths" securing one-to-one privacy only by isolating themselves!

9. The Evanescence-in-Time Characteristic: *Signals in the vocal-auditory channel fade rapidly in intensity over time.* The advantage of such evanescence, of course, is that it minimizes "cluttering up" of the channel—as anyone who has tried to understand what another is saying across an echo chamber fully appreciates. The disadvantage is that it puts a heavy load on short-term as well as long-term memory—the latter undoubtedly being the major reason for the development of writing systems of various types, apparently independently in different human societies as they reached certain levels of complexity. (Parenthetically, it is sobering in this nuclear age to realize that humans have had writing systems for only about 5,000 years.)

10. The Integration-over-Time Requirement: *The distribution of message forms over time on a linear "left-to-right" basis requires temporary storage and integration of information.* Although there is simultaneous patterning within sounds (e.g., chords in music), it is minimal in comparison with vision. A familiar example of such temporal integration in human speech is *prosody*—a falling intonation pattern over time signaling a statement, a rising pattern a question. This constraint also leads speakers to shift "leftward" (earlier in time) message elements that are salient to them (e.g., creating a passive, "Pierre was stung by that bee!"). Of course, our Octopian receivers would have to integrate information over *space* within the "panels" of their bulbous senders' bodies, as well as store it temporarily for integration with information in succeeding "panels."

11. Availability of Prompt Feedback: *The speaker of a human language is normally capable of hearing his own messages as he produces them.* This property of the vocal-auditory channel has significance for development of language in the young of the species as well as for production of language in the mature. Because it is a maxim in language development that, at all stages and in all phases, comprehension typically precedes production, it follows that the sounds of understood adult

forms (like "ball") and combinations of forms (like "that's Mommy's shoe") can serve as models against which the child can correct his own productions ("bawh," "dah Mommy show"), and even more complexly develop the syntactic niceties. In the ordinary speech of adults, one notes not only filled and unfilled pauses (time for cognizing to catch up with sentencing) but also retracings with corrections (usually of full constituent length, e.g., "Well, my dear, I did it all in one swell foop . . . /ah/ . . . in one fell swoop and was on my way!"). Under abnormal conditions of *delayed* feedback (via the intervention of tape), one finds he cannot speak, or even read, naturally (as I found when the late Grant Fairbanks had me try to read the statement on a pack of cigarettes, ". . . the Amer-eric-c-can To-to-BACCO Comp-comp-COMPNY! . . ."); under abnormal condition of *no* feedback (via masking with noise), patients in psychotherapy have been found to talk more freely (but often rather incoherently) and without as much self-critical backtracking (Mahl, 1972). One wonders how the Octopian "speakers" would monitor their own communicative displays—by seeing them from within?

The signing of deaf-mutes would be ruled out, as far as being a *natural* human language, by criterion 7 (use of the vocal-auditory channel), but of course it would still satisfy the requirements for being *a language*, even in the chimp, as Washoe has demonstrated. And what about our Cave Midgets—in their domain far beneath the floors of the Mammoth Cave? While we were trying to determine if our visitors from Arcturus had something that could be called "a language," other intrepid human explorers (linguists) were doing the same with the pale little Cave Midgets. Tape recordings of their high-frequency pipings left no doubt but that nonrandom recurrent sound forms were being reciprocally produced and received; the nonrandom dependencies of their use of artifacts in mushroom-and-worm cultivating activities upon these distinctive piping forms clearly satisfied the pragmatic and semantic criteria.

Testing for syntactic structuring and combinatorial productivity took a bit of doing, particularly because our linguists were struggling with very sore throats brought on by continuous whisperings—the big-eared Cave Midgets fly into panic at any loud, low-frequency sound. However, after many sleepless days analyzing visual displays of ultrasonic piping patterns, one linguistic genius demonstrated "noun/verb" selection rules, and, a bit later, another had a brainstorm (not surprisingly, after consuming a worm-and-mushroom pizza) and created a computer-based Cave-Midgetese synthesizer, at least for very simple utterances—and combinatorial productivity was firmly established. So there was no question but that these Cave Midgets had a language—

and, given the piping sounds that went whistling around the cavern passageways plus the big ears that rotated to receive them, it seemed obvious that this language met the *structural* requirements for being of the human type—but what about the *functional* requirements?

B. FUNCTIONAL CHARACTERISTICS OF HUMAN LANGUAGES

For something to be called a human language, it must also have the following functional characteristics: (12) the semantic relations between forms and meanings must, in general, be arbitrary rather than iconic, and (13) the forms in the channel that distinguish meanings must be discretely rather than continuously variable; further, the forms in the channel must (14) be analyzable hierarchically into levels of units-within-units, with (15) large numbers of units at each higher level being exhaustively analyzable into relatively small numbers of components at each lower level; and finally, (16) extension of a language within the species, both generationally and geographically, must be via experience (learning) rather than via inheritance (maturation). The complex, visual-patterning language of the Octopians seems to fit neither the arbitrariness (12) nor the discreteness (13) criteria, and its efficiency must lie elsewhere than in hierarchical (14) and componential (15) organization. Whether the Octopian language extends itself in time and space on the basis of experience (like human language) or of inheritance (like bee language) we do not know at this point. However, because the Cave Midgets are a somewhat humanoid species of this earth, we would be most interested in seeing how *their* language stacks up against these functional criteria.

12. Arbitrariness of Form-Meaning Relations: *In human languages the rules relating forms in the communication channel to events in other channels* (cf. criterion 4) *are typically arbitrary rather than iconic.* We must say "typically" because (as noted earlier) human languages do display both onomatopoeia and phonetic symbolism; however, for the most part form-meaning relations are arbitrary (witness *Pferd* in German, *cheval* in French, and *horse* in English). Noting the prevalence of phonetic symbolism in the communication of affect—in both natural chimp ("oh-oh-oh" for joy vs. "uu-uu-uu" for sorrow, "eeee!" for fear) and natural human ("boy-oh-boy" for pleasure vs. "ugh" for disgust, "eek!" for the "shriek" of fear)—one might speculate that there has been social evolution from iconic affective signs toward arbitrary denotative signs, particularly as languages became more complex and abstract in their references.

13. Discreteness of Form Shifts Signaling Differences in Meaning: *In human languages, the changes in form that convey changes in meaning are discretely rather than continuously variable.* This characteristic

certainly holds at the phonemic level (the abrupt shifts in distinctive features of sound that distinguish, for example, *fail, gale, male, sail* and *tail*), the morphemic level (the productive pluralizing morphemes for nouns in English are always *either* [-s], [z] or [-iz], conditionally dependent on the voicing or sibilance of the preceding sound, as in *cats, dogs,* and *horses* respectively), the lexical level (a graded speeding up of *walk* into say *wok* doesn't yield the meaning of *run*), and the syntactic level (an NP being signaled by *the singing* and a VP by *was singing,* for a simple example). Such discreteness has certainly simplified the descriptive task for linguistic science. Whether such discrete either/or-ness holds at the level of semantic features is highly debatable —but then meaning is not usually overtly signaled in the surface forms of human languages.

14. The Hierarchical Organization Criterion: *In human languages, the stream of forms in the channel is analyzable into levels of units-within-units.* Complex sentences are analyzable into clauses (or "sentoids"), clauses are analyzable into immediate constituents (concatenations of NPs "hanging on" a VP), constituents into word forms (heads, modifiers, and modulators), words into morphemes (stems and affixes), morphemes into phonemes, and phonemes into distinctive phonetic features. To some extent semantic systems also display hierarchical organizations (particularly for nouns) that are describable in the form of "taxonomic tree" structures—thus the meaning of *bird* is entailed in the meanings of all its exemplars (*sparrow, robin, eagle,* etc.), the meaning of *animal* is entailed in those of *bird, fish, mammal,* and so forth. Implicit in this criterion (and in criterion [15]) is the constraint that no higher-level unit can be embedded in a lower-level unit—and this raises some interesting questions about what is the proper linguistic analysis of, for example, sentences with relative clauses (*I've met the girl who arrived late at the party,* where the *Wh*-clause is itself a sentential elaboration of an NP), what I call "commentative" sentences (like *I hope that John will be on time for the wedding* or *It is a fact that John has been married before*) or monstrous center-embedded sentences (like *The boy the girl Pierre likes likes likes spaghetti!*).

15. The Componential Organization Criterion: *In human languages, large numbers of units at each higher level in the hierarchy* (of criterion 14) *are exhaustively analyzable as near-simultaneous combinations of relatively small numbers of units at each next lower level.* Potentially infinite numbers of sentences are analyzable into near-infinite numbers of clausal constituents, these in turn analyzable into some hundreds of thousands of word units that are themselves analyzable into some thousands of morphemes, and these being analyzable into some 40 or so phonemes that can be analyzed into an even smaller number

of distinctive phonetic features for any given human language. And this componential analysis is exhaustive at all levels—no leftover pieces! Viewed from bottom to top, from combinations of the smallest units (distinctive features) to the uniquely varied patterns of the largest (sentences), this system represents a remarkably efficient way to satisfy the criterion of combinatorial productivity (6)—which anything must meet if it is to be called "a language." But this is obviously not the only *conceivable* way to achieve efficiency. If, for example, a species were able to increase the number and complexity of units at some lowest, unanalyzable, level (e.g., hundreds of thousands of meaningful "morphemes") and simultaneously increase the complexity of the simultaneous patterning of only one higher level (potentially infinite numbers and complexities of "sentences"), then perhaps even greater efficiency could be achieved, but it would take mental capacities far beyond those available to humans—perhaps those available to Arcturians, however.

In introducing this section on the defining characteristics of human languages, and proposing that they could be categorized as "structural" vs. "functional," I added the parenthetical "hedge" (*at least superficially*). Now, with specific reference to the hierarchical and componential organization criteria (14 and 15), although they are in no obvious way dependent upon the *peripheral sensory or motor structures* of primates, they may well reflect ways in which the *central nervous systems* of higher organisms have evolved—and hence be just as innately determined as those reflecting the constraints imposed by using the vocal–auditory channel. Note that the same hierarchical-componential organization appears in prelinguistic behavior as well: in the comprehension of complex facial expressions of emotion, with their variable component states (upturned vs. downturned mouth, V-shaped vs. Λ-shaped brows, etc.); in the production of complex skilled acts, like that of "door opening," where locomoting, arm extending, object grasping, and pulling constituents are sequenced in terms of perceptual feedbacks, are themselves composed of finer motor units, and participate in many different intentional acts (e.g., object grasping as part of the acts of "apple eating" and "hand shake greeting" as well as "door-opening").

16. The Transferral-via-Learning Criterion: *Human languages are transferred to other members of the species, both generationally over time and geographically over space, via experience* (learning) *rather than via inheritance* (maturation). There is no evidence whatsoever that the offspring of speakers of some particular human language find it easier to acquire *that* language than any other; in other words, children come into the world cognitively equipped to speak any human-type language—a Japanese infant can learn to speak English or Papago just as easily as Japanese. Of course, this Japanese infant couldn't learn

Cave-Midgetese very well (without special equipment), and the same would hold for Cave Midget youngsters learning any existing human language, but this could be due simply to the special adaptation of the Cave Midgets to their cavernous environment over the millennia.

How might our intrepid linguists determine whether or not Cave-Midgetese meets the functional criteria for a language being humanoid in type? Form-meaning arbitrariness (12) and discreteness rather than continuousness in signaling meaning shifts (13) would both require pretty thorough familiarization with the language; given that, one might then determine if the *components* of piping "word" units (analogous to our phonemes) have essentially random relations to their meanings (12) and also whether the shifts in pipings are discretely or continuously variable with respect to shifts in meaning (13) (e.g., if a "vowel" frequency shifted continuously from low to high in order to modulate the meaning of an otherwise constant form to convey "doing something very slowly" to "doing it very rapidly").

But both of these "tests" already presuppose satisfaction of both hierarchical (14) and componential (15) organization, and in some ways "tests" of these characteristics would be easier: One would merely need to demonstrate (using the ultrasonic visual displays) that distinguishable piping forms enter arbitrarily into diverse larger forms that have distinctive meanings, and that these larger forms enter similarly into more diverse, still larger piping sequences, probably separated by identifiable "pauses"—the differences in these larger forms, of course, displaying predictable contingencies with behavioral (pragmatic) and referential (semantic) phenomena, as indicated by the use of a vastly improved computerized Cave-Midgetese synthesizer. So, given such demonstrations, it would appear that "the language of Cave Midgets" is indeed a human-type language—developed by an early branch of humanoids that, in the search for bigger and juicier mushrooms and worms, happened to end up in caverns deep in the earth.

III. NONDEFINING CHARACTERISTICS OF HUMAN LANGUAGES

All of the defining characteristics considered so far are, ipso facto, universals. There are many other characteristics of human languages—some of them apparently absolute but many of them only statistical universals—which, I would argue, are not *defining* characteristics. That is, if one encountered something that was *a language* by criteria 1–6 and, further, was a human-type language by criteria 7–16, then, if it failed to display any one or more of the characteristics to be discussed in this section, it would *still* be considered a human language—albeit a rather strange one. We can categorize nondefining characteristics fairly reasonably into two types: (1) those that reflect certain *intellectual and cultural traits that are common to the human species* rather than linguistic regularities per se; (2) those which reflect dynamic *interactions among principles of psycholinguistic performance* and typically yield statistical rather than absolute universals of language. Only very small samples of such nondefining characteristics can be offered here by way of illustration.

A. BASED ON INTELLECTUAL AND
   CULTURAL CHARACTERISTICS OF HUMANS

1. Propositionalizing

All known human languages can be used to create propositional sentences that, in principle, are testable as to their truth or falsity. All humans seem capable of cognizing certain regularities and relations in their physical and social environments and expressing these in linguistic assertions—*the sun always rises in the east, a robin is a bird, bears hibernate in the winter*, and so on *ad libitum*. Without such capacities, there could be no science, to be sure, but would we wish to claim that the language of a society of humanoids *sans* science was therefore not a human-type language? The language of our Cave Midgets might well be so characterized. Interesting in this connection is the complete absence of propositional sentences (apparently) in Washoe's signings—and, in fact, McNeill (1974) points out that chimpanzee "syntax" seems to be based on sociality more than objectivity, with the addressee–nonaddressee distinction being crucial for word ordering (witness Washoean "utterances" like *you me out, Roger Washoe out, you Naomi peekaboo* and *you tickle me-Washoe*).

2. Prevarication

In all known human languages, messages can be intentionally false, deceptive, or meaningless. This, in a way, is a consequence of being able to propositionalize. All humans seem to be able to produce sentences analogous to *the moon is made of green cheese, I was not involved in planning the Watergate Caper*, and even *colorless green ideas sleep furiously*. If speakers of an otherwise humanoid language—let's say Cave-Midgetese—couldn't prevaricate, then, of course, they could have neither fiction nor poetry, would be unable to "grease" the social grind with convenient "little white lies," would be incapable of sarcasm ("Thanks a lot!") or irony (saying "Isn't that just great!" while looking at a flat tire on one's car) or any of the little clevernesses with language, like saying of a certain woman "she'll make someone a nice husband." But would such lackluster communication rule out a language as humanoid? I doubt it. One might note in passing that "play" in higher animals (e.g., Pierre making a ferocious growling charge at me that ends in kissing my hand) is a kind of prevarication.

3. *Reflexiveness*

In all known human languages, messages can be used to talk about other messages and/or their components. In all human languages one can say things like "the word *bachelor* can refer to 'an unmarried adult human male' but also to 'one who has received the lowest college degree' or even to 'a young male fur seal kept off the breeding grounds by the older males.'" In writing, we usually make use of tricks like italicizing, capitalizing, and quoting to signal the fact that such forms *are* words about words, rather than ordinary communications. And witness performative sentences like *I christen thee "the Jimmy Carter"* for some aircraft carrier of the future, or illocutionary speech acts more generally (see Searle, 1969) like *I state that S, I promise that S, I fear* (am amazed, am sorry) *that S*, and *I know* (believe, doubt, etc.) *that S* —what I have called "commentative" sentences where the so-called matrix sentence (*I verb* that . . .) is some kind of comment on the embedded sentence. If our Cave Midget friends lacked this ability to use language to comment on language, then of course they could have no philosophy, no linguistics, no psycholinguistics . . . and no puns. But they could still be said to have a humanoid language, I think.

4. *Learnability*

Any natural human language can be acquired by any normal human being. If the acquirer is a child, we speak of first-language learning; if it is an adult, already fluent in his native language, then we speak of second-language learning. We might sometime come across a language used by humanoids so primitive or unintelligent that they just simply were not capable of learning the complex structures of any ordinary human language—and this might well apply to the hypothetical Cave Midgets—but I still think we would have to classify it as *a human language* if it met all of the defining criteria. And the same, of course, would apply in reverse: If it were some humanoid species whose spaceship landed in our backyard, and if they used the vocal-auditory channel and obviously displayed all of our defining characteristics—but their language was so complex in lexicon and in both length and embeddings of sentences that no Earthly human could learn it—then I think we would still humbly have to admit it as a human language.

5. *Translatability*

Any natural human language can be translated into any other human language. Both the preceding nondefining characteristic (learnability) and this one (translatability) assume, of course, that the lexicon of the acquirer or of the destination language of the translation can be expanded as necessary *or* be handled by circumlocutions (e.g., the "iron horse" used by American Indians as a translation of "loco-motive"). And the same complexity constraints apply as above—either the ordinary human source language could be beyond the intellectual capabilities of the destination language users (translating English into Cave-Midgetese) or the extraordinary humanoid source language could be too complex for the users of ordinary human destination languages (translating the language of those godlike humanoids from outer space into ordinary English). But again, I would argue that these limitations would not rule out the essential "humanness" of the languages involved.

B. BASED ON LANGUAGE PERFORMANCE PRINCIPLES
   AND THEIR INTERACTIONS

1. Selection and Combination Rules

   Across all languages and levels of units, rules of selection and com-bination of alternative forms are statistical rather than absolute univer-sals (cf. criteria 14 and 15, hierarchical and componential organization of human languages, above). At the phonological level, each language selects from those differences in sound which the human vocalic system makes possible a small subset of differences that will make a difference in meaning (i.e., are phonemic); certain differences (voiced vs. non-voiced) are much more probable statistically than others (lip flattening vs. lip rounding) across languages. At the syntactic level, each language selects as its grammar a limited subset of "rewrite rules" (for expansion in expression and for contraction in comprehension) from an indefi-nitely large number of possibilities; again, certain types of grammatical rules are statistically more probable than others (e.g., NP $\leftrightarrow$ N + A about twice as likely across languages as NP $\leftrightarrow$ A + N and for good psycholinguistic reasons). At the semantic level, each language selects from a potentially infinite number of features some subset for differ-entiating among the items in its lexicon; although many semantic fea-tures are universal, many are not—and, in any case, the distributions of feature weights in languages are statistically variable. This differential rule selection and combination at all levels is the reason why any par-ticular human language must be learned—yet is learnable.

2. A Progressive Differentiation Principle

   Across all languages and levels of units, a principle of progressive differentiation of meaning-signaling forms operates, but the extent of differentiation varies statistically. In phonology, for example, only if a high–low vowel distinction is phonemic will a lips flattened–rounded distinction also be phonemic—never the reverse order of differentiation. In syntax, one example would be the Keenan-Comrie (1977) "Accessi-bility Hierarchy" for relative clause formation: Only if a language permits relativization of the subject NP will it also have relativization of the object NP, and only if these are both developed in the language will relativization of the indirect object NP occur—and so forth, but never with the reverse order of differentiation. Greenberg (1966) documents evidence for progressive differentiation across languages for units at all levels; at the semantic level, for example, only if a language already makes a distinction between singular and plural will it also have a further distinction of plural into dual vs. indefinitely plural. Berlin and Kay (1969) offer evidence for progressive differentiation of color terms cross-linguistically—from the most primitive bright vs. dark, to differentiation of the bright into red vs. nonred, further in the red region into red vs. yellow, and later in the blue region into blue vs. green. Our own cross-cultural studies of affective meaning (Osgood, May, & Miron, 1975) suggest that generalized affective Positiveness vs. Negativeness differentiates into $\pm$Evaluation $+$ $\pm$Dynamism and thence differentiation of Dynamism into $\pm$Potency $+$ $\pm$Activity (i.e., from a one- into a three-feature system). Although the principle of progressive differentiation seems to be a universal of human languages, its interaction with other principles results in a statistical distribution of degrees of differentiation.

3. A Least Effort Principle

Across all languages and levels of units, a principle of least effort operates statistically, such that the higher the frequency-of-usage level (1) *the shorter the length of forms,* (2) *the smaller the number of forms,* and (3) *the larger the number of different meanings* (senses) *of the forms used.* This principle comes from G. Kingsley Zipf (1949), and he offers the entirely delightful analogy of a skilled artisan working at a long bench, with his production (sentence composition) space at one end and his various tools (here, lexical forms) spread out along it; obviously, it would be most efficient to have the tools most often used closest at hand along the bench, and these tools themselves lightweight, few in number and multipurpose in function. Using language data from English mainly, but also some from Chinese and Latin, Zipf was able to report functions that very neatly supported these hypotheses, and there seems to be no reason to doubt that the same would appear for languages generally. Does the Least Effort Principle hold for linguistic levels other than the lexicon? Greenberg (1966), noting Zipf's pioneering studies (p. 64), reports relevant data at the phonological level. Although I know of no explicit evidence, one would expect the same to hold for NP and VP constituents—e.g., that unmodified head nouns would be more frequent than elaborated ones (indeed, that diachronically there would be pressures toward simplification, e.g., from *knob of the door* to *door's knob* to *doorknob*) and that unmodulated verbs (simple presents and pasts, *walks* and *walked*) would be more frequent in ordinary language than modulated ones (like *was walking* or *had been walking* or certainly *would have still been walking*).

4. Affective Polarity

Across all languages and levels of units, it is statistically universal that affectively positive forms are distinguished from affectively negative forms (1) *by marking (either overt or covert) of the negative members of pairs and* (2) *by priority of the positive members of pairs in both development (in the language and in the individual) and form sequencing in messages.* Again Greenberg (1966) provides massive evidence at all levels: thus in phonology, marked nasal vowels are never more frequent in a language than unmarked nonnasal vowels, and Jakobson's general theory of phonemic development (Jakobson & Halle, 1956) includes the principle of priority for unmarked poles of features; thus in syntax it appears to be a universal (Greenberg, 1963) that affirmation is unmarked (X *is* Y) and negation is marked (X *is NOT* Y), and the unmarked active construction (X *verbed* Y) is universally the basic, natural form and the marked passive (X *WAS verbed BY* Y) is always viewed as a transformation; thus, in semantics, Animate is unmarked but INanimate is marked overtly, and affectively Positive *tall* is unmarked but Negative *short* is marked covertly (note that we normally say *how tall is John,* not *how short is John,* unless we are already assuming he is to some degree short). As far as priority of Positive members in the development of language in the species is concerned, the mere fact that it is characteristically Positives that are marked to produce Negatives (*happy/UNhappy* but not *sad/unsad,* although this, too, is only statistically universal, as witness *untroubled/troubled*) clearly implies that the Positives already exist *to be marked;* as far as priority in individual language development is concerned, DiVesta (as reported in Boucher & Osgood, 1969) has shown that in qualifier elicitation from children of various ages the Positives of familiar opposites (*good–bad, big–little,* etc.) typically appear earlier and hold tighter frequencies than the Negatives. As to sequencing of such pairs in language production, note first that in stating opposites one usually goes from Positive to Negative (*strong–weak* rather than *weak–strong, fast–slow* rather than *slow–fast,* and so on), and then that familiar idiomatic phrases tend to follow the same rule (see Cooper & Ross, 1975)— *no more ands or buts, they hunted fore and aft, are you for or against me, the pros and cons of it,* but definitely not the reverse orders.

5. The Pollyanna Principle

Across all languages and levels of units, it is statistically universal that affectively Positive forms and constructions are more diversified, more frequently used, and more easily processed cognitively than affec-

tively Negative forms and constructions. The greater diversity of Positives shows up nicely in our cross-linguistic semantic differential data
on (now) some 30 language-culture communities around the world—
in the eight-octant space defined by ±Evaluation, ±Potency and ±Ac-
tivity factors (which system is itself a human universal), the + + +
octant (Good, Strong, and Active) is much more densely populated
with concepts than the − − − octant (Bad, Weak, and Passive), and
the same holds for the Positive vs. Negative directions of each factor
taken separately. Greenberg (1966), Boucher and Osgood (1969), and
Hamilton and Deese (1971) all present evidence that the Positive members of pairs of word forms are significantly more frequent in usage
than their Negative counterparts. As to the ease of cognitive processing, both H. Clark and his associates (Clark, 1971; Clark & Chase, 1972)
and Hoosain (1973) in my own laboratory have shown that simple
sentences with overt (*nots*) or with covert negatives (*short, ugly, weak,*
etc.) take significantly longer to comprehend, and both also find that
the same holds for incongruent complex sentences conjoined with *but*
as compared with congruent ones conjoined with *and*—incongruence
being itself a form of negativity. Perhaps the most striking evidence
for the Pollyanna Principle will be offered in a paper in preparation
by Osgood and Hoosain (1979): Measuring the times required for
simply saying appropriately "positive" or "negative" to single words
from all sorts of pairs presented randomly, there was a highly significant difference of about 50 msec favoring Positives. In other words,
it is easier to "simply get the meaning" of affectively Positive words
than the meaning of affectively Negative words, and this even when
usage frequency was biased in favor of the Negatives.

IV. HOW MAY HUMAN LANGUAGES
HAVE ORIGINATED?

This is a question that has intrigued speculative philosophers of all
periods—and it is as purely speculative as anyone could hope, because
there is little likelihood that any of the hypotheses will ever be tested
empirically. There is no question but humans have the *propensity* for
vocal–auditory language: All known normal human groups have such
a language; all normal children develop competence in a native language of great complexity in what has often been called "a remarkably
short time" (although there are many hours in the busy days of childhood); and, as we have seen (criteria 1–16), all human languages are
fundamentally of the same type. Yet, given the essential *arbitrariness*
of the phonological, syntactic, and semantic rules of each, particular
human languages must be learned.

A. SPECULATIONS ON THE ORIGIN OF LANGUAGE

How did some genius man-ape "get the idea" of communicating with others of his kind by means of vocalizations having distinctive referential properties, thereby enabling him to influence their behaviors? All of the speculations I briefly characterize below—except the first, "mystical" theory—will be seen to contain a grain or two of probable truth, but they are all obviously insufficient. Furthermore, they are limited to "wording" (usually emoting or labeling) and have nothing to say about "sentencing"—but, like the holophrastic stage in child language, it seems certain that the expression of ideas (whole cognitions) would be the fundamental communicative unit.

1. The "Ding-Dong" (Mystical) Theory

Assuming it to be given (1) that meanings are somehow inherent in words and (2) that objects have the power to evoke the words that refer to them, the process of language origin is simply that man-ape sees object DING, DING causes him to say "dong," and "dong" contains the meaning *ding*. Nonsensical as this is, it nevertheless has understandable roots in primitive (?) human behavior—the strong tendency toward *reification of words:* The infant in its random babbling happens to produce the noise "ma-ma" and the fond parent exclaims "Why, the little darling knows me!"; Malinowski (1938) has aptly dubbed this the "bucket theory" of meaning—words, like little buckets, are assumed to pick up their loads of meaning in one person's mind, carry them across the intervening space, and dump them into the mind of another—and he notes that in some societies a man never reveals his real name (rather, inscribing it on a piece of wood or stone and burying it in some secret place) lest some ill-wisher practice magic on it. Other obvious criticisms are: (1) why don't all languages have the same names for things? (2) what about names for object-less "things" like function words, verbs, and abstract concepts generally?

2. The "Bow-Wow" (Imitative) Theory

Assuming it to be given (1) that animals and many other things make or have characteristic sounds and (2) that our man-apes had a spontaneous tendency to imitate noises heard, the process of language origin is simply that dog-produced "bow-wow" already has *dog* meaning as a perceptual sign and man-aped imitative "bow-wow" elicits the same meaning via stimulus generalization. Suggestive evidence would be the use of imitative sounds in most tribal ceremonies and the commonness of onomatopoeia across human languages. Critique: (1) most words in languages are not onomatopoeic; (2) because in different languages there are quite different "natural" imitations of the sounds that *dog, cow, cat, rooster*, etc., make, and they all follow their own phonological rules, we would have to assume that our man-apes already had a language. However, this theory has a grain of probable truth *as a "starter"* on the path toward vocal–auditory language.

3. The "Pooh-Pooh" (Interjectional) Theory

Given (1) that, like ape, man-ape has a repertoire of unlearned vocal expressions of affect (grunts, groans, screams), (2) that these are nonrandomly occasioned by the situations he is in, and (3) that these situations (as complexes of perceptual signs) have meanings for him, the "idea" of language originates in the transfer of the meaning of a situation to the vocal interjection as a sign of that situation. Thus Man-ape A breaks the thong he is using to tie his stone axe-head to its handle-stick and mutters a disgusted "pooh-pooh"; and later he says "pooh-pooh, pooh-pooh, pooh-pooh" to ridicule Man-ape B for tripping clumsily over a log—and soon the whole tribe is going around "pooh-pooh"-ing each other! Not only does this theory seem quite reasonable as a "starter" for vocal–auditory language, but it has a pretty solid grain of probable truth in it—prelinguistic cognizing (the meanings of perceived situations) is prior to, and necessary for, linguistic cognizing, a speculation on which I will elaborate momentarily. However, by way of critique: (1) how does the man-ape get beyond the ape—in the naming of entities (NPs) and relations (VPs)? and (2) how does he get from emoting into describing, explaining, warning and the like—that is, into sentencing?

4. The "Yum-Yum" (Gestural) Theory

This was what E. L. Thorndike (see below) dubbed the speculations of Sir Richard Paget (most recently, 1944) about the origin of human languages. Given (1) that our man-ape was a fluent and total gesture maker (with noisy mouth gestures accompanying other bodily gesturings and posturings) and (2) that his gesturing behavior followed the same principle of least effort as that proposed by G. K. Zipf (earliest in *The Psychobiology of Language*, 1935—see Section III,B,3), language originates as the least effortful and least interfering vocal parts of the gesturing are substituted for the total. Thus anticipatory behavior toward a juicy food-object includes tummy rubbing and lip smacking; when the latter is accompanied by voiced exhaling, "yum-yum-yum" is produced. Now imagine two hungry man-apes squatting beside a grubby rotten log: if they keep rubbing their tummies they can't keep on digging for juicy grubs, but they can keep on "yum-yum"-ing (except when swallowing!)—so the vocalizations become the signs. This also seems reasonable as a "starter" on the path to a human language, and it is consistent with evidence for short-circuiting and amplitude reduction in the acquisition of representation mediators in sign learning (cf. Osgood, 1956, 1979). Critique: (1) we are still left with the problem of how the *meaning* of "yummy" is abstracted from the situational context (so that Man-ape A can point in some direction, say "yum-yum" to Man-ape B, and get B to go to the grubby log); and again, (2) how do we get beyond the ape and satisfy functional criteria 12–16?

5. The "Babble-Lucky" (Associational) Theory

This is E. L. Thorndike's "dubbing" of his own theory (1943) of the origins of language. Given (1) that man-apes already had strong tendencies for vocalic play ("babbling," like human infants), (2) that they already existed in social groups and were surrounded with various natural and artifactual objects, and (3) that they had the cognitive capacities for symbolizing the meanings (Thorndike simply called these X's) of such objects, language evolves as a result of chance associations of certain random babbles with certain objects and events, these *happening* to be observed and imitated by the group, and thus becoming socially standardized (hence the "lucky"). Imagine that a bright man-ape spies some clams along the lake shore and happens to babble "uk-uk"; since he already has a meaning for the perceptual sign of CLAM, he associates "uk" with that meaning; gathering up some clams, he brings them back to the cave, calling "uk-uk-uk!" as he comes; the other, less gifted, man-apes imitate him, while observing and feasting on the clams—and "uk" thus comes to refer to CLAM object and all that it signifies. This theory includes the referential properties of others, but it has the advantage of allowing arbitrariness of form-meaning relations while permitting "bow-wow"'s, "pooh-pooh"'s and "yum-yum"'s as starters. It also introduces the critical notion of *social standardization*. Critique: (1) maybe this mechanism is *too* chancy and (2) too susceptible to social confusion (what with some man-apes in the group "uk-uk"ing, others "yum-yum"ing, and still others "whiss-whiss"ing about the same clams); most critically, (3) it remains simply a theory of "wording," with nothing to say about "sentencing."

B. SPECULATIONS ON THE EVOLUTION OF LANGUAGES

Is it possible that some prehuman simian species like Pithecanthropus had a human-type language? If so, we would expect it to have been more primitive than existing human languages, which presumably have evolved from simpler origins. It seems most unlikely that humanoids suddenly started talking as they dropped from the trees. Many writers have suggested what at least some of the lines of language evolution must have been. For example, in a paper submitted to a volume *To Honor Roman Jakobson*, J. Bronowski (1967) suggests the following: (1) increasing capacity to delay outgoing vocalization to an incoming auditory message; (2) increasing capacity to separate the affective reactions to, and the denotative significances of, messages; (3) the "prolongation of reference," thus increased ability to refer backward and forward in time; (4) increasing internalization of language, from being primarily a means of social communication to becoming a means of reflecting and reasoning; (5) the "structural activity of reconstitution," increasing analysis and synthesis of messages into rearrangeable components. One might also consider my defining *functional* characteristics— (12) arbitrariness of semantics, (13) discreteness of signals, (14) hierarchical organization, (15) componential organization, and (16) transferral via learning—as *variables* that increase in complexity as languages evolve. Unfortunately, unlike skulls and tools, languages leave no traces in or on the earth, and so there is no *direct* evidence available on language evolution. But what about *indirect* evidence?

1. The Question of "Primitive" Human Languages

Among the many thousands of extant human languages, are there some less and some more "evolved"? The Old Look answered "yes": It was suggested that there were stages in development—from isolating languages like Chinese, through agglutinating languages like Turkish, to highly inflecting languages like . . . of course! . . . Latin; this notion was dropped when it was realized, with some embarrassment, that most modern Indo-European languages, along with English, were *less* inflecting, *more* isolating, than Latin. The New Look answers with a resounding "NO!": Ethnolinguists have found the languages of *culturally* primitive (near Stone Age level) peoples fully as complex as those of highly civilized (??) peoples "like us"; complexity of language-based conceptual systems (for kinship relations, mythology, etc.) appears to vary quite independently of levels of technological development; so the very question of "relative primitiveness" of extant human languages is meaningless.

But perhaps we need to take a Fresh Look—and ask ourselves just what the *criteria* of "primitiveness" might be.

a. Structural Simplicity Vs. Complexity? Just how this would be indexed—numbers of phonemes, of semantic features, of syntactic rules, or maybe ease of descriptive linguistic analysis?—is entirely unclear; if anything, it would appear that there probably was prehistoric increase in overall complexity but decrease during recent historic times.

b. Size of Vocabulary? This clearly covaries with cultural development (but one should use lay speakers in such comparisons), and, in principle (given criterion 6, combinatorial productivity) any language *can* be used to talk about anything.

c. Efficiency in Communication? In the information-theoretic sense, most languages at most levels (e.g., N-features/N-phonemes) run at about a 50% redundancy level in order to maximize the probabilities of messages "getting through"; in my foreign research travels, however, I have noticed rather marked differences in the length of signs used to communicate the same messages in airlines (e.g., *no smoking, fasten seat belts*)—but then, cultures where we might expect language primitiveness usually don't have airlines! Maclay and Newman (1960) devised an interesting measure here: the number of *morphemes* needed to communicate the same information when Person A tells Person B on the other side of a screen which forms to select from a set to match his own; there were marked effects of both negative feedback and homogeneity of forms upon increasing the N of morphemes, but unfortunately no comparative studies across languages were made—only American English subjects being used.

d. *Degrees of Concreteness?* Roger Brown (1970, pp. 19–22) reports a comparison of the nouns and verbs used by adults vs. children in terms of their concreteness (vs. abstractness)—a kind of "picturability" (a point-at-able/non-point-at-able ratio). For nouns, 67% of the children's but only 16% of the adults' 1000 most frequent were "picturable"; for verbs, 67% of children's but only 33% of adults' were "picturable." Might *this* be used as an index of "primitiveness"? Perhaps —but this too, would seem to be more cultural than linguistic, when adult speakers are being compared.

e. *Ease of Learning?* It seems reasonable that more primitive languages should be easier to learn, but the "how" of going about this is obscure. Could one show that isolating, uninflected Chinese is learned more quickly *as a first language* than is, say, highly agglutinative, inflected, and left-branching Turkish—and just what criteria of "learning" would be used? Could it be shown that Chinese can be learned more quickly by Turks *as a second language* than Turkish can be learned by Chinese? As Uriel Weinreich has amply documented in his *Languages in Contact* (1953), the interactions at all levels of units in second-language learning are incredibly complex and bi-language specific. A related index would be the degree of difference (linguistically described) between adult and child language—comparatively across languages, of course—but at just what level do we define the "child" language?

So, having taken a Fresh Look at the question of relative "primitiveness" of extant languages in terms of criteria that might be used, we seem to be about where we started—with a set of possible criteria but little or no available evidence.

2. *The Notion of Recapitulation*

The notion that ontogeny (development of the individual organism) recapitulates phylogeny (evolution of its species) is a familiar one. Could we get some idea of how language might have evolved in human species from the regularities of language development in its contemporary offspring? In an early tracing of stages in language development, Ervin and Miller (1963) report that in the course of language development there are increases in the number of phonemic distinctions, the number of grammatical classes, and the average length of utterances; holophrastic words (with contextually redundant remainders of full cognitions unexpressed) appear before word combinations (constructions), lexical word forms (distinctively semantic) before function word forms (primarily syntactic), and ordering rules (e.g., Agent-Action-Recipient) before inflections (which permit permutations in ordering).

More recently, Brown (1973), taking a more sentential approach, specifies five stages in development: (1) expression of relations or roles within simple sentences (the case roles of various noun phrases in relation to the verb phrase); (2) modulations of meaning within the simple sentence (modulating the N with number tags, with qualifiers, and the like, and the V with tense indicators and adverbials); (3) diversifying the modalities of simple declarative sentences (into yes–no questions, *wh*-constituent questions, negations, imperatives and the like); (4) embedding of sentences, expressing simple cognitions, within others (relative clauses, object noun-phrase complements, and the like); and (5) coordination of simple sentences and propositional relations (simple *and/but* complexes, adverbial main/subordinate clauses, and so forth). It should be stressed that Brown believes this 1–5 ordering to be that of development in children.

If we have some faith that ontogeny *does* tend to recapitulate phylogeny, then we might speculate as follows about the evolution of human languages:

1. They probably began with holophrastic expressions of complete perception-based cognitions, with purely semantic (often affective) and pragmatic functions.
2. As the sheer numbers of such expressions increased, the number of phonemic distinctions and grammatical classes had to increase, along with socially agreed upon rules of sequencing the expression of such classes.
3. Starting with the simplest sentential expressions of full cognitions (single-word nominals related in action and stative relations by single-word verbs, like *dog took leg-bone* and *woman (is) in cave*), the pressures to express finer semantic distinctions led to modulations into NPs and VPs (*your mangy mutt sneakily stole away with my juicy leg-bone* and *my woman must have*

been in your warm cave) and the needs for more pragmatically effective social communication led to diverse modalities of sentencings (like *where is my woman?, she is not in our cave,* and *tell her to come home*).

4. Relatively late in the evolution of languages, complexes of cognitions came to be conjoined in coordinate and embedded sentential forms, with the rather aesthetic need to avoid repetitive orderings within sentoids (clauses) leading to diverse inflections and transformations—all of which eventuated in sentence lengths getting longer and longer (like this one!).

C. A "NATURALNESS" (REPRESENTATIONAL) THEORY OF THE ORIGIN OF LANGUAGES

I've been unable to come up with a catchy, rhyming dubbing for my own speculations—but perhaps some reader will succeed where I've failed and let me have his suggestion. The broadest notion underlying the general theory of cognizing and sentencing I've been working on (Osgood, 1979) is this: *that, both in the evolution of the species and in the development of the individual human, the cognitive structures that interpret sentences received and initiate sentences produced are established in prelinguistic experience, via the acquisition of adaptive behaviors to entities perceived in diverse action and stative relations.* I suppose one might also call this an "article of faith." However, it follows from two assumptions that would rather obviously seem to be true: (1) that humanoids, before they had language, must have had capacities (a) for cognizing the significances of events going on around them, and (b) for learning to behave appropriately in terms of such significances—if the species were to survive; and (2) that children of contemporary humans, before they have language, display exactly the same capacities for acquiring the significances of perceived events and reacting with appropriate intentional behaviors.

This notion implies what I have called a *Naturalness Principle* for sentencing in language behavior—namely, *that the more sentences produced or received correspond in their surface structures to the cognitive structures developed in adaptive prelinguistic perceptuomotor experience, the greater will be the ease of processing them.* This functional principle in turn has potentially testable implications for what should be *universal* (1) in the development of the language by the young of our species, (2) in the processing of language by the adults, and (3) in the evolution of language in the species itself. As to children (1), the greater the correspondence of alternative structures to the prelinguistically established ones, the earlier should be the acquisition of their processing—in imitating, in comprehending (Simply Acting out), and in expressing (Simply Describing)—both within any given language and cross-linguistically for bilingual children (cf. Slobin, 1973); as to adults (2), the greater the correspondence, the greater will be the speed of comprehending and producing sentences and the more frequent will be the use of such sentences in various communication tasks (e.g., in Simply Describing perceived events); as to language evolution (3), the greater the correspondence, the earlier such structures should appear in, and the more universal they should be across, human languages.[6]

1. A Bit of Behavior Theory

The specification of what is "natural" involves hypotheses deriving both from Representational Neobehaviorism (see Osgood, 1979) and from psychological intuitions about *what should be natural* in the prelinguistic cognizing of young children[7]—in contrast to linguistic intuitions about *what is grammatical* in the sentencing of adults. So a bit of behavior theory is in order. Our concern here will be limited, first, to presenting a basic *sign-learning principle* and its extension to an equally basic *feature-learning principle*—both being part of my own generalization of classical Hullian (Hull, 1943) mediation theory to a representational and componential mediation theory of meaning—and, second, to emphasizing the intimate parallelism between nonlinguistic and linguistic cognizing (or between "Things and Words," reversing appropriately the title of Roger Brown's justly famous book, 1958) by offering *an "emic" principle* and *an "ambiguity" principle of neo-behaviorism.*

a. A Sign-Learning Principle. Just like apes (and even rodents) before them, it seems likely that humanoids developed the capacity for "getting the meanings of" wholistic perceptual signs of things prior to the capacity for analyzing out the distinctive features that make the differences in meanings. This behavioral principle may be stated as follows: *When a percept that elicits no predictable pattern of behavior has repeated, contiguous, and reinforced pairings with another percept that does elicit predictable behavior, the former will become a sign of the latter as its significance, by virtue of becoming associated with a mediation process, this process (1) being some distinctive representation of the total behavior produced by the significant and (2) serving to mediate overt behaviors to the sign appropriate to ("taking account of") the significate.* Such a principle has been implicit in all of the speculations above (except the "ding-dong" theory) about the origins of language (e.g., the X's in Thorndike's "babble-lucky" theory). Note that, both in evolution of the species and in development of the individual, nonlinguistic percepts of familiar entities in diverse action and stative relations (DADDY SPANKING FIDO; KITTY BEING ON PILLOW) will acquire meanings prior to the linguistic percepts (word forms) that will later represent ("stand for," "refer to") them—and, indeed, the representational processes formed in such prelinguistic experience will typically provide "prefabricated" mediators in later language acquisition. The representational mediation process that comes to be associated with a sign (perceptual or linguistic) as a dependent event in the nervous system is its *significance* (in comprehending); the same process as an antecedent event is the *intention* behind the overt behaviors mediated by a sign (in expressing).

b. A Feature-Learning Principle. Just as the overt behaviors made to significates are typically a *set* of overt responses which together constitute and "act," so also in theory are the mediation processes derived from this total behavior, and now elicited by a sign, a *set* of mediator components. To the extent that pairs of signs elicit *reciprocally antagonistic* mediator components, these componential antagonisms will become the "differences that make a difference" in meaning.

A simple, but paradigmatic, demonstration (Lawrence, 1949) will illustrate: In a simple T-maze, with the upper "arms" at the choice point having both BLACK vs. WHITE walls and CHAINS vs. NO-CHAINS (soft curtain) distinguishing right from left sides (but with random right–left locations across trials), members of one of four possible groups of rat subjects will be rewarded with food pellets if they go toward the BLACK and punished by sudden loss of support if they go toward the WHITE, with the CHAINS/NO CHAINS location being random with respect to differential reinforcement; being reasonably bright little fellows, these rats rapidly learn to get food and avoid falls. The crucial thing here is that, after this experience, *they will learn to go to the WHITE and avoid the BLACK much more rapidly than to go to the CHAINS and avoid the NO-CHAINS;* in other words, they have learned to "pay attention to" the differences that make a difference in meaning—here, anticipated reinforcement ("hope") vs. anticipated punishment ("fear")—in an otherwise constant behavioral situation and to "disregard" differences that do not make a difference.

I call this little experiment "paradigmatic" because it suggests a general model for the development of both phonemic and semantic distinctive features in human languages. In this connection, it is interesting to me that, although many linguists and most psycholinguists assume that phonemic and semantic feature distinctions must be acquired via experience (given the obvious fact that languages differ in *what* features come to "make a difference"), I have searched in vain for any explication of the crucial *how* of this learning. Note that this feature-learning principle is a logical extension of the sign-learning principle, *once a componential conception of the mediation process is substituted for an undifferentiated global conception.* This is the entrée, I think, of Neobehaviorism to a theory of meaning and reference—and, with structuring of the semantic system, ultimately to a theory of sentencing.

The "emic" principle of Neobehaviorism. By virtue of the fact that both things and organisms are mobile with respect to each other, along with the fact that environmental contexts are changeable, it follows that the distal signs of things will be variable through many stimulus dimensions. Thus, for the human infant, MOTHER'S FACE will vary in retinal-image size as she approaches him and in brightness and hue as time-of-day shifts from dawn through midday into twilight; similarly, for man-ape on the hunt, retinal size of ANTELOPE percept must have varied in size and hue as he moved stealthily in on his prey. But because these varying percepts are associated with the same significate and the behavior it produces (cf. the sign-learning principle above)—mother eventually coddles and comforts baby and antelope eventually gets killed and eaten—there will be extension of the common mediator (meaning) across such sets of percepts. Therefore the differences within such sets will be differences that do *not* make a difference in meaning.

This is the "that-ness" or "thing-ness" in perception, and it is the basis for the *constancy phenomenon*—long familiar to psychologists. Note that what we have here is *a class of variable signs having a common significance:* if we substitute *sounds* for *signs,* we have the definition of the "phoneme" (a class of physically different sounds having the same significance in the phonemic code, e.g., the /k/ in *key, cope* and *coo*); similarly, at the lexical level, word forms like "mother" and "linguist" retain their denotative significance regardless of variations in intonation, stress, or voice quality of the speaker. Equivalently on the output side of the equation, classes of nonlinguistic and/or linguistic behaviors come to be associated with the common mediation process and therefore can be said to be *expressions of the same intention*—the child (older now) or the man-ape locomoting toward, reaching for, grasping, and biting the APPLE object . . . but *not* for a percept-class having a different significance, e.g., a RED-HOT COAL!

But there is also a "how-ness" or "where-ness" in perception. Neither human child nor man-ape emits the various responses expressing the same intention at random. Neither would emit biting, then grasping, then reaching movement—in thin air—in that order or before approaching the APPLE, anymore than Caesar would have announced "Vici, vidi, veni"! Rather, *the distinctive percepts as stimuli converge with the stimulus effects of the common mediator to modulate the probabilities of alternative movements* (expressions)—thus, the small visual angle of APPLE (ON-TABLE-OVER-THERE) plus its meaning as an edible object converge on locomoting toward, a larger visual angle plus the same meaning converge on reaching for, and so on. This fusion of convergent and divergent hierarchies is what is called *control* and *decision* in representational neobehaviorism. Note that there is thus *a syntax of behaving* just as there is a syntax of talking—and again, the former is clearly prior to the latter and therefore can serve as a cognitive model for the latter.

  c. The "Ambiguity" Principle of Neobehaviorism. When percepts are constant, but the mediators associated with them are variable, we have the conditions for *perceptual ambiguity*—the same sign having more than one meaning. Familiar examples from the psychological laboratory would be the Necker Cube (an outline cube which flips between "from the side" to "from above" perspectives) and the Miles Kinephantoscope (where the shadow of a rotating bar on a rod can be seen as "flapping toward me," "flapping away from me," "shrinking and expanding," "rotating left or right," etc.), and there are many others. The child may be ambiguated by a fuzzy black something on the floor (BALL OF THREAD or SPIDER?)—until it moves; our man-ape may be ambiguated by a sudden movement of some bushes (WOMAN-APE or SABER-TOOTHED TIGER?)—until it growls!

  This is strictly analogous to *linguistic ambiguity*—homonomy, and more generally (and finely) polysemy of forms, at lexical (*he went to the BANK*), syntactic (*the SHOOTING OF THE HUNTERS was terrible*), and pragmatic (*CAN you open the window?* as an indirect request or an inquiry as to capability) levels. *Disambiguation* via contextual signs can occur *within channels:* perceptual-by-perceptual, as when that pretty, long-haired person says "where's the toilet?" in a DEEP BASS VOICE; linguistic-by-linguistic, as in *he ROWED to the bank*. Or it can be *across channels:* perceptual-by-linguistic, as when the experimenter induces irresistible shifts in the Kinephantoscope perceptions of the subject from "pirouetting to the left" to "flapping behind" just by saying those words; linguistic-by-perceptual, as when one co-ed says to her companion as another co-ed in a *mini*-miniskirt just passes them on a campus path, "she also dyes her hair"! The cross-channel disambiguations have a most significant implication—namely, *that at some deep cognitive level, nonlinguistic (perceptual) and linguistic "wordings" and "sentencings" must share the same representational system*—otherwise, events in the two channels would pass each other like ships in the night.

2. *Some Speculations About Naturalness in Sentencing*

  In discussing the syntactic criterion (5) for anything to be called a language, in connection with Octopian, I introduced this Naturalness notion. It is assumed that the prelinguistic structures of the simple cognitions underlying sentoid (clause) comprehending and expressing are *tripartite* in nature (cf. Greenberg, 1963), and further that these cognitions are "SVO" in their ordering of components (ENTITY$_1$-RELATION-ENTITY$_2$). This makes the very strong prediction that human languages that are SOV in adult type will display evidence of originating from SVO: There is diachronic evidence for many shifts in type from SOV to SVO in historic times, but not a single case of an SVO-to-SOV shift, without external pressures (invasion, cultural dominance, etc.); in the "diachronics" of language in children, one would expect evidence for SVO ordering in the two- to three-word stages of development in SOV languages before the adult language ordering takes over.[8]

It is also assumed that there are two basic types of SVO cognitions: (1) expressing *action relations* (where ACTOR-ACTION-RECIPIENT is the natural ordering in cognizing, because of the characteristically +animate—and often +human—semantic coding of actors as against the ¯animate—or at least relatively passive—coding of Recipients); and (2) *stative relations* (where FIGURE-STATE-GROUND is the natural ordering, because of the Gestalt-like characteristic +Salience of Figures and ¯Salience of Grounds). Thus, both for all human children and for our hypothetical man-apes *en route* to language, one would expect prelinguistic cognizings like MAN KICK DOG (action) and DOG ON FLOOR (stative) to be more natural than DOG KICKED BY MAN or FLOOR UNDER DOG. If the underlying Naturalness Principle is valid, then one would expect the earliest sentencings—by contemporary child and by now-extinct man-ape—to be active (rather than passive) and "figure-ative" (rather than "ground-ative"). The fact that we don't even have any names for the latter suggests that the cognizing of stative relations may well be more basic and primitive than the cognizing of action relations (again, cf. Osgood, 1979, for elaboration).

What about evidence for these naturalness predictions? Only a bit of the most relevant evidence can be given here. Osgood and Bock (1977) present a reanalysis of data on the simply describing of a variety of little demonstrations with balls, blocks, tubes, poker chips, and the like by adult American English speakers (previously reported in a paper by the first author, titled "Where Do Sentences Come From?"). Evidence for naturalness in describing both action and stative relations was overwhelming: For stative relations, despite the grammatical availability of GROUND-STATE-FIGURE sentencings (e.g., *a plate is holding a ball, a spoon and a poker chip* or *a ball is being held by the man*), these rarely occurred (we got equivalents of *a ball, a spoon and a poker chip are on a plate* [20/0/6][9] and of *the man is holding a ball* [24/1/1]); for action relations, despite the availability of ordinary passives (e.g., affirmatives like *the tube was hit by the orange ball* and negatives like *the tube was not hit by the orange ball*), again they practically never occurred (we got equivalents of *the orange ball hit the upright tube* [21/0/5] and of *the orange ball did not hit* [*missed, passed,* etc.] *the tube* [21/5/0—the "flubs" not expressing negation in any way]). Our Center for Comparative Psycholinguistics is right now in the process of collecting such simply describing data from native speakers of some 20 languages around the world, using a color-film containing 70 similar demonstrations designed with "psycholinguistic malice aforethought"; we want to see how diverse languages equivalently take account of various cognitive distinctions (presumably universal) in the surface structures of their sentences.

At this point one might reasonably ask why do "unnatural," yet grammatical, sentencings ever occur? The title of the Osgood and Bock (1977) paper, "Salience and Sentencing: Some Production Principles," implies the answer: *All languages provide ways for their speakers to move constituents of messages that are salient to them forward (earlier) in time of production;* this, by the way, is consistent with the Hullian motivation principle (Hull, 1943)—performance equaling habit strength times drive. The *Naturalness* Principle itself is based on the notion of the relative salience of Actors over Recipients and Figures over Ground, other things being equal; the principle can be overridden by (1) the *vividness* (inherent salience, affective intensity, of semantic features) and/or (2) the *motivation of speaker* (attributed salience, due to topicality, interest, identification, etc.) with respect to nonactor or nonfigure constituents.

Kay Bock's thesis (summarized in Osgood and Bock, 1977), investigated the effects of vividness, using a variety of optional transformations in English. In the following examples, I capitalize the noun-phrase alternatives that were assumed to be ⁺Vivid in each case: the dative (*the boy tossed the FRISBEE/ball to the dog/ST. BERNARD / the boy tossed the ST. BERNARD/dog the ball/FRISBEE*), the passive (*the BULLDOZER/truck crushed the flowers/DAFFODILS / the DAFFODILS/flowers were crushed by the truck/BULLDOZER*), the genitive (*the powwow was held in the WIGWAM/tent of the chief/SITTING BULL / the powwow was held in SITTING BULL'S/the chief's tent/WIGWAM*), and a number of others. The prediction was that where the ⁺Vivid alternative was already in the temporally *prior* position (*the boy tossed the FRISBEE to the dog* or *the boy tossed the ST. BERNARD the ball*) there would be few shifts in reproduction, but where the ⁺Vivid was given in the temporally *subsequent* position (*the boy tossed the ball to the ST. BERNARD* or *the boy tossed the dog the FRISBEE*) there would be significant transformational shift tendencies. These vividness predictions had to be tempered by the Naturalness Principle, of course: If the given structures were already ⁺Natural, they would tend to be reproduced that way; if they were ⁻Natural, they would tend to be shifted back into the natural form in reproduction, regardless of the Vividness relations. In other words, 50% of the time Vividness and Naturalness Principles would reinforce each other and 50% of the time they would compete with each other. The results were generally consistent with these expectations.

An hypothesis derived from "putting on the booties of childhood" received interesting support from both cross-language linguistic data and from experimental psycholinguistic data, as reported by Osgood and Tanz (1977). The intuition was about the prelinguistic child's cognizing of bitransitive situations (prototypically, Person A transfers inanimate object X to Person B), where the X is perceptually a part of the transfer relation and Person B perceptually the real object (little Suzie perceiving BIG-BROTHER GIVES-BOOK-TO BIG-SISTER) —and this led to the title of our paper, "Will the Real Direct Object in Bitransitive Sentences Please Stand Up?"

For the cross-language data, a number of predictions were verified such as: (1) that the so-called indirect object (D for dative) should be more frequently marked than the so-called direct object (O for objective) and that this should be more often the case when D is closest to the verb (i.e., the unnatural transform); (2) the strong prediction—that in languages where O is marked in unitransitive clauses but not in bitransitive, the same marker will be applied to the D—was upheld in a surprising number of cases; (3) that in languages where nouns are incorporated in verbs, O-incorporation should be greater than D-incorporation (clearly upheld); and (4) that the natural SVOD structure should be less constrained transformationwise than the unnatural SVDO structure. Three psycholinguistic experiments supported the predictions (5) that natural SVOD forms would be more faithfully recalled as given than SVDO forms; (6) that unnatural SVDO forms would be more frequently shifted to SVOD in recall; and (7) that as probes for single-word associations, V should produce O more often than D, and O should produce V more often than D does. So it would appear that, despite what grammarians have been telling us for centuries, the *real* direct object in bitransitive sentences is the so-called indirect object!

Finally, the Naturalness Principle makes certain predictions about the ordering of clauses in complex, conjoined sentences—namely, that where there is a natural order in prelinguistic experience with complex events, this order in sentencing will be either required or at least preferred across languages. In the simple junction mode of conjoining, either order is natural (*Mary sang and John played the guitar* or the reverse). But for the temporal mode there is a natural order in experience (and thus *Mary got dressed and went to the party*, but not !*Mary went to the party and got dressed*);[10] similarly for the causal mode (*it was raining and John got wet*, but definitely not !*John got wet and it was raining*) and the combined causal-temporal mode (*Dan ate some poisonous mushrooms and got sick* but definitely not !*Dan got sick and ate some poisonous mushrooms*).

Opačić (1973) measured processing times (for judging whether a given pair of clauses, then a given conjoiner, was "possible" or "impossible") and then the complex sentence the subject produced *if* he had said "possible"—for these and other modes of conjoining. For all modes in which two orders are possible, one natural (N) and the other unnatural (U), natural-given and natural-retained (NN) had the shortest latencies, UN were next in ease of processing (i.e., where the subject *restores* the natural order), UU came next (literal memorizing), and NU (shifting from the natural *to* the unnatural ordering) was the most time-consuming.

Results of this sort are most encouraging and support the general notion that the cognitive structures developed in prelinguistic perceptual experience do in fact provide the "most natural" cognitive bases for comprehending and producing sentences—both in the evolution of language in the human species and in the development of its contemporary children. But, of course, neither this nor the demonstrably intimate parallelism between nonlinguistic and linguistic cognizing means that such prelinguistic capacity in itself constitutes "a language." It lacks three of the criteria for *anything* being a language—nonrandomly recurrent signals in some channel, reciprocality in sending and receiving such signals, and combinatorial productivity—precisely because such prelinguistic cognizing cannot be *abstracted* from the perceptual and motor chains that bind it to reality.

NOTES

1. In formulating my own notions about "what is a language" here and in the sections on human languages that follow, I am indebted to the participants in a conference I attended on *Universals of Language*, sponsored by the Social Science Research Council in 1961 and later published in a volume under the same title edited by Joseph H. Greenberg (1963)—particularly papers by Greenberg, Charles S. Hockett, and Uriel Weinreich.

2. See Osgood (1979) for detailing of these Naturalness Principles—including, of course, the fact that human languages also utilize adverbial substitutes for simple junction (*and*) and disjunction (*but*) which permit clausal permutations (which might well be unnecessary in Octopian).

3. See K. von Frisch (1974) and James L. Gould (1975) for updating references on communication in the bee.

4. With regard to semantics, particularly impressive to me was the fact that Sarah would make the same "semantic-feature" choices for the plastic *sign* of, say, an APPLE (Round rather than Square, Stemmed rather than Nonstemmed) as for the apple object itself—when the sign itself happens to be a flat purple triangle!

5. I can't resist noting (with no little remorse) that during my tenure on the University of Illinois Research Board in the early 1960s a request for support of precisely this type of study was voted on favorably, but the young couple who were to raise the baby chimp backed out—otherwise this breakthrough might have occurred at the University of Illinois!

6. And, I would add, the greater the correspondence of competence-based grammars to prelinguistically based cognitive structures, the higher should be their evaluation in competition with alternative grammars.

7. In preliminary mimeographed versions of my evolving APG (Abstract Performance Grammar) I have used as a parenthetical subtitle "Picking Oneself Up by One's Booties"!

8. During the summer and fall of 1977, two of my students tested this radical hypothesis—S. N. Sridhar and Annette Zehler in Bangalore and Hiroshima, respectively, Kannada and Japanese both being SOV languages, but otherwise rather different (cf. Osgood, 1979).

9. With an *N* of 26 subjects, the first value is the number fitting the naturalness prediction, the second the number of "flubs" (e.g., a subject opened his eyes too late!), and the third is the number contrary to the prediction.

10. I use the ! symbol to emphasize the fact that although such sentences as these may be completely unacceptable (indeed, mind-boggling), they are *not* ungrammatical—which raises some interesting questions about the notion of grammaticality, which we cannot go into here.

REFERENCES

Berlin, E., and Kay, P. *Basic color terms: Their universality and evolution.* Berkeley: University of California Press, 1969.

Boucher, J., and Osgood, C. E. The Pollyanna hypothesis. *Journal of Verbal Learning and Verbal Behavior,* 1969, *8*, 1–8.

Bronowski, J. In *To honor Roman Jakobson.* The Hague: Mouton, 1967.

Bronowski, J., and Bellugi, U. Language, name and concept. *Science,* 1970, *168*, 669–673.

Brown, R. *Words and things.* Glencoe, Ill.: Free Press, 1958.

Brown, R. *Psycholinguistics: Selected papers.* New York: Free Press, 1970.

Brown, R. *A first language: The early stages.* Cambridge, Mass.: Harvard University Press, 1973.

Clark, H. H. *The chronometric study of meaning components.* Paper presented at the CRNS Colloque Internationale sur les Problèmes Actuels de Psycholinguistique, Paris, December 1971.

Clark, H. H., and Chase, W. G. On the process of comparing sentences against pictures. *Cognitive Psychology*, 1972, *3*, 472–517.

Cooper, W. E., and Ross, J. R. World order. In *Papers from the parasession on functionalism.* Chicago: Chicago Linguistics Society, 1975.

Ervin, S. M., and Miller, W. R. Language development. In *Child psychology*, 62nd Yearbook, National Society for the Study of Education. Chicago: University of Chicago Press, 1963.

Gardner, B. T., and Gardner, R. A. Evidence for sentence constituents in the early utterances of child and chimpanzee. *Journal of Experimental Psychology: General*, 1975, *104*, 244–267.

Gardner, R. A., and Gardner, B. T. Teaching sign language to a chimpanzee. *Science*, 1969, *165*, 664–672.

Gould, J. L. Honey bee recruitment: The dance-language controversy. *Science*, 1975, *189*, 685–692.

Greenberg, J. H. Some universals of grammar with particular reference to the order of meaningful elements. In J. H. Greenberg (Ed.), *Universals of language.* Cambridge, Mass.: MIT Press, 1963.

Greenberg, J. H. Language universals. In T. A. Sebeok (Ed.), *Current trends in linguistics: III. Theoretical foundations.* The Hague: Mouton, 1966.

Hamilton, H. W., and Deese, J. Does linguistic marking have a psychological correlate? *Journal of Verbal Learning and Verbal Behavior*, 1971, *10*, 707–714.

Hoosain, R. The processing of negation. *Journal of Verbal Learning and Verbal Behavior*, 1973, *12*, 618–626.

Hull, C. L. *Principles of behavior: An introduction to behavior theory.* New York: Appleton-Century-Crofts, 1943.

Jakobson, R. C., and Halle, M. *Fundamentals of language.* The Hague: Mouton, 1956.

Keenan, E., and Comrie, B. Noun phrase acceptability and universal grammar. *Linguistic Inquiry*, 1977, *8*, 63–100.

Lawrence, D. H. Acquired distinctiveness of cues: I. Transfer between discriminations on the basis of familiarity with the stimulus. *Journal of Experimental Psychology*, 1949, *39*, 770–784.

Maclay, H., and Newman, S. Two variables affecting the message in communication. In D. Wilner (Ed.), *Decisions, values and groups.* New York: Pergamon Press, 1960.

Mahl, G. F. People talking when they can't hear their voices. In A. Siegman and B. Pope (Eds.), *Studies in dyadic communication.* New York: Pergamon Press, 1972.

Malinowski, B. The problem of learning in primitive languages. Supplement in C. K. Ogden and I. A. Richards (Eds.), *The meaning of meaning*. New York: Harcourt Brace, 1938.

McNeill, D. *The acquisition of language*. New York: Harper, 1970.

McNeill, D. Sentence structure in chimpanzee communication. In K. J. Connolly & J. Bruner (Eds.), *The growth of competence*. New York: Academic Press, 1974.

Opačić, G. *Natural order in cognizing and clause order in the sentencing of conjoined expressions*. Doctoral dissertation, University of Illinois, 1973.

Osgood, C. E. Behavior theory and the social sciences. *Behavioral Science*, 1956, *1*, 167–185.

Osgood, C. E. *Lectures on language performance*. Berlin, Heidelberg, New York: Springer, 1979.

Osgood, C. E., and Bock, J. K. Salience and sentencing: Some production principles. In S. Rosenberg (Ed.), *Sentence production: Developments in research and theory*. Hillsdale, N.J.: Lawrence Erlbaum Associates, 1977.

Osgood, C. E., and Hoosain, R. *Pollyanna II: It is easier to 'simply get the meanings' of affectively positive than affectively negative words*. Manuscript in preparation, 1979.

Osgood, C. E., May, W. H., and Miron, M. S. *Cross-cultural universals of affective meaning*. Urbana, Ill.: University of Illinois Press, 1975.

Osgood, C. E., and Tanz, C. Will the real direct object in bitransitive sentences please stand up? In *Linguistic studies presented to Joseph Greenberg*. Saratoga, Calif.: Anma Libri, 1977.

Paget, R. A. The origin of language. *Science*, 1944, *99*, 14–15.

Premack, A. J., and Premack, D. Teaching language to an ape. *Scientific American*, 1972, *227*, 92–99.

Premack, D. Language in chimpanzee? *Science*, 1971, *172*, 808–822.

Searle, J. R. *Speech acts: An essay in the philosophy of language*. London: Cambridge University Press, 1969.

Slobin, D. I. Cognitive prerequisites for the development of grammar. In C. A. Ferguson & D. I. Slobin (Eds.), *Studies in child language development*. New York: Holt, Rinehart and Winston, 1973.

Thorndike, E. L. The origin of language. *Science*, 1943, *98*, 1–6.

von Frisch, K. Decoding the language of the bees. *Science*, 1974, *185*, 663–668.

Weinreich, U. *Languages in contact*. New York: Linguistic Circle, 1953.

Winograd, T. Understanding natural language. *Cognitive Psychology*, 1972, *3*, 1–191.

Zipf, G. K. *The psychobiology of language*. Boston: Houghton Mifflin, 1935.

Zipf, G. K. *Human behavior and the principle of least effort*. Cambridge, Mass.: Addison-Wesley, 1949.

Human Communicative Behavior: A Biological Model

WILLIAM ORR DINGWALL

A. LINGUISTICS AND LANGUAGE

THE DEFINITION OF LANGUAGE

The vast majority of texts dealing with the subject of linguistics define it as "the science of language" (Robins 1964) or, less cryptically, as "the scientific study of language" (Lyons 1968). The prominent inclusion of the term *science* in this definition is probably premature, since the manner in which scientific method can apply to an essentially descriptive discipline such as linguistics is far from clear (cf. Botha 1968; Derwing 1973; Dingwall 1978). Our concern here, however, is not directly involved with questions of methodology, but rather with the object of study, *language*. Definitions of this phenomenon run the gamut from "[the] set (finite or infinite) of sentences, each finite in length and constructed out of a finite set of elements" (Chomsky 1957: 13) to "a communication system that is capable of transmitting new information" (Lieberman 1975:6). Either of these extreme definitions would appear quite applicable to various zoosemiotic systems (see Thorpe 1972:28–29) as well as to the output of various mechanical devices such as a digital clock. This is clearly *not* what the majority of linguists mean by language.

For them, language is equivalent to *human* communication only. Cairns and Cairns make this abundantly clear when they state in a recent introductory text:

> The most complicated communication system in the animal kingdom is, of course, that of human beings, Language. One purpose of linguistics is to describe those properties of Language that are common to all human beings and that differentiate it from the communication systems of other animals. [1976:5]

Tables and figures are reprinted with the permission of the publisher from *Die neueren Sprachen* 77:3/4 (1978):271–99. Verlag Moritz Diesterweg, Frankfurt am Main, West Germany.

Since the aim is to define language as a species-specific communication system, the output modality of this system is often stressed, since it clearly distinguishes it from systems employed by other animals (see Dingwall 1975). Thus, the standard definition of language adds this feature for good measure, as the following definitions demonstrate:

> Language . . . refer[s] to that verbal communication system developed and used by humans. [Glucksberg and Danks 1975:23]

> . . . [t]he subject matter of linguistics is confined to verbal messages only. [Sebeok 1977:1056]

The problem with using an output modality as the defining characteristic of language is that it is inconsistent with the goal set forth by Cairns and Cairns of describing "those properties of Language that are common to *all* human beings" (emphasis added). While it is true that only humans use articulate speech to communicate, it is not true that all humans who communicate use articulate speech. Either one defines language in such a way as to exclude humans that communicate nonverbally or one defines it in such a way as to include all humans who communicate. If the latter option is chosen, one cannot claim that it is a communication system confined to humans alone (see fig. 1).

Despite all protestations to the contrary (see Chomsky 1972), linguistics has remained essentially a descriptive discipline devoted to the study of corpora that consist of sets of sentences. Language is a noun with no verbal form. The goal of linguistics is the structural analysis of an entity, not a behavior. Until very recently, this entity has been studed in virtual isolation from the organism in which it resides and from the contexts in which it is produced. The isolation is reinforced by the distinction between competence and performance that separates knowledge of the structure of language from its use and asserts that competence alone is the appropriate domain of theoretical linguistics (Chomsky 1965).

Recent suggestions for broadening the scope of linguistics to include pragmatics have certainly been steps in the right direction. It is unfortunate, however, that many of these suggestions involve simply adding various formal devices to a grammar of competence in the above sense (see Lakoff 1971; Ross 1970) and that they are restricted to one output modality—speech.

It is not my intention here to argue whether the definitions of language outlined above are appropriate for linguistics. They are certainly not inconsistent with the traditional descriptive approach of the discipline. I will argue, however, that such definitions are inappropriate for interdisciplinary fields such as psycholinguistics and neurolinguistics

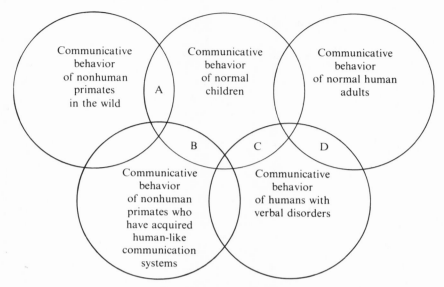

Fig. 1. The continuum of communicative behaviors evinced by various populations of primates. The interesting areas of overlap are labeled. A: Various reflexive and affective aspects of communicative behavior. B: Similarities in developmental sequences of communicative behavior. C: Similarities between communication systems in development and in dissolution. D: Continuities between dysphasic and normal communicative behavior, e.g., slips of the tongue, the tip-of-the-tongue phenomenon, etc.[1]

which study a behavior rather than an entity. In these interdisciplinary fields, all behavior bearing on communication is subject to study; study is not limited to behaviors such as judgments of grammaticality, synonymy, etc., that are needed to establish a corpus, or to speech and its derivatives. The communicative behavior of populations that would be considered distinct by linguists intersects, as suggested in figure 1. Human communicative behavior is not an entity such as language which one either possesses in its entirety or not at all. Rather, it is a mosaic of structures, skills, and knowledge that does not develop in children as a whole, does not disappear in dysphasics as a whole, and undoubtedly did not evolve as a whole. Finally, such behavior cannot profitably be studied in isolation from the environment in which it takes place or from the peripheral and central structures of the organism that subserve it.

What is being argued, then, is that the definition of language proposed by linguists is both too narrow and too monolithic to character-

ize adequately the types of communicative behavior addressed by fields
such as psycholinguistics and neurolinguistics, which study performance (as opposed to competence). Furthermore, it is suggested that
an adequate model for these interdisciplinary fields must be tied to
what is known about the biological bases of behavior in general and
about communicative behavior in particular. Before attempting to elaborate such a model, let us first consider how we might define communicative behavior in primates. (See Chomsky 1980 for an exposition of
his latest views on the issues raised in this section together with extensive invited comment on these views.)

B. BIOLOGY AND
COMMUNICATIVE BEHAVIOR

THE DEFINITION OF COMMUNICATIVE BEHAVIOR

While, as we have seen, the linguists' definition of language is too
narrow for our purposes, definitions of communicative behavior formulated by those working within a biological framework often appear
too broad. Many definitions simply require some correlation of behaviors between two organisms. Thus, for Altmann, it is "a process by
which the behavior of an individual affects the behavior of others"
(1967:326), a statement which is so general that the event of two individuals bumping into each other accidentally would constitute an instance of communication. Certainly, the factor of an external stimulus
affecting behavior of an organism in some manner is a necessary but
not sufficient condition for communication to take place. If one is interested solely in the transfer of information, one can concentrate on the
receiver organism alone. For information transfer to occur, it is only
necessary that signals fall within the acuity range of the receptor organs
of the organism and that the signals are interpreted unambiguously by
its nervous system. The nature of processing that occurs in the nervous
system will depend on the type of nervous system and type of stimulus.
In general, what one observes is a progression both phylogenetically
and ontogenetically in primates from reflexive to affective to cognitive
processing systems. While even so broad a term as "transfer of information" may seem inappropriate for reflexive behaviors such as jump-
ing at a loud noise, surely this term does apply to behaviors involving
a degree of cognition, such as the interpretation of a cloud formation
to signify rain. But is this really what is meant by communication?

MacKay (1972), in a most perceptive analysis of communicative
processes, suggests that the kind of behavior we have been discussing
does indeed involve transfer of information, but that it should not be
termed communication. Communication in his view involves an inter-

action between organisms such that the sender organism's behavior is *goal directed* towards the receiver organism. The essentials of MacKay's proposal are schematized in figure 2.

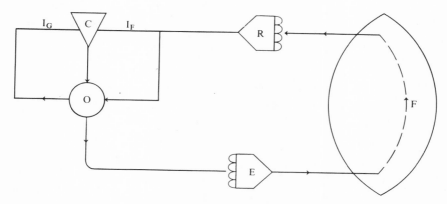

Fig. 2. The essentials of MacKay's model of the sender organism. The receptor system R of the organism monitors the action of its effector system E in field F. *Goal direction* involves essentially the comparison of the current state of field F (I_F) with the goal criterion I_G in evaluator C, so that a mismatch may be communicated to the organizing system O.

In this figure, the receptor system R of the organism monitors the action of the effector system E in field F. Goal direction involves essentially the comparison of the current state of field F (I_F) with the goal criterion I_G in evaluator C, so that a mismatch may be transmitted to the organizing system O. Many organisms, including man, appear to possess neural feature detectors which would determine to some degree the information included in I_F. Thus a bank of feature filters might be added to the model between the receptor system and I_F. One might also complicate O by including in it the capacity to produce a variety of responses as well as a mechanism for determining priorities in the production of these responses. Once again, one can imagine a progression here from a relatively small repertoire of stereotyped and automatic responses in communication systems of the reflexive and affective type to an extremely large and potentially infinite repertoire of novel and propositional responses in communication systems of the cognitive type.

Note that goal direction as defined in this model resembles somewhat Austin's concept of "speech act" when defined in a modality-free manner (see Bates 1976). The *locutionary act* is the joint result of the organizing and effector systems. The *illocutionary act* might be equated with I_G, the goal criterion, while the *perlocutionary act* is analogous to the comparison of I_F (the state of field F) with I_G (the goal criterion in the evaluator).

There is one basic difference between my interpretation of Mac-Kay's system presented above and his own. In order for his system to provide for the continuities in communicative behavior schematized in figure 1, it is essential that goal-directed behavior not necessarily imply volitional control. In large measure, what I have termed reflexive and affective communication systems do not involve such control. If we do not make this distinction, then a vast proportion of what has been termed animal communication cannot be considered communication at all. Such a distinction allows us to differentiate between non-human primate communication in the wild, which is goal directed but largely nonvolitional, and the acquired communicative behaviors of great apes in the laboratory, which is both goal directed and volitional. But what about the person who blushes in embarrassment or the poker player who cannot keep a poker face? Are they communicating in terms of this model? There can be no doubt that there may be a transfer of information in these situations and that it is nonvolitional. That such behaviors are goal directed in MacKay's sense appears doubtful. On the other hand, a dog who, after whining and nudging his master in order to gain attention, scratches at the door to be let out is certainly engaging in goal-directed behavior.

Goal direction on the part of the sender organism is not enough to ensure communication, as MacKay seems to imply. The receptor organism must, of course, be equipped to process such goal-directed behavior. This requires, as noted before, that the behavior can be perceived by the organism and that its central nervous system, operating in terms of a relatively closed or open genetic program (see Mayr 1974), is capable of interpreting the behavior of the sender organism unambiguously. Thus, if we should approach the cage of a rhesus monkey who in turn approaches us with teeth bared, we might interpret its expression anthropocentrically as a smile and even act on this interpretation by reaching out to pet it. Criteria for the communication process would have been met, save for the last stage, interpretation; the receiver must have knowledge of the communication system being employed, and in this case the receiver did not. It is not necessary, however, that both communicators be of the same species.

A GENERAL BIOLOGICAL MODEL OF COMMUNICATIVE BEHAVIOR

Our attempt to clarify the nature of communicative behavior in the previous section reveals that we have already begun to operate within a biological framework—one that involves monitoring the environment as well as considering peripheral structures (such as receptor and effector systems) and central processing structures (such as the evaluator and the organizing system). We are now ready to investigate a biological model of communication in more detail. We shall confine ourselves to primate communication, particularly that of the great apes, since it is reasonable to expect that if homologies in communicative behavior (i.e., behaviors that could in principle be traced back to a common ancestor) are to be discovered, they will be discovered among our closest relatives (see Hodos 1976 for a discussion of the concept of *behavioral homology* and Dingwall 1979 for a detailed application of this concept to the evolution of human communication). Unfortunately, much of the research on the evolution of human communicative behavior has been based on a classification of animals termed the *scala naturae* or Great Chain of Being, in which animals are arranged according to their imagined complexity, with man (or God) at the top. Comparisons of animals arranged in such a manner are meaningless if one is interested in the phylogeny of traits (see Hodos and Campbell 1969). It is not obvious to me what can be learned about the evolution of human communication from comparisons in terms of a set of features, such as those proposed by Hockett (1960), which are derived from the logical analysis of communicative behaviors and are applied helter-skelter throughout the animal kingdom, without regard to the structures that subserve the behavior and without regard to phylogenetic proximity to man. It is interesting that when such features are applied to primates alone, they fail to distinguish man from other members of the order (Altmann 1967).

Hierarchical Input/Output System

In biology, models of behaviors such as communication are typically presented in the form of hierarchical input/output systems. Such systems generally include specification of peripheral receptor and effector structures as well as some details of the routes taken by the tracts relaying neural impulses to and from a central processor that encompasses much of the central nervous system. A model of this type is depicted in figure 3 and, with further simplification, in figure 4, panel B.

In the latter figure, it is proposed that three basic transductions are involved in communicative behavior. The first (T_1) can be labeled *cognition* and involves the capacity of the brain of an organism to produce and to comprehend, if they impinge upon it, a variety of concepts which may be either simple or complex. Cognitive psychologists such as Piaget have to some extent clarified the nature of this transduction as it develops in humans. Ethologists and comparative psychologists have investigated its nature in other species.

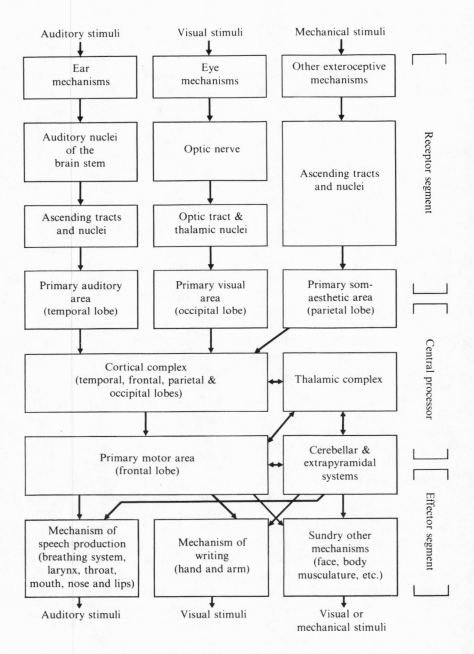

Fig. 3. Schematic diagram of neural mechanisms for human communication.

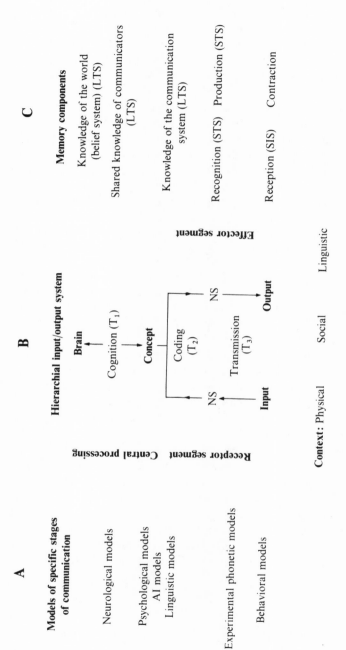

Fig. 4. Aspects of a general biological model of the communicative behavior of primates. (T_1 = transduction₁; LTS = long-term store; STS = short-term store; SIS = sensory information store; NS = neurosign.)

One cannot at present judge whether an animal is in command of a particular concept unless the animal signals it in some manner. This involves linking the concept with a neurological state, the neurosign (NS), that mediates either its production or its recognition. T_2, or what might be termed *coding*, involves the linkage between an abstract conceptual structure and an equally abstract sensorimotor representation, which is only imperfectly reflected in the various states of its production and recognition. When speech alone is considered, it is this transduction that theoretical linguistics regards as its major concern. (Thus, meaning is generally taken to involve an abstract conceptual structure, while speech sounds are taken to involve an equally abstract phonetic representation.) Recent work by Sachs (1967), Bransford and Franks (1972), Kintsch (1974), and others has provided the first clear evidence of the nature of conceptual structure, while at the same time neuroscientists have demonstrated in event-related potential studies that what is being termed the neurosign is more than a theoretical construct (see Dingwall and Whitaker 1974). On the other hand, a decade of work in experimental psycholinguistics has made it abundantly clear that current linguistic theory fails to provide a viable model of either the processes underlying T_2 or its endpoints (cf. Fodor et al. 1974; Watt 1970, 1974; Dingwall and Shields 1973; Wanner 1977; Wanner et al. 1977).

The third transduction (T_3), which we shall term *transmission*, involves the processes of signal production and detection. It is this transduction, because of its relative accessibility to study, about which most is known, thanks to the efforts of physiologists, physiological psychologists, hearing and speech scientists, experimental phoneticians, and others interested in this aspect of communication (see Lass 1976).

It should be noted that in a biological model of communication, effector and receptor segments involve quite different neurological substrates, as even the simplified account in figure 3 clearly shows. There is considerable psychological as well as neurological evidence that production and comprehension (of which these segments represent the late and early stages, respectively) involve quite different processes. This is true whether one examines these aspects of communication in normal adults, in children acquiring communicative abilities, or in persons whose communicative abilities are impaired in various ways (see Straight 1976 for a review of some of the evidence). Similarly, while it is clear that man is the only species that is capable of producing articulate speech, it is not at all clear that he is the only species that can process it (see Burdick and Miller 1975; Fouts et al. 1976; Kuhl 1978).

To what extent is the processing represented by the three transductions independent of each other? Let us first consider T_3. We know that trained phoneticians can abstract from a language phonetic elements which they cannot further process. In clinical cases of pure word deafness and pure alexia, words are heard or seen, yet are not further processed, even though they represent elements of the native language of the patient. Cases exhibiting neologistic jargon or glossolalia may represent the random production of sound sequences without further encoding. There is evidence that both transmission and coding can take place without cognition. We have all had occasion to process materials we could not understand; Lewis Carroll's "Jabberwocky" is an extreme example. There are cases of aphasia known as "isolation of speech area," where the patient shows little evidence of comprehension or volitional production of speech, but does repeat verbal material that has been presented. Despite the fact that such material does not appear to be processed cognitively (i.e., via T_1), it nevertheless appears to be processed by T_2. Thus, if the patient is presented with a grammatically incorrect sentence such as (1):

(1) She buy a dress yesterday.

it is corrected to form (2):

(2) She bought a dress yesterday.

Presented with items in a foreign language, a patient will pronounce them, but with an accent characteristic of his or her own language (see Whitaker 1976 for a detailed discussion of such a patient). A similar type of automatic processing is observed in speech errors. Thus, a German speaker intending to say (3):

(3) Er hat in Berlin drei *Tage* in der *Woche* gearbeitet.

exchanged the italicized words to produce (4):

(4) Er hat in Berlin drei Wochen im Tag gearbeitet.

Note that all appropriate inflectional changes have been made, even though this was not the intended sentence (see Bierwisch 1970). There is an automatic character to coding and transmission which is also typical of other overlearned outputs, such as driving a car and dancing. This factor of automatization appears to be tied to a critical period in individual human development, at least in the case of speech output (Oyama 1976), and has a plausible neurological explanation (see Dingwall 1975).

Can the processes represented by T_1 take place independently of T_2 and T_3? This question involves the essential problem of the relationship of language and thought. Most investigators agree that thought is possible without language (see Slobin 1975a for a recent discussion). If one narrows the definition of language to include only T_2 and T_3, then the evidence we have discussed above would indicate that language can occur without thought, whereas communicative behavior as defined in this paper clearly must involve T_1.

It is conceivable that communicative behavior can occur without coding (T_2). Halliday (1975:13) has noted that the earliest stages in language development do not involve T_2, but rather involve a direct mapping of concepts onto expression. Thus, each complex concept is tied to one unanalyzed unit of expression. This system lacks duality of patterning in Hockett's sense (1960). Similar by-passing of T_2 may characterize much of the reflexive and affective vocalizations of primates.[2]

Finally, it should be pointed out that two elements which are essential for communication have not been specified in either figure 3 or figure 4B: a series of feature filter systems to provide *feedforward* (defined by MacKay 1972 as "information in advance of any external action"), as well as a feedback mechanism providing visual, tactile-kinesthetic, and auditory information of ongoing activity. (See Borden 1979 for a detailed review of evidence relating to the role of feedback in human communication.)

Memory Components

Associated with each transduction are various kinds of knowledge stored in either long- or short-term memory which are necessary for the processing that goes on at the levels of these transductions (see fig. 4C).

On the input side of the hierarchical model in figure 4, there is evidence that after initial auditory or visual analysis, which undoubtedly involves feature detectors of some sort, information is stored briefly in a relatively gross form in a *sensory information store* (SIS). This preliminary processing may be sufficient to determine whether a signal engages the dominant hemisphere of the brain in further processing. There is considerable empirical evidence that what we term *coding* is carried on in this hemisphere. If the coding mechanism is engaged, then the signal is further processed, utilizing knowledge of the communication system held in long-term storage (LTS). The recognition process involves periods of short-term storage (STS) at various levels of analysis. As processing continues, perhaps in parallel with the above stages, employing not only shared knowledge of the communicators but also general knowledge of the world, the form of the signal is stored in short-term memory only long enough to abstract the *gist* of the message (see Pisoni and Sawusch 1975).

Thus, very shortly after hearing a sentence, one's memory for lexical items or syntax is near chance levels, but memory for semantic content is extremely good (Sachs 1967). If materials containing identical semantic content are presented in a simple versus complex linguistic form, then the complex materials will take longer to process; however, questions about content are answered equally rapidly once the material is processed (Kintsch and Monk 1972).

Bransford et al. (1972) have clearly shown that sentence processing is constructive (i.e., involves inference based on knowledge of the world). Thus, when sentences are inferentially related, as in the case of (5) and (6) below, subjects in recognition tasks are invariably confused about which one they were presented during the acquisition stage.

(5) The racoons raced up the tree and the dogs circled around them.

(6) The racoons raced up the tree and the dogs circled around it.

On the output side, knowledge of the world also plays a role in almost any conversational exchange. If, for example, I mention to a detective that I was held by my abductors in a car, he might ask me if I were put into the trunk. He asks this because his general knowledge of cars and abductions makes it a reasonable question. I might continue by telling him that I was driven to the mall where I was finally released. This statement assumes shared knowledge of the identity and perhaps location of the mall in question. What Grice (1968) has termed *conversational postulates* clearly involve both kinds of knowledge associated with T_1.

Note that on both the input and the output sides of the system model knowledge of the communication system is directly involved in performance, rather than abstracted away from it, as in Chomsky's model involving the competence/performance distinction. I agree with other investigators who question the validity of this distinction for interdisciplinary fields such as psycholinguistics and neurolinguistics (see Watt 1974; Whitaker 1970). If such a distinction is to be employed at all, it must be redefined so that competence applies to cognition (T_1), which appears not to be lateralized in the brain, while performance relates to coding (T_2) and transmission (T_3), which are.

Finally, in the last stage of output, short-term memory once again plays a role, providing a buffer for strings, perhaps of syntagma length, being readied for transmission (Laver 1970). It is at this stage that errors in ordering can occur, which happens in slips of the tongue and

Fig. 5. Elaborated models of the transductions involved in coding and transmission. These particular models, which are based on Pisoni and Sawusch (1975) on the input side and on Fromkin (1971) (for T_2) and on Cooper (1972) (for T_1) on the output side, are confined to the verbal input/output modality of humans.

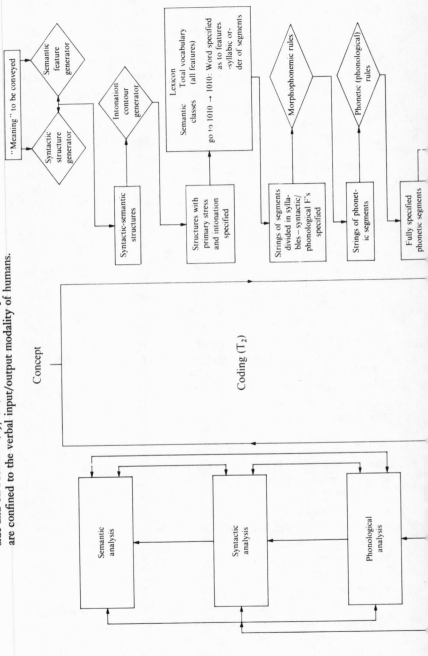

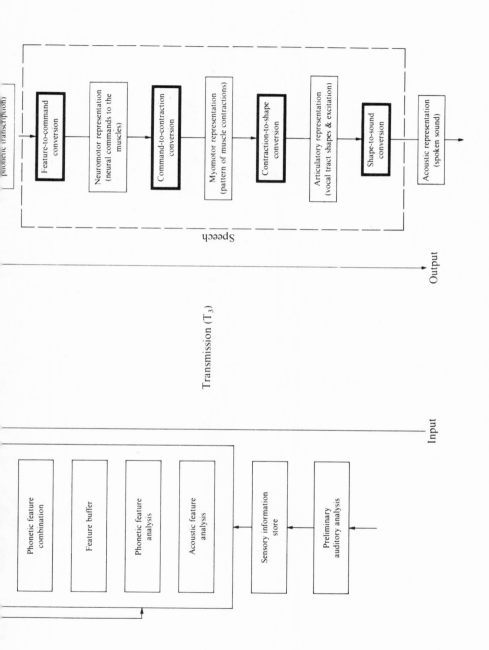

in dysphasia. Whether storage at later levels of the output process exists is not yet known.

It is clear that at each stage in processing a different code is employed in memory. The code of the sensory information store involved in transmission differs from that of the short-term store involved in coding. The form of storage differs in turn from the conceptual memory for semantic content, which we might term *mentalese* following Fodor (1975).[3]

Elaborated Models of Specific Stages of Communication

Investigators from many fields have provided us with elaborated models, based on a variety of empirical data, of the processes and structures involved in the transductions we have been discussing (see fig. 4A for a listing of models). While psychologists have generally concentrated on the representation of conceptual structures in memory (see Kintsch 1974; Frederiksen 1975), scholars working in artificial intelligence (AI) and in linguistics have been more interested in the coding processes that link the neurosign to such structures (see Chomsky 1965; Winograd 1972). Researchers in the area of experimental phonetics have, as one might expect, concentrated on aspects of the transmission stage (T_3) of communication. Figure 5 presents representative models of coding and transmission on both the input and output sides. Unfortunately, such models have been almost exclusively confined to speech processing.

We have already discussed in some detail the types of processes represented on the input side in figure 5. The model schematized there is based on that of Pisoni and Sawusch (1975). Note the parallel nature of the processing involved, as indicated by the double-headed arrows interconnecting various components. Exactly how such processing proceeds is far from understood. There is little evidence, for example, to support either the motor theory of speech perception or the related analysis-by-synthesis models of such processing (cf. Lieberman 1977; Fodor et al. 1974).

The output side presents a model of coding based on Fromkin's study of speech errors (1971) and on a model of transmission based on the work of the Haskins Laboratories group (Cooper 1972). While both models are based on empirical evidence, it is doubtful that either Fromkin or Cooper would claim that their proposals represent more than a gross approximation of the highly complex psychological and neurological processes that must be involved.

The most elaborate general model of the neurological bases of communicative behavior is that developed by Lamendella (1976, 1977). Its main features are summarized in figure 6. This model can be applied to the development of communicative behavior in the child, given the

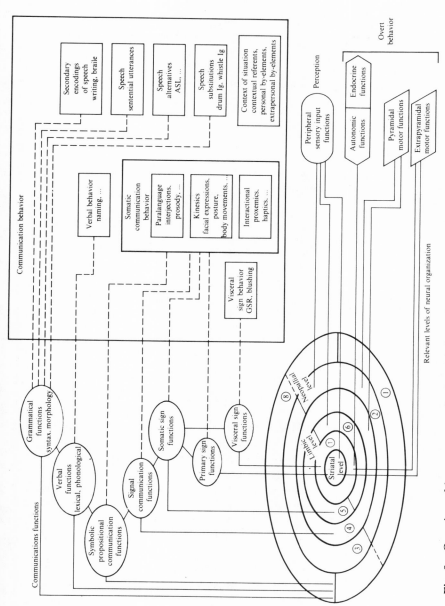

Fig. 6. Overview of human communication. (1) Lateralized systems of right hemisphere; (2) primary neocortical sensory systems; (3) primary neocortical motor systems; (4) volitional subsystem; (5) anterior affective subsystem; (6) posterior affective subsystem; (7) appetitive subsystem; (8) lateralized system of left hemisphere.

general rule of caudal to rostral maturation of the brain. The application is illustrated in table 1, where I have arranged communicative functions with behavioral examples under the rubrics of the reflexive, the affective, and the cognitive processing systems referred to earlier. In light of Lamendella's views on recapitulation (1976), the developmental sequence outlined in table 1 gives insight into the phylogeny of communicative behavior in the primate order.

Reflexive system (Striatal)	Affective system (Limbic)	Cognitive system (Neocortical)
Primary sign behavior (Global crying)	Visceral sign complexes (Differentiated crying) Somatovisceral sign schemata (Cooing) Somatovisceral sign learning (Tracking affective states of the communicator) Volitional signal communication (Babbling)	Propositional communication Gestural stage Naming stage Holophrastic stage Two-word stage Telegraphic stage Language stage

Table 1. The development of communicative behavior in children based on Lamendella's neurological model. These behaviors develop in the sequence from left to right and from top to bottom and are grouped under the neurological substrate that is held to be principally responsible for them.

In general, I find this grand scheme quite plausible and am in complete agreement with Lamendella that there is no reason to think that the brain divides behaviors into the neat packages that our taxonomies indicate. Although the model may be generally plausible, it should be noted that its representation of the localization of functions is based on scant empirical evidence. An example which may prove very important on this point is American Sign Language (ASL). It is by no means clear that ASL is lateralized to the dominant hemisphere in the deaf (cf. McKeever et al. 1976; Manning et al. 1977), as Lamendella's diagram indicates. This may be the reason that ASL can be processed by the great apes, who, as far as we now know, do not evince lateralization of communicative functions. Furthermore, the limbic system may not play as great a role in human and nonhuman communicative behavior as Lamendella and others have imagined (see Jürgens and Ploog [1976] and Dingwall [forthcoming] for further discussion).

Lamendella's view of human communication, however, differs significantly from my own in several ways. First, he embraces the linguists' definition of language, stressing that it is a communication system of a definite type, "characterized by quite specific syntactic, morphological, and phonological organization" (Lamendella 1976:401). Such a communication system is qualitatively different from that of nonhuman primates, and this narrow view of language leads to many of the problems discussed above, particularly the arbitrary exclusion of many humans who communicate from the class of language-users. Schnitzer, in a review of evidence from various types of aphasia that clearly demonstrated that phonological processing could be bypassed in human communicative behavior, came to the conclusion that "language without phonology *is* language" (1976:159). I concur with Schnitzer's conclusion, but not with his nomenclature. I would prefer to reformulate his finding by stating that human communicative behavior cannot be defined in terms of a particular input/output modality.

Second, I disagree with Lamendella's view that the stages of communicative development listed in table 1 do not represent a gradual accretion of the elements that make up a human communication system. I have stated earlier that human communication is a rich mosaic of structures, skills, and knowledge, and that it develops gradually in the child. If the child develops normally, then a particular input/output modality using the auditory medium will gain primacy over other modes, although the other communicative skills displayed in figure 6 will be present in the background. If the child does not develop normally or if speech becomes no longer available in adulthood, then other communicative skills, typically involving visual or tactile sensation, may be used predominantly. In fact, this multimodal backup system is one characteristic I would use to differentiate primate communication systems from those of other animals.

Now let us consider behavioral models of communication. Such models generally consist of taxonomies of observable communicative behaviors relating to the inputs and outputs of the organism and to the contexts in which such behaviors take place. As Savage and Rumbaugh (1977) have pointed out, such taxonomies may concentrate on (1) the physical aspects of the communicative act (the input/output modalities, the media used, etc.), or (2) the functions served by such acts (identification, contact, expression, etc.), or (3) abstract properties (*design features*) of such acts (openness, duality of patterning, etc.). Sebeok (1968) provides detailed examples of these approaches. Many of the best known taxonomies, such as those of Hockett (1960) and Hymes (1962), combine all three characteristics listed above. Sets of design features selected to characterize properties of animal communication in a general sense can provide insight into similarities and differences between communication systems, but such comparisons

provide little insight into phylogeny. Thus, if one compares the signing behavior of pongids and the songs of birds with human communication following Hockett, then one finds seven and nine differences
respectively out of a possible sixteen (see Dingwall 1979). The similarities found between birdsong and human communication are due to
the bias in Hockett's system towards a particular input/output modality. At the end of this paper, I shall propose a set of features based
on characteristics of the biological model. These features, in contrast
to those presented by Hockett, can be used to measure the complexity
of primate communication systems, and, at the same time, they are
phylogenetically relevant.

At least three aspects of the observable communicative behavior
of primates are of importance in the development of a general biological model. First, we need to survey the totality of communicative
behaviors in terms of the input/output modalities that man and other
primates are capable of using. This will give us some insight into the
nature and the complexity of primate communication systems. Second,
we need to discuss the role of context in communication. Biology has
always been concerned with the interaction of the organism and its
environment. Although we have recognized for quite some time the
sensitivity of the communicative behavior of nonhuman primates to
various aspects of the environment, we are only beginning to appreciate the existence of that quality in human communication. Third, we
need to investigate the aspects of the biological model that are engaged
by varied tasks involving the same communicative behavior. We shall
see that communicative behaviors to which we assign a single designation, such as *writing,* are indeed not monolithic capacities but rather
aggregates of skills.

Table 2 provides an overview of the diversity of factors involved
in primate communication systems. Communication by primates typically makes use of a variety of media, which are usually employed
simultaneously. We may isolate articulate speech as the central element
in face-to-face communication in normal humans, but we must realize
that it is nevertheless embedded in a complex of acoustic, visual, tactile,
and even olfactory signals, which may on occasion contradict the message the words transmit. Similarly, if we look at signing behavior in
deaf persons, we find that even though hand gestures are the predominant means of communication, various aspects of facial expression and
body movement interact with those gestures to help convey information. It is interesting to note that studies of nonhuman primate communication in the wild are unclear whether the acoustic or the visual
medium is more important (see Menzel 1971).

Input/Output Modality	Medium	Signal Types

ear/vocal tract (± articulation)	acoustic	prosodic feature
		  pitch
		  pause
		  loudness
		  tempo
		* segmental features
		  consonants
		  vowels
		voice qualifiers
		affective vocalization
		  laughter
		  cries
		  groans etc.
		vegetative sounds
		  cough
		  sneeze etc.
		* whistling

ear/hand		clapping finger-snapping drumming
eye/body	visual	body posture body movement proxemics spatial orientation piloerection

eye/hand-arm		hand gestures
		  sign languages
		  * fingerspelling etc.
		writing
		  * phonemic
		  * morphophonemic
		  * syllabic
		  ideographic
		  plastic cutouts etc.

eye/face		facial expression * lip-reading
cutaneous (usually hand/hand)	tactile	* braille writing grooming touching * petting
nose/body	chemical	body odor * perfume

Table 2. Primate communication systems: input/output modalities, media, and signal types. (Asterisks mark signal types presumed unique to human communication.)

In humans, and perhaps in some degree in nonhuman primates, almost any imaginable type and combination of input/output modalities can be recruited for purposes of communication. One can learn to write with a pencil grasped between one's teeth or to gesture with one's feet. One can learn to "read" using a series of electrodes attached to one's stomach or through letters traced on the palm of one's hand. The recent success in teaching great apes to communicate using the visual medium has sparked attempts to use similar modes of communication with humans who lack the ability to speak. As one might expect, these efforts have met with considerable success.

Communicative behavior is highly complex not only because of its varied and simultaneously occurring signal types, but also because it occurs in multifaceted environments. While it may be true that the ability to function in isolation in a *physical context* is a unique characteristic of human communication,[4] it can hardly be termed the norm. Where physical context is lacking or is not part of the shared knowledge of the communicators, it is usually supplied by descriptions, illustrations, or (on radio, for example) sound effects. Communication can be degraded by lack of knowledge of the communication system (as is often the case when dealing with foreigners, and is possibly the case when dealing with children) or by pathology. Contextual cues then become even more important for proper interpretation. Bloom (1970) was the first to point out the need for "rich interpretation" of early childhood utterances, taking into account aspects of the physical context. In cases of aphasia, the physical context becomes extremely important for cuing the meaning of communicative acts.

As sociolinguists have documented in detail, the *social context* is highly relevant to communicative behavior. This is as true of nonhuman primate societies as it is of human societies. For example, while the use of various lexical and grammatical devices in a human communication system such as Japanese to signal differences in sex, age, and status may be more subtle, it parallels nonverbal behavior among primates that signals the same types of sociological distinctions (see Lancaster 1975).

Finally, the *linguistic context* of communication must be considered. If we regard normal verbal behavior simply as a set of sentences unrelated to one another, we neglect to explain many phenomena such as anaphora, stress placement, article choice, and use of connectives. (See Isenberg 1968 for an early formal treatment of discourse phenomena.) Both monologue and dialogue must take account of linguistic context in order to function adequately. The linguistic context clearly has effects on performance. Thus, Wright (1972) has demonstrated that subjects make fewer errors when responding to questions if the questions are cast in the same grammatical form as the linguistic material upon which they are based. Thus, given a sentence such as (7):

(7) The crowd was held back by the police.

a question in the passive, such as (8), will probably be answered correctly, as well as more rapidly, than one in the active such as (9):

(8) Was the crowd held back by the police?

(9) Did the police hold back the crowd?

There may well be parallels to the role played by linguistic context in human communication systems in the communicative behavior of nonhuman primates. For example, Savage and Rumbaugh (1977) have recorded a definite ordering in the nonverbal exchanges that take place between chimpanzees. While physical context naturally plays a role, it is difficult to determine from the available evidence if either social or linguistic contexts are involved in the communicative behavior of great apes who have mastered humanlike communication systems.

The study of presupposition in pragmatics deals with the conditions under which a sentence is appropriate to the context in which it is used. There is no reason why this concept of presupposition cannot be broadened to cover the appropriateness of communicative behavior to the contexts in which it takes place.

Communicative Behavior as an Aggregate of Skills

Finally, one must not forget that the complex behavioral phenomenon we have been describing is the product of an equally complex organism that is ultimately controlled by the brain. There is no a priori requirement for the ultimate control mechanism to compartmentalize behavior in a manner isomorphic with human systems of nomenclature. It should therefore be obvious that behaviors instinctively felt to be monolithic because they have a single designation in some language are actually a complex aggregate of skills.

This is perhaps most graphically demonstrated in various aphasic syndromes. The array of deficits displayed by patients suffering from one of the so-called pure aphasias termed "alexia without agraphia" is a typical example (see Benson and Geschwind 1969). In such patients, verbal comprehension and production are typically uninvolved. However, these patients cannot read letters, words, or musical notation, although they may be able to read numbers (even roman numerals) as well as familiar logos. They can write, either voluntarily or to dictation, but cannot read what they have written. Objects, but not colors, can be recognized and appropriately named. Patients can verbally spell

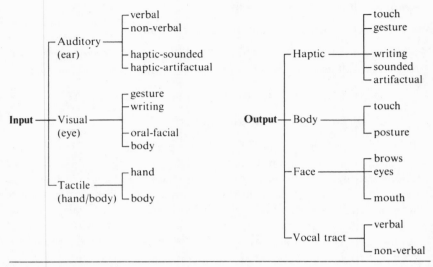

(a) input versus output
(b) modalities and types of input and output (cf. chart above)
(c) transformation of input
   imitation
   copying
   transcribing
   writing to dictation
   reading aloud etc.
(d) nature of transduction
   -isolation or by-passing of transductions
   -levels of processing involved in particular transductions (cf. Figure 5)
(e) memory components involved
(f) reflexive versus affective versus cognitive processing systems in communicative behavior (cf. Figure 7)

> **Table 3.** An aggregate of skills involved in communicative behavior. ("Haptic-sounded" refers to sounds made with the hands, such as finger snapping; "haptic-artifactual" refers to the use of mechanical means to make sounds with the hands, e.g., drumming.)

words, can understand spelled words, and can copy letters, but they cannot transcribe print into script.

The example describes an aphasia that is a breakdown in communicative behavior due to brain injury, and it reveals an aggregate of skills that is characteristic of the entire continuum of communicative behavior presented in figure 1. Some of these skills are listed in table 3. As already noted, input and output, comprehension and production, are different processes neurologically, and it is clear that they are differentially involved in this type of aphasia. At a finer level of resolution, it is clear that particular modalities and types of input and output are implicated. The patient cannot read, but inputs using other modalities or types can be processed by the system. Various transformations of inputs are affected in this syndrome. While letters and pictures can be copied slavishly, it appears that they are not being decoded, because they cannot be transcribed. Just as the phonetician imitates sounds or words of an unfamiliar verbal communication system, this patient can copy letters; transduction (T_3) alone is operating. There is evidence that some graphic symbols can bypass various levels of processing and be comprehended directly, that numerals and logos appear to be processed as gestalts (see the discussion of parallel phenomena in Schnitzer 1976). Even more detailed aspects of particular transductions may be involved. Thus, particular semantic categories of items such as colors cannot be named. Various aspects of the memory components listed in figure 4C are involved in aphasias such as anomia, as well as in the tip-of-the-tongue phenomenon characteristic of normal speech. Finally, there is clearly a continuum of communicative behavior ranging from the reflexive to the affective to the cognitive (propositional) that may be quite differentially affected in aphasia. Note, however, that this same continuum is evinced in the development of communicative behavior in children (see table 1). Some of the types of speech behaviors that make up this continuum, following research by Van Lancker (1975), are listed in figure 7.

C. ASPECTS OF CHANGE IN COMMUNICATIVE BEHAVIOR

Behavior implies flux. Whereas language may be regarded as a static entity, a corpus of sentences, to be analyzed at a particular point in time, communicative behavior must be regarded as ever changing. The aspects of this behavior which we have focused on in this paper are dynamic, whether they involve evolution, development, or dissolution (see fig. 1).

Slobin (1975b) has discussed with numerous examples four competing forces which he believes contribute to change in human communication systems. He expresses these as imperatives: (1) *to be clear,* that is, to express what we have termed simple and complex concepts with as little distortion as possible, (2) *to be humanly processible in ongoing time,* (3) *to be quick and easy,* that is, to relay as much information as possible within a given time span, and (4) *to be expressive,* both in the sense of relaying all that one has in mind (*being se-*

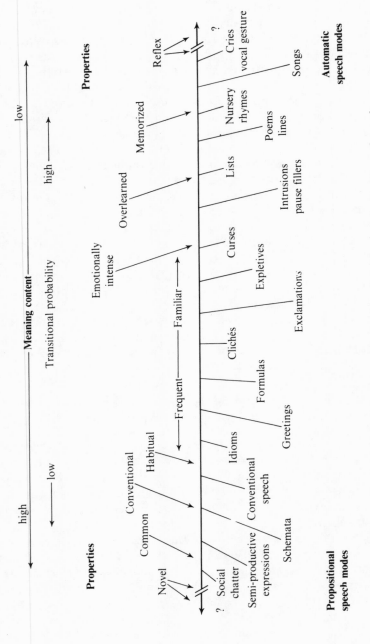

Fig. 7. A hypothetical continuum of propositional and automatic speech modes and their properties. (Van Lancker 1975:173)

mantic) and in the sense of relaying what one wishes in an effective manner (*being rhetorical*). It is clear that these forces are basically incompatible with stasis. The first two may be regarded as constraints on change, while the second two are stimuli for change.

What is the goal towards which such unstabilizing forces strive? If one were to give it a name, it might be *efficiency*. An efficient communication system may be defined as one that is capable of transmitting the greatest amount of information in the least amount of time with the least ambiguity and the greatest intelligibility. The complex of changing environmental pressures that would call for increased efficiency are easy to imagine. They involve a number of factors in a complex feedback relationship, such as more efficient toolmaking, more control over the environment, more learning, and more efficient social organization (see Dingwall 1979).

How does the pressure for more efficient communication affect the biological model we have been discussing? At least three basic changes can be imagined: (1) changes in the character and the amount of storage required, (2) changes in the character and the amount of processing required in each transduction, and (3) changes in the character of the predominant input/output modality.

As the amount of knowledge required for survival increases, there is obviously pressure for the memory components of cognition to expand. Table 4 presents the changes involved in increasing the efficiency of a communication system within the primate order. As the shifts in communication shown here take place, both the amounts of storage and of processing required for coding (T_2) and transmission (T_3) increase. Whereas the child, as noted earlier, initially links concepts directly to output, he or she later develops the type of complex intermediary processing suggested in figure 5. Finally, the character of the predominant input/output modality may change from that which is based on some combination of body movement plus affective vocalization to that which involves articulate speech, possibly with an intermediate stage where hand gestures rather than speech are predominant. There is good evidence to believe that speech is one of the most efficient means of relaying information between organisms that has evolved (see Lieberman 1975). Note that the changes outlined above apply to ontogeny and quite plausibly to phylogeny and are accompanied in both instances by increase in brain size.

D. DETERMINANTS OF COMPLEXITY IN PRIMATE COMMUNICATION SYSTEMS

It makes little sense to ask whether any of the populations depicted in figure 1 (to which one might add computers, for good measure) are

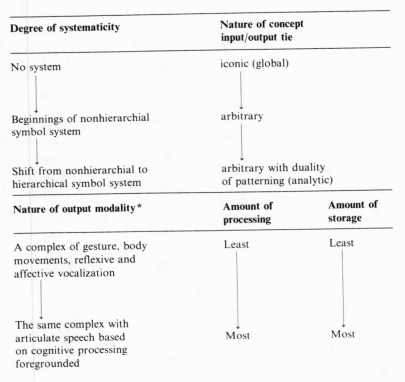

Degree of systematicity	Nature of concept input/output tie
No system ↓	iconic (global) ↓
Beginnings of nonhierarchial symbol system ↓	arbitrary ↓
Shift from nonhierarchial to hierarchical symbol system	arbitrary with duality of patterning (analytic)

Nature of output modality*	Amount of processing	Amount of storage
A complex of gesture, body movements, reflexive and affective vocalization ↓	Least	Least
The same complex with articulate speech based on cognitive processing foregrounded	Most	Most

Table 4. Some of the changes involved in moving towards a more efficient communication system within the primate order. All the transitions indicated are gradient rather than absolute. (*It is possible that there was an intermediate stage where gesture rather than speech was foregrounded.)

in possession of some uniform capacity called language or human communication. It should be evident by now that the determination whether one communicates in a human manner cannot be made in absolute terms; rather, some gradient measure must be employed. In conclusion, I should like to suggest the following set of six gradient features based on our biological model—each of which could be associated with a scale from 1 to 7 as a measure of comparative degree of applicability. I would also like to submit that, unlike Hockett's design features, these appear capable of producing a taxonomy within the primate order that is in accord with phylogenetic proximity.

1. *Length of Immaturity.* It is well known that there is a trend toward prolonged growth and maturation periods in primates.

The longer the period of immaturity, the greater the time available for learning.

2. *Multimodality.* The extent to which the communication system makes use of a complex of media simultaneously and to which alternative input/output modalities can sustain communication.

3. *Degree of Volitional Control.* The extent to which the communication system is of the cognitive type as opposed to the reflexive or the affective.

4. *Efficiency.* The extent to which the communication system is capable of transmitting a great amount of information in a small amount of time with little ambiguity and great intelligibility.

5. *Degree of Coding.* A measure of the complexity of the coding processes on both the input and the output sides.

6. *Degree of Context-Freeness.* The extent to which communication can take place in isolation from contextual cues.

Suppose we could quantify these features and then apply them to random samples of the populations we have been discussing throughout this paper, namely:

A. Nonhuman primates in the wild.

B. Nonhuman primates who have acquired humanlike communication systems.

C. Normal children acquiring language.

D. Humans with verbal disorders.

E. Normal human adults.

What would we find? My speculation is that nonhuman primates in the wild and normal adult humans would be significantly different on these measures. But what of the remaining populations? While length of immaturity would place children and the verbally impaired in a group with normal adults, the remaining features would most probably differentiate these two populations from the latter. Of the groupings that might occur, the following three appear most plausible on present evidence:

$$\text{(A)}\ \boxed{\text{B}\quad \text{C}\quad \text{D}}\ \text{(E)}$$
$$\text{(A)}\ \boxed{\text{B}\quad \text{C}}\ \boxed{\text{D}\quad \text{E}}$$
$$\text{(A)}\ \text{(B)}\ \boxed{\text{C}\quad \text{D}}\ \text{(E)}$$

Other possibilities are not ruled out entirely, however.

SUMMARY

We have seen that neither linguistics nor biology offers at present a viable framework for the study of human communicative behavior. In this chapter, I have attempted to develop a biological model of such behavior which combines the positive aspects of both linguistics and biology while avoiding their shortcomings. In elaborating this model, I have made use of insights, both theoretical and empirical, from such allied fields as neurolinguistics, psycholinguistics, artificial intelligence, experimental phonetics, and ethology.

Human communicative behavior is viewed as a hierarchical input/output system which is mediated by the central nervous system and peripheral structures of the human organism, and is carried out within a complex context involving physical, social and linguistic aspects. Language, the subject matter of linguistics, forms but one element of this complex behavior. This element, which I have termed *coding*, involves the transduction between an abstract conceptual structure and an equally abstract sensorimotor representation. Coding may be mediated by various input/output modalities, not just the ear and vocal tract, as is often assumed by linguists.

Neither language nor human communicative behavior, of which it is a part, is a unitary phenomenon. Rather, as has been demonstrated, both involve a mosaic of structures, skills, and knowledge. Numerous examples have been provided, showing: that comprehension and production involve different processes; that the three transductions we have discussed (*cognition, coding,* and *transmission*) can occur independently of one another; and further, that each transduction involves an aggregate of dissociable skills. These examples characterize not only the dissolution of human communicative behavior in instances of pathology, but its normal development in children as well as its normal usage by adults. That dissociations of transductions can be demonstrated provides some support for the view that language (coding) is task-specific (see Chomsky 1972, 1980).

On the other hand, it cannot be assumed a priori that human communicative behavior viewed in its totality constitutes a species-specific behavior without parallel in the animal kingdom. It seems likely that a behavior as complex as human communication did not evolve by some sudden genetic saltation, but rather in a mosaic fashion. Using the concept of *behavioral homology* developed by Hodos (1976) and elaborated in Dingwall (1979 and forthcoming), we may even be able to trace to some extent the probable evolutionary course of this behavior. Some aspects of this question are addressed in the final two sections of the chapter.

It should be clear that after hundreds of years of writing grammars and studying their properties, we have only begun to investigate in an empirical manner the broader question: what is the nature of the communicative behavior of our species, and how did it evolve?

NOTES

This chapter represents a modified and somewhat expanded version of an article with the same title, which appeared in a special issue of the journal *Die neueren Sprachen* (77:3/4, 1978), devoted to language and behavior.

1. The extent to which great apes have been able to acquire language-like behaviors is at present a hotly debated question. For an evenhanded discussion, from an evolutionary point of view, of the issues involved in this debate see Desmond (1979).

2. If information can be conveyed without coding, then what pressures could conceivably result in the emergence of such a transduction and its elaboration? As depicted in figure 8, Liberman and Studdert-Kennedy

A) CONCEPT
    ↑↓
    SIGNAL

PROBLEM: The number of concepts to be communicated vastly outnumbers the signals available to the organism

B) CONCEPT
    ↑↓
    SYNTAX
    ↑↓
    SIGNAL

PROBLEM: The limited number of signals available to the organism would require extremely long strings in many cases to express complex concepts

C)   CONCEPT   *ADVANTAGE:* Allows for a large lexicon
                          constructed from a limited number of elemen-
                          tary signals thus limiting the length of strings
     SYNTAX   necessary to express concepts

     PHONOLOGY

     SIGNAL

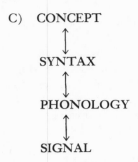

Fig. 8. A rationale for complex coding in human vocal communication (derived from Liberman and Studdert-Kennedy 1977).

(1977) have recently suggested that the elaboration of this transduction allows for the communication of a large number of concepts employing relatively short strings of lexical items that are constructed from a limited inventory of elementary signals. Thus, as the child grows in cognitive capacity and, perhaps, as early hominids came under selection pressures for such growth, the system of communication had to change in order to remain efficient, that is, capable of transmitting the greatest amount of information in the least amount of time with the least ambiguity and the greatest intelligibility. Other aspects of the communication system may also be affected by this drive for increasingly efficient transfer of information. Some of these are outlined from a phylogenetic perspective in table 4 of this paper.

3. There appear to be memory stores specific to language, since neither anterograde or retrograde amnesias affect language per se.

4. It should be noted, however, that chimpanzees who have mastered sign language have been observed to retrieve reliably objects which are not physically present. This is true even if the object in question is one among many different objects stored in a chest at some distant location. Thus, it is possible that the characteristic mentioned above is not unique to human communication.

REFERENCES

Altmann, S. A. 1967. The structure of primate social communication. In *Social communication among primates*, S. A. Altmann, ed., 325–62. Chicago: University of Chicago Press.

Bates, E. 1976. *Language and context*. New York: Academic Press.

Benson, D. F.. and Geschwind, N. 1969. The alexias. In *Handbook of clinical neurology*, vol. 4, P. Vinken and G. Bruyn, eds., 112–40. Amsterdam: North-Holland.

Bierwisch, M. 1970. Fehler-Linguistik. *Linguistic Inquiry* 1:397–414.

Bloom, L. 1970. *Language development*. Cambridge: MIT Press.

Borden, G. J. 1979. An interpretation of research on feedback interruption in speech. *Brain and Language* 7:307–19.

Botha, R. P. 1968. *The function of the lexicon in transformational generative grammar*. The Hague: Mouton.

Bransford, J.; Barclay, J.; and Franks, J. 1972. Sentence memory: A constructive versus interpretive approach. *Cognitive Psychology* 3:193–209.

Bransford, J., and Franks, J. 1972. The abstraction of linguistic ideas: A review. *Cognition* 1:211–49.

Burdick, C., and Miller, J. 1975. Speech perception by the chinchilla: Discrimination of sustained /a/ and /i/. *Journal of the Acoustical Society of America* 58:415–27.

Cairns, H., and Cairns, C. 1976. *Psycholinguistics: A cognitive view of language*. New York: Holt, Rinehart and Winston.

Chomsky, N. 1957. *Syntactic structures*. The Hague: Mouton.

————. 1965. *Aspects of the theory of syntax*. Cambridge: MIT Press.

————. 1972. *Language and mind*. New York: Harcourt Brace Jovanovich.

————. 1980. *Rules and representations*. New York: Columbia University Press, 1980.

Cooper, F. S. 1972. How is language conveyed by speech? In *Language by ear and by eye*, J. Kavanagh and I. Mattingly, eds., 25–45. Cambridge: MIT Press.

Derwing, B. 1973. *Transformational grammar as a theory of language acquisition*. New York: Cambridge University Press.

Desmond, A. J. 1979. *The ape's reflexion*. New York: The Dial Press/James Wade.

Dingwall, W. O. 1975. The species-specificity of speech. In *Developmental psycholinguistics: Theory and applications*, D. Dato, ed., 17–62. Washington, D.C.: Georgetown University Press.

————. 1978. Towards a reconstruction of the methodology of experimental linguistics. In *A survey of linguistic science*, W. O. Dingwall, ed., 135–57. Stamford, Conn.: Greylock Publishers.

————. 1979. The evolution of human communication systems. In *Studies in neurolinguistics*, vol. 4, H. Whitaker and H. A. Whitaker, eds., 1–95. New York: Academic Press.

————. Forthcoming. *The evolution of human communicative behavior*. New York: Academic Press.

Dingwall, W. O., and Shields, J. 1973. From utterance to gist. Four experimental studies of what's in between. Unpublished manuscript.

Dingwall, W. O., and Whitaker, H. A. 1974. Neurolinguistics. *Annual Review of Anthropology* 3:323–56.

Fodor, J. 1975. *The language of thought.* New York: T. Crowell.

Fodor, J.; Bever, T.; and Garrett, M. 1974. *The psychology of language.* New York: McGraw-Hill.

Fouts, R.; Chown, W.; and Goodin, L. 1976. Transfer of signed responses in American Sign Language from vocal English to physical object stimuli by a chimpanzee (*Pan*). *Learning and Motivation* 7:458–75.

Frederiksen, C. 1975. Representing logical and semantic structure of knowledge acquired from discourse. *Cognitive Psychology* 7:371–458.

Fromkin, V. 1971. The non-anomalous nature of anomalous utterances. *Language* 47:27–52.

Glucksberg, S., and Danks, J. 1975. *Experimental psycholinguistics.* New York: John Wiley and Sons.

Grice, H. P. 1968. The logic of conversation. Unpublished manuscript.

Halliday, M. A. K. 1975. *Learning how to mean: Explorations in the development of language.* London: Edward Arnold.

Hockett, C. F. 1960. The origin of speech. *Scientific American* 203(9):89–96.

Hodos, W. 1976. The concept of homology and the evolution of behavior. In *Evolution, brain and behavior: Persistent problems,* R. B. Masterton, W. Hodos, and H. Jerison, eds., 153–67. New York: John Wiley and Sons.

Hodos, W., and Campbell, C. B. G. 1969. *Scala naturae:* Why there is no theory in comparative psychology. *Psychological Review* 76:337–50.

Hymes, D. 1962. The ethnography of speaking. In *Anthropology and human behavior,* T. Gladwin and W. Sturtevant, eds., 13–53. Washington, D.C.: Anthropological Society of Washington.

Isenberg, H. 1968. *Überlegungen zur Texttheorie.* ERIC/PEGS Paper #57. Washington, D.C.: Clearinghouse for Linguistics, Center for Applied Linguistics.

Jürgens, U., aud Ploog, D., 1976. Zur Evolution der Stimme. *Archiv für Psychiatrie und Nervenkrankheiten* 222:117–37.

Kintsch, W. 1974. *The representation of meaning in memory.* New York: John Wiley and Sons.

Kintsch, W., and Monk, D. 1972. Storage of complex information in memory: Some implications of the speed with which inferences can be made. *Journal of Experimental Psychology* 94:25–32.

Kuhl, P. 1978. Predispositions for the perception of speech-sound categories: A species-specific phenomenon? In *Communicative and cognitive abilities —Early behavioral assessment,* F. Minifie and L. Lloyd, eds., 229–55. Baltimore: University Park Press.

Lakoff, G. 1971. On generative semantics. In *Semantics,* D. Steinberg and L. Jakobovits, eds., 232–96. New York: Cambridge University Press.

Lamendella, J. 1976. Relations between the ontogeny and phylogeny of language: A neorecapitulist view. *Annals of the New York Academy of Sciences* 280:396–412.

———. 1977. The limbic system in human communication. In *Studies in neurolinguistics,* vol. 3, H. Whitaker and H. A. Whitaker, eds., 157–222. New York: Academic Press.

Lancaster, J. 1975. *Primate behavior and the emergence of human culture.* New York: Holt, Rinehart and Winston.

Lass, N., ed. 1976. *Contemporary issues in experimental phonetics.* New York: Academic Press.

Laver, J. 1970. The production of speech. In *New horizons in linguistics,* J. Lyons, ed., 53–75. Baltimore: Penguin.

Liberman, A. M., and Studdert-Kennedy, M. 1977. Phonetic perception. *Haskins Laboratories Status Report on Speech Research* 50:21–60.

Lieberman, P. 1975. *On the origins of language: An introduction to the evolution of human speech.* New York: Macmillan.

————. 1977. *Speech physiology and acoustic phonetics.* New York: Macmillan.

Lyons, J. 1968. *Introduction to theoretical linguistics.* New York: Cambridge University Press.

MacKay, D. M. 1972. Formal analysis of communicative processes. In *Nonverbal communication,* R. A. Hinde, ed., 3–25. New York: Cambridge University Press.

Manning, A.; Goble, W.; Markman, R.; and LaBreche, T. 1977. Lateral cerebral differences in the deaf in response to linguistic and nonlinguistic stimuli. *Brain and Language* 4:309–21.

Mayr, E. 1974. Behavior programs and evolutionary strategies. *American Scientist* 62:650–59.

McKeever, W.; Hoeman, H.; Florian, V.; and Vandeventer, A. 1976. Evidence of minimal cerebral asymmetries for the processing of English words and American Sign Language in the congenitally deaf. *Neuropsychologia* 14:413–23.

Menzel, E. W. 1971. Communication about the environment in a group of young chimpanzees. *Folia Primatologia* 15:220–32.

Oyama, S. 1976. A sensitive period for the acquisition of a nonnative phonological system. *Journal of Psycholinguistic Research* 5:261–83.

Pisoni, D., and Sawusch, J. 1975. Some stages of processing in speech perception. In *Structure and process in speech perception,* A. Cohen and S. Nooteboom, eds., 16–35. New York: Springer-Verlag.

Robins, R. H. 1964. *General linguistics.* London: Longmans, Green.

Ross, J. 1970. On declarative sentences. In *Readings in English transformational grammar,* R. Jakobs and P. Rosenbaum, eds., 222–72. Waltham, Mass.: Ginn.

Sachs, J. 1967. Recognition memory for syntactic and semantic aspects of connected discourse. *Perception and Psychophysics* 2:437–42.

Savage, S., and Rumbaugh, D. 1977. Language and communication: A perspective. In *Language learning by a chimpanzee: The Lana project,* D. Rumbaugh, ed., 287–309. New York: Academic Press.

Schnitzer, M. 1976. The role of phonology in linguistic communication: Some neurolinguistic considerations. In *Studies in neurolinguistics,* vol. 1, H. Whitaker and H. A. Whitaker, eds., 139–60. New York: Academic Press.

Sebeok, T. A., ed., 1968. *Animal communication*. Bloomington, Ind.: Indiana University Press.

Sebeok, T. A. 1977. Zoosemiotic components of human communication. In *How animals communicate*, T. A. Sebeok, ed., 1055–77. Bloomington, Ind.: Indiana University Press.

Slobin, D. 1975a. Language and thought. (Audiocassette). Berkeley: University of California, Extension Media Center.

———. 1975b. *Language change in childhood and in history*. Working paper #41. Berkeley: University of California, Language Behavior Research Laboratory.

Straight, H. S. 1976. Comprehension versus production in linguistic theory. *Foundations of Language* 14:525–40.

Thorpe, W. H. 1972. The comparison of vocal communication in animals and man. In *Non-verbal communication*, R. A. Hinde, ed., 27–47. New York: Cambridge University Press.

Van Lancker, D. 1975. *Heterogeneity in language and speech: Neurolinguistic studies*. Working Papers in Phonetics #29. Los Angeles: University of California.

Wanner, E. 1977. Review of *The psychology of language* by J. Fodor, et al. *Journal of Psycholinguistic Research* 6:261–70.

Wanner, E.; Teyler, T.; and Thompson, R. F. 1977. The psychobiology of speech and language—An overview. In *Language and hemispheric specialization in man: Cerebral ERPs*. Progress in clinical neurophysiology, vol. 3, J. E. Desmedt, ed., 1–27. Basel: S. Karger.

Watt, W. C. 1970. On two competing hypotheses concerning psycholinguistics. In *Cognition and the development of language*, J. R. Hayes, ed., 137–220. New York: John Wiley and Sons.

———. 1974. Mentalism in linguistics, II. *Glossa* 8:3–40.

Whitaker, H. 1976. A case of the isolation of the language function. In *Studies in neurolinguistics*, vol. 2, H. Whitaker and H. A. Whitaker, eds., 1–58. New York: Academic Press.

Whitaker, H. A. 1970. *A model for neurolinguistics*. Occasional paper #10. Colchester: University of Essex.

Winograd, T. 1972. Understanding natural language. *Cognitive Psychology* 3:1–191.

Wright, P. 1972. Some observations on how people answer questions about sentences. *Journal of Verbal Learning and Verbal Behavior* 11:188–95.

Semantics and Pragmatics of Sentence Connectives in Natural Language

ROLAND POSNER

> When a diplomat says "yes", he means "perhaps"; when he says "perhaps", he means "no"; and when he says "no", he is no diplomat.
>
> When a lady says "no", she means "perhaps"; when she says "perhaps", she means "yes"; and when she says "yes", she is no lady.
>
> —Voltaire

One need be neither a diplomat nor a lady to use the word *perhaps* to mean 'yes' one time and 'no' another. But what is the meaning of a word like *perhaps* if everyone can make it mean either 'yes' or 'no' as he pleases? Can one in any sense talk about a fixed word meaning here? But if not, what is it Voltaire is telling us when he maintains that the diplomat's uttering "yes" as well as the lady's uttering "no" *means* 'perhaps'?

What is *said* and what is *meant*, coded information and its use in communication, do not seem to coincide in all cases. But, when they don't, which content elements of an utterance should be traced back to *word meanings* and which to the specific *use of the words* in the situation in question?

In semiotic terms, I am going to deal with the delimitation of semantics and pragmatics in the description of verbal communication. In treating this problem, I shall discuss the following points:

1. Two strategies for the description of verbal communication
2. The monism of meaning
3. The monism of use
4. The identification of meaning and use

Reprinted from *Pragmatics and Speech Act Theory*, edited by Ferenc Kiefer and John Searle, © 1980 by D. Reidel Publishing Co.

1. TWO STRATEGIES FOR THE DESCRIPTION OF VERBAL COMMUNICATION

In uttering verbal expressions to achieve communicative goals, we must be able to use these expressions appropriately. But how do we proceed? Does every word have a fixed meaning that language users reproduce in their utterances? Or are there no fixed meanings but only rules of use that guide the language users in their formulations?

These questions delineate two competing strategies for the description of verbal communication. For linguists pursuing the first strategy, verbal communication can be exhaustively described by reference to word meaning, sentence meaning, and the meaning relations holding among verbal expressions. Linguists pursuing the second strategy seek to avoid assuming the existence of meanings; they try to describe the same phenomena in terms of language use. Both approaches have come to develop highly elaborated and finely articulated systems of terminology:

— While proponents of the first strategy speak of meaning, semantic features and the realization of semantic features, proponents of the second talk about use, rules of use and the application of rules of use;

— while one side speaks of semantic categories, of literal versus transposed meaning, of uniqueness of meaning versus ambiguity, the other is concerned with modes of use, literal versus transposed use, consistent versus inconsistent use;

— while one side speaks of hierarchies of semantic features, involving union, intersection, and opposition of features, the other discusses hierarchies of semantic rules, involving union, intersection and opposition of rules;

— while one side speaks of presuppositions, the other talks about conditions of use; constraints on the realization of semantic features appear as constraints on the application of semantic rules; feature change appears as rule change; modifications in the meaning of a word appear as modifications in the use of that word.

These two strategies I will call *the monism of meaning* and *the monism of use*.[1]

Comparing the two strategies in such an abstract manner might lead one to regard them as merely terminological variants of the same theory, equally applicable and equally efficient in the description of verbal communication, were it not for the fact that they involve different empirical hypotheses and apply different methods of investigation: Monists of meaning usually assume that we have direct empirical access to word meanings and that rules of word use, if such things exist, are easily derivable from word meanings. Monists of use tend to believe that only the use of a word is empirically accessible, and that the meanings of that word, if such things exist, must be derived from its use. Common to each monism, however, is the assumption that its respective approach can give a complete linguistic explanation of how language functions.

In what follows I will show that both positions fail to satisfy some rather simple theoretical and methodological requirements for the description of language. Focusing on sentence connectives, I am going to argue against monistic approaches and in favor of a theory that assigns complementary roles to the meaning and to the use of words in verbal communication.

Since the discovery of truth-tables in the logic of the late 19th century, many logicians have offered an explication for the so-called logical particles of natural language. Nevertheless, doubts about the adequacy of such explications have never stilled. Recently, this century-long discussion has been given a new turn by the American philosopher of language Herbert Paul Grice, whose 'Logic of Conversation' indicates a new and promising direction to take in the description of sentence connectives in natural language.[2] Grice's approach has not been received without controversy, however, and the essential arguments against it must be taken into account as well. In order to show the proper role Grice's approach can play in empirical semantics, I shall begin by sketching the history of the monisms of meaning and of use, including some of their psycholinguistic ramifications.

2. THE MONISM OF MEANING

At the end of the 19th century the conceptual semantics inherited from the Age of Enlightenment came under the influence of a newly developed empirical discipline, psychology. This interaction resulted in a linguistic conception that can be characterized as follows. To communicate is to transmit concepts and in order to transmit concepts one must utter words whose meanings are concepts. According to Wilhelm Wundt, "every independent conceptual word [. . .] elicits a certain conceptual idea that is vivid to the degree to which the meaning of the word is concrete."[3] Edward Titchener taught, "The word *dog* has a meaning for us because the perception of this word elicits the idea of a dog in us."[4] While not every word is an independent conceptual word and, as such, able to transmit an idea, every word has (at least) one constant meaning which, when combined with the meanings of other words, contributes to the meaning of the expression as a whole. Thus, a speaker transmits the intended concepts by uttering the appropriate words, with which the addressee associates appropriate conceptual ideas of his own. Associations can be interpreted and tested according to the mechanism of stimulus and response. In order to find out which ideas are associated, addressees are subjected to standard tests such as drawing the associated objects or picking out their putative qualities from a list.

Unfortunately, the association experiments did not, when carried out on a large scale, confirm this theory in the expected way. The ideas elicited by a particular word differed greatly according to the context. Thus, it gradually became a commonplace of meaning-monist word semantics to claim, "The boundaries of word meaning are vague, blurred, fluid."[5] Even linguists like Karl Otto Erdmann, who took such statements as the starting-point for the introduction of new distinctions in his 'Essays from the Borders of Psycholinguistics and Logic', were not able to neutralize their force.

3. THE MONISM OF USE

The consequences of this failure were drawn by behaviorist psychology. If the association test does not provide reliable access to word meaning, it is useless as a linguistic method. And, if we are forced to assume that word meanings are fluid, then the concept of meaning loses its theoretical value for the description of verbal communication as well. John Watson formulated this insight most emphatically, "From the position of a behaviorist the problem of meaning is a mere abstraction."[6] And Burrhus F. Skinner laconically concurred, "The speaker does not utter any ideas or images but only words."[7]

Even Charles W. Morris prided himself on being able to do away with meanings altogether. Indeed, he thought he had renewed the connection with experimental psychology by taking dispositions into account in his semiotic program.[8] Whereas association psychologists had put word and meaning on the same level with stimulus and response and had regarded word meaning as a directly observable variable, Morris took word use to be a disposition that mediates between stimulus and response in the communication situation. Being dispositions, the rules of use cannot be directly observed but must be inferred from manifest behavior in the form of intervening variables. Thus, in the case of word use the hypothesis of direct empirical accessibility was abandoned just as it had been in the case of word meaning.[9] Not even the difficulty encountered by Erdmann disappeared for monists of use; it merely became more clearly formulated. How one and the same word can play a role in fundamentally different behavioral dispositions is a question still looking for an answer.

4. THE IDENTIFICATION OF MEANING AND USE

These empirical problems and methodological difficulties deprived the two monist positions of their initial theoretical attractiveness. To be sure, it was not only for methodological reasons that Ludwig Wittgenstein advised, "Don't ask for the meaning, ask for the use."[10] He believed that he could also give this maxim theoretical underpinnings, claiming, "For a large number of uses of the word 'meaning'—even if not for all its uses—this word can be explained thus: The meaning of a word is its use in the language."[11] But Wittgenstein failed to develop satisfactory methods for systematically collecting and describing word uses and restricted himself to analyzing examples. For this reason, he prepared the way for an elaboration of the use-monist terminology rather than for the introduction of explicit criteria justifying its application. What survived was the slogan in its truncated version: "The meaning of a word is its use." Because of the lack of guiding criteria it was no surprise that this identification of meaning to use was soon made to apply in the opposite direction. This has led to today's uncritical contamination of the terminology of meaning with the terminology of use.

Of course, even such contamination can be justified, if only in the form of an analogy: are not meaning and use just two aspects of one and the same phenomenon, like temperature and particle velocity in thermodynamics or like wave and corpuscle in quantum physics? Yet, whoever holds this view, must take into account that physics has confirmed each of the two aspects experimentally so that the coexistence of the two terminologies is justified empirically.

But, can this be said of the two aspects of language?

The lack of direct experimental evidence for the existence of meanings and of rules of use has already been pointed out. Nevertheless, it must be conceded that there are phenomena in language that are more easily describable in terms of meaning and that there are other phenomena for which a description in terms of use is more convincing.

For example, consider the German color words *gelb* and *blond*. If we take these words to denote those parts of the color spectrum that are reflected by yellow and blond objects, respectively, then *gelb* and *blond* have approximately the same meaning. They are, however, used in different ways; indeed, their uses in German are mutually exclusive: *blond* generally refers to human hair; everything else reflecting the color waves in question is called *gelb* or *gelblich*. It is true, there are certain marginal uses as in: *Herr Ober, bitte ein kühles Blondes!* ("Waiter, please bring me a light ale'). But even here there is no mutual substitutivity, since no one would say, *Herr Ober, bitte ein kühles Gelbes!* The words *gelb* and *blond* can therefore be said to have the same meaning but to be in *complementary distribution*.

The following example is equally instructive. When we hear little Peter say at the hairdresser's: "Mommy, look, Annie is being mowed," we smile, but we understand what he wants to say. *Mow* means the same as *cut*, but its use is restricted in such a way that human (and animal) hair is excluded.[12] What we must take into account here are the *conditions of use* that restrict the occurrence of a word beyond what its meaning would allow. In the lexicon such conditions of use normally appear as parenthetical supplements to the specification of meaning, e.g., "*blond:* 'yellow (of human hair)' " and "*mow:* 'cut (of grasslike vegetation)'."

In recent years it has become commonplace to regard conditions of use as presupposed semantic features of a word and thus to integrate them into the meaning of the word. Correspondingly, *blond* would mean something like 'having yellow human hair' and *mow* something like 'cut grasslike vegetation'. But such a solution can be maintained only with great difficulty.[13] Once again color words demonstrate quite clearly how indispensable the specification of conditions of use can be. If the color of a cotton coat that Germans call *rot* ('red') occurs on a plastic wall, they tend to call it *braun* ('brown'). Thus, the color word is changed when the area of application changes, even though the color waves have remained the same. Monists of meaning might try to cope with this situation in the same way as they did in the cases of *gelb* and *blond;* they might say: The meaning of *rot* includes the presupposed semantic feature of 'having a rough surface', and the meaning of *braun* includes the presupposed semantic feature of 'having a smooth surface'. But this is plainly wrong, for it would also be perfectly acceptable to call a rough surface *braun* and a smooth surface *rot*. In contrast to the cases of *gelb* and *blond*, the transfer from one area of application to another does not affect the acceptability of use of the words *rot* and *braun*, but their meaning. If applied to smooth surfaces, *rot* denotes a different section in the color spectrum than if applied to rough surfaces.

The same is true for *braun*. There seems to be a mutual dependency here between the meaning and the context of use and that makes sense only if meaning and use are independently characterizable.

These brief examples may suffice to call into question the identification of meaning and use and to show that the two kinds of terminology are not interchangeable in all areas of lexical semantics.

5. THE USE OF MEANINGS

The difference between semantic features and conditions of use has been elaborated most clearly by Grice. In his William James Lectures, held at Harvard in 1968, he succeeds in liberating himself from the simplistic opposition of "meaning versus use."[14] In contrast to Watson and Skinner, Grice is prepared to claim that in communication we deal not only with words or concatenations of words but also with word meanings and sentence meanings. What is involved here is the use of meanings. Grice strives to discover the rules according to which we use meanings in order to achieve our communicative goals.

Let us compare the following five sentences:

(1) Please take the garbage out.
(2) (a) I want you to take the garbage out.
    (b) Can you take the garbage out?
    (c) Will you take the garbage out?
    (d) Have you taken the garbage out?

In everyday family communication each of these five sentences evidently can be uttered for the same purpose, that is, to express a request for someone to take out the garbage. Nevertheless, when we isolate each of these sentences from its context and describe it as such, we rightly say: (1) is an imperative sentence, (2a) is a declarative sentence, and (2b) through (2d) are interrogative sentences. But how can one, in uttering an assertion or question, get someone to fulfill a request? How can we explain that the son who hears his mother ask, "Have you taken the garbage out?" understands this as a request for him to take the garbage out? This is the sort of problem that concerns Grice.[15] In order to solve it, we must take into account the context of utterance and apply certain principles from the theory of rational behavior. Let us begin with the situation in which mother and son are standing in the kitchen in front of the full garbage can. Both can see with their own eyes that the garbage can is full and can infer that it has not yet been taken out and emptied. Nevertheless, the mother asks her son, "Have you taken the garbage out?" If he takes this sentence in its literal meaning, its utterance can only be a question for information. But as such it would lack any communicative function. The son knows that the question would have to be answered in the negative and he knows that his mother knows that, too. In this situation that question seems to be absurd and its utterance by the mother irrational. Rational behavior would conform to the following maxim:

(M1)   Make your contribution such as is required, at the stage at which it occurs, by the accepted purpose of the action in which you and your partners are engaged.

This maxim is called "cooperation principle" by Grice; by appropriate specification it can also be applied to communication, understood as verbal cooperation:

(M2)   Make your utterance such as is required, at the stage at which it occurs, by the accepted purpose of the talk-exchange in which you and your partners are engaged.

What purpose might the mother be pursuing when standing with her son in the kitchen in front of the full garbage can? From the rest of his mother's behavior the son knows, "Mother likes everything to be clean and neat and wants me to be so, too." But does the mother's question serve this purpose? "If taken literally, no." Does it serve another purpose? "If taken literally, no." Did the mother want to say something pointless? "No, this is something she normally does not do." In order to avoid such a conclusion, the son prefers to reinterpret the sentence and to give the utterance a new meaning by relating it to the accepted purpose of the talk-exchange: "Mother likes everything to be clean and neat and wants me to be so, too. I would be neat if I took the garbage can out and emptied it. Mother's question evidently is supposed to draw my attention to a fact which she and I already know but from which I have not yet drawn the desired consequence. Evidently, it is desired that I should now take out the garbage can and empty it. Since I would like to continue communicating with my mother and to achieve my own communicative purposes, too, I will take the present purpose of communication seriously and behave as if mother had requested me to take out the garbage can and empty it." These considerations lead the son to the result that he has to treat the question as a request. Reasoning of this kind is normally performed automatically and remains below the threshold of consciousness. But it has to be taken into account if the behavior of the addressee is to be adequately explained.

Of course, the utterer regularly anticipates such reasoning. In fact, the mother only formulated her utterance as a question because she could assume that her communication partner was in a position to reconstruct the intended request from it. She used the literal meaning of (2d) in order to convey the literal meaning of (1). In doing so, she not only combined words with lexical meanings according to grammatical rules to produce the literal meaning of a sentence, but also used the sentence meaning according to pragmatic rules to convey a message normally conveyed with different words and different grammatical rules. She used an assertion or a question in order to suggest a request.

But in what kind of situation does one prefer to rely upon the reasoning of the addressee instead of saying literally what one wants to convey? The answer becomes obvious if we consider how an obstinate son could respond to the utterances (1) and (2) if he took them literally:

(1′)   No, I won't.
(2′)   (a′) You can do it.
       (b′) I can, but I don't want to.
       (c′) I will, but right now I'm doing something more important.
       (d′) No, because I have more important things to do.

As these examples demonstrate, the utterances under (2) leave open to the addressee the possibility of understanding them not as requests but as assertions or questions and to respond to their literal meanings. Interpreted in this way, they can provide an opportunity for a discussion whether the conditions for a sensible request are satisfied at all. In using such a formulation the utterer makes it possible for his addressee to argue against making a request before such a request has in fact been uttered; he spares him an open conflict and avoids losing face himself. In short, the use of meanings like those of (2a) through (2d) to suggest a request is more polite than the use of the literal meaning of (1).

If this explanation of the function of suggestions proves right, it gives us a strong argument for the existence of meanings; for, the entire explanation would collapse if meaning were reducible to use.

6. MEANING VERSUS SUGGESTION

The construction of suggestions originates in the effort of the addressee to interpret the verbal behavior of his communication partner as rational behavior. If the speaker utters a sentence whose meaning, taken literally, does not contribute to the recognized purpose of communication, then the addressee asks himself if the speaker means something different from what he has said literally. He evaluates the verbal and non-verbal context of the talk-exchange, looking for supplementary information that, applied to the literal meaning, will let him infer a message conforming to the recognized purpose of communication.[16]

This reasoning is a heuristic operation; it follows certain rules, but its results are not strictly deducible since it often remains unclear what the purpose of communication is and which circumstances of the context are relevant to it.

In order to get such a reasoning process going, it is important to discover which maxim of rational behavior the utterance would have violated if it had been taken literally. Therefore, Grice has tried to supplement his principle of cooperation with a series of special maxims which are valid in particular for the exchange of information during a conversation.[17] Grice sets up these conversational maxims by facetiously employing Kant's table of categories:

(M3)   I   Maxims of Quantity
            1. Make your contribution as informative as is required . . .
            2. Do not make your contribution more informative than is required . . .
        II Maxims of Quality
            1. Do not assert what you believe to be false.
            2. Do not assert that for which you lack adequate evidence.
        III Maxim of Relation
            Say only things which are relevant . . .
        IV Maxims of Manner
            1. Avoid obscurity of expression . . .
            2. Avoid ambiguity . . .
            3. Be brief (avoid unnecessary prolixity) . . .
            4. Be orderly . . .

The dots following these formulations indicate that the maxims of quantity, relation and manner can only be understood with respect to the purpose of communication accepted for a particular stage of a conversation.

This list of maxims is neither complete nor systematically organized in a satisfying way, and the individual maxims are neither of equal importance nor completely independent from one another (e.g., compare the relationship between I/2 and III). However, these flaws do not rule out the possibility that the maxims mentioned are actually applied in the production and interpretation of conversational suggestions. Therefore one must also take them into account when describing these processes.

How this is done may be illustrated with an example that has given logicians many headaches: A First Mate does not get along well with his Captain. The Captain is a prohibitionist and the Mate is often drunk.

Therefore the Captain is looking for a pretext to have the Mate fined when the ship comes to port. One day, as the Captain has the watch, the Mate starts bellowing out a sea chantey again. The Captain can stand the Mate's excesses no longer and writes in the log:

(3)　　(a) Today, March 23rd, the Mate was drunk.

A few days later, when the Mate himself has the watch, he discovers the Captain's entry in the log and wonders what he can do about it without compromising himself any further. Finally, he also makes an entry in the log, which reads:

(3)　　(b) Today, March 26th, the Captain was not drunk.

This is not an ordinary conversation, but Grice's conversational maxims are nevertheless applicable, since the institution of the log serves an accepted purpose of communication that can be realized by following the maxims. Both entries are true statements; however, there is an important pragmatic difference between them, which is revealed by the reader's reaction. Whereas the Captain's entry is interpreted and understood without hesitation, any reader who comes across the Mate's entry cannot help asking, "Why is that written in here? What relevance can the statement have in a log that the Captain was not drunk on a certain day?" Once the reader has established that this entry would, if taken literally, violate the maxim of relation, the next steps of his reasoning are easy. "If the writer wanted to establish communicative cooperation with the reader of the log at all, he must have considered this entry relevant himself. A log serves to register exceptional occurrences on a voyage. Evidently the writer wanted to indicate that the Captain's sobriety on March 26th was exceptional. Sobriety is, of course, exceptional if one is usually drunk. Under these circumstances the writer wanted to suggest with his entry that the Captain was usually drunk during the voyage." Thus the reasoning prompted by the Mate's entry has, on the basis of assumptions about the purpose and context of communication, turned a trivially true statement into a false statement of a rather defamatory nature. This example shows how one can lie with true statements when the utterance of those statements violates one of Grice's conversational maxims. In our case it is the maxim of relation (III) that is involved. There are similar examples for the violation of other maxims.

What is peculiar in this defamatory suggestion is the fact that it is hardly possible to take legal action against it. When confronted with the alternative of calling the Mate to account for false statements or for disorderly conduct, any court would choose the latter.

The two examples from household and sea demonstrate that the discrepancy between what an utterer formulates and what he intends to convey can be explicated on the basis of the distinction between literal meaning (which is determined grammatically) and suggested content (which is determined pragmatically). Furthermore, our analyses of these examples have shown how the utterer proceeds to produce conversational suggestions on the basis of literal meanings and how the addressee proceeds in his efforts to reconstruct these suggestions from the literal meanings. If these analyses are not misguided, they force the linguist to postulate *duality* in the description of verbal communication. He must not only determine the literal meaning of the verbal expression uttered but must also examine how the utterer uses this meaning.

Illuminating as this conception may seem, it leads to theoretical and methodological questions that are hard to answer. How can a linguist determine which content elements of a given message must be considered as the literal meaning of the words or sentences uttered? Can we rightly claim that the sentence *Have you taken the garbage out?* is an interrogative sentence, if it can obviously be used as a request? If the negation of the word *drunk* can be used to indicate that the person in question was the opposite of sober, why do we continue connecting its affirmative with the opposite of sobriety?

One thing is certain: an undifferentiated treatment of all the uses we can find will not bring us any nearer to the literal meaning of a word or sentence. Rather it is necessary to select from among the many uses of a word or sentence those uses in which the literal meaning does not appear to be subjected to any modifications required by specific features of the verbal or non-verbal context.

However, by being asked in this way the question is in danger of becoming circular. We are saying: (a) the meaning of a verbal expression will not be submitted to a context-dependent reinterpretation if its utterance does not violate any conversational maxims; (b) the utterance of a verbal expression does not violate a conversational maxim if it is unnecessary to reinterpret its literal meaning in a context-dependent manner. In this perspective, the literal meaning appears to be like Wittgenstein's beetle in a box: even if we assume that the beetle exists, we cannot tell how big it is.[18]

There seems to be only one way out of this dilemma, and that is the attempt to reconstruct the process of comprehension itself.

1. According to our initial assumption, the addressee proceeds from the literal meaning of an expression and, on this basis, establishes certain conversational suggestions corresponding to the particular features of the verbal and non-verbal context. A comparative analysis of the comprehension processes for all essential uses of an expression could thus furnish us with those content elements which are always

involved, as against those elements that play a role only in certain classes of context. We may assume that the content elements involved in the comprehension of all the uses of an expression belong to the literal meaning of that expression; as to the other content elements, we may conclude that they are dependent on special circumstances of communication and are produced only in the process of special interpretive reasoning. This is the *postulate of variability* for suggestions.

2. Since conversational suggestions change as the situation of conversation changes, we can cancel them through the choice of certain contexts. Even simple verbal additions will do the job, and by claiming the contrary we can annul an alleged suggestion without giving rise to a contradiction. This is the Gricean *postulate of cancellability* for suggestions.[19] If, after asking one of the questions (2b) through (2d), the mother in the kitchen had added, "But I'm not requesting you to do it now," no request would have been suggested. Likewise, the Mate could have avoided a defamatory use of his entry without contradicting himself, if he had supplemented (3b) by the sentence, "The Captain is never drunk." Such additions cannot, however, prevent other suggestions from arising, in case the complete utterance, understood literally, still violates *some* conversational maxim.

3. Finally, one cannot avoid a conversational suggestion by simply choosing another formulation with the same literal meaning. Suggestions of the relevant sort do not result from the use of special words but rather from the specific use of meanings. Therefore a suggestion generated by a particular utterance in a given situation is detachable from the words, but not from the literal meaning of that utterance. This is the Gricean *postulate of nondetachability* for suggestions.[20] In our examples, the mother's suggestion would not have been changed if she had said, "Has the garbage been taken out?" and the Mate's suggestion would not have been changed if he had written, "Today, March 26th, the captain was sober."

Variability, cancellability and non-detachability are useful indications, but, unfortunately, they are not sufficient as criteria in determining which content elements have to be excluded from the literal meaning of an expression.[21] Nevertheless, we have to work with them, as long as there are no better analytical instruments. The imperfections of this procedure only confirm once more what meaning-monists and use-monists had to discover by experience, namely that neither the meaning of a word nor the rules for the use of a word are directly accessible to the empirical linguist, but must be inferred from manifest verbal behavior.

Now if it is theoretically certain that all verbal behavior is based upon literal meanings as well as upon rules for the use of meanings it becomes necessary in the course of linguistic analysis to estimate how much of the content of a given utterance may be traceable to its literal meaning and how much is to be construed as suggestion. This is a procedural problem that gains importance in view of the fact that there is hardly any word of a natural language whose uses have been exhaustively analyzed. As long as we are in the position of creating hypotheses, we can again choose between two strategies that take up the positions of the old monists in a weakened form. *Meaning-maximalists* attempt to deduce as much as possible from the literal meanings of verbal expressions and tend to assume richness and ambiguity in the meanings of words. On the other hand, *meaning-minimalists* attribute more importance to the pragmatic rules of reinterpretation as opposed to literal meanings and tend to accept only minimal meanings and unambiguous words.[22] Let us now consider the consequences of these strategies for the analysis of sentence connectives in natural language, particularly, of the word *and* in English.

7. SENTENCE CONNECTIVES: MAXIMIZATION OF MEANING

When the logical particle *et* (written as "&", "∧", "." according to the various notational conventions) occurs between two propositions, it turns them into one complex proposition that is true if and only if both constituent propositions are true. This statement, which defines the connective *et* of propositional logic, also seems to apply to the word *and* as found between declarative sentences of English. What would then be easier than to assume that this definition also characterizes the meaning of this sentence connective?

However, the truth-functional definition of *and* has consequences that run counter to many uses of the word *and* in natural language. For example, it allows sentences to be connected to one another without regard to their meaning. But any speaker of English would consider the following expressions absurd and unacceptable:

(4)   (a) $2 \times 2 = 4$ and it is impossible to analyze further the concept of *intention*.

         (b) Müller just scored a goal and eels spawn in the Sargasso Sea.

Moreover, the truth-functional definition of *and* places exactly the same condition on the two connected declarative sentences; so they should be interchangeable. But any speaker of English will interpret (5a) differently from (5b):

(5)   (a) Peter married Annie and Annie had a baby.

         (b) Annie had a baby and Peter married Annie.

Of course, these observations are not contested by anybody. What is controversial is how they should be explained.

The meaning-maximalist draws the following conclusions: The meaning of the word *and* is richer than the meaning of the logical connective *et;* it includes not only the truth-functional feature of *conjunctivity*, but also the feature of *connexity* and the feature of *successivity*. On the basis of connexity, the *and*-sentence conveys that the facts described in the second constituent sentence are part of the same situation as the facts described in the first. On the basis of successivity, it conveys that the facts described in the second constituent sentence appear at a later time than the facts described in the first.

Such an analysis of meaning, however, is liable to quite a number of objections.

1. What about the three postulates of variability, cancellability and nondetachability? It is by no means true that every use of the sentence connective *and* implies a temporal sequence between the facts described:

(6)   (a) $2 \times 2 = 4$ and $\sqrt{4} = 2$.
        (b) The moon revolves around the earth and the earth revolves around the sun.

This shows that successivity is variable and not fixed to the word *and*. The assumption of successivity can also easily be cancelled by an additional utterance of the right kind. Continuing with:

(7)   But I don't know in which sequence that happened.

after having said (5a), rules out the basis for the conclusion that the baby came *after* the wedding. On the other hand, one cannot get around the successivity assumption by merely reformulating the constituent sentences in such a way as to preserve their meaning. The successivity assumption is non-detachable.

These observations indicate that successivity should be regarded not as a semantic feature of the word *and*, but as a conversational suggestion. Whenever we use coordinate sentences to describe events in time, we relate the sequence of the sentences uttered to the sequence of the events they describe, even without the help of the word *and*. The utterer would volate the conversational maxim "Be orderly . . ." (IV/4), if he were not to keep the temporal sequence parallel on both levels.

However, such an objection will not deter a meaning-maximalist, since, according to him, the absence of assumptions about the sequence of the facts described in (6) should be explained in a different way. Even when we speak of *chocolate hearts, paper tigers,* or *roses of glass,* we do not imply that the hearts beat or that the tigers and roses are alive. Evidently, quite simple syntactic procedures like the addition of an attribute to a noun can lead to the deletion of semantic features of this noun.[23] This deletion occurs during the amalgamation of the semantic features, in order to satisfy a requirement to avoid contradiction. Let us apply this explanation to our example (6): If one had to assume both that the facts described in (6) are time-independent and that they occur one after another, a contradiction would arise. So the addressee, preferring a non-contradictory interpretation, will delete the feature of successivity in his interpretation, according to the meaning-maximalists.

With this procedure we now have two proposals for grasping variable content elements. These approaches impute converse operations to the process of comprehension. According to one approach, the addressee proceeds from a literal meaning with few semantic features and reaches the required interpretation with the help of conversational maxims relying on additional information specific to the verbal and non-verbal context of utterance. According to the other approach, the addressee proceeds from a rich literal meaning and deletes, according to certain preference rules, those semantic features which would come into conflict with the verbal or non-verbal context.

What is remarkable here is that both approaches are based on a similar theoretical apparatus. As shown by the requirement to avoid contradiction, even the meaning-maximalists need additional pragmatic maxims of interpretation besides grammar and the lexicon. And if even meaning-maximalists cannot manage without pragmatic rules, then we are justified in asking why they trust this instrument so little, why they apply it only to restrict meaning and not to produce new content. One might suppose that they have become victims of hypostatizing their own concept of meaning.

2. In order to support the meaning-maximalist analysis of the word *and*, one often compares it with the word *but*.[24] *But* seems to share with *and* the semantic features of conjunctivity and connexity. Instead of successivity it has *adversativity* as its third semantic feature. Someone who says *but* implies that the facts described in the following sentence are unexpected or contrary to the present context.[25]

However, this parallelism is misleading. In contrast to the successivity of *and* the adversativity of *but* is not cancellable. Someone who says:

(8)   (a) Annie is Martha's daughter, but she is married to Peter.

and then goes on to say:

(9)   However, I don't mean to say that there is an opposition between the two facts.

will not be taken seriously, since there is then no way to explain his saying *but* in (8a). Finally, non-detachability does not hold for adversativity. In many cases the assumption of adversativity will vanish if the *but*-sentence is reformulated in such a way that the rest of its content is preserved. Let us compare (8a) with (8b):

(8)   (b) Annie is Martha's daughter and she is married to Peter.

In (8b) there is no longer any trace of unexpectedness or opposition.

Besides, whereas an *and*-sentence may or may not convey successivity, depending on the context and on the facts described in the constituent sentences, *but* without adversativity is unthinkable. In contrast to *paper tigers* and *chocolate hearts*, this semantic feature never disappears, even in the face of a possible contradiction:

(10)   (?) $2 \times 2 = 4$, but $2 \times 2 = 4$.

We will tend to simply reject an utterance like (10) as unacceptable instead of asserting that the meaning of *but* is reduced to the features of conjunctivity and connexity here.[26]

This and other observations will also make us wonder about the meaning-maximalist explication of *and*. It seems that the model of feature amalgamation in attributes and nouns is inappropriate as a model for the interpretation of sentence connectives.

3. There are, however, stronger objections to the meaning-maximalist description of utterances with *and*. Let us compare the sentences (11a) through (11g) with the versions under (11'), in which the word *and* has been replaced with a lengthier formulation and at least one possible interpretation of the respective initial sentence is preserved.

(11)   (a) Annie is in the   (11')   (a') . . . and there . . .
             kitchen and she
             is making dough-
             nuts.
         (b) Annie fell into a   (b') . . . and during
             deep sleep and   this time . . .
             her facial color
             returned.
         (c) The window was   (c') . . . and coming
             open and there   from it . . .
             was a draft.
         (d) Peter married   (d') . . . and after
             Annie and she   that . . .
             had a baby.

(e) Paul pounded on
the stone and he
shattered it.

(e′) . . . and thereby
. . .

(f) Give me your
picture and I'll give
you mine.

(f′) If you give me
your picture, I'll
give your mine.

(g) The number 5 is a
prime number and
it is divisible only
by 1 and itself.

(g′) . . . and there-
fore . . .

The reformulations show right away that successivity need not play a
role at all in *and*-sentences, even for events bound in time. The strategy
of deletion of semantic features in the examples under (11) will not
help either since *other* relations besides conjunctivity and connexity are
expressed between the facts described by the constituent sentences. And
those relations can in no way be acquired on the basis of successivity.

The sentences under (11) leave the meaning-maximalist no other
choice but to assume that the word *and* is ambiguous. He will say:
There is not only a successive *and* (as in (d)), but also a simultaneous
and (as in (b)), a local *and* (as in (a)), a directional *and* (as in (c)),
and an instrumental *and* (as in (e)), a conditional *and* (as in (f)), and
an explanatory *and* (as in (g)). He will be inclined to assume that all
these different *and*s share the semantic features of conjunctivity and
connexity and differ only with regard to the third semantic feature.

However, even this position seems plausible only as long as no further questions are asked. To begin with, one must observe that the
word *and* also occurs in the reformulations under (11′), which are supposed to make the content of the original sentences more explicit.
If the word *and* on the left means the same as one of the expressions
listed on the right, i.e., *and there, and during this time, and after that,*
etc., then what does the word *and* mean *in these expressions?* It is obvious that none of the seven meanings already mentioned can be considered. Now what about obtaining the meaning of this *and* by deleting
the third semantic feature of one of the complete *and*s on the left? This
proposal could be pursued. But from which of our seven *and*s should
we proceed? From the successive or the simultaneous, the instrumental
or the conditional *and?* As long as such a question cannot be answered,
it would seem to be easier to postulate an eighth meaning. This one,
though, would already closely approximate the truth-functional meaning of the connective of propositional logic, *et.*

4. An even stronger objection to the meaning-maximalist position
can be found in the observation that the *and* in the sentences under

(11) can also be omitted without involving a change of content.[27] Let us replace the *and* with a semicolon, as in the sentences under (12), or with some other punctuation mark:

(12)   (a) Annie is in the kitchen; she is making doughnuts.
              (b) Annie fell into a deep sleep; her facial color returned.
              (c) The window was open; there was a draft.
              (d) Peter married Annie; she had a baby.
              (e) Paul pounded on the stone; he shattered it.
              (f) Give me your picture; I'll give you mine.
              (g) The number 5 is a prime number; it is divisible only by 1 and by itself.

We can communicate practically the same information with (12) as with (11) or (11'). This may make us ask how the content elements explicated by the formulations of (11') are conveyed in (12). Should we say that the semicolon itself has a meaning—or rather seven different meanings? Or should we say that the meaning is somewhere in the air and that it must be read "between the lines"? If one proceeds, like a meaning-maximalist, from seven different meanings and projects them, in (11), all on the word *and*, then, to be consistent, one would have to say the same about the semicolon (and about the articulatory pause between the utterances of the constituent sentences) in (12).

The only possibility left for someone who rejects this solution is to talk about contextual determination of content elements. But he must then be ready to answer the question as to whether such a solution would not be just as appropriate for the *and*-sentences under (11).[28]

5. The conclusive argument against the meaning-maximalist analysis of the sentence connectives, however, is based on the fact that the list of sentences under (11) could be extended at will and thus give rise to a virtually infinite number of new meanings of *and*. Depending upon what the communication partners take to be the actual relationship between the facts described in the constituent sentences, one could speak about an adversative *and*, a consecutive *and*, a diagnostic *and*, etc., as in the sentences under (13):

(13)   (a) Peter is a reactionary and he is crazy about Mao.   (13')   (a') ... and nevertheless ...

              (b) The locks were opened and the ship was able to move on.   (b') ... so that ...

(c) The control lamp   (c′) ... which showed
     went on and the   that ...
     oil pump was
     broken.

   .   .   .
   .   .   .
   .   .   .

In the case of ambiguous words we can usually count the number of individual meanings on the fingers of one hand. Words with three meanings are not unusual and one could even accept a word with twenty-seven meanings, but a word with an infinite number of meanings would be a contradiction in itself. Besides the practical difficulty that the lexicon cannot allow infinitely long entries, such a word would also raise theoretical difficulties: how could a language user learn to cope with a word of infinitely many meanings? The only solution here would be to assume a generative system of rules for the production of such an infinite number of meanings. Such a rule system cannot, by definition, be part of the lexicon, but would have to be assigned either to a prelexical linguistic component or to a postgrammatical component. However, after all that has been said, it is superfluous to assume that we are dealing with an infinity of word meanings.

8. SENTENCE CONNECTIVES: MINIMIZATION OF MEANINGS

The collapse of the meaning-maximalist position now brings us back to the beginning of the last section. So let us restrict ourselves to the content elements common to all previously mentioned uses of the word *and*: to *conjunctivity*, which requires that two sentences connected by *and* are true if and only if the entire complex sentence is true; and to *connexity*, which requires the facts described by the constituent sentence to be part of the same situation. And let us attempt to reconstruct all the supposed additional content elements on the basis of conversational maxims.

A meaning-minimalist would most probably go one step further; he would ask if conjunctivity and connexity could not be explained away in the same manner as successivity. It is easy to see how this would work in the case of connexity. The examples under (4), whose absurdity had led us to postulate such a semantic feature for *and*, do not lose any of their characteristics when one omits the *and*:

(14)   (a) $2 \times 2 = 4$, it is impossible to analyze further the con-
            cept of *intention*.
        (b) Müller just scored a goal, eels spawn in the Sargasso
            Sea.

Even when formulated asyndetically, these sentences are odd, as long
as the utterer cannot rely on additional information specific to the situation of utterance that would allow the addressee to establish a connection between the facts described. This shows that the construction
of a relation between the facts described by coordinate sentences is
not at all specific to the use of the word *and*. It must always be possible
if the addressee does not want to assume that the utterer has violated
a conversational maxim. The maxims concerned here are particularly
those of manner (IV, especially IV/1 "Avoid obscurity of expression . . . ," and IV/4 "Be orderly . . ."). Reasoning involving these
maxims is available at any time; nothing prevents the addressee from
also applying it in the event that the coordinate sentences are connected by *and*. Therefore it really is unnecessary to consider connexity
to be a special semantic feature of the word *and*.

However, these considerations should not mislead us into trying
to eliminate conjunctivity from the meaning of *and*. Of course, it is
true that conjunctivity survives in many cases in which one omits the
sentence connective *and;* that is especially so for coordinate sentences
(cf. the examples under (12)). But what is interesting here is the co-
occurrence of *and* with other sentence connectives in complex sentence
structures. Let us consider the following conversations:

(15)   A: Annie has married, she has had a baby.
        B:

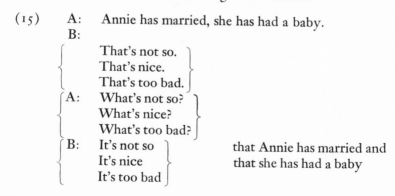

In B's last utterance it is not possible simply to omit the word *and* or
to replace it with a semicolon. The *raison d'être* of this word lies in
its combinatory function (not in its connecting function). In using his

last utterance to elucidate the meaning of his comment, "That's not so," B makes it clear that he thinks one of the constituent sentences of A's initial utterance is false, but that he does not want to specify which. It is the semantic feature of conjunctivity that enables B to do this, as can easily be seen from the following truth-table:

(M4)

p	q	$p \wedge q$	$\neg(p \wedge q)$
T	T	T	F
T	F	F	T
F	T	F	T
F	F	F	T

(The lower case letters "p" and "q" stand for the constituent propositions, "$\neg$" stands for *it's not so that . . .* , and the capital letters "T" and "F" stand for truth-values 'true' and 'false'. For the operators *It's nice that . . .* and *It's too bad that . . .* we arrive at analogous results.) If one claims that the formula in the right hand box of the truth-table is true, one actually leaves three possibilities for the distribution of truth-values among the constituent propositions p and q (cf. the truth-values of p and q as noted in the corresponding lines of the left hand boxes). This example shows that in certain cases we cannot do without the word *and* if we want to communicate conjunctivity: when *and* is removed, conjunctivity is also lost. This, then, is a case where conjunctivity is detachable from the meaning of the rest of the sentence.

Conjunctivity also violates the other two criteria for the occurrence of a conversational suggestion: it is neither variable nor cancellable.[29] To assert:

(16)   Peter married Annie and Annie had a baby; the complete sentence is true, but one of its constituent sentences is false.

is to contradict oneself.

Now that we have demonstrated that conjunctivity is a semantic feature of the literal meaning of *and*, we must show how it is possible to construe as conversational suggestions at least the seven other content elements discussed earlier.

re (11a): If someone explicitly states that Annie is in the kitchen and then adds *without specifying another place* that she is making doughnuts, then he is guilty of *suppressing relevant information* if he thereby wants to convey that the doughnuts are being made outside of the kitchen. This would be a violation of maxim I/1. In order to avoid assuming such a violation, the addressee interprets the formulation of (11a) as a *suggestion of identity of place* (. . . *and there* . . .).

re (11b): If someone explicitly states that Annie fell into a deep sleep but then adds *without specifying another time* that her facial color returned, then he is guilty of *suppressing relevant information* if he thereby wants to convey that the two events took place at a completely different time. This would again be a violation of maxim I/1. In order to avoid assuming such a violation, the addressee interprets the formulation of (11b) as a *suggestion of simultaneity* (. . . *and during this time* . . .).

re (11c): If someone explicitly states that a window is open and then adds *without specifying another source* that there is a draft, then he is guilty of *communicating irrelevant information* if he does not want to convey that the draft is coming from that window. This would be a violation of maxim III. In order to avoid assuming such a violation, the addressee interprets the formulation of (11c) as a *suggestion of the source* of the draft (. . . *and coming from it* . . .).

re (11d): If someone begins by reporting that a woman got married and then immediately adds *without specifying another time* that she had a baby, then he is guilty of *distortive reporting* if he thereby wants to convey that the wedding took place after the baby was born. This would be a violation of maxim IV/4. In order to avoid assuming such a violation, the addressee interprets the formulation of (11d) as a *suggestion of a temporal parallelism* between the reporting utterances and the reported events (. . . *and after that* . . .).

re (11e): If someone explicitly reports someone's action upon a certain object and then, *without specifying another action*, reports a result of that person's acting upon that object, then he is guilty of *communicating irrelevant information*, if he does not want to convey that this result was brought about by the action mentioned. This would be a violation of maxim III. In order to avoid assuming such a violation, the addressee interprets the formulation of (11e) as a *suggestion of an instrumental relation* between the action and its result (. . . *and thereby* . . .).

re (11f): If someone asks a favor and, in the same sentence, predicts an action of his own that can be considered as compensation for that favor, then he is guilty of *communicating irrelevant information* or of *obscure procedures of negotiation* if he does not want to make a conditional promise dependent on the accomplishment of the favor. This would be a violation of maxims III or IV, respectively. In order to avoid assuming such a violation, the addressee interprets the formulation of (11f) as a *suggestion of a conditional relation* between the two actions mentioned (*if . . . , then . . .*).

re (11g): If someone uses one and the same sentence to make two statements about a number each of which implies the other, he is guilty of *prolixity* if he does not use one statement to justify or explain the other. This would be a violation of maxim IV/3. In order to avoid assuming such a violation, the addressee interprets the formulation of (11g) as a *suggestion of an explanatory relation* between the two statements (*. . . and therefore . . .*).

These paradigms of the sources of conversational suggestions would not be complete without the following comments:

1. Conversational suggestions are dependent on the context of utterance. Any addition of a verbal utterance or of a detail of situation can direct the reasoning of the addressee in another direction. The seven paradigms should be read *with this reservation.*

2. Each reasoning process takes reference to the formulation of the sentence in question. Instead of doing this in an *ad hoc* way one could systematically compare the suggestion-producing qualities of sentences. On this basis, it should be possible to arrive at generalizations about the production of conversational suggestions and to approach explanatory adequacy. This can be an important methodological starting-point for progress in *descriptive stylistics.*

3. Conversational suggestions arise for the most part from specific qualities of the literal meanings conveyed. If a sentence manifests several such qualities at the same time, then several suggestions can arise. Thus

— (11a) is interpretable not only as local, but also as simultaneous;
— (11b) is interpretable not only as simultaneous, but also as explanatory and local;
— (11c) is interpretable not only as directional, but also as simultaneous and explanatory;
— (11d) is interpretable not only as successive, but also as explanatory;
— (11e) is interpretable not only as instrumental, but also as simultaneous, explanatory, and local;
— (11f) is interpretable not only as conditional, but also as successive.

The fact that we obtain *multiple suggestions* is a further confirmation of the meaning-minimalist approach, since it explains the vague and expressive character of the suggestive use of language. Which of the possible suggestions dominates in each case depends amongst other things on how the corresponding semantic dimensions are realized in the sentence in question. Thus, time plays a less significant role in (11a) than in (11b) through (11e), since (11a) is formulated in the present and not in the past tense. Place plays a more important role in (11a) than in (11b) or (11d), since (11a), in contrast to the other sentences, contains an explicit specification of place (*in the kitchen*). Abstract conceptual relationships play an exclusive role in (11g), since the facts described in both its constituent sentences are valid at any time and place.

4. From the structure and results of the reasoning processes sketched above we can conclude that the given suggestions are not to be added to the conjunctivity of *and* as semantic features of the same sort; rather, they are made possible only through the combinatory function of this word. Nor do those suggestions have the same status as connexity, since they embody rather special kinds of connection between the facts described, a connection whose existence is suggested by the contiguity of the utterances of the constituent sentences. Therefore, I propose to call them *connexity-suggestions*. With his "thesis of the dual control of linguistic structure" Charles W. Morris drew attention to this phenomenon as early as 1938, when he wrote: "From the interconnectedness of events on the one hand, and the interconnectedness of [communicative] actions on the other, signs become interconnected [. . .]."[30]

The paradigms of suggestion-producing reasoning have shown the usefulness of Grice's maxims and have made it plausible that the other possible suggestions a speaker of English may intend in uttering *and*-sentences are also reconstructed pragmatically by the addressee. The truth-function defined in propositional logic has revealed itself to be the only semantic feature of the sentence connective *and* in English. And the hypothesis that other sentence connectives of natural languages also have a purely truth-functional meaning has gained in plausibility. A fresh start should be made in considering in detail whether it is possible to identify at least the literal meanings of the sentence connectives *and*, *or*, *if*, and *not* with the meanings of the connectives of propositional logic *et*, *vel*, *si*, and *non*, even if their use occasionally appears to be radically different.

At this point the meaning-minimalist position seems to have won the argument. However, this judgement may still be somewhat premature since here again things are not quite so easy. Therefore, I do not want to end this discussion without at least touching upon those difficulties.

9. THE DUALITY OF SEMANTIC AND PRAGMATIC INTERPRETATION

Problems arise in the use of *and* in complex sentence structures. Let us consider the utterance of a conditional sentence that contains the word *and* in the first clause and suggests successivity:

(18)   If Annie has married and has had a baby, grandfather will be happy.

Let us assume that (18) is true. The truth-functional analysis of the word *if* indicates that, if the antecedent clause is true, the consequent clause must also be true. The truth-functional analysis of the word *and* indicates that the entire sentence is true if and only if both constituent sentences are true. Under these conditions the grandfather would have to be happy if it is true that Annie has married and if it is true that she has had a baby. But sentence (18) is not normally so interpreted. Even if (18) is true, it can also happen that the grandfather will not be happy at all, if he hears that the child came before the wedding. So the truth of the consequent clause is dependent here upon the realization not only of the literal meaning of the antecedent clause, but also of its successivity-suggestion.[31]

Thus conversational suggestions arising from constituent sentences can be crucial in the evaluation of the truth of the entire sentence. In these cases one can no longer speak of a purely truth-functional use of the sentence connectives. The choice of explanations available creates a dilemma:

— whoever wants to save the truth-functionality of *and* by asserting that the subordinate clause of (18) is true because each of its constituent clauses is true, sacrifices the truth-functionality of *if*, since he must admit that the consequent clause can still be false.

— whoever wants to save the truth-functionality of *if* by asserting that the consequent clause in (18) is only false if the antecedent clause is false, sacrifices the truth-functionality of *and*, since he must admit that the antecedent clause can be false even if each of its constituent sentences is true.

In view of this dilemma we are on the verge of losing our motivation for a truth-functional treatment of the sentence connectives: it would only be of theoretical importance if it could be extended to all relevant sentence connectives.

A homogeneous treatment of the sentence connectives concerned seems possible only if we weaken the thesis that in natural language the truth-value of the entire sentence is a function of the truth-value of the constituent sentences. This thesis cannot be held in the sense that in complex sentence structures the truth-value of the entire sentence is directly deducible from the truth-values of the smallest constituent sentences. Rather, after each step in the truth-functional deduction, it must be considered whether the resulting conversational suggestions alter the derived truth-value. Each deduction in the value distribution of the complex sentence on the basis of the value distributions of two constituent sentences must be open to reinterpretation according to the context in which the sentence has been uttered.[32]

This is certainly not a very elegant solution. It complicates the process of interpretation to such an extent that we might have doubts about the presuppositions of this analysis, in particular, the division of the content elements into word meaning and word use.

However, another solution is hard to find, considering the arguments against the meaning-maximalists given above. Moreover, there is a series of additional arguments that make this solution more plausible than any imaginable alternative:

1. Let us compare the following versions of sentence (18) with one another:

(18)   (a) If Annie has married and has had a baby, grandfather will be happy.
      (b) If Annie has married and she has had a baby, grandfather will be happy.
      (c) If Annie has married and if she has had a baby, grandfather will be happy.
      (d) If Annie has married and if Annie has had a baby, grandfather will be happy.

Only the subordinate clause differs each time. The number of syntactic transformations performed on the subordinate clause is greatest in (a) and is reduced progressively until (d).[33] What is significant is that in (18) the strength of the successivity-suggestion also varies. It is strongest in (a) and diminishes progressively down to (d). Obviously, the intensity of the communication of a connexity-suggestion depends on the *degree of syntactic connectedness* of the constituent sentences concerned. What we have here is a typical iconic relationship between content and syntactic form. The effect of this relationship is also noticeable, although to a lesser degree, where *and* is the only sentence connective involved:[34]

(17)   (a) Annie has married and has had a child.
      (b) Annie has married and she has had a child.
      (c) Annie has married and Annie has had a child.
      (d) Annie has married. And Annie has had a child.

2. The difference between the sentences under (17) and the sentences under (18) can be generalized in the following way: the strength of a connexity-suggestion depends on the *degree of embedding* of the clause concerned in the entire sentence. Compare (19) with (18), (20) with (19), as well as (20), (19), and (18) with (17):

(19)   If grandfather finds out that Annie has married

$$\left.\begin{array}{l} \text{and} \\ \text{and she} \\ \text{and that she} \\ \text{and that Annie} \end{array}\right\} \text{has had a baby,}$$

he will be happy.

(20)   If grandmother finds out that Fritz has told grandfather that Annie has married

$$\left.\begin{array}{l} \text{and} \\ \text{and she} \\ \text{and that she} \\ \text{and that Annie} \end{array}\right\} \text{has had a baby,}$$

she will be happy.

This generalization also proves valid when we reverse the sequence of sentences connected by *and* and formulate:

(17′)   Annie has had a baby

$$\left.\begin{array}{l} \text{and} \\ \text{and she} \\ \text{and Annie} \\ \text{. And Annie} \end{array}\right\} \text{has married.}$$

(18′)   If Annie has had a baby

$$\left.\begin{array}{l} \text{and} \\ \text{and she} \\ \text{and if she} \\ \text{and if Annie} \end{array}\right\} \text{has married, grandfather will be happy.}$$

(19′)   If grandfather finds out that Annie has had a baby

$$\left.\begin{array}{l} \text{and} \\ \text{and she} \\ \text{and that she} \\ \text{and that Annie} \end{array}\right\} \text{has married, he will be happy.}$$

(20′)   If grandmother finds out that Fritz has told grandfather
          that Annie has had a baby

$$\left.\begin{array}{l} \text{and} \\ \text{and she} \\ \text{and that she} \\ \text{and that Annie} \end{array}\right\}$$ has married, she will be happy.

In all these sentences the strength of the successivity-suggestion diminishes according to the degree of embedding, and the content of the
sentence connectives *if* and *and* comes progressively closer to their
truth-functional meaning. In the most expanded version of the sentences
under (20), it surely is irrelevant to the grandmother's joy whether the
events occurred in one sequence or another.[35]

3. The force of embedded connexity-suggestions correlates with
still other factors. Let me only mention as a last case the *meaning of the
higher verb:*

(21)   If Fritz  grandfather
         that Annie has had a baby and has married, grandfather
         will be happy.

In a "report," the sequence of the events conveyed is essential. Here, the
person reporting tends to make his utterances follow the events. If he
should happen to deviate from the natural sequence he would make sure
that his addressees realize that. Thus, if Fritz reports something to the
grandfather and the grandfather is happy about it, the sequence of the
events must undoubtedly be considered among the reasons for his being happy. In a simple transmission of information, however, the sequence of the utterances can depend on any kind of accident and does
not allow any conclusion about the sequence of events. Here, then,
the sequence of events will not be among the reasons for the grandfather's joy. In this way, the strength of a connexity-suggestion can
be controlled by the choice of the higher verb.

These last three observations make it clear that connexity-suggestions are characterized not only by considerable variability, but also
by change of intensity—a property never found in literal meanings. No
grammar describes cases in which the syntactic qualities of the surrounding sentence exert an influence on the semantic value of a word

such that one of its semantic features is either foregrounded or suggested with varying strength or even eliminated entirely.

All this indicates then that connexity-suggestions are not lexical phenomena but have to be accounted for by pragmatics. And since that is so, there seems no way to avoid the dual procedure previously discussed for the interpretation of complex sentences. It is not without irony that pragmatic rules should play an essential role in the interpretation of expressions the analysis of which has for decades been considered the core of semantics.[36]

After this general conclusion it may be appropriate to summarize the individual results to which we were led by our discussion of the sentence connectives:

1. The delimitation of *semantics* and *pragmatics* in language description must follow the difference between *meaning* and *use* of words in verbal communication.

2. The meaning and the use of a word are not just two sides of the same thing, but have to be distinguished systematically. Speakers of a natural language master not only fixed word-meanings, but also fixed rules for the use of words. Both are *empirically testable*, even if there is *no direct experimental access to them.*

3. The criteria of *variability, cancellability* and *non-detachability* can help to answer the question of which content elements of a given utterance come into play through the literal meaning and which through the use of words in verbal communication.

4. On the basis of these criteria, the meaning of sentence connectives such as *and, or, if,* and *not* in natural language may be equated with the defining properties of the connectives of propositional logic *et, vel, si,* and *non.* Corresponding to the special purpose and circumstances of communication further content elements can be acquired by a sentence connective on the basis of the formulations, the meanings and the facts described in the connected sentences. These content elements occur as *conversational suggestions,* more specifically, as *connexity-suggestions.*

5. The differentiation of semantics and pragmatics in language description, and the differentiation of meaning and use in verbal communication are *theoretical* distinctions; it would be false to assume that in the actual process of comprehension one begins by applying all and only the semantic rules and then continues with the pragmatic rules. Examples with a sentence connective occurring in the scope of another sentence connective show that the meaning of a complex sentence depends not only upon the meanings of its parts, but also upon their conversational suggestions, and thus, upon their use.

6. To summarize this summary:

a. The use of a verbal expression is partially determined by the meaning of this expression.

b. The meaning of a complex verbal expression is determined not only by the meanings of its constituents, but also by their specific use.

In short, in verbal communication we not only make use of meanings but this use even makes sense.

NOTES

For helpful comments on earlier versions of this paper I am grateful to Jerry Edmondson, Donald Freeman, Frans Plank, and David Schwarz. I also want to express my gratitude for stimulating discussions of the material involved to students of linguistics, semiotics, and philosophy of the universities of Hamburg, Montreal, Chicago, Los Angeles, Berkeley, and Stanford. The usual disclaimers apply, of course.

1. The two *façons de parler* can be found in any historic-systematic presentation of linguistics, cf. Lyons (1968) and Ebneter (1973). A book exclusively applying the terminology of meaning is Schmidt (1967); presentations applying the terminology of use are Leisi (1953) and Brown (1974).

2. Cf. Grice (1968) and Grice (1975).

3. Cf. Wundt (1900, p. 596).

4. Cf. Titchener (1912, pp. 367 ff.). See also Hörmann (1970, pp. 166 ff.).

5. Cf. Erdmann (1900; 4th edition 1925, p. 5).

6. Cf. Watson (1919; 2nd edition 1924, p. 354).

7. Cf. Skinner (1937). See also Hörmann (1970, p. 165).

8. Cf. Morris (1938, pp. 43–48).

9. Cf. Kutschera (1971, 2nd edition 1975, pp. 87 f.).

10. Cf. Alston (1963, p. 84).

11. Cf. Wittgenstein (1953, I, 43).

12. Cf. Leisi (1953; 4th edition 1971, pp. 73 f.).

13. Cf. Kempson (1975) and Wilson (1976).

14. Cf. Grice (1968).

15. For this example cf. Gordon and Lakoff (1971).

16. Cf. Dascal (1976, p. 23).

17. Cf. Grice (1968), 2nd lecture.

18. Cf. Wittgenstein (1953, I, 293).

19. Cf. Grice (1968), 2nd lecture.

20. Cf. Grice (1968), 2nd lecture.

21. For the methodological value of the three criteria cf. Walker (1975, pp. 169 ff.).

22. Cohen (1971), who makes a similar distinction, talks about "semanticists" on the one hand and "conversationalists" on the other. However, he does not distinguish between the literal meaning (of a word or a sentence) and the lexical meaning (of a word).

23. Cf. Cohen (1971, p. 56).

24. Cf. Cohen (1971, p. 57).

25. Cf. Wilson (1976, pp. 118 ff.). See also Abraham (1975).

26. Cf. Lang (1977, pp. 230 ff.).

27. However, sentences (12d) and (12g) are ambiguous for many speakers of English. The fact described in the second sentence in (12d) need not be taken to occur later than that described in the first sentence, it can also be taken to have been a reason for the first to occur. The fact described in the second sentence in (12g) need not be taken to be explained by the fact described in the first sentence, it can also be given as a reason for it.

28. Naess (1961) has conducted a series of tests which show that even the decision whether the sentence connective *or* must be interpreted as an exclusive or inclusive disjunction depends on the facts described by the disjuncts involved. See also Seuren (1977, pp. 371 ff.).

29. Of course, we are dealing here only with the *and* that occurs between sentences or their transformational variants, not with the phrasal *and*, as occurring in *Peter and Annie went to Saarbrücken*. The proposed treatment can easily be applied to all cases where *and* is used to connect the propositional content of two sentences, even if these sentences are uttered with non-declarative illocutionary force. The treatment of the *and* that connects speech acts of different illocutionary force must, however, be postponed to another occasion.

30. Cf. Morris (1938, pp. 12 f.).

31. Cf. Cohen (1971, pp. 58 f.). There are a number of other interpretations possible for (18). Even if the order of wedding and birth is as it should be, it is possible that the grandfather is not happy because Annie's husband was not the baby's father. On the other hand, it is conceivable that the truth of all constituent sentences still does not entail the truth of the entire sentence in its intended sense because the grandfather could be happy about something else that he has learned simultaneously. These interpretations are eliminated if we formulate (18) in a more explicit way: *If Annie has married and has had a baby, this is a reason for grandfather to be happy*.

32. Of course, the criteria of variability, cancellability, and non-detachability also apply to embedded sentences. E.g., a cancellation of an embedded conversational suggestion is achieved by the following context: *If Annie has married and has had a baby, grandfather will be happy. But the sequence of these events will not leave him unaffected.*

33. The first and second versions are generated by conjunction reduction, and the second and third by pronominalization; in the underlying structures of the first three versions *if* dominates *and*, in the last *if* is dominated by *and*.

34. Cf. Freeman (1978), as opposed to Boettcher and Sitta (1972), who consider sentences like those under (17) to be different forms of realization of the same (semantic) category and the same (pragmatic) structure. Such a characterization would make it impossible to account for the semantic and pragmatic differences of these sentences.

35. Of course, these analyses should not make us blind to the fact that the sequence of the formulations can also express other aspects than the sequence of the events described. Compare *Annie now is a young mother. The fact that she has had a baby and that she has married has made grandfather very happy.* Here the sequence of the embedded clauses is rather used to foreground Annie's new role of a young mother.

36. Compare the procedures of formal logicians, who admit only a truth-functional relation between the complex sentence and its constituents and exclude all pragmatic aspects.

BIBLIOGRAPHY

Abraham, Werner. 1975, 'Some Semantic Properties of Some Conjunctions,' in S. P. Corder and E. Roulet (eds.), *Some Implications of Linguistic Theory for Applied Linguistics*, Brussels and Paris: Aimav and Didier, pp. 7–31.

Alston, William P. 1963, 'The Quest for Meanings,' in *Mind* 72 pp. 79–87.

Boettcher, Wolfgang and Sitta, Horst. 1972, *Zusammengesetzter Satz und äquivalente Strukturen* (= Deutsche Grammatik III). Frankurt a. M.: Athenäum.

Brown, Cecil H. 1974, *Wittgensteinian Linguistics*, The Hague and Paris: Mouton.

Chao, Yuen Ren. 1968, *Language and Symbolic Systems*, Cambridge: University Press.

Cohen, Jonathan L. 1971, 'Some Remarks on Grice's Views about the Logical Particles of Natural Language,' in Y. Bar Hillel (ed.), *Pragmatics of Natural Languages*, Dordrecht: Reidel, pp. 50–68.

Creelman, Marjorie B. 1966, *The Experimental Investigation of Meaning— A Review of Literature*, New York: Springer.

Dascal, Marcelo. 1976, 'Conversational Relevance,' Working paper, Colloquium on 'Meaning and Use', Jerusalem.

Douglas, Mary (ed.). 1973, *Rules and Meanings—The Anthropology of Everyday Knowledge*, Harmondsworth/England: Penguin.

Ebneter, Theodor: 1973, *Strukturalismus und Transformationalismus—Einführung in Schulen und Methoden*, München: List.

Erdmann, Karl Otto: 1900, *Die Bedeutung des Wortes—Aufsätze aus dem Grenzgebiet der Sprachpsychologie und Logik*, Leipzig: Avenarius, 1900. Reprint of the 4th edition of 1925, Darmstadt: Wissenschaftliche Buchgesellschaft, 1966.

Freeman, Donald. 1973, 'Keats's "To Autumn": Poetry as Pattern and Process,' in *Language and Style* XI (1978).

Gazdar, Gerald. 1978, *Formal Pragmatics for Natural Language*, London and New York: Academic Press.

Gloy, Klaus. 1975, *Sprachnormen I.—Linguistische und soziologische Analysen*, Stuttgart and Bad Cannstatt: Frommann-Holzboog.

Gloy, Klaus and Presch, Gunter, (eds.). 1976, *Sprachnormen III. Kommunikations-orientierte Linguistik—Sprachdidaktik*, Stuttgart and Bad Cannstatt: Frommann-Holzboog.

Gordon, David and Lakoff, George. 1971, 'Conversational Postulates,' in *Papers from the Seventh Regional Meeting of the Chicago Linguistic Society*, Chicago: Chicago Linguistic Society.

Grice, Herbert P. 1968, 'The Logic of Conversation,' Working paper. Berkeley: University of California.

Grice, Herbert P. 1975, 'Logic and Conversation,' in P. Cole and J. L. Morgan (eds.), *Syntax and Semantics. Vol. 3: Speech Acts*, New York: Academic Press.

Grimm, Hannelore and Wintermantel, Margret. 1975, *Zur Entwicklung von Bedeutungen—Forschungsberichte zur Sprachentwicklung II*, Weinheim and Basel: Beltz.

Heringer, Hans Jürgen (ed.). 1974, *Der Regelbegriff in der praktischen Semantik*, Frankurt a. M.: Suhrkamp.

Hörmann, Hans. 1967, *Psychologie der Sprache*. Berlin, Heidelberg and New York: Springer. Translated into English by H. H. Stern: *Psycholinguistics —An Introduction to Research and Theory*. Berlin, Heidelberg and New York: Springer, 1970.

Isenberg, Horst. 1971, Überlegungen zur Texttheorie,' in J. Ihwe (ed.), *Literaturwissenschaft und Linguistik*, Vol. 1, Frankfurt a. M.: Athenäum, 1971.

Kasher, Asa. 1974, 'Mood Implicatures: A Logical Way of Doing Generative Pragmatics,' in *Theoretical Linguistics* 1, pp. 6–38.

Kempson, Ruth M.: 1975, *Presupposition and the Delimitation of Semantics*, Cambridge: University Press.

Kutschera, Franz von: 1971, *Sprachphilosophie*, München: Fink; 2nd edition, 1975.

Kutschera; Franz von. 1975, 'Conventions of Language and Intensional Semantics,' in *Theoretical Linguistics* 2, pp. 255–283.

Lang, Ewald: 1977, *Semantik der koordinativen Verknüpfung* (= studia grammatica XIV), Berlin (GDR): Akademie-Verlag.

Lehrer, Adrienne and Lehrer, Keith, (eds.). 1970, *Theory of Meaning*, Engelwood Cliffs, N.J.: Prentice Hall.

Leisi, Ernst. 1953, *Der Wortinhalt—Seine Struktur im Deutschen und Englischen*, Heidelberg: Quelle and Meyer; 4th edition 1971.

Lewis, David. 1969, *Convention—A Philosophical Study*, Cambridge: Harvard University Press. Translated into German by R. Posner and D.

Wenzel: *Konventionen—Eine sprachphilosophische Abhandlung*, Berlin and New York: de Gruyter, 1975.

Lorenzer, Alfred: 1970, *Sprachzerstörung und Rekonstrukton—Vorarbeiten zu einer Metatheorie der Psychoanalyse*, Frankfurt a. M.: Suhrkamp.

Lyons, John. 1968, *Introduction to Theoretical Linguistics*, Cambridge: University Press.

Mooij, Jan J. A. 1976, *A Study of Metaphor—On the Nature of Metaphorical Expressions, with Special Reference to Their Reference*, Amsterdam, New York and Oxford: North-Holland.

Morris, Charles W. 1938, *Foundations of the Theory of Signs*, Chicago: University Press. Translated into German by R. Posner and J. Rehbein: *Grundlagen der Zeichentheorie*, München: Hanser, 1972, 2nd edition, 1975.

Naess, Arne. 1961, 'A Study of "or",' in *Synthese* 13, 49–60.

Posner, Roland. 1972 a, *Theorie des Kommentierens—Eine Grundlagenstudie zur Semantik und Pragmatik*, Frankfurt a. M.: Athenäum.

Posner, Roland. 1972 b, 'Commenting—A Diagnostic Procedure for Semantico-Pragmatic Sentence Representations,' in *Poetics* 5, pp. 67–88.

Posner, Roland. 1972c, 'Zur systematischen Mehrdeutigkeit deutscher Lexeme,' in *Linguistik und Didaktik* 12, pp. 268–276.

Presch, Gunter and Gloy, Klaus, (eds.). 1976, *Sprachnormen II. Theoretische Begründungen—ausserschulische Sprachnormenpraxis*, Stuttgart and Bad Cannstatt: Frommann-Holzboog.

Raz, Joseph. 1975, *Practical Reason and Norms*, London: Hutchinson,

Richards, David A. J. 1971, *A Theory of Reasons for Action*, Oxford: Clarendon.

Rollin, Bernard E. 1976, *Natural and Conventional Meaning—An Examination of the Distinction*, The Hague and Paris: Mouton.

Sadock, Jerrold M. 1974, *Toward a Linguistic Theory of Speech Acts*, New York: Seminar Press.

Schmerling, Susan F. 1975, 'Asymmetric Conjunction and Rules of Conversation,' in P. Cole and J. L. Morgan (eds.), *Syntax and Semantics. Vol. 3: Speech Acts*, New York: Academic Press.

Schmidt, Wilhelm. 1967, *Lexikalische und aktuelle Bedeutung—Ein Beitrag zur Theorie der Wortbedeutung*, Berlin (GDR): Akademie-Verlag.

Searle, John R. 1969, *Speech Acts—An Essay in the Philosophy of Language*, Cambridge: University Press.

Seuren, Pieter A. M. 1977, *Zwischen Sprache und Denken—Ein Beitrag zur empirischen Begründung der Semantik*. Wiesbaden: Athenaion.

Skinner, Burrhus F. 1937, 'The Distribution of Associated Words,' in *Psychol. Rec.* 1, pp. 71–76.

Slobin, Dan I. 1971, *Psycholinguistics*, Glenview, Ill. and London: Scott, Foresman and Comp.

Titchener, Edward B. 1912, *Lehrbuch der Psychologie*, Part 2, Leipzig: Barth.

Travis, Charles. 1975, *Saying and Understanding—A Generative Theory of Illocutions*, Oxford: Basil Blackwell.

Ulmann, Gisela. 1975, *Sprache und Wahrnehmung—Verfestigen und Aufbrechen von Anschauungen durch Wörter*, Frankfurt a. M. and New York: Campus Verlag.

Walker, Ralph C. S. 1975, 'Conversational Implicatures,' in Simon Blackburn (ed.), *Meaning, Reference and Necessity*, Cambridge: University Press.

Watson, John. 1919, *Psychology from the Standpoint of a Behaviorist*, Philadelphia and London: Lippincott; 2nd edition, 1924.

Wilson, Deirdre. 1976, *Presuppositions and Non-truth-conditional Semantics*, London, New York and San Francisco: Academic Press.

Wittgenstein, Ludwig. 1953, *Philosophical Investigations*, ed. by G. E. M. Anscombe and R. Rhees, Oxford: Basil Blackwell.

The Bridge between
Semantics and Pragmatics

WILLIAM P. ALSTON

According to the hallowed trinity of syntax, semantics, and pragmatics, syntax is concerned with the internal structure of a system of signs; semantics with the relations between signs and their designata, referents, or meanings; and pragmatics with the use of signs as vehicles of communication. The mutual dependence or independence of these areas of inquiry has long been a thorny issue, the most visible form of which is the debate over the possibility of developing the syntax of a language without recourse to semantic considerations. In this paper I shall exhibit one mode of dependence—that of semantics on pragmatics. My concern is with conceptual rather than methodological or any other form of dependence. My explicit concern is restricted to *language* and to the *meaning* aspects of semantics, rather than to reference, truth, or anything else one may be inclined to put into that basket. My claim is that the concept of linguistic meaning is to be elucidated by reference to pragmatic concepts of the roles of meaningful units in communication—what speakers *do* with those units in communication. I am not suggesting that specific facts, principles, or phenomena of pragmatics must be used to work out the semantics of a language. That is not the kind of bridge I want to build. Indeed, I do not attempt here to draw any methodological consequences from my thesis. I am concerned instead with gaining a reflective understanding of the concepts we use in semantically describing a language, however such a description may be most fruitfully developed.

Most of those currently concerned with the semantic side of language—linguists, philosophers, and others—concentrate on applying semantic concepts to language or to particular stretches of language—definite descriptions, adverbs, tenses, token reflexives, mass terms, natural-kind terms, and so on. There is relatively little interest in making explicit *what it is* for a word, phrase, or sentence to have a certain meaning. When conceptual problems are addressed, it is usually by way of defining certain semantic concepts in terms of an initial set of semantic primitives. Only occasionally does anyone seek to throw light on our most basic semantic concepts or on the system as a whole.[1]

As already advertised, I am attempting to do this job by exhibiting the conceptual dependence of semantics on pragmatics. This dependence can be stated in its most general form as what I call the "Use Principle":

> I. To have a certain meaning is to be fitted to play (to be used for) a certain distinctive role in communication.

I must say that the Use Principle has seemed overwhelmingly plausible, even truistic, to me from the day I first formulated it explicitly. It seems to me constitutive of our concept of linguistic meaning that the meaning of a linguistic expression is what fits it to play a distinctive role in communication. Surely it is obvious that by meaning what it does, the sentence "What time is it?" is standardly usable for one sort of communicative act rather than another, in this case, for asking someone for the time. How could we change its meaning without changing what it is standardly usable to communicate? And how could we change its standard communicative potential without changing its meaning? No doubt, the identification of meaning with communicative potential will be acceptable only if we carefully restrict the kinds of communicative roles we put into the equation. But considerations of the sort just indicated encourage us to suppose that there is some way in which this can be done.

First we must determine what kind of communicative role can constitute the meaning of what kind of linguistic unit. The best strategy would seem to be to start with the linguistic unit that is usable to perform a complete act of communication, namely, the sentence. Having identified the communicative potential that constitutes sentence meaning (SM), we can then construe word or morpheme meaning more abstractly, as the capacity of the word or morpheme to make a certain distinctive contribution to the communicative potentials of sentences in which it occurs. Thus, in the implementation of this program, the concept of sentence meaning is the first semantic concept to be elucidated, and the concept of word meaning is elucidated in terms of that.[2] In this paper I shall restrict myself to sentence meaning.

My basic thesis identifies sentence meaning with *illocutionary-act-potential* (IAP). The "IAP Thesis" can be stated as follows:

> II. A sentence's having a given meaning consists in its having a certain illocutionary-act-potential.

A few preliminary points should be made about the concepts involved in this principle. For a preanalytic demarcation of the category of *il-*

locutionary acts (IA), I rely on the familiar indirect discourse form. We have, in ordinary language, a variety of locutions for making explicit *what someone said* (where this does not mean what sentence he uttered), that is, what the content of his utterance is, what message it conveyed. Here is a small sample:

1. U asserted (admitted, replied, insisted, etc.) that his garden gate was open.
2. U promised to meet Jones for lunch tomorrow.
3. U asked A for a match.
4. U predicted that the strike would soon be over.
5. U remarked that the weather was warming up.
6. U assured A that everything would be all right.
7. U congratulated A on his performance.
8. U exhorted A to finish by tomorrow.
9. U expressed considerable enthusiasm for A's proposal.
10. U expressed his intention to stay here all summer.
11. U declared the meeting adjourned.
12. U called the batter out.

Note that each of these items involves an action verb (*promise, predict, advise*, etc.) followed by what we might call a *content-specifying phrase*. We may follow John Searle[3] in saying that the verb specifies the *illocutionary force* (IF) of the utterance, while the ensuing phrase specifies the *propositional content* (PC).

Although most of the examples yielded by my criterion would be recognized by other theorists, there are some differences. First, I use a third-person approach based on the ways in which we report utterances; on this approach, an illocutionary verb is not necessarily usable in the performative formula. *Express*, for example, is not. I do not express admiration for your performance by saying, "I express admiration for your performance." Second, I do not share the tendency exhibited by some others to individuate IA-types solely by what I have called IF. In my scheme, *predicting that it will rain tomorrow* is just as much a different IA-type from *predicting that Jones will come to the party* as it is a different IA-type from *asking Smith what time it is;* albeit the first difference is only in PC, while the second is also in IF.

Now a word about the P in IAP. It is clear that if statement II above is to have any chance of being acceptable, we must restrict *potential* to something like *standard potential*, that is, *usability by virtue of the constitution of the language*. For if we consider private codes or special conventions for special subgroups, it is clear that any sentence (S) can be used to perform IA's of any type. (But by the same token, given the proper arrangements, a given sentence can be used to mean anything.) Since we are interested in established meanings of S's, we are correspondingly focused on what makes an S *standardly usable* to perform IA's of a certain type.

Next I must note some counterexamples to the unqualified identification of SM and IAP.[4] To deal with them we shall have to complicate the thesis.

SM can be unqualifiedly identified with IAP only if for each distinguishable SM there is exactly one IA-type for the performance of which the S is thereby fitted; and, vice versa, for each IA-type there is exactly one SM that fits an S for being used to perform it. If this were true, then whenever I used an S with a given meaning and thereby performed some IA, it would always be the same IA; and whenever I performed an IA of a certain type, by making a normal use of an S, I would always be uttering that S with the same meaning. But the world is not that simple.

There are, first of all, cases of the sort used by Austin to introduce the concept of IF originally, those in which a sentence can be used with the same meaning to perform acts with different IF's.[5] As Austin pointed out, one can use the sentence "It is going to charge" without changing its meaning either to state or to warn that a certain bull is going to charge (and, we may add, to admit, to agree, to conclude, or to announce that it is going to charge). Clearly the meaning of one's sentential vehicle cannot be depended on to determine fully the IF of one's IA. Austin took this to show that the IF of an utterance was something over and above meaning "in the sense in which meaning is equivalent to sense and reference." But it is important to note that insofar as it shows this, a parallel argument also shows that PC is not determined by meaning. For just as my sentential vehicle may not make completely explicit the IF of my utterance, so may it not make explicit the PC. By saying "It will," I may be asserting that a certain bull is going to charge, that the interest rate will go down, that a certain ladder will hold steady, and so on. And, given the appropriate stage setting, I can express any propositional content by saying "Yes," surely a limiting case of the underdetermination of IA by sentential meaning.

Involved in all these cases is the familiar fact that if we have enough contextual clues, we need not use a sentence rich enough to carry all the details of the intended IA. This point applies equally to the IF and PC aspects; but for any IA-type it is possible (with a possible exception noted below) to construct a sentence the (or a) meaning of which *does* fully and unambiguously determine that type. Thus the Austinian IF ambiguities could be resolved by augmenting the sentence with a performative verb to make it "I warn you it's going to charge" or "I admit it's going to charge." My first PC ambiguity can be resolved by replacing "It will" with "The bull over there is going to charge" or "The interest rate will go down." The only aspect of IA's that seems not fully determinable by meaning is reference (meaning by "meaning" *meaning* rather than Austin's "sense *and reference*"). Note that my enlarged sentences did not make explicit which bull or which interest rate. But this is controversial, and in any event our present concern is with determination in the opposite direction. For any SM there is an IA-type that is fully determined by that meaning, in the sense that if someone seriously and literally utters a sentence with that meaning, then, just by knowing that, we can determine that the person intends to be performing an IA of that type. We do not need any supplementary contextual clues for that determination. This criterion gives us what we may call the *matching IA-type* for a given SM. Here are the matching IA-types for some of the above sentences and some others (assuming a familiar meaning for each sentence).

1. "It will"—asserting of something that it will do something.
2. "It's going to charge"—asserting of a certain animal that it is going to charge.
3. "I agree that it is going to charge"—agreeing to the proposition that it is going to charge.
4. "The bull is going to charge"—asserting of a certain bull that it is going to charge.
5. "Jones's prize bull is going to charge"—asserting of a certain prize bull belonging to a person named "Jones" that it is going to charge.

To construct a matching IA-type we have to find just the degree of specificity that is explicitly embodied in the SM in question—with respect to the identity of referents, the predicative aspects of the PC, and the IF. Note that an IA-type can be too poor for the sentence meaning, as well as, like all our initial examples, too rich. Thus while *admitting that Jones's bull is going to charge* is too rich for "It is going to charge," *asserting of something that it will do something* is too poor. Again, there are dimensions of mismatch other than specificity. The sentence "The Norwegian banners fan our people cold" can be used metaphorically to assert that the Norwegian Army is making our people afraid; but that IAP is not directly determined by any of its established meanings in the language. And second-order uses, such as ironically using "What a beautiful day" to remark that the weather is nasty, are not directly determined by meaning.

In sum, although it is not unqualifiedly true that SM amounts to IAP, we can say that for any SM there is a matching IA-type such that the SM can be identified with whatever renders a sentence usable to perform IA's of that type.

It may help you to appreciate the distinctive character of IAP theory if I contrast it with another form of "communicative role" theory, one which identifies sentence meaning with the usability of a sentence to produce or elicit certain effects in a hearer, for example, the production of a certain belief, intention, or emotion, or the elicitation of a certain action. Using Austin's correlative concept of a *perlocutionary* act,[6] we might term this the "Perlocutionary-Act-Potential (PAP) Theory." The PAP Theory is found in many thinkers, from Locke to Grice. Suppose, contrary to what I believe, that we could find a matching PAP for each SM, just as I have claimed we can find a matching IAP. Then each SM would be extensionally equivalent to a certain PAP. Even so I would not consider PAP theory a serious rival to IAP theory, for I would hold that an S has a distinctive PAP only by virtue of having a correlated IAP. A given SM determines a distinctive PAP *through* determining a distinctive IAP. Consider what makes the sentence "The house is on fire" an effective vehicle for getting the addressee (A) to realize that a certain house is on fire, or to realize that the utterer (U) believes of a certain house that it is on fire. Why should we suppose that uttering that sentence is a good way of getting one's addressee to realize *that*? It is because the rules of the language and the conventions of communication are such that when U utters that sentence, A (in the absence of indications to the contrary) takes U to be performing the IA of asserting of the house in question that it is on fire. Unless A has reason to doubt U's sincerity or reliability, A will draw the conclusion that the house is on fire, or at least that U believes it to be. But this inference would never get started if A did not suppose U to be performing the IA of asserting that the house is on fire; and, in the normal case, A has no basis for this supposition other than the fact that the sentence uttered is tagged in the language for performing IA's of that type. Thus, even if each SM does determine a correlated PAP, that relationship is derived from the more basic determination of a correlated IAP. Even if the PAP Thesis passes the test of extensional equivalence, the equivalence will be correctly viewed as a consequence of the IAP Theory, rather than as the basis for a rival account of what meaning is.

It may be thought that the IAP Theory purchases complete coverage at the price of remaining so close to the analysandum as to be unilluminating. According to IAP theory, the sentence "The house is on fire" means what it does because it is standardly usable to tell someone that a certain house is on fire. And isn't the concept of telling someone that a certain house is on fire too close to the concept of the sentence's meaning that a certain house is on fire to be the basis of an illuminating account of the latter? I would agree that if we leave the concept of IAP in an unanalyzed state, we have not thrown sufficient light on the matter. To make further progress, we must develop an analysis of IAP. And to do that in an illuminating way, we must develop an account of the structure of IA's, of what it is to perform an IA of a certain type. (An understanding of potentiality requires an understanding of the corresponding actuality, as Aristotle taught us.) This is a very large subject, and here I can do no more than present the bare bones of my account.

Let us begin with flat assertions, which, in the light of the completed account, turn out to be a case of limiting simplicity. What is it to assert that my garden gate is open? What is added (or subtracted) when I move from using a certain sentence, for example, "It's open," to practice pronunciation or to assert that my front door is open, to using it to assert that my garden gate is open? When I began to make a determined assault on this problem, I was surprised to find how little attention it has attracted from scholars, so the following account does not confront much overt competition.

First we must specify the requirements that an adequate answer must satisfy. The crucial condition that makes the utterance an assertion that p must contain the following elements:

1. It must involve the proposition that p. Otherwise, how could it turn the utterance into an assertion that p rather than an assertion that q?

2. It must connect the proposition that p with the utterer, U. Otherwise, how could it turn U's utterance into an assertion that p? The most obvious way to satisfy these first two requirements would be to make the condition require a certain stance or propositional attitude of U toward p.

3. This attitude must be within U's voluntary control. For it seems that, given the appropriate equipment, I can, at will, use the sentence "It's open" in any of the three ways enumerated above, as well as in many others.

We can satisfy these constraints by the condition that U utter a certain sentence, S, in order to get the addressee, A, to believe that p, or, in a more complex version, to get A to believe that U believes that p. This kind of suggestion is worked out in a very complicated form in Stephen Schiffer's book, *Meaning*[7]; but however complicated, it seems clear to me that it does not provide complete coverage. For example, I may have absolutely no hope of your believing what I say, or even of your believing that I believe what I say, but nevertheless I may feel an obligation to tell the truth in answer to a direct question. Hence, in the interest of finding an account that applies straightforwardly over the whole range, I am motivated to look elsewhere.

Consider the following natural ways of bringing out what U did in making a flat assertion that p.

1. He represented himself as knowing that p.
2. He purported (claimed) to know that p.
3. He committed himself to its being the case that p.
4. He vouched for its being the case that p.
5. He lent his authority to the belief that p.

The last three items indicate that when one makes an assertion one changes one's normative status in a certain way; that one sticks one's neck out or goes out on a limb. When I vouch for something or lend my authority to its being a certain way, I render myself liable to censure, reprimand, correction, or the like, in case things are not as I have claimed they are. I have put myself in such a position that I can be called to account provided things are not that way. (Of course, whether I am actually "called to account" in that case, and if so how, depends on various features of the social situation.) The first two items indicate that the condition that must hold if one is to escape liability to negative sanction is not simply that p (where p is what is being asserted), but that U knows that p. We can conclude that what makes an utterance of S into an assertion that p is that in uttering S, U takes on a liability to negative sanction (if otherwise appropriate), provided he does not know that p.

Let us add one more bit to the picture. If we may assume that what renders me liable to negative sanction in case that $\sim p$ is the existence of a rule that requires that p, we may reformulate the crucial condition in terms of the holding of a rule that requires U to know that p. Remembering that the crucial condition is supposed to be under the voluntary control of U, we are then forced to recognize that the crucial condition cannot be merely that the rule does hold, that it does apply to U's utterance, but that U recognizes it to hold, utters S *as subject to* that rule.[8] Putting this all together, we may formulate our crucial condition (for asserting that p in uttering S) as follows:

III. U uttered S as subject to a rule that, in application to this case, implies that U's knowing that p is a necessary condition of U's permissibly uttering S.

So far we have explicitly considered only one small corner of the IA terrain, namely, asserting; however, I believe that we can extract from our account of asserting a general account of IA's. The crucial step in this extraction is the recognition that in performing an IA of whatever type we are presupposing or implying that certain states of affairs obtain. Here are some examples of what is presupposed or implied in nonassertive IA's of several types.

1. U ordered A to open that door.
   a. That door is not now open.
   b. It is possible for A to open that door.
   c. U is in a position of authority vis-à-vis A.

2. U promised A to meet him for lunch tomorrow.
   a. It is possible for U to meet A for lunch tomorrow.
   b. A would prefer U's meeting him for lunch tomorrow to U's not doing so.
   c. U intends to meet A for lunch tomorrow.

3. U declared a certain meeting (M) adjourned.
   a. M is in session at the time of the utterance.
   b. U has the authority to terminate M.
   c. Conditions are appropriate for the exercise of that authority.

It seems clear that the account we have given of asserting that p will apply equally well to presupposing or implying that p. For if, in ordering A to open a certain door, I am implying that the door in question is not already open, it would seem that I am purporting to know that the door is not already open, just as much as I would if I were asserting that the door is not already open. If I order you to open the door without knowing that the door is not open, my utterance is out of order as unequivocally as if I had asserted that the door is not open without knowing that it was not open. This means that insofar as we can construe these nonassertive illocutionary acts as nothing other than presupposing and implying certain things in uttering a certain sentence, we can analyze them along the same lines as assertions. To be sure, there are various difficulties which must be overcome before we can pursue this analysis to its conclusion. First, we will have to explain the difference between asserting that p and presupposing or implying that p. Second, we will have to take account of the point that associated with each of a certain range of IA-types (e.g., declaring a meeting adjourned) there is a distinctive *conventional effect* (e.g., the meeting is no longer in session). At this point I can only consider the second problem, and can only indicate briefly how I might deal with it.

On the one hand, it seems clear that it is a conceptual truth that declaring a meeting adjourned has as its natural outcome the conventional effect just mentioned. On the other hand, it is clear that so long as an IA concept involves only what is said (the content of the message communicated), we cannot take the actual production of such a conventional effect to be a necessary condition for the actual performance of an IA of that type. For if we contrast a case in which the speaker actually terminates the meeting and a case in which the speaker does not although the speaker had intended to do so (some essential procedures were overlooked), it is clear that *what the speaker said* is (or could be) exactly the same in the two cases. Hence what we may call the *pure* IA is not "adjourning the meeting," but rather "declaring the meeting adjourned," where the latter description leaves it open whether the meeting actually is terminated.

But if this is the case, how are we to accommodate the first of the two points mentioned above—that somehow the notion of the meeting being terminated is involved in the pure IA concept of declaring the meeting adjourned? I suggest that we do it by adding to the list of conditions presupposed or implied the following:

By uttering S, U brings it about that the meeting in question is terminated.

Thus we lay down as a necessary condition of U's declaring the meeting terminated that U *imply* that by this utterance U is terminating the meeting, but we do not require that U actually do this. In this way we accommodate both the points made at the beginning of the previous paragraph.

One virtue of the account of IA performance in terms of rule recognition that is embodied in statement III above is that it presents us with a ready-made answer to the questions "What gives a sentence a certain IAP?" "By virtue of what is a sentence rendered standardly usable to perform IA's of a given type?" If performing an IA of a certain type consists of uttering a sentence as subject to a certain kind of rule, then the condition that would render a sentence standardly usable for performing an IA of that type is simply that it be governed by a rule of that sort. That is, the sentence will have a certain IAP if there exists in the language community a rule that stipulates the appropriate requirement for permissible utterance of that sentence. This is, of course, only the general outline of an answer. It merely indicates the lines along which detailed specifications of IAP's are to be developed. Actually working them out will be an enormous task. It will require us to determine what kind of rule, applied to an utterance, would imply that the utterance was out of order in the absence of a given appropriate condition, taking account of such complications as multivocality and the underdetermination of reference by meaning. For the present, I shall have to be content with having indicated in outline how sentence meaning can be thought of as constituted by IAP, and thus how semantic concepts are conceptually derived from pragmatic concepts.

NOTES

1. For some noteworthy recent attempts see: H. P. Grice, "Meaning," *Philosophical Review* 66 (1957):377–88; H. P. Grice, "Utterer's Meaning and Intentions," *Ibid.* 78 (1969):147–77; H. P. Grice, "Utterer's Meaning, Sentence-Meaning, and Word-Meaning," *Foundations of Language* 4 (1968): 1–18; John Searle, *Speech Acts* (Cambridge: At the University Press, 1969); Stephen R. Schiffer, *Meaning* (Oxford: Clarendon Press, 1972); David Lewis, "General Semantics," in *Semantics of Natural Language*, D. Davidson and G. Harman, eds., 169–218 (Boston: D. Reidel, 1972); Jonathan Bennett, *Linguistic Behavior* (Cambridge: At the University Press, 1976).

2. One might think that the claim that sentence meaning is prior to word meaning conflicts with the universally accepted, and undeniable, point that the meaning of a sentence is a determinate function of the meanings of its constituents plus its syntactic structure. This latter principle takes sentence meaning to be derivative from, among other things, word meaning. So how can word meaning be derivative from sentence meaning? It seems we can't have it both ways.

But it can work both ways, provided the orders of priority are different, or, more precisely, provided the terms of the opposite priority relations are not the same; and that is the case here. *The fact that a given sentence has a certain meaning* is derivative from *facts about the meanings of its constituent words;* whereas the general *concept of word meaning* is derivative from the general *concept of sentence meaning.* It is in the order of derivation (or explanation) of particular semantic facts that word meaning is prior, while it is in the order of derivation or analysis of semantic concepts that sentence meaning is prior. It is not my position that the same kind of derivation can be carried out in both directions. I do not claim that the fact that a particular word has a certain meaning can be profitably construed as a function, among other things, of the meanings of sentences in which it occurs; nor do I claim that the concept of sentence meaning is derivative from the concept of word meaning.

It is quite common in many spheres of thought to find an opposition between the order of concepts and the order of facts or things, whether the latter be a causal, compositional, explanatory, or other kind of order. For example, a popular position in the philosophy of science holds that although micro facts and micro processes (atomic structure, electron movements) are responsible for observable macro phenomena (such as rusting and the movements of electric motors) and thus are prior to the macro phenomena in the order of causality and the order of causal explanation, nevertheless our *concepts* of the micro phenomena are necessarily derived, at least in part, from the ways in which they enter into the explanation of the macro phenomena and so are posterior in the order of conceptual analysis to *concepts* of macro phenomena. This is an exact parallel to my position on the relation of sentence meaning and word meaning. On my view sentence meaning (macro phenomenon) is explained by reference to its micro (semantic and syntactic) structure; but we cannot explicate our concepts of that micro structure except by reference to the ways in which aspects of the structure enter into the explanation of particular sentence meanings.

Here are some other examples of the same duality. According to Thomism, God is the cause of all other things including men (God is prior in the order of causality), but our concept of God is derived from our concepts of men and of other creatures (creatures are prior to God in the order of conceptual analysis). According to sense-datum theory, the concept of a physical object is derivative from concepts of sense-data, even though particular sense-data are caused by physical objects.

3. *Speech Acts*, 30–31.

4. I have presented the IAP Thesis in an unqualified and a somewhat different form in W. P. Alston, "Meaning and Use," *Philosophical Quarterly* 13 (1963):107–24, and in W. P. Alston, *Philosophy of Language* (Englewood Cliffs, N.J.: Prentice-Hall, 1964), chap. 2.

5. J. L. Austin, *How to Do Things with Words* (Oxford: Clarendon Press, 1962), lect. 8.

6. *How to Do Things with Words*, lect. 8. Roughly, to perform a perlocutionary act is to produce some effect "upon the feelings, thoughts or actions of the audience, or of the speaker, or of other persons" (101) by saying something.

7. *Meaning*, chap. 4.

8. We will not be able to consider here the complicated issue of the extent to which it is U's recognition that constitutes the applicability of the rule to his utterance, and the question whether this is true of different sorts of cases in varying degrees.

Semiotic and Linguistics

JOSEPH RANSDELL

INTRODUCTION

A semiotic linguistics would differ significantly from linguistics as usually conceived in recent decades. The extent and nature of this difference became increasingly clear to me as I transformed the oral address I presented at the conference into the paper now before you, in accord with a growing understanding that the semiotic conception cannot be of real use to the linguist—or to any other student of the meaningful and the significant as such—until the methodic basis of this approach is understood. This involves assumptions about what the empirical objects of such studies are, and how such objects are to be regarded, which differ radically from what has usually been assumed in linguistics, and the attempt to understand the semiotic perspective within the context of the usual assumptions can only result in confusion. Consequently, I focus here primarily on what seems necessary (in the present intellectual situation) to bring about an understanding of the relevant assumptions, rather than on the development of the analytic conceptions of semiotic. I do hope, though, to provide a way toward a more authentic and useful understanding of the icon/index/ symbol distinction in particular than has been available heretofore.

In the first part of the paper I focus on the contrast between a semiotic approach and what I call "hermetic" linguistics, the term *hermetic* being my own term for a certain way of conceiving the science which I believe to be common to what is usually called "structuralist" linguistics, to Chomskyan linguistics, and perhaps to some others as well. I argue that linguistics, so conceived, cannot be a genuinely empirical science. (Hence such knowledge of language as linguists of these schools have achieved—and I do not question any substantive achievements, but only a certain conception of linguistics as a science— has been in spite of serious confusion about the nature of their enterprise.) The formal *validity* of my argument is one thing, however, and its *application* to this or that particular conception of linguistics quite another. I do not adduce textual evidence here that it applies to this or that school of thought—though I see no reason not to make clear to whom I think it applies—because this would invite responses in which the two distinct questions were confused. Thus you must regard what I say as an "if-the-shoe-fits" argument, and make your own decision as to whom it fits, if you think it valid. The second part of the paper focuses on the assumptional basis of the semiotic approach. In the third part, I try to convey a working sense for a few of the basic analytic conceptions, particularly the icon/index/symbol distinction. The conception of semiotic explained here is due to Charles Peirce, who discovered it more than a century ago in an attempt to provide a radically new basis for the science of logic.[1] My representation of Peirce's theory can fairly be said to be an informed one; however, it is not a textual exegesis but rather an attempt to restate some of his ideas in a way appropriate to the present audience and to the contemporary intellectual context generally.

I

During this century, the dominant conception of linguistics as a science has been that the primary task of the linguist is to describe languages, that is, to write grammars and dictionaries. Many linguists have also held that a further task is that of developing a single canonical form for such descriptions (a "universal grammar," with the term *grammar* used in an extended sense to include principles of dictionary writing, and perhaps still other principles not usually thought of as grammatical). Languages are thus regarded much as if they were Aristotelian "primary substances," that is, individual entities (albeit inferred rather than observed individuals) having form or structure; and the task of the linguist is to describe, by inference from linguistic phenomena, the structural properties of these individual entities at particular points in time, and perhaps also to observe and describe their changes across time (much as one might write biographies of individual persons). Then if one believes in "universal grammar," one attempts to describe the "essence" or "secondary substance" they all have in common that makes them the kind of thing they are. Whether the inferences from linguistic phenomena to the individual language are inductive or hypothetical in character, whether the properties consequently to be assigned to the phenomena are supposed to be at a "surface" or "depth" level, whether the inferred structures are of this sort or that—all such disputes fall within the general agreement that the description of languages is the primary task of the linguist, if not the final one.

In view of this basically Peripatetic conception of the science, it is surprising that so much has been made of the difference between what John Lyons calls "modern linguistics" and the previous linguistics traditions.[2] Lyons specifies five supposedly differentiating features of "modern" linguistics: (1) recognition of the priority of the spoken to the written language; (2) a nonprescriptive approach to language description; (3) recognition of the priority of synchronic to diachronic description; (4) recognition of the *langue/parole* distinction; and (5) the adoption of a "structuralist" view, defined as regarding a language as a system of relations "the elements of which—sounds, words, etc.— have no validity independently of the relations of equivalence and contrast which hold between them."[3] But these differences are more apparent than real.

Feature (1) would betoken a methodological shift of some importance if it meant that the differentiating characteristics of the spoken word (e.g., kinesic factors) had been integrated into linguistics; but I see little evidence that the focus on the spoken language has in fact made any great difference in this respect. It has given rise to an extensive and sophisticated development of phonology, and this is surely important, but it is no more than an extension of the traditional concern, constituting no fundamental reconceiving of the science.

Feature (2) is of no significance: a prescription is simply a description functioning prescriptively, and linguistics of the sort in question here has had little concern with such functional differences. Moreover, language descriptions are always relativized to the speech habits of some specially selected class of persons in any case, and it is of no consequence that linguists now *say* they are not prescribing the "best" usage. Whether their works actually function prescriptively is a matter of how they are responded to by those who consult them, not of the linguists' pious avowals and intentions.

Feature (3) is misleadingly stated. Anybody who has accepted the conception of "synchronic" and "diachronic" description could hardly have failed to realize that any "diachronic" description must be based on (or imply) at least two "synchronic" descriptions. What differentiates so-called "modern" linguistics is rather the formulation and acceptance of the distinction itself. I have argued elsewhere that the conception is bogus, and I cannot repeat that argument here.[4] It will have to suffice to say that its apparent plausibility depends upon a pseudo-analogy with state-descriptions in the physical sciences, and that it is illegitimate because it overlooks the fact that a physical state-description does not describe *laws*—much less *rules* (which are the linguist's pseudo-analogue to laws)—but rather singular states-of-affairs. If this is correct, then "modern" linguistics differs from traditional linguistics in this respect only in having fallen into a pretentious and unhealthy confusion.

Feature (4) is formulated by Lyons in such a way that it does not affirm the priority of *langue* to *parole*, perhaps because not all modern linguists have accepted that priority. But if it is only a matter of the recognition of the distinction itself (vaguely conceived, as it must be if he is not referring only to some particular school of thought), then it is questionable whether it has ever gone unrecognized. In any case, its importance is a matter of where the priority is conceived to lie.

Only feature (5) seems to point to a substantial difference, unless (4) includes an affirmation of the priority of *langue*. It is apparently formulated with an eye to the Saussurean "associative" and "syntagmatic" relations. "Associative" relations, which include relations of logical contrariety, are doubtless of great importance; but concern with these has been far more prominent in Europe than here, and it is still not clear *precisely* what these relations are supposed to be, inasmuch as contrariety relations of quite different types, with importantly different relations to empirical fact, are cited as examples (e.g., color contrariety would appear to be quite different from familial contrarieties). Saussure's "syntagmatic" relations are analogous to the "syntactical" relations discussed in North American linguistics, but these are, of course, relations of traditional linguistic interest. However, the force of this supposed differentiation probably lies in what Lyons is trying to capture in saying the elements have no "validity" independently of the relations, etc. I take it that by *validity* he means linguistic identity (*validity* perhaps being his translation of Saussure's *valeur*), and that he means the relations are "unmotivated," that is, logically ungrounded in the terms related. Lyons may be confusing or conflating several distinct things here, as is indicated by his citing both words and sounds as examples of elements. Thus he might mean: (*a*) that relational linguistic predicates are ungrounded in nonrelational linguistic predicates, or (*b*) that relational linguistic predicates are ungrounded in nonrelational *nonlinguistic* predicates, or (*c*) both of the above, or (*d*) that no linguistic predicates of any sort (relational or monadic) are grounded in any nonlinguistic predicates.

I am not certain that everything with a right to be called "modern" linguistics is committed to any of these doctrines, or that there is any sense whatever in the idea—something of a shibboleth in Continental structuralism, in particular—that a "structure" can be constituted on the basis of the relations of identity and otherness ("equivalence" and "contrast") only. However, the ungroundedness of linguistic predicates in nonlinguistic predicates (the fourth alternative mentioned above) seems to be an important feature of the dominant schools and tendencies in contemporary linguistics, and it would seem to be another way of expressing the dictum that *langue* is prior to *parole*. For I understand this dictum to mean that linguistic properties are indefinable in non-linguistic terms; consequently a linguistic phenomenon *is* linguistic *only* because of the de facto application to it of a coexisting rule of language (*langue*) which assigns a linguistic property to it thereby. The term is *assigns*, rather than *attributes*, because there are no perceptible properties a phenomenon could possess which would *justify* the application of the rule, not even if the phenomenon should happen to conform to some perceptible pattern specified in its antecedent clause. (The reason is that it would otherwise be possible for something clearly nonlinguistic —a sound made by an animal or nonliving being, or a randomly occurring visual pattern, for example—to conform to it accidentally.)

Let me say this another way. On the view in question, a *langue* is a set or system of rules, and a *langue* rule applies *itself* to a particular phenomenon such that, if the phenomenon to which it applies itself satisfies its antecedent (which presumably describes a perceptual configuration), then the phenomenon ipso facto has whatever linguistic property is described in the predicate in the rule's consequent. An individual person, on the other hand, can only believe or assert or judge that the phenomenon has that property, presumably on the basis of a perception of its configurational type and knowledge of the *langue* rule that describes that type in its antecedent, plus the assumption that the rule has *already* been applied to that case to constitute its linguistic identity. For if we do not suppose that the rule applies *itself* to the case, thereby assigning or bestowing the linguistic property on the phenomenon, then no given person's judgment ("intuition," as some prefer) that the phenomenon has that property could be either true or false. Or to put it the other way around: were the individual person the applier of the rule to the case, that person would be simultaneously bestowing *and* recognizing the presence of the property bestowed, which is not only nonsense but also collapses the *langue/parole* distinction. So, on this view, we have to suppose that the *langue* has the power to do its own applying. What sense that makes I do not know; but since it is not my theory I suppose I am not obligated to explain such a mystery. (One is tempted to say that a *langue* is conceived as a sort of superior and benevolent Mind which goes about giving things linguistic properties so we can have words with which to talk!) Such appears to be what the dictum of the priority of *langue* to *parole* comes to, and I understand it to be another way of saying that linguistic properties are not definable in terms of nonlinguistic properties.

In any case, I refer to any linguistics so conceived as a "hermetic" linguistics, since it regards linguistic properties as "sealed off" from extralinguistic properties (i.e., recognizes no extralinguistic implications of the words for such properties), and I am primarily concerned here with contrasting the hermetic conception—which appears to be shared in common by the leading Continental schools, the Chomskyans, and at least some of those whom the Chomskyans characterize as "taxonomists" —with the semiotic approach to linguistic phenomena. I do not address myself to behaviorist linguistics (except insofar as there are any behaviorists who are also hermetic linguists, which may be a contradiction in terms), other than to distinguish Peirce's approach from a behavioristic one.

Any hermetic linguistics could be called "structuralist" (notwithstanding the Chomskyans' aversion to the term as applied to themselves) because the logical effect of sealing off linguistic predicates—treating *langue* as prior to *parole*—is to satisfy an essential condition for regarding languages as individuals which have an internal and independent structure. Without such a logical seal, the linguistic properties of phenomena would be grounded in part in something external to the *langue*, which would mean the relevant "structures" would not be *langue* structures proper, but rather relations between the *langue* and something else. The question would then arise as to whether there *is* any such thing as a *langue*, considered as a describable individual; for if a *langue* is a bearer of relational predicates, it must have some monadic (nonrelational) properties: one cannot ascribe relational predicates to a blank *Ding an sich*. But what monadic properties could be ascribed to something which is unobservable, and about which the only things supposedly known are precisely the relational properties in question? We can see, then, that the idea that the basic task of the linguist is to describe languages, that languages are individual entities with structures (i.e., are Aristotelian "primary substances"), that *langue* is prior to *parole*, that linguistic properties are hermetic (i.e., indefinable in nonlinguistic terms)—we can see that all of this is a package; and I suggest it is simply the traditional but vague conception of linguistics as language description brought to its logical conclusion, rather than the radically innovative or "revolutionary" new conception of the science it has been widely touted as being.

In fact, it would seem that, apart from phonological developments, "modern" linguistics is basically just traditional grammar and dictionary writing, minus any latent tendencies to explain what it means for something to be linguistic in character: the "Copernican revolution" in linguistics was nothing more than a decisive and intentional rejection of any possible demand upon the linguist to explain how linguistic things, as such, *function* or *act* (unless the inscrutable operations of the *langue*, as it goes about "arbitrarily" bestowing linguistic identities on things, is to count as a functioning). Thus it was, in effect, a formal reduction of the possible scope of linguistics, at a time when it might instead have conceived itself more broadly than before. Moreover, instead of subjecting the vague (and confused) traditional idea of grammar to close critical scrutiny, perhaps refining this conception or even replacing it by something more sophisticated, the very possibility of explaining the term *grammar* was definitively ruled out. Why? Because if the predicate *is grammatical* were defined in empirical terms, directly or indirectly, the logical "seal" would therewith be broken—and, indeed, I believe no such definition will in fact be found in the writings of such linguists (though of course one may find it defined intratheoretically by other nonempirical terms). Thus the traditional idea was simply formalized and protected from critical scrutiny without being analyzed. I do not find it surprising that some of these "scientists" have subsequently extended the use of the term *grammar* to everything with which they wish to concern themselves, so that "semantic" and even "pragmatic" considerations are now also said to be a part of "grammar." Who can object when there is no way to know what it is to which one is objecting?—unless, of course, one objects in principle to the forging of a carte blanche for the vagaries of a priori "theorizing."

In contrasting the structuralist (hermetic) approach with a functional one, I do not mean by *function* the uses to which linguistic entities may be put. This would imply that linguistic entities are *tools* or *instruments*, ready-formed and awaiting their use for whatever jobs one finds their structure fits them to perform; and a functional approach so conceived would in fact imply a prior structuralist theory, rather than being an alternative to it. Thus I agree with the structuralist rejection of the idea of linguistic entities as being basically of the nature of tools (though I should point out that the metaphor of *langue* as a machine nonetheless occurs with remarkable frequency in their writings). Words can of course be put to use, in some sense of *use*, but it is precisely the unlimited variety of their possible uses which makes the conception of use improper for explicating what linguistic entities are as such. In view of this, I understand why such linguists insist on regarding language as *intrinsically* functionless. But when I speak of the "function" or "functioning" of linguistic entities, I mean what words do *as words*, not the extrinsic purposes which their doings may happen to serve. More on this later, however. For the moment let us keep our focus on the peculiarities of the type of linguistics I am criticizing.

If a linguistics is hermetic in the way it treats its concepts, this will show definitively in its evidential methodology. We owe it to the

Chomskyans, in particular, to have made it clear that such a linguistics will have an "intuitive" evidential base, though I cannot think much of their attempt to palm off intuition as an empirical (I don't mean "empiricist") base. Moreover, I find their pretension to homologize hermetic linguistics with a science like atomic physics reprehensible: this smacks more of academic strategizing than of serious philosophy of science, and it does a disservice to their linguistics colleagues by fostering a misleading self-conception that discourages clear thought about what linguistics actually is—and could be. Let me now try to explain why hermetic linguistics must be "intuitional," and why such intuitions cannot be regarded as providing an empirical scientific base.

Since languages (*langues*) are unobservable entities, all *langue*-descriptions are the result of inference from their observable manifestations, insofar as such descriptions can lay claim to empirical grounding. Let us call such observable manifestations "*parole*-examples." A *parole*-example must be described as having some linguistic property if any inference is to be drawn from it: let us call that "the linguist's *parole*-description." The terms in this description (i.e., the predicative terms) must have conceptual relationships with the terms in the *langue*-description if any inference is to be made from a *parole*-description to a *langue*-description; for the rules which the *langue*-description describes should be such as to generate logically the linguist's *parole*-descriptions, though of course the linguist's inferential task is, as it were, to go "upstream" to the generating source. This means the linguist's *parole*-description *must use theoretical predicates*, which means in turn that this description is not itself empirically evidential, except insofar as it is in turn evidentially grounded. Thus we must distinguish between (*a*) the inference *from* the linguist's *parole*-description to the *langue*-description, and (*b*) the inference *to* the linguist's *parole*-description from the evidential base.

These distinct inferential moves have frequently been conflated and confused, especially in connection with the topic of hypothetical inference. It is clear enough that an inference of type (*a*), from a case to a rule, or from a rule to the rule which generates *it*, may fairly be construed as a hypothetical inference. However, it is far from clear that an inference of type (*b*), to the linguist's *parole*-description, is also a hypothetical inference, in the case of hermetic linguistics in particular. My claim is that there is not only no possibility of a hypothetical inference here, there is no inference possible at all for the hermetic linguist. Hence, such a linguistics has no empirical evidential base: just "intuitions" without evidential force. Let us see why.

The problem, then, is the logical movement from a *parole*-example to the linguist's *parole*-description. No one supposes that linguistic properties are monadic or nonrelational. Hence, the *parole*-example must be regarded as relative to something else if there is to be a *parole*-description with any pretense to an empirical base. A behaviorist, for example, will put the *parole*-example in relation to a person (or persons), as an element in a stimulus-response complex in which both participate. We need not specify exactly how; the point is that it will be the descriptions of that complex which will constitute the behaviorist's evidential base. A hermetic linguist will also put the *parole*-example in relation to a person (or persons) and look for a response. However, the only response of interest in this case will be a response which is an *assertion* about a linguistic property of the *parole*-example by some person (possibly the linguist in another capacity) regarded as representative of the *langue* being investigated. Thus somebody will be designated as a "fluent" or "native" speaker, will be presented with the *parole*-example, and the assertional response will be recorded as *evidence*. The evidence is thus of that special type called "testimony." Let us refer to this as "*parole*-testimony," bearing in mind that this is quite distinct, in terms of logical function, from the linguist's *parole*-description, even in the case where the linguist is his own informant and his *parole*-description is verbally identical with his own *parole*-testimony. For without this distinction all claim to an evidential base for the *langue*-description is thereby nullified. (As I pointed out above, the hermetic linguist's *parole*-description cannot itself have any empirical evidential value, since it must be formulated in theoretical rather than empirical terms if inference to the governing rule is to be possible.)

Before seeing why the hermetic linguist's evidence—or what is supposed to be such—must be testimonial in character, let us note the *prima facie* oddness of appealing to a testimonial evidential base for a nomic theory. I know of no true parallel to this in the history of nomological science, not even in the case of introspective psychological experimentation. For in such experimentation the testimony is treated as indicative of facts which *caused* the experiences to which the testimony testifies, and the latter facts are those which provide the evidential base for inference to an explanatory theory; such facts, however, are not themselves testimonial in type. For example, Peirce himself conducted (with Joseph Jastrow) one of the first psychological experiments in this country (published in 1884).[5] The test was of the Fechnerian hypothesis that there is an *Unterschiedsschwelle* or *Differenzschwelle* (i.e., a threshold of perceivable difference) for sensation, and it consisted in the production of controlled differences in sensory stimulation to which the subjects responded by testifying whether they could detect any difference. Their testimony—including responses to requests to guess whenever they could seem to perceive no difference—was then systematized and correlated with the facts of actual stimulation differences. The correlation between actual and testimonially attested differences indicated no such threshold. (Peirce also regarded this as evidence for awareness of perceptual differences of which one is not reflectively conscious.) For our purposes, the point is that the testimony itself functioned as only one element in the process of acquiring the evidential base, but was not regarded as having evidential value relative to the hypothesis insofar as it was just testimony. I suggest that testimony will never be found to have functioned as an evidential base *per se* in any reputable experimentation in a nomological science. Its proper role as evidence is in the law courts and as a basis for historical inference, not for inference to laws or regularities.

The reason why the hermetic linguist as such must nonetheless make appeal to such "evidence" is that such a linguist cannot define the predicative terms in his *parole*-description in extratheoretical terms (since this would break the logical "seal" which makes the theory hermetic), and therefore can establish no basis for a hypothetical inference. For it is an indispensable requirement of all hypothetical inference that the conclusion hypothetically inferred deductively imply that from which it was inferred, given appropriate instantiating conditions, which means that the *parole*-example must be described in terms which are present (by implication) in the theory or hypothesis inferred.[6] But this is precisely what is precluded by the hermetic linguist's refusal to provide extratheoretical definitions for his theoretical terms. Nor can any relevant sort of inductive inference be made. The only thing induction could do here would be to generalize the scope of application of a predicate; but what the hermetic linguist requires at this point is the *replacement* of the predicate in the evidential *parole*-description by a theoretical (and hermetic) predicate in the linguist's *parole*-description, and only hypothetic inference could do that. This is why the hermetic linguist must instead appeal to testimonial evidence, the idea presumably being that since the testimony is *already* in terms of distinctively linguistic properties, there is no need to replace the testimonial predicates by the linguist's theoretical predicates through an inferential move. Thus the appeal to testimony is an attempt to circumvent the need for a hypothetical inference from evidential facts.

But this is, of course, only logical sleight-of-hand. If the informant's testimony is already in the linguist's terms (these terms being understood in the same way), then the *parole*-testimony is on a logical par with the linguist's *parole*-description as regards its lack of extratheoretical implications, and can no more be regarded as evidential than can the linguist's description. Hence it cannot be regarded as evidential relative to his description. If, on the other hand, the testimony is not in his terms, or if the terms are apparently the same but not understood as the linguist understands them, then the linguist must establish some determinate relation between what his terms mean and what the testimonial terms mean in order to infer from the testimony, *taken as true*, to his description. But this the linguist cannot do without defining his terms so that they imply (directly or indirectly) the predicates in the testimony. For no matter how reliable the informants are supposed to be, the most that can be inferred from their testimony is that the facts about the *parole*-examples are as they say they are. But what they say about the facts is not what the linguist says about them in his *parole*-descriptions (and cannot be if they are to have any evidential weight). Nor is there any use in saying that the linguist does not infer from their testimony as true, but only from the fact that they testify as they do. For whatever the linguist infers from such facts *cannot* be the description needed without some conceptual relation being established between that description and those facts (however they be construed). Hermetic linguistics is thus essentially devoid of any empirical evidential base.

I believe it can now be seen that this peculiar talk of "intuitions" is just logical misdirection. An appeal to an intuition could only establish that someone is certain a *parole*-example has this or that property. But such certainties are not to the logical point. Let the informant's intuition be felt by him as powerfully as you like: it cannot make any difference as regards the linguist's logical right to infer from their testimony to his description. And let the linguist's intuitions about his own descriptions be as powerfully felt as you like: it cannot add an iota of evidential force to a description which can have no such force except as derived from something which can count as evidence for it, and that cannot be a feeling of certainty. The idea, promulgated by the Chomskyans in particular, that intuitions are evidential is surely a debasement of the concept of evidentiality to such a state of confusion that anything resembling a *scientific* method in linguistics is out of the question as long as that conception is operative in the thinking of linguists. It is not that there is no place in scientific inquiry for intuitive perceptions and certainties, provided this only means that there is always an evidential starting point in something not doubted. Unquestioned (though not unquestionable) beliefs are at the basis of any science. But the logical problem is not whether anybody is certain of this or that, but whether there is any way in which those certainties, or rather the expression of those certainties in assertional form, can function evidentially. I see no possibility for that in any hermetic linguistics.

I submit, therefore, that such linguists have simply been attempting to devise a new and more general way of doing what grammarians have always done, namely, identifying and systematizing certain patterns of speech and writing recurrent in the discourse of people whom they regard as linguistically proficient (including themselves, needless to say). But what is proficiency? The traditional grammarian meant by a proficient speaker one who speaks in accord with the patterns of a reference class, and who therefore can communicate effectively and without embarrassment in such a milieu. But the kind of linguistics I have been criticizing does not differ significantly in this respect, except that the contemporary linguist disavows interest in this use of his work and focuses instead on trying to develop standard methods of representing such patterns for all languages. I have no objection to such an enterprise, but I cannot think it a worthy conception for a science of linguistics. A truly "modern" linguistics—one which would address itself to what is important about the linguistic dimension of our lives—would surely have set as its first task not that of systematizing and universalizing the description of prevailing grammatical patterns, but rather that of asking what grammar *is*. Grammatical patterns have at least two distinct functions. On the one hand, they provide indications of what one is talking about, what one is saying about it, how this is being qualified, and so on; on the other hand, they present esthetically pleasing and rhetorically effective forms: in short, they have both logical and stylistic functions. Any writer or teacher who reflects on what he or she is doing will have experienced conflicts between the imperatives of logical rigor, on the one hand, and communicational effectiveness, on the other, and will have noted the ambiguous role of grammatical form in resolving these conflicts. It is possible that grammatical functions could be so conceived as to reconcile these two prima facie distinct functions—and perhaps others as well—in a unitary conception of what grammar *does*. (I think myself that a suitably reconceived idea of rhetoric could do this; that is, that what is now called "grammar" would reappear in an adequate theory of rhetoric as a standardized rhetorical function.)[7] But, however that may be, hermetic linguistics—structuralism, as I prefer to call it—definitively and formally rejects the task of sorting these things out openly, and instead relies on the fogginess of the notion of "intuition"—and the fogginess of intuitions—to permit itself to systematize with maximum freedom, and with maximum irresponsibility when it comes to explaining *what* they are systematizing and *why* they are doing so, anyway.

To me, this requires explanation, and I have a hypothesis. In introducing this hypothesis I may offend some of you, who may think it logically shoddy to move to motivational matters at this point. But I do not rest my case against the kind of linguistics I have been criticizing on this hypothesis,[8] and, more to the point, I think that we—as students of human life—need to think far more about the consequences of what we are doing in our theoretical work than we usually do, particularly in view of the technology which our work generates insofar as it is successful. The atomic physicists—some of them—were brought (temporarily) to the realization in 1945, and B. F. Skinner's blatant claim that he and his like should be allowed to rule the world surely makes it clear that, whatever our personal motivations may be, we are engaging in researches of a sort which, if successful, will be fraught with practical moral implications of the first importance. So I ask you to take a look at something here.

The type of linguistics I am criticizing begins with the laying down, a priori, of a general theory of language ("universal grammar") which is, in effect, a logic. I mean the term *logic* in a very broad sense, according to which it is a general theory of the human mind, at least insofar as the mind is linguistic in nature, as such theorists usually do suppose it to be. I say they *begin* with this because, in spite of all the sober-sounding talk about how "linguistic universals" are something to be inferred from a basis of descriptions of various languages, the fact is that the universal grammar is present already in the rules laid down for language description. For example, Chomskyan linguistics— linguistics conducted as Chomsky says it should be—*is* the universal grammar which he nonetheless keeps talking about as if it were something *to be discovered*. But what sort of "discovery" is it that consists in "inferring" the general rules implicit in the very cases which have been described in open accordance with precisely those rules to begin with? Had the name of Chomsky's first book been *Universal Grammar* instead of *Syntactic Structures* it would have been obvious to anyone that the "discovery" was in fact made by Chomsky himself before he ever wrote the book, and that what purports to be a theory of universal grammar is just a set of prescriptions for writing the very grammars which are supposed to be its evidential base. Linguistics is thus conceived from the beginning as a priori cryptophilosophy.

I have no objection to cryptophilosophy insofar as it is good philosophy, but I object to it as cryptic because this is a way of avoiding intellectual responsibility for what one is doing; nor do any of the cryptophilosophical "linguistics" with which I am acquainted persuade me that I am mistaken in thinking that taking full and open responsibility for what one is doing is essential if one is to do it well. Moreover, I do not think the ambitions of such "linguists" are limited to doing irresponsible philosophy of mind. (I mean what is implicit in the tendencies of their work, not how they consciously regard themselves.) To the contrary, it seems obvious that it is the development and defense of a *metaphysics*, a doctrine of the basic nature of reality in general, which lies beyond—or perhaps rather within—this movement. For one need only adduce the premise that the real is the knowable to convert a theory of mind into a metaphysics; then if one adduces the further premise that the ultimate form of the real is divine in nature one has a *theology* (and such a premise is nearly axiomatic in theological thinking). Thus I suspect that linguistics has been unwittingly put in the service of an unacknowledged religious drive which has been unable to satisfy itself within the confines of traditional religious forms and is in this respect much like, say, Marxist "social science."

One of the forms or guises such an unsatisfied impulse may adopt is political, and it is perhaps here that what I am trying to bring to your attention can be most clearly seen. The European semiological movement, with several decades' head start on Chomskyanism, has already extended structuralist principles—or at least what purport to be such—to a number of paralinguistic areas (e.g., fashions, aesthetics, anthropology). The question is, when is it going to be—or has it already been—extended to the political sphere in the form of a structuralist "political science"? And what kind of political understanding would result from such an extension? (Bear in mind that, from the very beginning of speculation about the nature of language in the West, that is, from the time of Greek Sophism and the Socratic/Platonic response to it, theories of language and political doctrines have gone hand in hand: in fact, one of the most fruitful strategies for understanding philosophers is to identify the isomorphisms holding between their political/ethical models and their logics and theories of meaning.)[9] Consider, then, the hermetic or structuralist model for linguistics reinterpreted as a political model.

The *langue* is, of course, analogous to the law of the land. *Parole* is citizen behavior. Being a citizen is behaving in accord with the law (which, like a *langue*, is definitive or constitutive—not merely regulative —of what it is to be a citizen). Failure to so behave is to be a political deviant or perhaps even a political nonentity, outside the law altogether and devoid of legal identity (including rights). Whether or not one is behaving in such a way as makes political "sense" is to be determined by qualified citizen informants who "intuit" the facts about one's behavior relative to the law and assess its "acceptability." The informant class is selected by the legal expert as exhibiting "obvious" proficiency in nondeviation, and of course the expert may function as his or her own informant. The legal expert—the analogue to the linguist—is the one who definitively determines whether the behavior is in the State as deviant or normal, or is not a part of the political reality at all. If my criticisms earlier are correct, this "scientist" will necessarily do so on the basis of no empirical evidence. It is true, of course, that the State— the law, the *langue* of political behavior, as it were—tends to change

across time in virtue of deviant acts (though how this is logically possible I do not know), and that persons formerly classified as deviant, or
perhaps even as beyond the pale of law altogether (wild animals, in
effect), may subsequently be recognized as fully "acceptable" after all,
and their corpses (or reputations) duly exhumed for belated public admiration. The experts who originally "misidentified" them because of
"faulty intuition" or the testimony of "unqualified citizen informants"
will be replaced by new experts (such is the usual fate of such "scientists"), though how the new experts are to avoid the same sort of error
is not clear. But I need not elaborate this obvious isomorphism further.
If you think it is a fanciful picture . . . I hope you are right! (But before
you so conclude, reflect upon the present political role of the "science"
of psychiatry in certain countries.)

   These linguistics theorists do not, of course, regard what they are
doing in this light, and they would doubtless protest—quite sincerely, I
should think—that it is a mere accident that their linguistics model is
so remarkably isomorphic with the familiar type of authoritarian political order just sketched. But then Oedipus—I mean the Greek rather than
the Austrian version—didn't know who he was looking for either when
he looked about for the source of pollution. In any case, I intend no
personal criticism, and perhaps it would be appropriate if I offered in
justification of mentioning these matters some words from Chomsky
himself:[10]

> When certain ideas are dominant, it is very reasonable to ask why.
> The reason could be that they are plausibly regarded as true, they have
> been verified, etc. But in the case where they are without empirical
> foundations, and have little initial plausibility, the question arises more
> sharply: the answer may actually lie in the domain of ideology.

I would add that the ideology involved might be in radical conflict with
the ideology consciously held by the theorist.

II

   In conveying to you something of what I understand of Peirce's
basic semiotic conceptions, particularly as they bear on the analysis of
linguistic phenomena, I will go about it in my own way, for the most
part, rather than follow the letter of Peirce's writings. The course of
discussion in the past fifty or sixty years—much of it highly idiosyncratic in verbal usage—on such topics as meaning, significance, sense,
signification, reference, and so on, has so thoroughly anarchized the
terminology in this area that Peirce's own way of talking about and
explaining these things would almost certainly be misunderstood unless

I were to interpret his words to you at far greater length than would be possible or appropriate here. Another reason for attempting a somewhat different way of explaining his ideas than is to be found in his own writings is that due account must be taken of reigning metaphysical conceptions which make some things seem to us "obvious" or "self-evident" or "natural," and some other things "unintelligible" or "odd" or "confused," though such responses may only indicate compatibility or incompatibility with questionable metaphysical assumptions so totally taken for granted that we are quite unaware of them and do not realize they are unnecessary and perhaps even undesirable.

The perspective Peirce articulates in his semiotic is an attempt to achieve, on a theoretical level, something equivalent to a metaphysical innocence: a premetaphysical way of thinking about the things with which semiotic is concerned. It is not a matter of actually being innocent, of course, but rather of intentionally thinking of things in the most innocent way possible. Such a stance is artificial and difficult both to achieve and to maintain. Yet only to the extent that such a stance is achievable in theoretical work of this sort can we escape the stultifying effects of the ethnocentricity which hidden metaphysical commitments necessitate. Whether Peirce's semiotic actually succeeds in staying free of such commitments is another matter, as is the question whether I have understood the basic isues well enough to do justice to what he attempted. But, in any case, since I must myself try to subvert any metaphysical assumptions that might hinder your understanding of his ideas, I think it best if I take a somewhat free approach and present his ideas in a somewhat unusual way.[11]

The icon/index/symbol distinction concerns what I call the "sign powers" of objects, and any object which has such powers is ipso facto a sign. Such terms as *meaningfulness, significance, sense, intelligibility*, and so forth, are vague nontechnical equivalents, in some contexts, for what I call "sign power," and I occasionally use some such terms as an informal reminder of what sort of thing we are talking about. Bear in mind, though, that these are not technical terms (nor are they usually so used by Peirce), and I only use them here because of their suggestiveness.

The major difficulty you may have in getting a reliable sense for the semiotic approach lies in the fact that it is the signs themselves—not people who use signs—which are regarded as the primary agents, so that the introduction of reference to people (or any other entities which use or respond to signs) in a semiotic analysis means that a shift in analytic level has occurred, from concern with sign properties and actions as such to some more specialized investigative concern. In particular, the occurrence of terms such as *mind, interpreter, user*, and *use* usually indicate that such a shift has occurred from the basic level to a more specialized perspective, such as that of, say, psychology or sociology. (The shift to a more specialized perspective is, of course, legitimate, as long as one is aware of what one is doing).[12] Perhaps it will help, then, if we define the term *use* at this point. For present purposes, let us understand the use of signs as being the intentional presentation of signs in accordance with what one thinks or hopes the signs will do. (Do not construe the term *intentional* as equivalent to or as implying *reflective* or *selfconscious*.) All sign use—as distinct from sign behavior, which is what use exploits and therefore presupposes—involves, then, an exercise of skill-knowledge, comparable to the employment of any other sort of object in accordance with one's understanding of its powers and of the conditions under which these powers are actualized.

So deeply entrenched in contemporary theorizing is the assumption that people—whether individually or socially—somehow *give* meaning, significance, and the like, to meaningful, significant, and sensical things, particularly as regards linguistically meaningful things, that it may seem strange at first that sign powers are not conceived, from a semiotic point of view, as essentially constituted by their relation to people or other sign users. (Nor, I might add, by relation to a *langue*, which is a queer sort of group mind, nor by relation to the "linguistic competence of an ideal speaker/hearer," which is a fictitious individual or group mind.) According to the semiotic view, nobody gives meaning to any sign of any sort, *if* this is supposed to be a transfer of intended meaning from people's minds to objects, as a sort of infusion or transfusion through intentionality, will, stipulation, fiat, or any other sort of direct psychic injection. There is a sense in which people can and do create meaning, particularly as regards linguistic signs, but it is not the sense usually involved in discussions of the "conventional" or "arbitrary" or "unmotivated" character of linguistic meaning. Sign powers are in the signs themselves, and any changes in these powers, or the accruing of such powers to objects not previously having them, are due primarily to the signs themselves and *their* actions, not to people's actions (though the action of people is usually contingently instrumental in this respect).

Let me show you a sign which will, I am sure, be willing to perform for you if you will watch it for a few moments:

It is difficult to stop some of these things once they get started: watch it some more and see whether you can stop it from "going through its act." (Persistent, isn't it?) Linguistic signs are similar in this respect: concentrate on any of the linguistic signs on this page and try to stop them from "doing their thing," that is, try to see them as meaningless marks. (They are rather persistent, too, aren't they?)

You may say this is due to the innate and/or acquired perceptual dispositions of the perceiver. But we are not concerned with the psychology of perception here, and the fact is that it was the signs, not your dispositions, that you just *observed* to be doing something: the role of your dispositions in this is something inferred—and obvious only as a familiar inference—to account for what the signs were doing, and that inference is certainly somewhat less certain than are the observed facts about the phenomena for which it is supposed to account. Words as such do what they do differently than what the line-figure above does, of course, and it is to get clear on just such differences that the icon/index/symbol distinction (among others) is developed; but my purpose at the moment is simply to introduce you experientially to the idea that signs themselves *do* things that are empirically observable, while at the same time making it clear to you that this is *not* to say that signs "stimulate responses" in people. They do that, too: one can observe signs stimulating people (and other responsive beings as well), and one can hypothesize that somehow this sort of thing is involved in every case of observed sign behavior (i.e. behavior *of* signs). But that is a hypothesis about—and thus presupposes—the observable behavior of the signs themselves. (Semiotic is not behavioristic, except in the sense that it regards signs as behaving. The behavior of people can perhaps be explicated in terms of signs, but the behavior of signs is not to be explicated in terms of people on the basic level of semiotic analysis.)

It is also important to understand that Peircean semiotic is "phenomenologically" based. It is not essentially a part of psychology or sociology or dependent upon them (though semiotic conceptions can enter into psychological or sociological theories or analyses). It involves no "introspection," either, unless this just means paying close attention to what one experiences, that is, unless it simply means *observing*. In Peirce's sense of the term *phenomenology*,[13] to say that semiotic is phenomenologically based is to say that the objects studied by semiotic are not limited to any particular existential category (including the category of nonexistence or unreality). They may be things sensed or they may be only imagined or dreamt or hallucinated or fictionally created. They may be something arrived at only by a complex and lengthy inferential chain or they may be as immediately present as any object ever is. They may be in the physical world or the mathematical world or the mental world or not referred to any metaphysical order. The reason is that the power of a sign to act *as* a sign is not contingent upon its existential status; on the contrary, we must draw upon our knowledge of an object's sign powers in order to know how to classify it existentially: hence, the property of being a sign is attributable to an object simply as such, prior to any qualification or delimitation of the sort indicated.

"I have a dream," said Martin Luther King. That which he dreamt (the object in the dream), and tried to describe and to actualize in the existential order, acted by producing (among other things) his descriptions and actions, which were in turn capable of producing, and did in fact produce, replicas of what he dreamt in the experience of others (apparently in the form of nightmare for the head of the secret police). Did King act upon his dreams or did his dreams act upon him? From the semiotic perspective, the latter is the more basic description. In fact, we might say that it was his dream as a sign which produced Martin Luther King as the sign that he was—or rather is. (A sign of what? Well, interpretations vary, of course.)

Now let us consider linguistic signs in particular, because the idea that meaning is due to human agency seems particularly compelling in their case. (That is, it seems that way to the contemporary mind: the ancient Greeks—like archaic peoples generally—did not regard logos as man-made until the rise of egocentric humanism, which achieved its definitive expression in the conventionalism espoused by the linguistic entrepreneurs of fifth century Greece whom we call "the Sophists.") Consider, for example, the present communicational process: I mean the one occurring right HERE and right NOW. I probably don't know you, but even if I do I have no way of knowing that it is indeed YOU to whom I am presently talking. (By "presently" I mean HERE and NOW.) So to achieve my purposes I can only select, combine, and take steps to present such visual configurations as I think may behave for you, whoever you are, as I would wish them to behave in your presence. I know many of them will not behave as I wish. They can if they "want" to. I am sure of that. But, like living things,[14] they just do not always do what you want them to do. I can't even know which of them are unlikely to behave as I wish. (If I did I wouldn't bother you with them.) So I try to compensate for that by selecting, combining, and presenting them in a variety of ways in hopes of getting the right sort of sequences started for you, if not in virtue of one combination then perhaps in virtue of another. Now in the combinatorial presentation of them to you I may indeed achieve the creation of a more or less coherent and unique whole of resultant meaning in your experience; and it may be that certain of the signs—such as, say, *Peirce, semiotic, phenomenology, icon, index, symbol, linguistics*—will undergo some modification in their sign powers or meanings in virtue of the whole of meaning to which they are contributing here. I am not referring principally to a possible change in your *understanding* of their meaning as a result of your understanding of this entire paper, but rather to a change in the meaning or sign power of the words themselves. For as the words interact in combination here, some of them may undergo permanent changes in their sign powers as a reflexive result. In *this* sense I may indeed create meaning here, as we all create meaning in this way in much of our communication. (This is, in short, the locus of sign mutation or language change, which is a product of sign interaction in the *co*-operative creation of a unique communicational whole, always involving some spontaneity or unpredictability, which results reflexively in the change in sign powers of some of the signs responsible for that whole.)

The sense, then, in which I am (or may be) creating meaning here —which is not different in principle from any other linguistic transaction in which meaning change occurs—is roughly the same sense in which a breeder of animals can be said to create the progeny which results from the breeder's mating experiments: one arranges a promising conjunction and hopes for the best. Thus to the extent that I do have some measure of success in this it is a matter of chance and skill, not will: I cannot willfully infuse any of these configurations with my intentions or hopes, like a god breathing life into lifeless matter. Moreover, even though my intentions are responsible in part for the overall whole of meaning which is the matrix of meaning change (since it is I who have selected the parents, thereby bringing about indirectly whatever off-spring may be their issue), the result almost certainly will not be the result I vaguely intend, though perhaps it will be enough like it to have been worth the trouble. This is true even in the cases where I stipulate that certain signs are to be understood in certain ways for the purposes of this paper. Such a stipulation is no absolute fiat but rather a proposal, nothing more: man proposes; the sign disposes.

The chances are that you know little about me beyond the fact that I am the one who selected this batch of configurations which you are presently trying to understand. From where you are positioned it is even possible—wildly implausible, I hope, but possible—that I do not exist. Perhaps the editors of this volume are in collaboration with some psychologists who have taken seriously the old story about how the roomful of monkeys pounding away at typewriters produced the complete works of Shakespeare, and you are now reading (reading?) the results of a similar experiment. Suppose this were indeed the orzhlttt..-%va½q Suppose this wethrdddddddf4xx#8,nmh Supppppppppppppp

pppp etaion shrdlu! Suppose this were indeed the origin of this paper, and that you knew it. Would these configurations then be only meaningless marksmarksmarksmfksmmmmppppzz;89rt? Colorlessgreeeeeenideasszzz.... (What is this? Some kind of monkey business?) Would these configurations cease to *do* the sort of thing they are doing now, as you peruse them? And if they just kept right on "doing their thing," would this be a sort of pseudomeaning, rather like the pretense put up by a check written on a nonexistent account? Suppose further that, if one were nevertheless to read them as if they were intentionally and "intelligently" produced, they would not only make sense (i.e., be as if they made sense) but would also turn out upon investigation to be true, valid, cogent, and so forth (i.e., be as if true, valid, cogent, and so forth). What would be the force of the *as if* in that case? Does it signify a diminishment in value, or even an annulment of it? And if it were subsequently discovered that these configurations really were, after all, a "product of intelligence," would this in turn result in an elevation or reinstatement of their cognitive worth? I pose these as rhetorical questions because one cannot settle such matters in brief fashion; but what I am suggesting—or those monkeys may be causing you to think—is that, whatever the role of intentionality in discourse may be, it is not that of giving meaning to things which otherwise would not have it.

Human agency in the production of words is, from a certain point of view, no different in principle from the skillful manipulation of materials with their own energetic propensities that is typical of any craft. Human creation is never ex nihilo, whether it be the creation of a pot, or a piece of music, or a painting, or a discourse; nor is it a peculiar sort of emanation from a mental substance. Voluntaristic conceptions of language—by which I mean both intentionalistic and conventionalistic conceptions—are perhaps just displaced theological doctrines decked out in the form of humanism. "Let there be light!" God says (in Hebrew?), and, Lo!, light is. "Let there be *langue!*" the conventionalist imagines people to say, and, Lo!, *langue* is. But this cannot account for the fiat itself, which is already linguistic. "Archaic" peoples—those closer to the basics (ἀρχαί) than we moderns—regard crafts, including speechcraft, as a natural process *in* which the craftsman participates and *co*-operates, but does not dominate: the craftsman gives direction, to be sure, but then so do the materials through their own propensities. In fact, it is "nature" (cf. the Greek φύσις) which is the true craftsman because craft is only a special case of growth. Thus nature itself makes receptacles, for example; and such things as holes in the ground, caves, nests, baskets, pots, tombs, houses, and so on, are just so many products of nature's various propensities for receptacle making. Is this a naive and inferior way of regarding such matters? It is no doubt true that, for certain purposes, it is profitable to conceive the human craftsman as a manipulator of materials which are passive relative to the craftsman's agency; but do we reach a still higher stage of "sophistication" when we go so far as to elevate the craftsman to transcendent status and invest him with the powers of a god or magician? There is surely a fine irony in the fact that our "advanced" theoreticians of language, who talk so earnestly of their belief in "human universals," proceed ab initio as if from a completely unquestioned assumption that the key to the nature of language is to be found in one version or another of a seventeenth century metaphysical doctrine according to which meaningfulness is something "arbitrarily" bestowed upon or infused into brute matter by the inscrutable will or wish of transcendent individual or group minds. But if any true human universality is to be discovered, perhaps it would be advisable to abandon the idea that the role of human agency in the production of signs is fundamental, without thereby denying that there may be special reasons in special contexts of inquiry for recognizing a relatively basic role for intentionality and will.

It is equally important to understand that human agency in the interpretation of signs is not fundamental either, as regards the constituting of significance or meaning. For if signification is not essentially relative either to sign producers or sign interpreters, then a semiotic linguistics need not be conceived as a part of psychology (as is usual in the United States) or of sociology (as is usual on the European continent), though of course its conceptions and theories may enter into those sciences, much as mathematics enters into the natural sciences. The interpretation of linguistic signs—the sort of thing you are doing right now—is first of all an intelligent and active *experience* of them, similar in many ways to sense-perception experience of any sort. Thus as your eyes scan a line of type, you experience what the signs mean, that is, you experience them *as* meaningful; and although this involves perceiving them as visual configurations, it involves more than that. In fact, what you will "carry away" from the total experience of the text will probably contain little memory of the sign configurations themselves, but will instead consist mainly of what you retain from the experience of the *object(s)* of the signs. In the case of the present text, these objects would include such things as Peirce's theory in general, Peirce himself, me, linguistics, certain conceptions of linguistics, and certain things in Peirce's theory. The experience of the object of the text will be the result of the actualization of its sign powers, along with those of the other signs you will have provided as your own context (the ever present, ever unique, and ever changing accompanying text). Now these things or objects—I use the term *object* here as synonymous with *thing*, in the broad, vague, and colloquial sense of *thing*—

are what are presented phenomenally or experientially in and through the actualization of the powers of these signs, so that your experience of reading this text will have been an experience of things or objects which you will have *observed* in virtue of the powers of the signs to present them to you for your observation. The signs themselves are among those things experienced, and how they are experienced is also a result of sign powers; but the focus of your experience will be primarily on objects not present on these pages which the objects on these pages—the signs or words—will have made present to you.

It is of little importance what this is like as any particular person happens to experience it in the flow of their consciousness. Concern with that sort of thing arises only for special reasons, and it is not essentially pertinent to the question of your understanding of what you have read. For the answer to this question would not be ascertained by introspection, but rather by having you describe the object(s) you have experienced. Any attempt to reproduce the actual flow of experience would result largely in a fictitious account, anyway, because one would be unable to remember most of it and would have to reconstruct what it might have been and put that forth in place of what it actually was. But then there is rarely any reason for such a description. Generally speaking, many of the objects experienced in the course of reading will occur (phenomenally), function as signs by producing other objects, and then disappear after they have fulfilled their semiotic roles; however, some of them will keep recurring, will combine with others to form more comprehensive objects, and so forth, and may finally appear as constitutent parts in the resultant object or constellation of objects. Usually, it is only the final result—the object (or objects) which the entire reading results in experientially—which is of concern to us. But what I want particularly to stress here is that the experience of the meanings of words (the interpretation of them) is an experience of the same general sort as, say, the experience of sensory objects by alert sensory observation of them.

Let me explain something at this point about the idea of a "phenomenal object" and its relation to the idea of a "sign" which may help in understanding what I am trying to convey about sign interpretation being a kind of observation. A sign is a phenomenal object, by which I mean an object in the phenomenological sense of the term *object*, as I explained earlier.[15] The actualization of a sign's power consists in its presencing a phenomenal object. *To presence* is a transitive verb which I use as a synonym for *to present*, when the latter is first construed in its most generic sense and then delimited in application to only those cases where the presenting is a making present of something to some responsive being (not necessarily human). It is roughly equivalent to the

Greek verb φαίνω, which has no equivalent in common use in English, so far as I am aware. The idea of something being present to someone is quite familiar to you, and it could be operationally (that is, extensionally rather than intentionally) defined as being something to which any response of any sort is made, provided the concept of response is so modified as to permit phenomenal objects in general to be stimuli (rather than being so conceived that only objects in the spatiotemporal order can qualify as stimuli), and provided the stimulus-response process is so conceived as to take adequate account of the contribution of the directional word *to*, as it occurs in the phrase *response to something*. In that case, *to be presenced* would be the phenomenologically extended analogue to the word *to stimulate*. (Note that I say "analogue" rather than "equivalent"; for being presenced is only extensionally and not intensionally correlative with the idea of a stimulus.) But, so far as I know, no attempt has ever been made to so extend the idea of response (in its theoretical use), in spite of the fact that we all know perfectly well, on the common sense level, that responses are often to things which are not in the spatiotemporal order, such as objects merely dreamt, conceived, imagined, hallucinated, and so forth.

What has just been said does not imply that the powers of a sign as such are fundamentally dependent upon responses to it. The somewhat subtle conceptual connection to responses is necessary in order to insure that signs are conceived as publicly available, but the basic powers of signs are not per se powers of generating responses to the things presenced, but are rather powers of presencing things. In other words, nothing can be a sign which is not publicly available; but what makes a sign a sign is not that, but rather its power of presencing. Thus there is no contradiction with the thesis that human agency, whether it be in the form of the sign producer's intentionality or the sign interpreter's response, does not account for meaning properties.

Signs are themselves presenced by phenomenal objects acting as signs, and the phenomenal objects they presence will in turn act as signs. A sign-interpretational process is thus an ordered procession of phenomenal objects, directly or indirectly related to one another in certain ways, in virtue of what I call "presencing." To identify a phenomenal object as a sign is to impute to it the power to presence a phenomenal object. To identify it as specifically an iconic sign, or an indexical sign, or a symbolic sign is to say something about how it relates to other objects in the procession. A distinction must be made between what a sign can do and what it actually does. A semiotic description of an actually occurring sign process (i.e., of an actually occurring phenomenal sequence regarded as semiotic in character) would be a description of what each sign did or is doing or will do, and of how it relates to others in the process, the result being a description of a complex sequential process, usually involving many branchings and joinings of subsequences. A semiotic description of a particular sign *text* would be an account of some of the processes that *could* occur, starting from that text or any part of it. (Such descriptions of possible readings are infinitely extendable, even in the case of the simplest text; hence a semiotic analysis of any text will always be only partial.) To refer to a sign as a "text" is simply to refer to it as a starting point (usually composed of many subtexts) relative to some possible or actual sign process. Since one of the theorems of Peirce's theory is that every phenomenal object has sign powers (not necessarily known powers), every phenomenal object is a possible text. Moreover, it is at the same time something that can itself be regarded as semiotically derivable from a prior text. A semiotic theory of the Peircean type is basically a systematically developed set of distinctions for use in the analysis of sign processes and texts, actual or possible. In other words, semiotic is a method of describing phenomenal objects *as* functioning or functional units in actual or possible sequential processes which are structured according to certain principles implicit in the idea of "presencing" power.

Since a phenomenal object is any object,[16] regardless of existential status, it will not necessarily have properties which it will have *if* it is rightly classifiable as an individual existent in the historical order of nature, occurring at a certain place and a certain time (or existing continuously through time and moving through space). If it *is* classifiable as an individual within this existential order, then it follows, for example, that for any given predicate (within the class of predicates categorially relevant to it), it either has that predicate or does not have it. Or perhaps it would be more accurate to say that it is our practice to expect this particular "logical law" (the law of excluded middle) to hold true of any object thus classified, though it may be that some exceptions have to be made (as perhaps in the case of certain entities on the subatomic level).[17] On the other hand, a merely imagined object, for example, need have only a few properties and may be highly indeterminate—I mean indeterminate in itself, not merely as known to us—in respect to innumerably many others that would be either true or false of it were it in the space-time order instead. And this is true of any phenomenal object, unless it is especially classifiable as being an object of the sort which must meet such "laws" (the force of the *must* deriving from what we assume in so classifying it). Thus, like a denizen of Hades, a phenomenal object can be a "mere flitting shade"—or, indeed, a far more insubstantial thing than that—though it must be capable of being referred to (in order to be an object) and be minimally describable (in order to be phenomenal).

For example, I am at present writing with a cheap black pen. This pen is a phenomenal object in what we call "the real world," and thus it is a determinate individual, possessing innumerable properties of which I am not aware and for which I have no concern. But your idea of my pen (that is, the *object* of which you are now aware in virtue of my description of my pen), which is also a phenomenal object, is highly indeterminate; it is black, cheap, and a pen, but it neither is nor is it not made of a certain sort of plastic. (My pen either is or is not made of that kind of plastic, though, because it is an entity in "the real world.") Shakespeare's Brutus was an honorable man—or at least an "honorable" man (scare-quotes used to pacify the shade of Shakespeare's Antony), but it is neither true nor not true that he had a stiff drink on the morning of that fateful day, before setting out for the forum; for Shakespeare left him indeterminate in that respect. The "real" Brutus, however, may not have been so honorable and he either did or did not have a stiff drink the morning of the assassination. (The relation between one phenomenal object and another which is signified by saying that the one is an "idea of" the other is not a topic we can pursue here, though I should remark that nothing precludes a certain limited or partial identity of the two in the case where truth is involved; thus, for example, your idea of my pen, assuming I told you the truth about it, *is* my pen *as* it appears to you now, notwithstanding the fact that we can *also* speak of them as two phenomenal objects. This is because identity relations are far more various in type and are capable of being construed with far more flexibility than is usually realized. Moreover, the identity predicate has as many different ways of applying to things as there are differences in the ways of counting things.)

Such is the idea of an "object" or "thing" which you must keep in mind in what follows, and not suppose that a phenomenal object is always a "full-bodied" object of the sort we encounter when we are dealing with objects in the space-time order we call "the real world." But mere flitting shades though some of these objects may be, they all have sign powers nonetheless. Equipped with this initial understanding of the terms *phenomenal object* and *sign*, let us now return to the fact that the reading of a text of any sort is to be construed, for semiotical purposes, as the observation of phenomenal objects as presenced through the action of signs, which are themselves phenomenal objects.

When the subject matter of a text is a theoretical object (involving innumerable subobjects, also mostly of a theoretical nature), such as in the case of the present text, we tend to think of interpretation or understanding as something quite different from sense perception. In the case of reading a novel or a poem the difference is clearly not so great: thus no one would deny that in reading a description of a landscape, for example, the linguistic signs are so acting as to presence objects "in the imagination," and that this experience is, in many respects, quite similar to an experience of sense-perceiving them. A skilled reader, deeply immersed in the reading, will often have little significant awareness of the linguistic signs which are mediating the experience, and it will seem, experientially, very like "being there." Indeed, an unsophisticated cinematic version of a child's fantasy story—the sort of trash children watch on television now—is often experienced by them with a lesser sense of direct observation than the same story is experienced by children who read it or hear it told to them, the mediating images on the television screen being less powerful semiotically than the word-signs, even with regard to pictorial "realism." I find in my own case that the mediating images on a television or movie screen rarely have as much power to presence the objects depicted as do the word-signs in the corresponding novel or short story. This no doubt varies greatly with individuals, but the point is that we can and do in fact observe "through" words just as we do "through" any other sign configurations presented to us. Thus the semiotician will regard all of these cases—the reading of a theoretical text, the reading of a novel or poem, the seeing of a cinematic representation, and the direct sensory perception of something—as fundamentally alike, in that in all such cases (and in innumerable other kinds of cases), phenomenal objects functioning as signs produce other phenomenal objects which are themselves signs, which in turn function to produce still further phenomenal objects which are signs, and so on.

There are important differences, too: differences in the relative roles of the various kinds of signs; in the kinds of phenomenal objects; in the patterns and the sequences of interactions of signs as they actualize their sign powers; and still others. But in common would be the fact that some entities functioning as signs are actualizing their powers such that *objects* are being *observed* by the interpreter, whether the objects are imaginary or real, and whether they are correctly or incorrectly perceived.

— Well, if reading a theoretical text, such as the present one, is supposed to be basically like, say, watching a football game from the grandstand, then tell me this: What does Peirce's conception of semiotic *look* like (or smell like, or whatever)? I don't see how you can liken the sense perception of a physical object to the intellectual awareness of a theoretical conception, unless you mean by the phenomenal object the words themselves. And that is what a theoretical conception is, isn't it? A se-

quence of word-signs? But if that is what you mean, then it is
highly misleading to say that these words are in any sense producing or "presencing" a phenomenal object which *is* that
theory: the words *are* the theory, that is, they are the theory as
put in your own words. That is what you are saying, isn't it?
No, that is not what I am saying. The words in the present paper are
not Peirce's theory (or my conception of Peirce's theory), nor are
Peirce's words Peirce's theory either.[18] Nor is the atomic theory of
matter the same as the word-signs in which it is expressed (or the
class of all such word-signs), anymore than the history of England is
the word-signs which the historians have used to describe it. Peirce's
conception or theory of the sign-interpretational process *is the sign-
interpretational process itself*—as Peirce conceived it. And to the extent
that he conceived it correctly, we can drop the qualification.

Think of it this way. There is (1) a phenomenal object which
consists of all sign-interpretational processes that ever were or will be.
Then there is (2) a phenomenal object which is exactly like the one
just mentioned but which is highly abstract, lacking concrete details
and including only those properties which would be specified in a true
description of (1), if one were describing only the types of sign powers
involved in (1). Then there is (3) a phenomenal object which is Peirce's
idea (conception, theory) of (2). Then there is (4) a phenomenal object which is my idea of (3). Then there is (5) a phenomenal object
which is your idea of (4), and perhaps also of (3), if you are hearing
of Peirce's theory for the first time and put some belief in my account.
I could go on, of course, but this is enough to make my point. The
extent to which these various phenomenal objects are identical or different is another matter. For example, to the extent that Peirce is right,
and I am right about Peirce, (4) has some partial identity with (3),
(3) with (2), and (2) with (1).

My imaginary interlocutor asks what Peirce's theory *looks* like.
My answer is that one of the things it looks like is a set of Chinese
boxes, with no innermost or outermost box. That is, this is one of
several appearances of the sign-interpretational process itself, as I conceive that Peirce conceived it. (As it happens, I don't perceive Peirce's
theory in such a way that smell or sound or taste or tactile qualities have
any prominence, though I suppose others might possibly so perceive it.)
That is, there is a certain *isomorphism* between the form of the sign-
interpretational process, as Peirce conceived it, and the form exhibited
by a series of such boxes (though Peirce's own favorite isomorph of the
process was an onion with no outermost or innermost skin), so that if
I were teaching a class on Peirce's theory I might so present it and
explain the isomorphism, much as a teacher of atomic physics might

use the old Bohr solar system model at an early stage in his pedagogical explanations.

> — Now wait a minute! You surely aren't saying that an atom actually *looks like* Bohr's pedagogical image, in the sense that it actually *appears* in that form?

Yes.

> — But everybody knows that atoms don't look like anything, for the simple reason that they are imperceptible.

I don't "know" that. Speaking as expositor of Peircean semiotic, I say that neither atoms, nor electrons, nor quarks, nor any other such entities are imperceptible. If, for example, the Bohr model—inadequate as it may be for the sophisticate—still has some genuine use as an isomorphic representation of the reality it represents, then that which it represents does indeed look like that. This is one of its appearances, just as, say, a very poor photograph of a person may still be a genuine likeness of the person in some respect, even if not in a very useful respect. Thus if all one can discern from the photograph is that the person has a more or less human shape, it certainly wouldn't be of much use; but it would still be true that that person really does have such an appearance. Similarly, the Bohr image is a genuine appearance of an atom in certain superficial respects, even if its use is now quite limited.

> — But not all theories have accompanying models, if that is what you are getting at with this idea of the phenomenal object which word-signs "presence." Quantum mechanics was mistakenly criticized by some scientists on just this ground, namely, that every theory has to have a pictorial model accompanying it; but quantum mechanics has no such model. And in general, although such models may be helpful, when available, they are not necessary—and are not in fact constructable for some theories.

I didn't say the model must be pictorial, if that means visual, and the role of models vis-à-vis theories in scientific representation is merely one special case of what I am talking about (though an exceptionally interesting one because of the sophistication of the critical literature on this topic). But with regard to your critical point, one answer would be that mathematical representations also function in such theories, and can be regarded as having a modeling function; for mathematical signs are not in general identical with word-signs, though mathematical representation includes word-signs.

> — Not if the formalist theory of mathematics is correct, according to which all of mathematics is reducible in principle to word-signs.

That is *a* theory about mathematics, but it was not Peirce's theory and it is not the only theory held. Peirce was himself an accomplished mathematician, working at the leading edge of that science, and he was a master logician as well, whose contributions to the latter science are without parallel, as regards both scope and depth. Thus he was at least as qualified to analyze the nature of mathematical representation as anyone else, now or then, and he decisively rejected the formalist analysis. However, the reader should understand that there is nothing approaching the consensus opinion on this topic which would have to obtain to make it reasonable to accept *any* theory of mathematical representation as well established: in fact, it is precisely the lack of a generally agreed upon theory of meaning (semiotical or otherwise) which precludes any substantial weight being put upon any such theory at this time. Do not mistake the confident tone with which some philosophers of science and logicians pronounce their dicta as a sign of their *authority* in these matters. There are no authoritative opinions on these matters, even in the weak sense of *authority* according to which a scientist who is highly respected by his colleagues in a well-established science might be said to speak "authoritatively." I stress this because those not well acquainted with logic and philosophy of science often mistakenly believe that fundamental questions have been settled in this area, whereas in fact the situation in this area is not different than in any other part of philosophy.

In sum, then, the semiotic approach considers all sign interpretation—including the reading of linguistic signs—to be the *observation* of *objects* produced phenomenally by signs, which are themselves phenomenal objects produced by others and producing others still. Thus, interpretation is not regarded as a mental process distinct from what the signs themselves do in presencing phenomenal objects. In other words, what we ordinarily think of as a flow of thought (including feelings and the like) which is produced in us by the signs is regarded semiotically as an objective procession of phenomenal objects (even "feelings" being regarded as appearances of objects).[19] The mind, semiotically construed, is not something within which the flow occurs, nor is it a sort of spectator of the flow; it *is* the flow. (The operation of the interpretational process is a reflexive operation within the process itself, which can itself be the object of observation in virtue of another reflexive observation, and so on.)

This means that the concept of mind is gratuitous or redundant, strictly speaking. The sign-interpretational process, the processional flow of phenomenal objects functioning semiotically, is that in terms of which such terms as *mind, thought, thinking, feeling,* and so forth, are to be explicated. Such terms explain nothing and add nothing; they merely indicate something about how the process is to be regarded for some special purpose. So also with regard to the idea of the interpre*ter*:

to introduce this idea is either, as Peirce wittily put it, to "throw a sop to Cerberus," because one finds it expositionally convenient to avoid crossing existing theoretical prejudices in order to make a point which is not affected thereby; or it is to speak in shorthand of something which would be too complicated for exact expression in a given context (which is how I have used the term *interpreter* here); or else it signifies that one has shifted from a basic semiotic level of analysis to a special context wherein the concept of an interpreting mind or body is especially introduced because it has some useful meaning for that context.

In short, there is no place in the semiotic analysis (except as just qualified) for human minds as agents apart from or in addition to the agency of the signs themselves, either with regard to the sign user or the sign interpreter. There are only signs produced by signs and producing signs, with no absolute starting point and no absolute stopping point. Alternatively, there are only phenomenal objects presencing and presenced by phenomenal objects, such objects often becoming sub-objects within more comprehensive objects in various ways. The purpose of a semiotic analysis is to articulate the ways in which this can and/or does occur.

I said earlier that the phenomenological stance is an attempt to attain a sort of metaphysical innocence. I say "attain" rather than "regain," for I see no reason to suppose there was ever a time when human beings were metaphysically innocent, any more than there ever was a time when human beings were not social beings. But many conceptions we now take for granted (e.g., those expressed in such terms as *mind, feeling, imagination, dreaming, sense perception*, and so on) are actually of quite recent origin, relative to the length of time during which distinctively human life has existed, and they are intimately bound up with metaphysical conceptions of the real and the unreal which we organize our lives around. But the contemporary Western ways of organizing experience are significantly different even from those of the Greeks of the late classical period, and to move back only a few centuries earlier in that same culture is to move to ways of experiencing often astonishingly different from our own. This point has, of course, been stressed repeatedly by anthropologists in connection with contemporary "primitive" cultures. In fact, it has often been overstressed, to the point of implying that such people are so radically different in their *Weltanschauungen* that they are radically incomprehensible to us. We forget that the identification of them as human beings already supposes that they are not *radically* incomprehensible (and that, conversely, to regard their lives as incomprehensible is to dehumanize them in our thinking). But the difficulties in translating their ways of experiencing into our ways is due largely to our refusal to abandon the use of the kind of terms which preclude any such translation because they are essentially bound up with our taken-for-granted metaphysics. Yet it is surely possible to free ourselves, at least for theoretical purposes, from this sort of ethnocentricity, given the fact that some of the most basic elements in our present (and far from coherent) metaphysics have been incorporated not only within recorded Western history but within the past few centuries. The phenomenological point of view assumed by semiotic can be regarded as an attempt to establish a nonethnocentric theoretical base upon which to stand in the process of coming to understand both our own metaphysical presuppositions and those of others. Yet the difficulty in adopting and maintaining such a stance is shown in the difficulty we have in grasping what is meant in saying that thoughts, ideas, feelings, emotions, and so on, are to be regarded, one and all, as phenomenal objects, quite on a par with physical tables, chairs, and trees, in the basic phenomenological description.

The difficulty is not merely that we take it for granted that certain things are real and others unreal, some substantial and some insubstantial, such as people with other metaphysical assumptions would disagree with us about. A further difficulty lies in our habit of treating the idea of an unreal object as identical with the idea that there really is no object, that is, in our tendency to regard the phrase *real object* as equivalent to *really is an object*, so that *unreal object* is implicitly treated as a contradiction in terms. There is, of course, no possibility of understanding things phenomenologically insofar as this gratuitous equivalence is taken for granted, and there is, therefore, no way to step back, as it were, from our own metaphysics without stepping into another. Thus arises the characteristic twentieth century theoretical belief that we cannot truly understand another culture "from the outside," but if we understand it "from the inside" we lose the "distinterested" position from which we could assess and compare our findings. And on a less sophisticated level, the effect is that, while we may be willing, in a superficial sort of way, to look with a tolerant eye on persons or peoples who recognize "different realities," we cannot really make any sense of it because we assume all the while that their experience of these unreal objects (as we regard them) is an experience of nothing at all. Being unreal, they are not objects; not being objects, they cannot be referred to; not being referrable to, they are not there to be experienced; hence the experiences of them are just experiences of nothingness! Notice how odd it seems to us when we first learn that "primitive" peoples —and not only they—usually have no difficulty in recognizing that there are gods other than their own, and often assimilate them to their own pantheon enthusiastically. Perhaps this seems odd to us because a nonexistent god is, for us, no god at all; consequently our "tolerance" of religions and world views other than our own is the sort of tolerance we pay to lunatics, who are similarly prone to experiences of nothing-ness which are somehow at the same time not just experiences of noth-ing. I cannot here illustrate the way this stultifying assumption works in much contemporary logic, psychology, sociology, anthropology, and other scientific fields, nor consider the deleterious effect it has had on all esthetic criticism (imaginary objects being no objects at all); but I do want to underscore that it must be dropped if the semiotic point of view is to be utilized effectively.

III

Given this understanding of what is meant by *phenomenal object*, we need only consider one further aspect of the conception in order to take up directly the nature of sign action and distinguish the various types of signs. A phenomenal object must be capable of appearing. Con-sidered *as* appearing, a phenomenal object is a *phenomenon*. A phenom-enon is thus not itself an object but rather an appearance of an object.[20] But the English word *appearance* has two distinguishable (though re-lated) meanings; on the one hand, it is synonymous with *appearing*, as, for example, in the sentence

John's appearance at the party—after he told us all that he definitely wasn't coming—was quite a surprise.

On the other hand, it also refers to a perceptible Gestalt of the thing which is appearing, as, for example, in

John's appearance at the party—with all that scraggly long hair trimmed off and in his nice new suit—was quite a surprise.

(The Greek words εἶδος and ἰδέα are rough equivalents to the English word *appearance* in this second sense.) In order to avoid confusion, I will use the term *quality* for *appearance* in the second sense,[21] and *ap-pearing* for the other sense, and in neither sense are we to think of appearance as something "subjective," as in the appearance vs. reality distinction. A quality is an aspect of phenomena, and of phenomenal objects thereby, and in appearing an object may exhibit more than one quality. Thus this phenomenal object has both the quality of squareness and the quality of blackness. Since many things are square and many are black (have squareness or blackness as qualities), a quality as such is in some sense independent of particular phenomena and phenomenal objects. (Neither a quality, nor a phenomenon, nor a phenomenal object are what some philosophers call a "sense-datum." There is no equivalent in Peirce's philosophy to such a concept.)

We are to understand a sequence of phenomenal objects construed semiotically as being a sequence of consecutive presencings, with each object in the sequence being a *sign* insofar as it presences, and an *interpretant* insofar as it is presenced.[22] There is no assignable first or last member of the series. Hence, every member is at once a sign of the one which follows it and an interpretant of the one that precedes it in the series. The *object* of any given sign is the object of every member of the series *qua* sign. That is, there is a common and unifying reference throughout; and since there is no assignable first or last member of the series, the object is always assumed to have more signs referring to it than are represented in any given representation of the series. The object is not, however, anything other than the referential unity of the series.[23] (The incomplete representability of the object at any given time is, I think, essential to its being a genuine unit; but I cannot here go into the issues that arise in connection with the formal representation of such sequences.) Conceiving a sequence of phenomenal objects as a semiotic series is therefore tantamount to claiming that they can all be represented as in a single series, every member of which is a sign of the same thing. In other words, all of the phenomenal objects in a series are regarded as logical parts or components of the same comprehensive phenomenal object. (This does not preclude subidentification of phenomenal objects in the series as numerically identical or diverse; and, looking at the matter macroscopically, it does not preclude an entire series being related through numerical referential identity to other series, such that the comprehensive object which is the unity of one series becomes a subobject within a still more comprehensive object.) Construed dynamically, such a series of presencings is something like a "moving picture" of the object, which is itself the principle of unity of the series and is thus what *appears* in every member.

Strictly speaking, every sign of an object, regardless of the type of sign, is a presencing—an appear*ing*—of the object, which thus essentially manifests itself (since it is simply the principle of unity of a sequence of appearings). Thus the words on this page are, *as* signs, appearings of Charles Peirce's semiotic. But of course there is an important difference between types of appearings of an object. To take a more intuitively clear example: a physical description of a person—say Peirce himself—

is clearly different in some important way from a photograph of Peirce or from him as "appearing in the flesh." Semiotically, these are all equally Peirce's appearings, but there is still an important difference, such as is brought out by the fact that we might say that Peirce looked like his pictures (or that they looked like him), whereas we would hardly want to say that he looked like the words on this page.

In semiotic terms, the difference is that some of the signs in the semiotic series are of the sort to which *looks like the object*—or more generally, *is similar to the object*—is a pertinent predicate, while some are not of this sort. *Iconic* signs are signs of this sort: they are signs regarded as phenomenally exhibiting qualities which are similar to (perhaps the same as) qualities of the object itself, in the sense in which we would ordinarily understand the idea of the qualities of an object. Word-signs of an object are not usually like that: the word-signs on this page are appearances of Peirce, in one sense, but he didn't look like this page looks. (His semiotic theory doesn't look like this page looks either, which is what I meant earlier when I said that the word-signs of a theory are not the theory itself.) Iconic signs of an object are, then, signs which are appearings of the qualities of the object itself, as we would ordinarily understand that.

However, the difference between an iconic sign of the object which we would ordinarily say is not itself the object (e.g. a portrait, photograph, sketch, diagram, etc., of the object) and an iconic sign the appearing of which we would identify as the appearing of the very object itself (as, for example, when we are in direct sensory contact with the object) is not such a sharp or significant distinction as common sense and some philosophical theory takes it to be.[24] For example, I recall that when I visited Venice briefly a number of years ago I could never shake the feeling that I was seeing the city only through a movie travelogue; somehow I could get no more sense of "presence" or "reality" from actually being there than I would have had by seeing it "indirectly" on a movie screen. An odd reaction, no doubt; but my point is that, even from an experiential point of view, the difference in question is not always a significant one. And if we turn to the criteria of *physical mediation*, with the idea that we can differentiate by saying that I was seeing Venice directly, in a physical sense of *directly*, when I was in Venice, but would have seen it only indirectly, through physical mediation (film, camera, projector, etc.), if I had seen Venice in a movie, we still find no generally significant basis for differentiation; for all sense perception is physically mediated: the human body with its sense organs, and so on, is not a fundamentally different sort of thing than such artificial organs as are involved in filming and showing the film of something. Thus the need for a fundamental logical distinction here is questionable, and there is no such fundamental distinction in semiotic theory; but insofar as there *is* any need for such a distinction, it would simply be a matter of mustering criteria of numerical identity and diversity for the phenomenal object which is the iconic sign and the phenomenal object which is its object. These certainly can be identified (as a subidentity in addition to the numerical identity constitutive of the unity of the entire semiotic series), but apart from a special context which would provide such criteria we can only say that such identification (or differentiation) *can* be made, provided such cirteria are actually available in a specific area of inquiry or concern.

Let me elaborate on this, because of its practical importance in semiotic analysis. From the perspective of this paper, where the topic is the basic semiotic theory itself, we have no substantive criteria for numerical identity and diversity available to us. Such criteria are not provided a priori, but rather by concrete contexts of semiotic analysis. In the various areas of our experience and concern we do have various criteria for identity and diversity. But what counts as one or many is a function of predicates used in a given area and in accordance with what they require, whereas we are talking here in abstraction from the kind of predicates which so determine unity and plurality. In practice, we are often far from clear on what these criteria are, and we are also often inclined to use criteria of this sort where there is no necessity to do so, because of our adherence (conscious or otherwise) to metaphysical theories. Suppose, for example, that you have ten living human bodies, all behaving intelligently. Are there therefore ten minds, one per body? Cartesian metaphysics says yes. Materialistic metaphysics of the crasser sort says there are no minds there at all. Semiotic theory ignores the question, insofar as there is no specific context that makes it necessary or desirable to use such criteria (though when such a context does arise no one imbued with the semiotic point of view is likely to find either the Cartesian or the materialist answer satisfactory).

So, in sum, although a distinction of the common sense sort can be made between an iconic sign which *is* its object (numerically) and one which is not, the actual criteria for making this distinction are not available apart from some specific context. Iconic signs are, therefore, all alike in being appearings of the object which exhibit some intrinsic quality of it. If the Chinese box image is a good iconic sign of the semiotic sequence, from a certain perspective, then that *is* what it looks like, just as Peirce as seen "in the flesh" in his later years looked like a man with a rather longish beard. (I know he looked like that because I've seen him—in a picture.)

Let us now consider *symbolic* signs, which are actually a species of indexical signs. For a *symbol* is not the same thing as a symbolic sign. A symbol is a rule the relation to which differentiates a special class of indexical signs, which are accordingly called "symbolic signs." (Similarly, an icon is not the same thing as an iconic sign: an icon is the quality in the sign phenomenon which, because it is similar to or the same as a quality in the sign's object, constitutes the basis for the sign being an iconic sign of it.) Any indexical sign which is a symbolic sign is a *replica* of the symbol which "rules" the sign, thereby making it a symbolic sign. To understand the symbolic sign we must, then, first understand the nature of indexical signs generally.

All occurring signs are indexical signs, because an *indexical* sign is simply any phenomenal object with the power of presencing another. Even an iconic sign—though not an icon proper—is an indexical sign. (This is a consequence of the expository approach I have taken here, and it should be qualified by saying that all signs *which are phenomenal objects* are indexical signs. Neither icons nor symbols proper are phenomenal objects, as the term *phenomenal object* has been explained here, though this does not mean that they are *non*phenomenal objects but only that a deeper analysis of the concept of a phenomenal object—involving distinctions such as that between "qualisigns," "sinsigns," and "legisigns"—would be necessary in order to make clear the exact status of the icon and the symbol proper. It is not profitable to attempt to distinguish here between the terms *index* and *indexical sign*.) Now the following phenomenal object

is an iconic sign of a square. (What square? Any square you like.) But it also indexes (indicates). For example, it indexes a sign which looks like this:

square

Or if appropriate criteria for numerical identity and diversity were contextually available, we might, for example, wish to divide the phenomenal object above, which is an iconic sign of a square, into innumerably many different phenomenal objects, simply by regarding it as a numerically different object at each successive moment in time: we could then say that each such object is indexing or presencing a sign exactly like itself at each successive moment. Similarly with this one:

We could regard it as a new object every time a figure-ground reversal occurs, were it appropriate and desirable to do so, though of course we could not speak of an *it* which is doing a figure-ground reversal in that case. The general point is that iconic signs are also indexical signs, and they may be such in a variety of ways. But to regard them as iconic signs is not the same as to regard them relative to their indexical or presencing power, but rather in relation to their exhibitive or qualitative characters.

Indexical signs are not to be identified with "natural signs": the latter are a species of the former. The term *natural sign* could be defined here as meaning an indexical sign which occurs in the natural order and which presences, directly or indirectly, another object in the natural order. (Any sign in a series can be said to presence indirectly any sign subsequent to the interpretant it directly presences.) But signs do not operate only in the natural order; for the power of presencing is a property of phenomenal objects primarily, and it is not contingent upon their existential status. Generally speaking, the usefulness of a sign lies in its power of presencing phenomenal objects (their interpretants), such that an interpretant of the sign which satisfies the purpose animating one's interest in the sign is finally produced. I cannot here go into the formal structures involved in such series (i.e., the structures of representation involved in representing a phenomenal sequence as a semiotic series), but I should remark that the presencing power of a sign involves a kind of *causation* not the same as what is usually called "efficient causation." Efficient causation relates to signs as occurring in the natural order, but semiotic causation—the sort of causation implicit in the term *presencing*, as I have used that here—is of a sort which I can only hint at by saying that a sign (or complex of signs) may finally presence the interpretant that satisfies one's interest in the sign only long after one has lost all conscious interest in the matter, and by an interpretational chain which could not possibly have been predicted in advance. Yet long-range interpretational results of signs are by no means completely unpredictable in spite of that (which is why there is a basis for talking of causation in this connection).[25] For example, the revolutionary goes about saying "Oppression!," "Injustice!," "Freedom!," and so forth, in appropriate situations, and can often be reasonably certain that these signs will, *in due time*, and *in one way or another*, result in interpretants of the sort he hopes for, even though it may be several years away. To deny some kind of causation here would be obtuse; to claim that it can (in principle) be explicated in terms of efficient causation only would be mistaken, if it is true that sign power is a feature of phenomenal objects primarily. In any case, though, bear in mind that what a sign presences, directly or indirectly, is, like every sign of an object, the appearing of the object itself (in the sense explained earlier).

Symbolic signs are differentiated by their relation to a "rule" which somehow delimits or defines a range of interpretants of them *as* symbolic, and *as* the particular symbolic signs they are. But how is the idea of "rule" to be explicated? Contrary to the belief of many theorists, the term *rule* is far too anarchic in its sign power to bear the explanatory burden usually put upon it. (Peirce himself occasionally uses the term, but not regularly, and I use it here only because it has some helpful familiarity to the reader.) The idea that *langue* is prior to *parole* is tantamount to saying that the rule *gives* the meaning to the sign. But this exactly reverses the situation. What converts an indexical sign into a symbolic sign is rather a delimitation (cf. *definition*) or restriction, a narrowing down of the meaning or sign power it *already* has. The problem is not "How do words get their meaning?" but rather "How do meaningful entities come under control such that their meaning is made finite or limited?" An attempt at a precise answer to this cannot be attempted here, but an intuitive sense for this can be gotten by realizing that words and other symbols are, as it were, *moral/ethical* entities. (I say "as it were" because it is probably best to treat this idea as a metaphor here, though in fact it is no metaphor.)

Consider what we would call a "social role," such as that, say, of being a physician. Any person who purports to be such (e.g., by setting himself up in practice) thereby incites certain expectations about himself or herself: for example, it is expected that they have a certain knowledge and that they will act upon their patients only insofar as they are reasonably convinced that their actions will be conducive to health. The morality or ethics associated with social roles is not mysterious in origin: it is simply the standing expectations directed towards anyone identified as being in that role. We know, of course, that no individual will ever perfectly meet such expectations. But when they deviate sufficiently from such expectations we are inclined to say something like "That so-and-so is no surgeon, but just a greedy butcher," notwithstanding the fact that the person has all of the relevant credentials, and perhaps even the knowledge, we expect of a physician. So also with words as such. A word *is* a word, and is the word that it is, because it "lives up to" certain expectations about its sign powers, and insofar as it deviates from these it is not counted *as* a word, or at least not as the word it is supposed to be relative to the expectations. Thus the word may well have—normally does have—sign powers falling quite outside the expectations that make it a word: insofar, it is *merely* an indexical sign. But insofar as an indexical sign has the expected powers it is a symbolic sign, the expectations being the symbol. (By *expectations* I mean that which is expected, not the psychological state of expectation. A definition formulates such expectations, and thus a definition might be regarded as the symbol proper relative to the symbolic sign defined. But insofar as a definition *appears*, as a phenomenal object, it, too, is a symbolic sign with a corresponding symbol, and is not itself a symbol.)

The term *expectation* has its own problems, needless to say, and I am not supposing that it is any more clear than the term *rule*. However, my purpose is to move us toward a more fruitful way of thinking about words and other symbols than is suggested by the term *rule*. Thus I suggest that we provisionally understand by the term *symbolic sign* an indexical sign which is given special treatment when it occurs, with only some of its presencing powers being regarded as properties of it as the particular symbolic sign it is, the rest being regarded as properties of it only insofar as it is a nonsymbolic sign. What this means is that the interpretants of a symbolic sign identified as such are treated in a special way in the process of our observation of the presencing powers of signs. I have laid great stress on the idea that the sign-interpretational process is best regarded as primarily an observational or experiential process: instead of thinking of the reading of a text as a mental process accompanying a sense perception of it, for example, I have tried to encourage thinking of it rather as a perception of what signs are themselves doing. But of course all observation—perhaps all experience whatsoever—involves an active element also. For example, when one *looks* at an object one is doing something: first one focuses attention here, then there, deriving information from each perspective, synthesizing that information, and so on, finally arriving at a *seeing* which satisfies one. So also in reading a text of any kind: one observes a sign and perhaps experiences a certain interpretant sequence, moves to a new sign and its interpretants, perhaps returns to the first one again and reexperiences its powers, and so on, synthesizing interpretants from both, and so on, just as in sense-perceiving. The difference between the symbolic sign and the merely indexical sign has to be understood in relation to this active aspect of observation. A symbolic sign is one which can function *as* such only because one knows how to observe a symbolic sign as such, that is, only because one knows that it must be treated in a special way in "reading" it if its special sign value is to be made accessible.

The sign-interpretant series is not a simple linear chain. It is rather to be thought of as a complex of initially independent sequences which join with one another, branch, join with still others, branch, and so on, such that by the end of the process all have ultimately contributed (like contributory rivers) to a final resultant interpretant. The interpretational process is a process of *composition* of a phenomenal object, such that one begins with a number of unrelated phenomenal objects, follows out the interpretational sequences they generate *qua* signs, and ends up with a composite object which is the resultant of the sign powers of all of the phenomenal objects that constituted independent starting points. Thus, all of the signs in the present paper, for example, were put together by me with the idea that the reader might be led, by following out the sign powers of the individual signs, to a resultant single phenomenal object which is *the* object of the composite sign which is the complete paper. (That object is, of course, Peirce's conception of the sign-interpretant process.) The author's intention is not what I am underscoring here: that intention is available to the reader simply as more signs—more context—which, along with the context each reader individually provides, adds still more starting points (i.e., starting points in addition to the signs in the paper itself). The point is rather that the sign-interpretant process, construed as one in which the observer is trying to observe intelligently, is one which involves *strategies* and *techniques* of observation of the signs and their sign actions, and the symbolic sign in particular has to be understood in terms of the appropriate strategy for the observation of it. In fact, it can only be differentiated from nonsymbolic signs with reference to that strategy. Thus while an iconic sign can be defined in terms of de facto qualitative likeness to its object, and an indexical sign in terms of the de facto power of presencing another phenomenal object, the symbolic sign can be defined only relative to how it is to be treated or regarded by the sign observer (interpreter, reader, audience). Its unique sign value as symbolic is wholly dependent upon its being treated in a certain way by the intelligent sign observer in the observational process. (This is a shorthand way of speaking: it does *not* mean that we must introduce an external mind as an independent factor; it means rather that a certain reflexive operation must be introduced into the analysis of the sign-interpretation sequence whenever a symbolic sign as such is supposed to occur.)

It is not possible here to explain that treatment adequately because it would entail developing the formal principles involved in construing a phenomenal process semiotically, that is, it would entail explaining in detail how to represent such a process in semiotic terms. I can only say that the representation of a given reading of a text would involve starting a new sequence with every sign which is not an interpretant in a sequence already started; following that with its interpretants until one of them presences two or more objects directly, which means a branching; joining sequences whenever certain signs occur which would warrant it (each such joining representing a further composition of the object); guided all the while by semiotic conceptions construed as principles dictating and/or advising branching and joining moves, given the aim of arriving ultimately at a resultant object exhibiting maximum coherence. (Such a representation, which would itself be an iconic sign of an idealized experience of a text, would involve the use of judgment continually, and is far from being a representation of a *mechanical* process.) Whenever a sign is functioning at once in a symbolic, indexical, and iconic way (as often occurs) there is ipso facto a three-way branching, but there are other causes for branching as well. There will also be *level* moves involved, that is, moves in which signs take signs as such as their objects. (In fact, the differentiation of iconic, indexical, and symbolic signs cannot be adequately explicated in a formal way without understanding these level moves and how they relate to the branching and joining aspects.)

Take the present text, for example. As a whole, this paper is a single (but highly complex) symbolic sign whose object is Peirce's semiotic considered in relation to linguistics. In order to gain access to that object experientially through this sign (which I composed with that purpose in mind), it is necessary to interpret its constituent symbolic signs, though not in any strict order. Signs are not "logical atoms," that is, ultimate units of analysis, and there are no absolutely "simple" signs; hence, what counts as a constituent sign is a matter of what it is profitable to regard as such, given one's particular analytic aims (e.g., a word, a phrase, a sentence, a paragraph, or whatever). To simplify, though, let us suppose that the interpreter starts with the first word of the first sentence of this paper, which happens to be *A*. Now, this sign is iconic in visual shape with signs the interpreter already knows to occur in contexts in which it is customarily interpreted to signify symbolically that the sign which follows it in a certain customary order of interpretation is a symbolic sign which may signify any of a number of different objects (i.e., is a general sign); and the interpreter also knows that the sign *A* customarily signifies that in interpreting the sign it signifies—which is the sign *semiotic linguistics*, in this case—

one may select any one of its objects in the process of interpreting it, at least until such time as the interpreter may encounter a further sign which qualifies or restricts this in some way. (Were the first word *The* instead of *A*, the interpreter would be alerted to expect that such a qualification would shortly be forthcoming.) When we say that *A* (or *a* or *An* or *an*) is an indefinite article we are saying something more or less equivalent to this, and it would add nothing interpretationally pertinent to say also that it is in the English language; for it is not what language it is in but what signification it has which is to the interpretational point.

That the sign *A* is an indefinite article, that is, has that kind of ideal signification (ideal because it is a *symbolic* sign), is something which the interpreter has to infer from the evidence. In this case, the evidence consists in such facts as that it occurs with a space between it and the next sign (that is, the sign sequence is *A semiotic linguistics* instead of *Asemiotic linguistics*), the fact that it occurs in a book whose primary readership will be people who, as the reader knows, will in fact construe it as having the signification of an indefinite article, and the fact that the author must have known this, too, and surely would not have arranged for such a sign to be in that place had he not assumed that such an interpretation would be put upon it. Such considerations do not deductively necessitate the conclusion that *A* would be best interpreted in the way described above (i.e., as an indefinite article), but the interpreter would normally—and reasonably—draw that conclusion. Thus in order to determine the identity of *A* as a *symbolic* sign it is necessary first to interpret it as an *indexical* sign; and there is no way to determine, on that basis, what symbolic sign it is without interpreting it as an *iconic* sign in the way indicated at the beginning of the analysis. This is true of symbolic signs generally: there is no access to their symbolic identity without prior interpretation of the facts of their occurrence, their perceptible form, and their likeness and spatial or temporal relationships to other signs, which involves interpreting them both indexically and iconically. Moreover, the signification of the special sort of symbolic sign which *A* is, namely, the sort we call an "indefinite article," requires ascertaining in every case what it is in fact spatially adjacent to in that particular occurrence; for without that being ascertained there is no way to know which symbolic sign it in fact signifies in that occurrence. Because its signification can be determined only if this kind of fact is known, which involves construing it as an indexical sign in a special sort of way, indexicality plays a role in its interpretation which it does not play in the case of all symbolic signs, and that is why it—like definite articles and demonstratives—is regarded, rightly, as a special sort of sign relative to other symbolic signs. But, like all articles and demonstratives, it is still a symbolic sign, nonetheless, just as ⟶ and ☞ are symbolic signs.

Before proceeding through a few more steps of this—which will be enough to indicate to you something of what is involved in such an analysis—let me interject that this is not to be construed as a *psychological* analysis, as if the aim were to hypothesize about what would actually go on in the mind of the interpreter. I am describing this in a shorthand way in order to convey what I deem essential in as short a space as possible, but it should be thought of as an analysis of the inferential steps one might go through if one had to think through the justification of a claim that a certain text has a certain possible interpretation. I am assuming that the signs in question are themselves acting so as to produce a range of interpretants, among which the interpreter has to identify those interpretants which are their interpretants *as* specifically symbolic signs, and as the particular symbolic signs they are. In other words, the interpreter's task is not that of "reading meaning into them," for if they do not already have meaning, and are not in fact presencing those meanings, the interpreter can do nothing. The task is rather that of *isolating* those meanings which will ultimately yield the best overall interpretation of the text; and any sign the interpreter considers may in fact be yielding many meanings with which he has no concern because they are not germane to his interpretational purpose, regardless of what that purpose it. If the analysis I am giving seems to be too complex to be plausible, given the fact that we normally go through no such conscious thought process, I can only repeat that the psychology of the matter is not at issue here. I might suggest, though, that a person who knew no English but was working from a translational handbook might go through some such steps quite explicitly. (One might also compare the sort of minute analysis involved in the decipherment of archaeological texts.)

I should also emphasize that the semiotic analysis of a text need not start on such a microscopic level as this. There is no a priori principle which could decide what are to be taken as the analytic units, as this is entirely a matter of the purposes of a particular inquiry. For example, I have been working for some years on an analysis of Plato's dialogues in which I make use of semiotic principles. My hypothesis is that the object of the entire corpus of Plato's work, taken as a single sign, is a thing called "φιλοσοφία", this being effected through the symbolic construction of several other objects (the most important one being the figure of Socrates) which function as iconic signs of that object. In the process of analyzing the dialogues in this way I occasionally find it necessary to work with particular word sequences in a microscopic way, somewhat as illustrated here; for the Greek text is usually so badly misrepresented in translation that nothing can be taken for granted about the significance of most of the passages important for my purposes. But the extent to which I go into such minute detail is dictated solely by the need to confirm and support the hypothesis, and much of the analysis is in terms of relatively macroscopic objects yielded by the text which are themselves functioning as signs of objects which are in turn functioning as signs, and so on. For it is characteristic of literary works, myths, and so forth, that the objects ultimately signified are available only through several levels of signification, such that objects of signs are themselves signs (of one type and another) of objects which are themselves signs of objects, and so forth.

Let us return to the sample analysis. Having ascertained that the next sign to interpret is the sign *semiotic linguistics* (which is composed of the second and third words at the beginning of the present paper), the interpreter will then take account of the fact that this sign is composed of two signs, *semiotic* and *linguistics*, each of which is visually iconic with other signs which the interpreter already knows to be in customary use to signify things with which he or she has at least some familiarity (namely, semiotic things and linguistics things), and it will be reasonably assumed that the presence of signs of such shapes in this place are good evidence that they are indeed occurring with these symbolic significations. Moreover, their propinquity and relative spatial relationship, taken in conjunction with the fact that *semiotic* appears with no final *s*, whereas *linguistics* has one, is an indexical sign of the fact that the object of the sign *semiotic linguistics* is a linguistics of the semiotic type (rather than a semiotic of the linguistics type). Given the prior interpretation of the sign *A*, the reader can move from the sign *A semiotic linguistics* to any phenomenal object of his or her choice which has the property of being a semiotic linguistics. (This could be its only property, and of course it may be a merely possible object.) The next step, then, would be to go to the sign *would*, the interpretation of which would affect how the object of the sign *A semiotic linguistics* is to be represented in relation to the modalities of the possible and the necessary; it would therefore require the introduction of some signs of those objects—I mean the objects signified generally by the words *the possible* and *the necessary*—which would have to be situated appropriately within the interpretational sequence. I will not pursue the analysis further here.

In order to do this sort of thing carefully, a notation would have to be developed comparable in some ways to the notations developed for the purposes of deductive logic, though I am certain it would be rather more complex. It might even require the use of hints from topological mathematics. Such private attempts as I have made to work out the principles of such notation—and, so far as I know, no one else has attempted to understand Peirce's semiotic in this way to date—have led to frustration due to the limitations of two-dimensional representation. Peirce himself did some experimentation with three-dimensional graphical representations in connection with his Existential Graphs (an ingenious system of notation he developed as his preferred alternative to the algebraic type of representation for deductive logic), but whether any help for the present problem is to be found in his work on that I do not know at this time. In the absence of any such notation, it is difficult to know whether one is making a blunder even on a relatively simple level of analysis, and the sample analysis I give above is intended only to be suggestive of what this would be like, rather than being put forth with confidence as a correct analysis.

I should make it clear, though, that I am not saying that a semiotic linguistics—or any other form of applied semiotic—would have as its basic task the constructing of such analytic representations, or of the general method of such representation. A linguist working from the semiotic approach might well develop and use a special method of representation, but this would be merely a technique in the service of other ends. It would always be possible in principle—though, I think, prohibitively difficult in practice—to work without any such aid, just as the late Medieval logicians developed a way of doing in highly controlled Latin some of the same things contemporary logicians do with their specially devised notation. Such notational systems are like mathematics in some respects, but their purpose is not primarily that of a *calculus*—even though some calculating can be performed with them— but rather that of a highly controlled way of talking about certain properties of things. Thus, for example, the logician's form $(x)(Fx \rightarrow Gx)$ is a way of saying what *All men are mortal* says without saying anything about men and mortals or any other beings in particular, and without leaving any ambiguity as regards whether or not any existing things are being signified *as* existing. The primary purpose of developing such a notation is that of sharpening our theoretical ideas by developing what is, in effect, a highly controlled descriptive symbolism which can function as an organ of perception in the analyses of concrete phenomena. It would be quite wrongheaded, in my opinion, to see in such notational devices something comparable to the calculative role of mathematics when it enters into the natural sciences.

As regards the relevance of all this to linguistics, it seems to me to be something like this. A linguistic sign would be a special case of a symbolic sign. The differentiation of the linguistic sign from the symbolic sign in general, and thus the differentiation of linguistics itself, would be based on what it is convenient to regard as specifically linguistic, rather than on any fundamental principle within semiotic itself. Symbolism undoubtedly functions in all of the arts, for example, and the differences between the various arts are not differences of great importance at a theoretical level (or so I would guess), no matter how remote in type music may now seem from literature or painting. Still, there is sufficient prima facie difference between these sorts of things to make it reasonable to suppose they had best be regarded as importantly different areas of study at present, and I should think that linguistics, construed as the study of the principles and varieties of specifically linguistic symbolism, would in fact constitute a conveniently distinct scientific enterprise for some time to come.

As I hope I have made clear, semiotic is a general theory of the principles to follow in understanding how signs work, and it is thus essentially oriented toward the perfection of what the Greeks would have called the τέχνη—craft, art, skill—of understanding signs. Given what is meant by *sign*, this is tantamount to saying that it aims at the perfection of the learning process. But it is a nonpsychological conception of what learning is; for it assumes—through its basic phenomenological stance—that learning is the acquisition of skill in the intelligent observation of signs, and that this depends upon knowing what signs themselves can do, and on developing both mandatory and preferential techniques for observing them (experiencing them, understanding them, interpreting them) in order to be able to learn the most we can from them. A semiotic linguistics would thus be a science which aimed at making us maximally intelligent when it comes to observing—and of course using—signs of the special sort it would be concerned with.

From such attempts as I have made at understanding the nature of words from the semiotic point of view, I am myself convinced that they have systematically distinguishable powers and functions beyond anything existing theories are able to articulate, and that, moreover, there are possible linguistic powers—I mean powers of signs, not powers of sign users—beyond any that have ever yet been discovered and used by even the greatest of word users. If the basic idea of semiotic is sound, or capable of being made sound, then linguistics might in due time find a way through it to the nature of words and their workings which would reveal linguistic properties—both possible and actual—comparable in their marvelousness to the physical properties which the natural sciences have discovered. To discover these properties, however, linguistics would have to abandon the idea that its basic task is that of interrogating "native informants" about the "acceptability" of simple sentences in order to compile grammars and dictionaries, and instead direct itself toward studying human *discourse*—poems, plays, treatises, novels, conversations, and so on—with the aid of an analytic technique for discovering what is *going on* in such phenomena, and hypothesizing about what further kinds of powers the *logos* might be found to have, if we could learn how to orient ourselves toward it properly.

NOTES

1. The foundational paper is the 1867 essay "On a New List of Categories" (CP 1.545–59). The abbreviated reference is to Volume 1, paragraphs 545 through 559, of *The Collected Papers of Charles Sanders Peirce*, in 8 volumes, C. Hartshorne, P. Weiss, and A. Burks, eds. (Cambridge: Harvard University Press, 1931–1958). This collection is but a small part of the total corpus of Peirce's work, the rest being available in a variety of media, including some 80,000 manuscript pages now available in microfilm and xerographic form. See M. Fisch, K. Ketner, and C. Kloesel, "The New Tools of Peirce Scholarship, with Particular Reference to Semiotic," *Peirce Studies No. 1* (1979):1–17, for a comprehensive and reliable description of the present state of availability of Peirce's work.

2. John Lyons, *Introduction to Modern Linguistics* (Cambridge: At the University Press, 1969), sec. 1.4.

3. Lyons, p. 50.

4. J. Ransdell, "Semiotic Objectivity," *Semiotica* 26(1979):261–88, esp. 281f.

5. C. S. Peirce and J. Jastrow, "On Small Differences of Sensation," *Memoirs of the National Academy of Science* 3, Part 1 (1884):73–83, reprinted with corrections and later reflections at *CP* 7.21–48.

6. Peirce was the originator of the theory of hypothetical or "retroductive"—as distinct from inductive and deductive—inference. The *Collected Papers* contain so many discussions of this topic that the interested reader should simply consult the indexes to the volumes under the headings of *hypothesis, retroduction, abduction,* and, of course, *inference.*

7. This does not imply that logical form is a species of rhetorical form. Certain linguistic forms are indicative of (but never identical with) the pertinent logical forms, and such linguistic forms are themselves rhetorical forms. A logical form is something to which a linguistic entity is put in relation for the special purposes of logical assessment, and is "in" the linguistic entity only in that sense.

8. I present a second formal argument against the same type of linguistics in J. Ransdell, "Semiotic Objectivity," *Semiotica* 26(1979):261–88, esp. 281–84, though my argument is relativized there to the conception of objectivity I develop in the earlier part of that paper.

9. The discussion of the moral/ethical nature of the symbolic sign in

Part III of this paper may suggest why theories of meaning have so often been isomorphic with political doctrines.

10. Noam Chomsky with Mitsou Ronat, *Language and Responsibility* (New York: Pantheon, 1977), 89.

11. See Gérard Deledalle, *Théorie et pratique du signe: Introduction à la sémiotique de Charles S. Peirce* (Paris: Payot, 1979), for a sound and systematic account of Peirce's basic semiotic conceptions, particularly in relation to linguistics. I was not acquainted with Deledalle's book until after the present paper was written and I cannot make any helpful comparative comments here. I can say, though, that Deledalle has an informed and generally accurate grasp of Peirce's basic ideas, and that, while he perceives clearly that no mere eclectic synthesis of Saussurian and Peircean conceptions is possible, he does indicate how one can move from the Saussurian to the Peircean conceptual framework. He remarks on page 40: ". . . [I]l est possible et même relativement facile de retrouver dans la sémiologie de Saussure quelques-uns des concepts fondamentaux de la sémiotique de Peirce. Ce que ne veut pas dire qu'ils soient assimilables. Leur signification contextuelle interdit au contraire en principe toute assimilation des uns aux autres." Work in progress by David Savan will undoubtedly result in an especially penetrating account of Peirce's ideas on the purely philosophical level, and philosophers may also look forward to a revised version of John J. Fitzgerald's *Peirce's Theory of Signs as a Foundation for His Pragmatism* (The Hague: Mouton, 1961). Douglas Greenlee's *Peirce's Concept of Sign* (The Hague: Mouton, 1973), is, in my opinion, so vitiated by certain basic misunderstandings of Peirce's writings as to be worse than worthless as an introduction to Peirce's semiotic, though it will have some value for those with an independent understanding. See J. Ransdell, "Another Interpretation of Peirce's Semiotic" and Jarrett Brock, "Draft of a Critique of Greenlee's *Peirce's Concept of Sign*," both of which are in the same issue of *The Transactions of the Charles S. Peirce Society* 12(1976):97–110 and 111–26, respectively, and see also Greenlee's reply in the same issue, at 135–47.

12. Peirce's use of mentalistic terminology has been seriously misleading to his contemporary readers, who usually overlook the fact that Peirce began developing his semiotic theory prior to the existence of what we now think of as psychology, and who ignore his repeated statements in later years that semiotic is *not* psychologically based, as he conceived it. Peirce's use of mentalistic terminology does not usually indicate a shift to a psychological perspective, because these terms did not bear the meaning for him that they usually bear for the contemporary reader. In his later writings, when psychology was beginning to flourish, Peirce sometimes uses such terms with the awareness that they might be misconstrued, but with the idea that others probably will grasp little of his meaning unless they first understand him psychologistically. The purpose of his special semiotic terminology was that of making it possible to break out of a psychologistic stance toward meaning-phenomena. His dilemma—on the horns of which he impaled himself repeatedly—was that if he defined his terms in a non-

psychologistic way no one would understand him at all because his approach was too alien to the prevailing ways of thinking; whereas if he defined them psychologistically his readers might gain *some* idea, but a badly distorted one. One cannot read Peirce with any real understanding without a grasp of the desperate communicational situation he was in and the effect this had on how he expressed his ideas.

13. Neither the conception nor the term *phenomenology* was derived from Husserl, and Peirce subsequently changed to the neologism *phaneroscopy* in order to avoid confusion of his and Husserl's conceptions. However, in the past few decades the word *phenomenology* has come to be used in a sufficiently indeterminate sense to make it reasonable to use it now with reference to Peirce's theory, as an indication of its general type, though it would doubtless be advisable to use the word *phaneroscopy* whenever the differentiating features of his particular approach are under discussion. See J. Ransdell, "A Misunderstanding of Peirce's Phenomenology," *Philosophy and Phenomenological Research* 38(1978):550–53. (I should also remark that the word *semeiotic* is the preferred term in recent scholarship when one wants to differentiate Peirce's semiotic from other possible instances at that general type of theory. But I prefer myself to use *semiotic* for the same reason I prefer *phenomenology* to *phaneroscopy*, namely, because I think it is rhetorically preferable at present not to reinforce the reigning tendencies to perceive Peirce's thought as idiosyncratic.)

14. Peirce often used the word *psychical* as an equivalent of *semiotical*, drawing implicitly upon the meaning of the Greek word ψυχή during the classical period, according to which whatever possesses *psyche* is ipso facto alive, as in Plato's definition of ψυχή in *Phaedrus* 245E. (Perhaps it is needless to say that *psychical* in this sense has nothing to do with the unfortunate meaning the word *psychic* has acquired in virtue of its occurrence in the popular phrase *psychic powers*.)

15. *Presence* is my term, not Peirce's. His corresponding terms would be *suggest* (in a psychological context) and *determine* (in a logical context); but I could not use his terms here without extensive commentary. The term *phenomenal object* is also mine, and it corresponds roughly to his term *phenomenon* as he often *uses* the latter term in his later writings, and also to his use of the term *object* in many contexts. He sometimes uses the term *idea* in this sense, also; for he always understood by *idea* not a mental entity but *that of which* one is aware. (Compare the Greek term ἰδέα, which was not a mentalistic term.)

16. Such an object may be "a single known existing thing or thing believed formerly to have existed or expected to exist, or a collection of such things, or a known quality or relation or fact, . . . [or] a collection, or whole of parts, or it may have some other mode of being, such as some act permitted whose being does not prevent its negation from being equally permitted, or something of a general nature desired, required, or invariably found under certain general circumstances" (*CP* 2.232). In short, anything you can think of.

17. See Alberto Cortes, "Leibniz's Principle of the Identity of Indiscernibles: A False Principle," *Philosophy of Science* 43(1976):491–505.

18. Except in a somewhat recondite sense, as explained in Part III of this paper.

19. ". . . [A]s for feelings, they are always referred to some object, and there is no observation of feelings except as characters of objects" (*CP* 7.376; see also 5.244–49, 462).

20. My distinction between *phenomenal object* and *phenomenon* is not systematically made by Peirce in these terms, who tends to use *phenomenon* indifferently in this respect.

21. *Quality* is a Peircean term, and he sometimes uses the word *idea* as an equivalent, though he sometimes uses it as indicated in note 15 above.

22. This is not a *definition* of the sign-interpretant relation. I do not define that relation here.

23. My basic objection to Douglas Greenlee's *Peirce's Concept of Sign* (see note 11 above) is that he does not understand that the semiotic object is not something logically external to the semiosis process itself.

24. I develop this point in a paper on the iconic sign and its function in reconciling the ideas of "direct" and "indirect" perception. See J. Ransdell, "On the Epistemic Function of Iconicity in Perception," *Peirce Studies No. 1* (1979):51–66.

25. Peirce called it "final causation," which, as I explain elsewhere, is actually the idea of a self-corrective or "cybernetic" process, which is regarded by Peirce as involving efficient causation but not reducible to it. See J. Ransdell, "Some Leading Ideas of Peirce's Semiotic," *Semiotica* 19 (1977):157–78.

Thirdness and Linguistics

RULON S. WELLS

Peirce considers Thirdness to have many aspects: generality, universality, regularity and lawfulness (and their correlative, conformity to rule or to law), mediation, continuity, vagueness.[1] This paper considers the bearing of his doctrines about Thirdness upon language. It proceeds by first considering certain major facts of language, and then by asking how Peirce's system takes cognizance of them. The system turns out to perform rather poorly in this respect, and the paper ends by inquiring into the reasons for this.

Concern with the facts of language occupies the first two parts of the paper. Part One compares rules governing language with rules governing art, and draws some conclusions about rules in general. Part Two compares rules with laws (laws of nature, that is), emphasizing their specific differences even though both are varieties of Thirdness. Part Three comments on Peirce's treatment of rules and of laws, remarking the infertility of his system as a heuristic for ascertaining an adequate treatment of linguistic rules and analyzing the reason for this infertility.

I. PRELIMINARY REMARKS ON RULE AND LAW

By the seventeenth century, the concept of law had developed to the point where one distinguished the laws of man, of God, and of nature. Laws of nature are descriptive, not prescriptive or normative. Later, people thought of the differences this way: if you break a law of man or of God, so much the worse for you; but if you break a putative law of nature, so much the worse for that law of nature.

The word *rule* is, as the word *law* once was, primarily normative, but with the difference of connoting conscious or deliberate or witting obedience. Dante in *De vulgari eloquio* c. 3 (quoted in Leo Spitzer, *Essays in Historical Semantics* [New York: Vanni, 1948], p. 19) defines the *vulgar* way of speaking as that which we, imitating our nurse, adopt without any rule. In prevailing current linguistic usage, set by Chomsky (e.g., "What is a rule of grammar?"), a linguistic *rule* is neither deliberate nor normative. If we ask, Why call it a rule, then?, the answer could be given: Such a rule is not an absolute norm, but it is a conditional one. Take, for example, the rule which states that in order to speak correct English (or, on pain of not speaking English), if you use a plural subject you must use a plural verb. These rules are conditions, and, moreover, they are necessary but not sufficient conditions. All the rules of English together will not tell you what to say; they will only tell you what you may say. In popular parlance, they are *don't*'s, not *do*'s. In technical parlance, they impose constraints, or, as Bloomfield and Harris called them, limitations upon distribution. So it is possible to find normative character in Chomsky's sense of *rule*, whether or not he intended it: linguistic rules are norms.

Under this conception, rules are constraints upon us; but (*a*) they only constrain us from, prohibit us from, enjoin us against saying certain things, and (*b*) their constraint is not total. The speaker has freedom within constraint.

At this point, we temporarily leave language and turn to an area where the relation between constraint and freedom is even more striking than in language, namely, art. Then we will come back to language.

Pope, in his *Essay on Criticism* 1.88–91, makes a point which he then illustrates by Homer and Virgil:

> These rules of old, discovered, not devised,
> Are nature still, but nature methodized;
> Nature, like liberty, is but restrained
> By the same laws which first herself ordained.

It will turn out that this point holds not only for art (whether verbal or non-verbal), but also for language (or rather, for speech, the actualization of language). As the artist is bound by necessary conditions, but within these bounds has his freedom, so, too, is the speaker. There are other analogies: the artist, but likewise the speaker, has (*a*) his materials on which and (*b*) his implements with which he operates, as well as (*c*) the circumstances in which he operates; and artwork, like an utterance, is typically used—or at least intended and adapted—for communication. Most important of all, in both kinds of communication there is an active and a passive role.

On the subject of freedom and constraint in art, the great theorist is Kant. (Peirce has nothing of his own to say about esthetics, and does not seem to understand what Kant has to say.) In section 46 of his *Critique of Judgment*, Kant relates art to genius. He makes these points: (1) there are rules for producing art (i.e., great, good art), but it takes genius to find them; (2) art is different from science in this regard; and (3) the rules are subjective, as taste is; there is no rule of criticism. Kant's examples are: for a scientist, Newton; and for an artist (specifically, a poet), Homer and Wieland. In his second point—the difference between art and science regarding subjection to rule—Kant seems to be mistaken both in his conclusion and in the reason he gives for that conclusion (namely, that a genius is different in kind from a nongenius, whereas Newton differs from a tyro only in degree). But there is a consideration, unnoticed by Kant, that could be placed at his service; it involves something like the difference mentioned above between active and passive roles. There are many who can understand Newton though they cannot achieve anything like his achievement. They can follow but cannot lead, as Glaucon and Adeimantus in Plato's *Republic* could follow Socrates's insights but could not originate them. Just so, it is often remarked that in mathematics the ability to follow proofs is different from the ability to discover proofs. Genius, then—at least the kind we are interested in here—is genius at discovery. Any other kinds there may be (for example, genius at organization, genius at persuasion, genius as an infinite capacity for taking pains) are here left out of account.

Now let us begin to put this analogy between art and language to linguistic use. Both the speaker and the artist are both constrained and free within their constraints. Are these lines sharp? Is the constraint utter constraint, and the freedom utter freedom? It would please Peirce to find degrees and continuity.

In a first-approximation model, there is a sharp line between the grammatical and the ungrammatical. This is possible because utterances are atomistic, they are molecules built out of discrete atoms: the units of sound, the phonemes (or, according to prevailing contemporary theory, distinctive features; similarly mutatis mutandis for written language), and the units of vocabulary, the morphemes.

This capital point deserves some elaboration. Because there are units, we can with mathematical rigor speak of combinations. And because the number of units is finite, for any finite length, the number of combinations is finite. This gives us an enviable control. Even though the set of grammatical sentences is infinite, we can organize it, for example, alphabetically, into the one-unit sentences, the two-unit sentences, and so on. In our present discussion, the principal use of this control is that it lets us speak in an obviously meaningful way both of discovery and of creation as selection. It is a fiction, but one whose implications and presuppositions can be definitely stated, to say that it is as if all the possibilities are laid out for one to review, and all one has to do is to choose. We could analyze the difference between the genius and the duffer thus: that although each of them selects from a range or set of possibilities which he has considered, the set considered by the genius is larger than the set considered by the duffer.

When we are considering possibilities, it is advantageous, for certain purposes, to confine our attention to possibilities such that each possibility is sharply distinct from each other possibility. It is so advantageous in the discussion of creativity and of genius that we may now ask whether the possibilities of every art may be conceived after this fashion. We have already seen that it is possible with versification because of the discrete, atomistic nature of verse. So the only remaining question is whether the matter of every art other than versification is similarly atomistic. I believe that the answer is that in every art the matter either is naturally atomistic or else can, in an arbitrary but admissible way, be treated as atomistic. To give but a single and brief example: every painting, even the smoothest, can be conceived pointillistically; it is only a question of choosing points so small that adjacent points will not be perceived as distinct from each other (precisely as, in the cinema, adjacent frames are not perceived as distinct).

A slightly different way of characterizing creativity is, on the Greek (versus the Judeo-Christian-Moslem) model, an arrangement, a disposition of a preexistent matter. So far as this matter is discrete and atomized, one may speak of combination. At one time, the image of the kaleidoscope was used to suggest this model.

Let us now return to language and its actualization, speech. So far, we have the contrast between what one may (can, could, might) say and what one does say, with creativity placed inside the bounds of those possibilities. We have not challenged the sharpness of the constraining bound, nor of the freedom within the bound. Before we do that, I have in mind a last comparison with art.

On the model so far, one is entirely free to mean. If, given the constraint of grammar, one adds the constraint of circumstances, the constraints are increased, but the basic sharp contrast between constraint and freedom or license is not altered. And there is still room for creativity, for the selection which will make other people say, "I wish I'd said that." According to our model, it would be more appropriate to say, "I wish I'd meant that"; having settled on a meaning, how one says it follows automatically.

In art criticism, we speak of effectiveness; also, as elsewhere, of success. When we speak of art, we have in our minds (whether in the back or in the front) the distinction between bad and good art, good art including great art (*great* meaning very good or the best). The great artist, in making his selections, takes into consideration not only grammatical and circumstantial constraints, but also the question of effectiveness; and here, no doubt, psychological laws enter the discussion. So far as that is true, it is even easier to think of the creator (artist or speaker) as discoverer. However, psychological laws are not relevant here as rules which govern the creative genius (whether they do govern him or not), but as one more set of constraints that bound his liberty.

So far, no difficulty has been found with the view that bounded freedom divides sharply into a component of sheer bondage and a component of sheer freedom. To find difficulties we must turn elsewhere.

An important vista has appeared before us in this discussion. We have not discovered anything new, but we have been reminded of something old that we had neglected: the distinction between simple (pure) and composite (mixed) cases. The situations in speech and in art where we found an element or factor of bondage and an element of freedom are composite cases, which break cleanly apart into a component of sheer bondage and a component of sheer freedom. The possibility then immediately suggests itself, that this cleavability is true of all such cases. This would be a heavy blow for synechism to withstand: a whole class of cases of apparent continuity would be done away with, not as illusory (i.e., as merely apparent), but as composite. Synechism, to be interesting, must be concerned with simple (fundamental, irreducible, original, primary), not with composite (derivative, reducible, secondary) continuity.

But there is a kind of rule, yet to be examined, that has a better claim to exhibiting simple continuity. Consider the following rule of poetics. It is common in verse to allow substitutions; for example, in English iambic pentameter, to allow a trochee to substitute for an iambus. This substitution is more acceptable in the first foot than elsewhere; this is sometimes expressed by calling the first foot the *favored* position. We have not yet accurately stated the rule, though. It is not a mere permission, because if it were, there would be nothing wrong with making every first foot a trochee. It is possible, however, for something to be wrong; there is such a thing as excessive substitution. (Similarly, in various matters of morals and of mores, there is such a thing as abuse of a privilege.) So a more accurate formulation of the rule is: a *moderate* amount of substitution is permitted. In this more accurate formulation, the rule can be seen at a glance to be vague.[2]

From considering such a rule we also gain a further insight. It is sometimes said that rules are made to be broken; and we are sometimes urged to be an untrammeled Walter von Stolzing rather than a score-counting Beckmesser. In that witticism and this romantic advice two quite different things are confounded. The point may be that such and such a rule is not binding on y, even though x says it is binding; for example, that contrary to Beckmesser's claim, Walter is not subject to the Mastersingers' rules. Or, quite differently, the point may be that rules should not be followed literally and slavishly, but with discretion. The latter interpretation holds that the rules as formulated are a good approximation—and so are by no means worthless—but still are not perfect, and so should not be followed literally.

Both interpretations are common, but it is only the second that is of present concern. Many who agree with the witticism interpreted the second way would go further and hold that, in general, it is humanly impossible to achieve perfect formulation of the rules that people follow. Michael Polanyi's concept of *tacit knowledge* covers the case where someone *knows* something but cannot perfectly formulate or articulate it.

From the same example we can draw a further lesson. The class of rules that are difficult or impossible to formulate perfectly falls into two subclasses which are worth distinguishing from each other. Those of one subclass are difficult because of the amount of detail; those of the other subclass are difficult because of the subjective judgment that is expressed by terms like *moderate*. (Rules of this second subclass are like Aristotle's mean.)[3]

A rule in the first subclass is precise, in that persons render categorical judgments and agree with each other in their judgment whether a given expression conforms to or violates the rule; in the case of a rule in the second subclass, by contrast, a person's judgment will be gradational rather than categorical, or else one person's judgment will differ from another's, or else both situations will obtain.

Rules of the second subclass, such as the rule "Be moderate in substitution," correspond roughly to what would commonly be called rules of style. In fact, the correspondence is close enough so that we may consider making it even closer by changing our use of terms slightly. To state my proposal using the labels that Rudolf Carnap proposed, can the concept *rule of the second subclass* serve as a precise explicatum for the vague explicandum *rule of style?* It seems to me that it can, and, if so, then we can divide the province of grammar from the province of style in this neat way: grammar comprehends the rules of language and of speech that are easy to formulate, and those hard rules that belong to the first subclass; style comprehends the hard rules belonging to the second subclass. Poetics therefore falls into a linguistic and a stylistic component: for example, in metrics, a part of poetics, the linguistic component includes the rule (hypothetical imperative) that, for English verse, sets up iambic pentameter as a type; the rule enjoining moderation in substitution belongs to stylistics.

Finally, we can say that stylistics belongs to art. Ernst Cassirer is

right in contending that language and art are two distinguishable symbolic forms, distinguishable even though each is involved with the other.

II. LAWS VERSUS RULES

Let us now compare rules with laws. Peirce tries to assimilate them,
but there are fundamental differences. It would take us too far into the
realm of metaphysics—into what he calls realism; into his animistic, per-
sonifying conception that nature tries to conform to laws—if we were
to examine his claim that conformity of instances to law is essentially
like what Kant calls acting out of respect for a law. The following
argument enumerates, rather than elaborates, points of difference, and
therefore is conditional, not absolute. The essential difference is that
which exists between fact and value. Peirce endeavors to disunite the category of sheer fact by splitting it into varieties of two of his categories,
namely, Brute Fact (Secondness) and Law (Thirdness). My reply to
him is an ad hominem argument, not based on personalities, but based
on logical consistency: namely, Peirce reintroduces the familiar category of fact under the label of truth, without realizing what he is doing.
I mean *truth* in the sense subsequently termed the semantic conception
of truth, such that for any assertion p there is a necessarily equivalent
assertion "It is true that p." No doubt this conception of truth is fal-
lible, as is every conception, including Peirce's categories; therefore,
fallibility does not suffice to reduce a conception (*fact* is the conception
of present concern) to Peirce's categories. Peirce makes a distinction
between fact and truth that has some basis in ordinary use, but not
enough to warrant the identification of fact thus distinguished from
truth with Brute Fact, in his sense of Secondness. Peirce's insistence on
this distinction, however, is also insufficient.

Discussion of fact is complicated by actuality. This complication be-
deviled the Positivists' conception of laws as descriptions. When it was
said that if the laws of man or of God were broken, so much the worse
for the breakers, but if the putative laws of nature were broken, so
much the worse for those laws, it was meant that for laws of nature,
unlike laws of man and of God, to be broken and to be invalidated
are the same thing. The difficulties in moving from this formulation
to the formula that laws of nature are descriptions arose because
description was needlessly taken to mean *description of actualities*, thus
omitting altogether Peirce's element of *would-be* (Chisholm's *contrary-
to-fact*; Goodman's *counterfactuality*). Peirce made the mistake of moving from recognition of *would-be*—recognition that, as he put it, general
laws are really operative in nature—to an assimilation of this variety of

Thirdness to the variety known as norms or values. This mistake of confounding formal identity with material identity is discussed in detail in Part Three below. At present, it is my concern to point out that Peirce, in his 1898 "Lectures on Vitally Important Topics" (*Collected Papers* 1.616–77), accords due recognition to those properties of norms which distinguish them from laws of nature. There results a hard, sharp dualism which—this is the inconsistency I spoke of—is glaringly at odds with synechism and is of the sort which, when readers called such anti-synechistic dualisms to Peirce's attention, he defended with the airy observation that "the question cannot be decided in that way" (*CP* 2.116; see below p. 196).

Both rules of language and rules of esthetics are, therefore, subsumed under norms, and as such they can be distinguished from laws of nature. The distinction is probably partial rather than total; that is, there will be some properties that norms and natural laws have in common, and others that norms have but that natural laws do not, or vice versa. We may as well follow the convenient Aristotelian terminology and say that norms and natural laws are two species of one genus. The inconsistency of Peirce that concerns us is that he sometimes neglects—virtually denies—the specific differences, while at other times recognizes them. This paper assumes without further discussion that they must be recognized.

The circumstance that the same word, law, is used both normatively and factually—normatively of the laws of men and of God or the gods, factually of the laws of nature—is easily explained historically. The normative conception came first and the factual conception evolved from it. The transition must have been mediated by ambiguity in the word *why*. Why do people pay taxes? Because that's the law of the land. Why do people rest one day in seven? Because it was decreed in the Decalogue. Why does water freeze when it gets cold? Because Nature has made it so. Very likely, the personification of nature contributed to the mediation. The change of meaning, described in current linguistic terms, would be a metonymy. It is a law of nature—of human nature—that, by and large, laws of men and laws of God (or of the gods) are followed. (There are large exceptions: one class of exceptions is often labeled *dead letter;* another is the class involved in the witticism about rule-breaking described in Part One above, as interpreted in the second way.)

The transition from normative to descriptive law occurred in ancient Greece. The transition is almost complete in Aristotle, but he retains one major vestige, namely, the doctrine that laws of nature hold always *or for the most part;* in other words, that there are genuine exceptions to laws of nature. For Stoicism, on the other hand, as Peirce rightly says, laws have no exceptions. This same doctrine accorded with the Judeo-Christian belief in God's infinity and omnipotence. But on Aristotle's view, unnatural things (things contrary to nature) happen, though not often and not for long.

Nature, personified as female, is not completely the mistress of the matter which she rules. The interesting steps that lead to Aristotle's view may be retraced briefly. Cornford (*From Religion to Philosophy*) emphasizes the morality which pervades the archaic Greek view of nature. Destiny and Fate coincide with Right. Anaximander says that things perish because they are unjust to other things; Heraclitus (fragment 62 Bywater = 80 Diels-Kranz) says, contradicting this, that the universal strife is not universal injustice but universal justice. And why does the sun follow its regular course? Because if it strayed, it would be found and punished by the Erinyes (fragment 29 Bywater = 94 Diels-Kranz). In short, there is a Lawgiver who imposes his law; this echoes the phrase of A. N. Whitehead (*Adventures of Ideas* §§7.5ff.), who has especially Plato's *Timaeus* 41ff. in mind.

These doctrines make it seem that things are a certain way because some personal, divine power has decreed them to be so; but this is only one side of the Greeks' view. From the beginning, their view had an opposite side which retracted almost completely the first side. The first side tends to say, That is right which is decreed by the divine powers; the other side says, rather, That which is right is decreed by the divine powers. The way in which the Greeks accomplished this contradiction is by placing in the background, behind the personal gods in the foreground, impersonal divine powers such as the Lots (Moirai), to which the personal gods are subject. The two-sidedness already evident in Homer is clearly identified by Albin Lesky's *History of Greek Literature* (1966, pp. 65–66). How will the Trojan War turn out? Sometimes Zeus decrees his will, but sometimes he lifts his scales to find which one comes down. In the former case, he determines events in the sense that he decides the outcome; in the latter, he determines them in the sense that he learns, finds out. As a last attempt to evade the issue, the Greek mind claims that you can act against the Lots, but that the Lots will get even with you for it (Lesky 1966:66; Cornford 12 and n. 3, on *Iliad* 16.433). It is a further step—and a Stoic one—to replace the Lots, which one can disobey, though with penalty, by the Fates, which lead the willing and drag the unwilling (Seneca *Ad Lucilium* 107).

Something should be said about the neutralization, the desacralization, the secularization of the concept of rule. 'Law' (*nomos, lex*) was desacralized earlier, and then, centuries later, 'rule' (*regula*) followed suit. But the route by which this took place was different for the two concepts. With rule, as is obvious, for example, in Chomsky (a major recent agent in the conceptual change), the change is mediated by the distinction (Kant *Metaphysical Foundations of Ethics* §2) between categorical and hypothetical imperatives. A rule entails a command, expressed by an imperative. Unless we are instructed to the contrary, we are to construe a rule as a categorical imperative. What Chomsky has done, in effect, without instructing us, is to call any imperative a rule; and in fact he only applies the term *rule* to hypothetical, not at all to categorical, imperatives.

III. RULES, LAWS, AND THIRDNESS

Having considered rules of language and of art, and having pointed out the distinction between rules and laws, we are ready to look at Peirce and ask what he can contribute to the discussion. The answer that I find myself forced to give is "Not much." The observations that any adequate treatment of rules and of laws must include are compatible with, but not entailed by, Peirce's system. It follows, as a corollary, that his system has no heuristic power in leading us to insights about rules of language.

These are adverse, even harsh, contentions, but I believe with Peirce that truth has nothing to do with being agreeable to reason, and, moreover, I believe that I can locate within Peirce's system the reason for this impotence. I speak of the reason, in the singular, because there is only one, although it can be stated in several ways. The most startling way, perhaps, is: idealism; a more analytical way is: a failure to do justice to the difference between formal identity and material identity.

Peirce drew the distinction between the two clearly enough, but he failed to respect it. Indeed, he deluded himself that he was empirically sensitive and had taken due precautions against such hybris. But he slipped, and he slipped by believing in something that was agreeable to reason, namely, in continuity (mediation). He rejected any deductivism—any claim to deduce the singularities of the world from its generalities, such as Hegel's notorious youthful indiscretion of coming down against the possibility of an eighth planet—as breathing the spirit of the seminary rather than of the laboratory. But he thought he saw a way lying between aprioristic deductivism and utterly passive empiricistic inductivism; namely, a logic of inquiry, a heuristic, which would ask though it would not answer; would suggest though it would not insist. His belief in the reality of Thirdness led him to think in such a way; it led him to slip.

I make a double claim: not only did Peirce slip; but the slip is one that he would at least sometimes acknowledge as a slip.

It is easy to charge that Peirce is a "triadomaniac." Evidently Peirce has been chaffed about this, and is sensitive to the charge. What concerns us here is not his defense, but his exceptions, that is, the cases where he rejects a triadic treatment, and more particularly, the places where he rejects a mediating, synechistic treatment.

The most conspicuous exception is his mind-matter dualism. Peirce admits that at first glance mind appears to be distinct from matter, but he answers monistically that they are but two sides of one fact. (He gives the same answer to his dualism of inner and outer.) This answer seems triadic, because the thing of which mind and matter are two sides mediates, at it were, between them. But this answer backfires; neither side of x is closer to x than it is to the other side, so that the would-be mediation is unsuccessful; the third thing, which it sets up in order to unite the first two, is merely claimed to unite them. Showing that it is like the one in one respect and like the other in another does not necessarily show that it unites them. There are places where Peirce tries a genuine mediation (e.g., *CP* 4.87), but this attempt to establish that the difference between mind and matter is one of degree only is forced to the two concessions that (1) "the difference . . . is certainly very, very great" and (2) there is a "remarkable absence of intermediate phenomena," concessions which make the attempt silly.

On occasion, as in *CP* 2.116 (cf. 2.87), Peirce says that "one might antecendently expect that the cenopythagorean categories [i.e., Firstness, Secondness, Thirdness] would require three modes of being. But . . . the question cannot be decided in that way. Besides, it would be illogical to rely upon the categories to decide so fundamental a question." So, purporting "to make an entirely fresh investigation," he arrives in forty lines at the conclusion that there are three modes of being.

The dualism that this paper has focused on is the dualism between law and rule, between fact and value. Can Peirce's system do justice to this? In a superficial sense, yes. Peirce himself emphasizes the dualism in the 1898 "Lectures on Vitally Important Topics" (*CP* 1.616–77). But the question immediately arises, Was he true to himself in doing so? Isn't the position of these lectures at odds with other, and perhaps deeper, principles of his? He connects this dualism with three others: that between theory and practice, that between reason and instinct, and that between the time being and the long run; and, of course, each of these connections is a mediation in some sense, so that each of the dualisms is mediated—subordinated to Thirdness. But Peirce is less sensitive to the equally cogent consideration that the Thirdness in question is simply the general truth that there are radical, ineluctable dualisms, some of which lead to the others.

It is not hard to find a category for ineluctable dualisms: each member of a dualism is a Second to the other. It is hard, however, to find a heuristic. Let us return to the original question. What the linguist primarily wants from Peirce is a heuristic—a system, or a framework—that will help to discover significant facts, or to describe them. In the present instance, Peirce's system would justify itself if it directed the linguist's attention more forcefully than other writers do to the fact-value (or law-rule) distinction, or if it offered the linguist a more lucid exposition of the distinction. But the system does not do either of these things; and, moreover, its exposition, in spite of setting up a dualism at odds with his synechism, does not compensate for the inconsistency by being notably apt. The values Peirce deals with are ethical and logical values, and his purview is limited to these by the restriction to deliberate self-controlled conduct. Behavior that is unconscious, and largely innate, thus falls outside the scope of normative science.

It might not be hard to emend his system so as to abolish the restriction and thus enlarge the scope, but that would hardly support claims of adequacy and fruitfulness.

The question before us is whether Peirce's system helps us to characterize linguistic signs. A negative answer is harder to prove than a positive one, because proof of the positive need only prove that there is a place in his system which is helpful, whereas proof of the negative must prove that there is no place at all in his system which is helpful. The preceding argument may prove that the two places in Peirce's system, his treatment of norms and his treatment of laws, are not helpful in treating linguistic rules, but this obviously does not prove that *no* places are helpful.

In this paper, however, I am offering the difference between laws and norms not as a sample but as an example. I cite it not as evidence for an induction, but in the same way a diagram is employed in geometry. And just as the diagram by itself is not sufficient, so an example needs to be accompanied by an explanation of what the example exemplifies.

Briefly, the reason why Peirce does not adequately distinguish rules from laws is that he treats both of them as Thirdnesses. If we could say that rules = Thirdness and laws = Thirdness, his identification would be valid. But we could only make that statement if we forget, as Peirce tends to, a distinction that he draws between formal and material categories. In the case before us, there is formal but not material categorial identity between rules and laws. Thirdness itself is only a formal category.

Described in Peirce's own terms, Peirce's mistake is to move from formal to material categorial identity. The temperamental penchant that leads him to this mistake is, to give it his name for it, idealism. The reason why we can describe the mistake in his terms is that he was not always subject to it; he occasionally acknowledged that his usual idealism was a mistake.

Peirce even reveals the history of the mistake. In the 1860s, when he addressed himself to the topic of categories, he spent two or three years working at the problem, his work taking the external form of a critical study of Kant. He came to think (1) that there are two kinds of categories: formal and material; (2) that the formal categories are also aptly characterized as universal, and the material as particular; (3) that he could make no headway in dealing with the material, particular categories, but succeeded in establishing that there are three formal, universal categories; and (4) that his three formal categories—eventually labeled Firstness, Secondness, and Thirdness—substantially agree with Hegel's three *Hauptstufen der Gedenkens* (*Enzyklopädie* §83): *Sein, Wesen,* and *Begriff.* "On account of their connection with numbers," Peirce had by 1902 (*CP* 2.87) come to call his categories Ceno- or Kaino-Pythagorean, alluding (*CP* 1.521, of 1903) to Aristotle's remark at the beginning of his *De caelo* about Pythagorean Three. "They agree substantially," he says in the former place, "with Hegel's three moments." (Hegel does not use the term *moments* for his three *Hauptstufen;* the three moments of §79 are something quite different.) (The above is a synthesis based on §§1.284, 288, 300, 561; 4.3; 5.37–40, 43; and the passages already cited.)

It is important to note that while Peirce is ready to agree that there are material categories in addition to the formal ones, his lack of headway with them (*CP* 1.284, 525; 5.38) makes him neglect them. His semiotic, in particular, is developed deductively, in the main (as he acknowledges, in a limited way, in a letter of 1909[4]), from universal categories alone. Therefore, it, too, is merely formal and lacks content or substance. I imagine that if we were to ask Peirce why he is not disturbed by this limitation, he would give a twofold answer: (1) the formal categories are more important (*CP* 1.288), and (2) semiosis not only falls under one of them, Thirdness, but almost *is* that one.

Indeed, the word *almost* is an afterthought. His first published statement of the categories (1867) identified Thirdness and Semiosis outright, by calling his third category *representation;* when he came to see the inadequacy of that conception (two essays of three decades later, CP 1.564–65 and 4.3), he tried to repair it by admitting that representation (alias representability, intelligibility, reasonableness, destiny, regularity, law; see Note 1) is only one of two varieties of Thirdness, the other being growth (alias continuous growth, life, continuity). (In "The True Nature of Peirce's Evolutionism," p. 321, I argue against admitting disjunctive characterizations.[5])

The formal, deductive origin of Peirce's semiotics is unable to guarantee its fruitfulness. There are taxonomies that prove fruitful; in such cases, people are apt to say that they are more than mere taxonomies. The periodic table of the elements is a fine example. Employed heuristically, it suggested the hypothesis that the apparent gaps were not real gaps; in other words, that empty cells in the matrix of chemical elements represented ignorance, and that missing elements could be discovered. (Both Mendeleev and Newlands predicted gallium in 1871, and Boisbaudran discovered it in 1878.) One wants to employ Peirce's classifications of signs similarly, but efforts to do so have not proved fruitful. This paper has exposed a complementary deficiency. Instead of showing that a possibility presented by Peirce's taxonomy remains empty, it shows that a possibility not presented by Peirce's taxonomy is full, is actual. One might think of developing Peirce's semiotics so that places appeared to accommodate hitherto neglected phenomena, but what concepts would generate these places? Where would they come from? They cannot escape the dilemma of being either internal or external to the system as it stood before. If they are internal, then their previous apparent absence was a mere defect in the exposition of the system, not in the system itself; if they are external, then their introduction requires us to extend the system. In either case, the point remains that the system was not heuristically effective.

What does it mean to say that concepts are internal to the system? All concepts are internal to every system, in the respect that they may be introduced by the law of excluded middle. For instance, we could introduce the previously absent concept of stylistic rule at the point of legisigns by saying that every legisign is either a stylistic rule or not a stylistic rule. This would treat the legisign as a genus with two species. But the question raised by Aristotle in his discussions of taxonomy remains pertinent: is the specific difference that divides the genus into species internal to the genus? In the present example, we would have to answer no, or at least say that it has not been shown to be relevant. Internality on the basis of excluded middle is trivial, because excluded middle says that every concept is internal to every system. Any stronger claim that the concepts needed to describe linguistic rules are internal to Peirce's semiotic remains quite unsupported.

NOTES

1. Not to mention representation, intelligibility, reasonableness; destiny; growth, life. See below p. 199.

2. It is vague in the ordinary sense in which we speak of a vague boundary, as opposed to a precise one; it may not be vague in Peirce's sense, in which a vague assertion grants license to the hearer, in contrast with a general assertion which reserves license to the speaker. In Peirce's sense, every existentially quantified proposition is vague.

3. *Nicomachean Ethics* 2.6:1107a1; 2.9:1109a24, b19; 4.5:1126b3; 6.1:-1138b29; 6.8:1141b29–1142a31.

4. To Lady V. Welby, 14 March 1909; complete letter in C. Lieb (ed.), *Charles S. Peirce's Letters to Lady Welby* (New Haven: Whittock, 1953), 34–40. This passage (Lieb, p. 36) is also quoted in C. K. Ogden and I. A. Richards, *The Meaning of Meaning*, 5th ed. (New York: Harcourt Brace, 1938), 288. Peirce happens to make his remark in connection with his concept of interpretant, but it applies just as aptly to all of his semiotic concepts.

5. In E. C. Moore and R. S. Robin (eds.), *Studies in the Philosophy of Charles Sanders Peirce, Second Series* (Amherst: University of Massachusetts Press, 1964), 304–22.

The Nonverbal Inlay in Linguistic Communication

JOHN N. DEELY
with tables based on drawings by Brooke Williams

> In brief, each kind of animal has at
> its command a repertoire of signs
> that forms a system unique to it or is,
> in biological parlance, species-specific.
> Language is a species-specific trait
> of man; it is therefore counter-
> productive and misleading to ascribe
> language to any other animal, except
> perhaps, metaphorically.
> —Thomas A. Sebeok (1978:21)

The emergence of semiotics as the architectonic of communications study as such sheds new light on and, to some extent, calls for a re-conceptualization of linguistics in the traditional, scientific sense. Of course, the difficulty of defining "language" in a satisfactory way is celebrated, and is as much as any single factor responsible for the currently faddish but philosophically unsophisticated claims of animal experimenters to have taught "language" to chimpanzees, etc. I would agree simply with Professor Sebeok in regarding this current fad as "counterproductive and misleading"; and I would further argue that these widely heralded cases of language usage by carefully cued chimps are each one instances of the "clever Hans fallacy," that is, the fallacy of researchers finding in the animals' behavior what they themselves have put there by various muscular or behavioral cues (cf. Sebeok 1979).

But that would form the subject of a paper in its own right. Here I have a related but different objective, namely, to contribute to a clarification of the relationship between linguistics and semiotics by outlining a framework or model wherein the *function* of language in relation to behavior and social structure appears in its proper light. In other words, I want to suggest that the impossibility so far of achieving a satisfactory definition of "what language is" may be the result of a failure to appreciate the *proper functional status* of language in the context of social behavior; and that the rise of semiotics provides an opportunity to reconceptualize our understanding of language in a framework that makes this proper functional status for the first time generally apparent and directly accessible.

One of the first and broadest divisions of semiotics is into anthroposemiotics, or sign-systems as they function in a uniquely human context, and zoosemiotics, or sign-systems common to human and nonhuman animals. I think that language, properly conceived, is the key to rightly understanding the rationale of this contrast. To show my reason for thinking this, I want to introduce two distinctions. First, I want to distinguish zoosemiotic sign systems against the linguistic system that is species specific and unique to man. Then I want to set *both* of these systems in contrast with what I am going to call *post-linguistic* structures or systems,[1] by which I mean systems that come into existence on the basis of language and can only be understood in what is proper to them on that basis, but are not themselves linguistic; and once they have come into existence, they redescend, so to say, into the purely perceptual to become assimilated in a behavioral way to the society of non-linguistic animals. Thus, post-linguistic systems are normally simultaneous with language, and even, from the point of view of the individual language-learner, in certain ways *precede* 'language'; but they always depend upon language for their *proper* existence, which transcends the modalities of simple perception and zoosemiotic signalling. Post-linguistic structures exist beside, alongside, aside from, language— yet are based on and derivative from it. And they *react* upon language, by influencing the semiotic exchanges that transpire through language (just as sensation does in pre-linguistic ways). Thus we find in linguistic behavior, as it were, a *twofold non-verbal inlay* embedded in and influencing semiotic exchange, one from the pre-linguistic order of perception, and one from the *users themselves* of language, as they are products of and have been shaped—even in their eventual perceiving —by a world of *post-linguistic experience*.

Here, the expression, "post-linguistic," must not be separated from the notion of "experience." I want to say that "experience" can be *either* pre-linguistic or *both* pre- *and* post-linguistic (though not post-linguistic without being also pre-linguistic), and that this is the proper contrast between zoosemiotics and anthroposemiotics taken in their fullest amplitude.

To see what is involved in these distinctions, let me develop the discussion around a sequence of diagrams or tables, which illustrate the double dichotomy between language and pre-linguistic structures of experience, on the one hand, and language and post-linguistic structures of experience on the other hand.

Consider first of all pre-linguistic experience (where the first non-verbal inlay in linguistic communication comes from), in a purely zoo-semiotic sense. For ease of imagination, I am going to focus only on the peculiarly anthropoid structure of experience as it began to emerge, roughly from the time of the Australopithecines; because, of course, to take into account insect and other animal forms far removed from the human, a great many conceptual modifications irrelevant to our present purpose would have to be introduced into the scheme. I think we would not be far wrong in envisioning an experience structure for anthropoids somewhat along the following lines (Table 1):

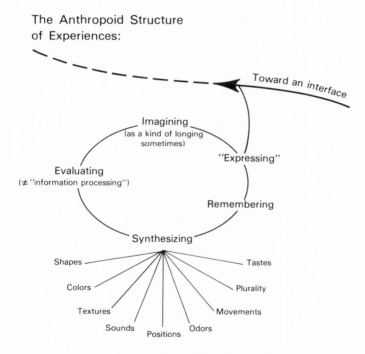

The Anthropoid Structure
of Experiences:

Toward an interface

Imagining
(as a kind of longing
sometimes)

"Expressing"

Evaluating
(≠ "information processing")

Remembering

Synthesizing

Shapes — Tastes

Colors — Plurality

Textures — Movements

Sounds   Odors
Positions

The initial and sustained immediate level of cognitive contact between organism and extra-organismic world is through the so-called "external senses," whence we encounter colors, shapes, tastes, textures, odors. But connected with these, inseparably, and with no temporal gap, is a great deal else besides: to see colors *is* to see shapes, places, a plurality of things—so, the whole series of notions in Table 1 below the term "synthesizing" (which takes place within the organism experiencing) comprises the first data of experience out of which, eventually, language itself (the *interface*, let us say, between pre- and post-linguistic structures of experience) will arise.

The situation here bears looking at more closely (Table 2):

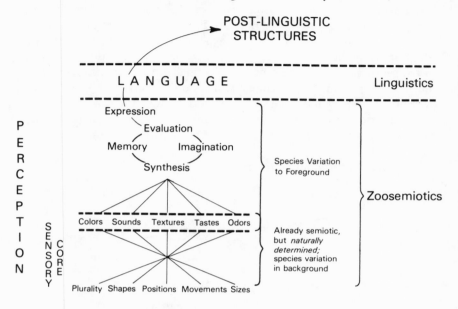

In this Table, we have the same picture of anthropoid experience, but broken down more clearly into its structural components. Note particularly the relation between the whole of perception and its immediate sensory core. Precisely here semiotic analysis enables us to give, for the first time, a satisfactory resolution to the controversy over "sense data," as that controversy traces back in empiricist philosophies from present-day positivism to its beginnings in John Locke with his "simple ideas" of sense. The empiricist tradition has always had a problem figuring out why the mind structures sensory objects in the ways that it does. The origin of this difficulty was twofold. First, the direct objects of each external sense—colors, sounds, textures, tastes, and odors —were considered to be wholly effects within the mind itself, perhaps *caused* by external objects, but certainly not properties of those external things as such. This was in contrast to an older, less critical "realist" tradition which simply considered color to *be* in the grass, etc.

What eluded our early modern forebears, as their successors, was yet a third possibility for these initial data of sense: they could be regarded as neither intrinsic properties of physical things nor mere modifications of our subjective faculties, but precisely as properties exhibiting how things are in their action here and now on an organism possessed of this determinate range of sensitivities. This third alternative would account for the experimentally demonstrated relativity of sensory qualities without making of them mere constructs of subjectivity—while preserving, that is to say, their status as here and now revelatory of "the way things are" so far as involves the experiencing organism. The initial contact between cognizing organism and environment, on this view, is indistinctly subjective and objective. The world appears thus (e.g., colored) only to a subject, but it really *is* that way *given that totality of conditions.*

Equally serious was the characteristic modern failure to see that the initial sensory data are not "atomic" in character, but strictly semiotic. Thus, the initial synthesis of sensations made by the mind is not arbitrary or habit-controlled, as the early moderns, notably Hume, opined, but *naturally determined* by semiotic means. Since a sign is anything functioning to bring something other than itself into an organism's awareness, and since colors, sounds, textures, etc., immediately bring along with themselves an awareness of plurality, positions, shapes, movements, and so on, one has only to regard sensation semiotically in order to realize that we are already given within it an outline of objective structure that is relative and changing, true, but naturally determined nevertheless. "Sense data," in other words, already comprise an objective structure (not atomic elements logically discrete but habitually combined) that is the same, in the above sense of naturally determined, for all organisms. Species variation, consequently—that is, subjective differences of sensory range and variety—are strictly background phenomena at the level of the sensory core; and that is why biological mechanisms of camouflage (such as protective coloration) and deception, though principally dependent on the "qualitative" appearances or "properties" of bodies, are so widespread and consistently useful in nature across species lines.[2] Species variation comes to the fore only in the interpretation of the "common" data and in the uses that they are put to in predation and social exchange.

Now, language, in the sense that linguistics studies it, and as it constitutes a species-specific system, is something that emerges, so to speak, "on top" of this common structure of anthropoid experience. To understand it in relation to that experience sufficient for present purposes, it is enough to indicate how the "natural" and the "conventional" relate in the separating off of specifically linguistic from purely behavioral sign systems in anthropoid interaction.[3]

Prior to the advent of cognitive organisms, relations are only physical, that is, obtaining between presently existing entities. Once cognition is introduced, the situation drastically changes. Now the physical relation of A to B (e.g., of clouds to rain, or of smoke to fire, etc.) acquires the possibility of a new, further dimension: A can *represent* B to C, a cognitive organism. What was formerly *only* a physical relation can now become *also* a recognized (a known) relation that makes A, besides being the *cause* of B (or B, besides being the *effect* of A), its *sign*. Nor is this all. Because the relationship as such has its proper being "between" A and B, while it has its reality independent of cognition from the existence of A as, say, cause of B (or from B as effect of A, depending on which relation is considered), it can now exist as "between" A and B in cognition (memory, say) even after A (or B) has gone out of existence. Essence and existence, in the case of relation, do not go together in a way that ties relation to a unique subjective ground. Thus the same relation existing independently of cognition can also exist dependently upon cognition, and can continue to exist in cognition after its physical ground no longer exists! Moreover, relations existing first in cognition can subsequently be introduced into the physical order by bringing about the proper conditions within that order; and relations can be established in cognition that can have no counterpart in the physical world, just as there are physical relations that have not yet or will not ever enter into the cognition of some organism.

Physical relations are the paradigm case of "natural" relations, but cognitive relations too are forms of "nature," and many such are exhibited in the instinctive behavior of animal species. The important thing for semiotics is simply that these two orders of relations are *functionally equivalent in perception* wherever it is a question of inter- or intra-specific interaction between individual organisms or between organisms and relevant features of the *Umwelt*. Comparatively "real" and "unreal" from the standpoint of what exists independently of cognitive activity as such, physical and cognition-dependent relations are strictly on a par from the standpoint of what works within experience to achieve some determinate end. Both types of relation are essential to the constitution of experience, as is clear from the above remarks; but within experience, it is not essential that the two be explicitly distinguished according to type, and indeed it is not always possible to separate out in experience what is the contribution of the subject and what is the contribution of the object to the experimental structure of a given interaction situation.

In philosophical tradition, one little-realized way of grounding the putative distinction between understanding and perception ("intellect" and "sense") was precisely in terms of relation: perception reveals objects as they are only relative to the dispositions, needs, and desires of the organism perceiving, whereas understanding reveals in these same objects the further dimension of existence in their own right independent of relations to the knower.[4]

It is this way of interpreting the difference between "sense" and "intellect," it seems to me, that is decisive for semiotics.[5] For within the interweave or mix in experience of cognition-dependent and cognition-independent relations, *only those organisms possessing the capacity to understand in its distinction from the capacities to sense and perceive, in the way just described, will ever be able even on occasion to discriminate between real and unreal elements in semiosis*, that is, in the process of communication through signs. Stipulation, as a distinctive semiotic process, presupposes exactly this ability; and it is *only* in relation to stipulative decisions and their consequences that language can be said to be "conventional." But stipulations, when successful, pass into customs, and customs into nature. Thus, sign-systems arise out of nature in anthropoid experience, become partially "conventionalized" in the sphere of human understanding, and pass back again through customs into continuity with the natural world as it is experienced perceptually by human and nonhuman animals alike (Deely 1978:7ff.). "Language," in short, in the sense that is species-specific to *homo sapiens*, is nothing else than the "unreal" component of semiosis explicitly segregated and seized upon in its unique signifying potential by the understanding in its distinction from perception and sense. As a result of the intervention of language, those organisms capable of seizing upon the difference between the "real" and the "unreal" elements of experience soon find themselves in an entirely different world. In prelinguistic experience, relations are not distinguished from the *objects related*. With language, it becomes possible to separate the two. The consequences of this simple feat are enormous, and without end—literally, for it is this that makes human experience an "open-ended" affair as a matter of principle (Table 3):

In this diagram, which looks very complicated at first glance, notice to begin with the same basic structure of anthropoid experiences—the zoosemiotic structure that is common to man and the higher anthropoids—that we examined in Table 2, retained in the lower half of the diagram. But in man, the processes eventuating that structure go up one step—but what a step!—higher. Passing through the layer of language, the social structures of anthropoid life "come out on the other side," so to speak, in the form of such things as military establishments, civil governments, religious traditions—things which are not linguistic, are much more than the linguistic system, but which *couldn't come into being apart from language*, enabling us as it does to systematically differentiate between relations (as offices and social roles, for example) and the things here and now related (the individuals concretely playing those roles in any given case). So, this diagram looks complicated, but when examined carefully, it appears that the upper portion is struc-

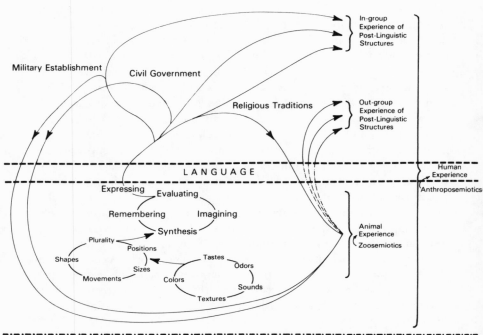

tured representatively by only three arrows (though indefinitely more, of course, could be added) each of which splits into two.

Follow, to begin with, the left-most arrow. As it splits toward the right, it leads toward a military establishment as it is experienced by linguistic animals belonging to the society of which that establishment is an expression. That same establishment, of course, has an impact within the experience of any non-linguistic animals having commerce with the society, and elements of it will be perceived and assimilated by semiotic processes, but now only insofar as these elements of the military establishment have "gone below" the linguistic layer. This is indicated by the left-most split of the leftward arrow, which leads back toward the sphere of simple perception and pre-linguistic experience. The domesticated dog, for example, will well perceive a relative social importance of individuals as they affect his own well-being; but without language,

he will never perceive the four stars of the general, the bars of the lieu-
tenant, or the stripes of the sergeant for what they are as properly *military* insignia. Post-linguistic structures, in what is proper to them, are
forever hidden from the standpoint of pure perception and pre-linguistic experience.

Thus we have animal experience in the sense of zoosemiotics below
the broken lines of language, and, both above and below the lines, and
indeed "centered" by them, human experience which, for the reasons
given, includes what the animals have, plus the post-linguistic institutions or structures which exist properly consequent upon language and
owing to it. It is thus that human experience is much broader than that
of even the highest of animal species in the total biological community
without "understanding."[6] Post-linguistic structures exist *properly above*
the linguistic interface; but they *also* exist *in some way other than what
is proper to them assimilated and accounted for* in animal experience
below that interface, and, as they are encountered perceptually, we
must further distinguish the sense in which they are encountered by
non-linguistic anthropoids from the sense in which they are encountered
by post-linguistically formed but alien organisms ("outgroups": the
broken arrows to the right of the diagram leading back up through the
interface).

In the taking account of things in experience by animals, one way
of describing what results from post-linguistic structures would be as
two levels of natural systems—a primary (or infralinguistic) level and
a secondary (or supralinguistic) level (Table 4).

If we adopt in imagination the point of view of an alien—an alien
in the sense of someone from outside the given culture, or even from
another planetary system—observing for the first time life in a given
human society, what would appear? A series of regularities, or "natural
systems," which, upon examination, would appear in one sense primarily as objects or patterns of perception, but in another sense, as
objects of understanding, as derivative from the unique indifference of
language to "reality" as perception alone reveals and grasps it. The
so-called "primary" natural systems comprise real (physical, i.e., cognition-independent) relations of the human organisms to one another and
to their *Umwelt*. Further observation would reveal, however, within
this primary network of perceptually accessible interactions, and *carried
by them* (*conflated* with them in social life), a secondary network of
(comparatively) unreal relations conveying the historical experience of
the group as something transcendent, not to individual and social reality,
but to the perceptually accessible elements as such expressing the "primary" systems. The so-called "primary," or perceptually available sys-

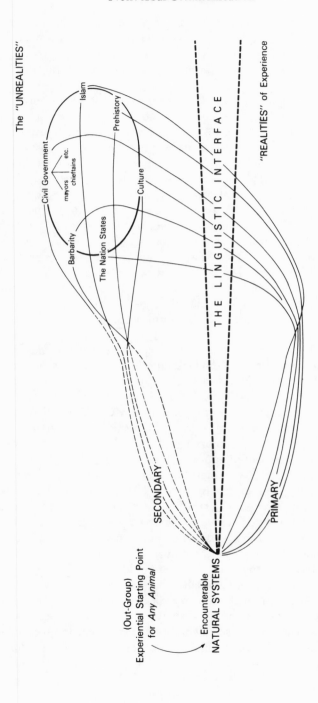

tems, thus, "feed into" the linguistic interface in and through social interaction; but what "comes out on the other side," so to speak, is not language, but society enculturated, society as a potential *cultural* system.[7]

The main point here is that the system of language, to be best understood, should not be conceptualized as a whole unto itself, but *as an interface*, a perceptually diaphanous network of unreal relations intervening as such between the specifically human language users and the layered manifolds of experience they seek to understand. It is in such a light, I conclude by suggesting, that the relation of linguistics to semiotics might well be further examined.

NOTES

1. So far as I have been able to determine, this distinction I am proposing between linguistic and post-linguistic systems does not appear anywhere in previous semiotic literature. This strikes me as somewhat improbable, so I should not be surprised to later learn that it does have a counterpart in some previous book or essay as yet unknown to me. Nevertheless, I must report that the only distinction found so far even analogous to the one I am proposing is Jurij M. Lotman's distinction between primary and secondary modeling systems, first called to my attention by Donna Jean Umiker-Sebeok in conversations preparatory to this paper: see Daniel P. Lucid (1977:7ff.), and J. Lotman (1977a:95–98; 1977b: *passim*); and that this distinction as it is employed in Soviet semiotics, though unquestionably related to the distinction being proposed here, is not the same distinction, and indeed is not yet clear in its foundation. Lengthy discussions with experts versed in the Soviet literature, notably Dr. David Danow of the University of South Carolina, served only to confirm the ambiguity as to the grounding of Lotman's usage. My choice of terminology for expressing the proposed distinction was a difficult one. "Paralinguistic" would have been my preferred term for what I am here calling "post-linguistic," but previous appropriation of this term by linguists (see Sebeok, Hayes, and Bateson 1964; Crystal 1974) made this choice likely to create endless and needless misunderstandings. The final choice of "post-linguistic" was influenced more than anything else by Charles Morris' discussion of what he called "post-language symbols" (1971:122–25); but whereas Morris is naming a particular group and functioning of signs as such, the structures I am referring to incorporate and generate signs without being in themselves semiotic, even though they owe their origin to semiosis and are normally permeated by semiotic dimensions.

2. Julian Huxley, in his classic study (1942:414), went so far as to say that Cott "has shown that concealing and revealing coloration, when properly investigated, remain the paradigm of adaptive studies, and has thoroughly turned the tables on captious objectors."

3. Elsewhere (Deely, 1978: especially pp. 7ff.), I have dwelt at length on the essential ambiguity of this traditional dichotomy between the "natural" and the "conventional." That account provides the background concepts for most of what follows here.

4. The 'sensory core' we have distinguished within perception (Table 2 above) consists of the impressions produced in the organs of sense by the action here and now of the surrounding environment on the organisms. Never given as such in our experience, which is always of perceptual wholes, pure sensations are known only derivatively and by an analysis which proceeds from the realization that unless there were such first elements or data at the base and core of perception, we would find that all knowing in every respect entails an infinite regress, and so could have no point of origin (cf. Price 1950:3, 7, 149, 155).

Now sensations are always given with and by perceptions, that is to say, within an elaborate and detailed network of objectivity that is the work of memory and imagination as well as of the so-called external senses. Moreover, the perceptual field is not only determined by the individual experiences of an organism, but, even more profoundly, by the anthropoid history of the higher organisms (which alone concern us at present) as it has been built into their genetic constitution over the centuries by the complex processes of 'natural' or evolutionary selection. Thus, a given organism has a 'natural' perception of certain objects as friendly or hostile, alluring or repulsive, prey or predator, etc., and these naturally given determinations of perception—sometimes called "instinct"—precisely consist in the catching of a given element of experience within a net of "unreal" or cognition-dependent relations whereby the perceiver apprehends its objects not principally according to what they are "in themselves," as it were, but rather according to what they are *so far as the perceiving organism is involved*. The same remarks apply to cognition-dependent relations attached to objects not by the a-prioris of organic constitution (the organism's genetic and selective history), but by the simple *learnings about* things built up through experiences the organism undergoes.

Now outside the human species, and indeed often enough inside the human species, this difference between relations obtaining among objects *so far as the actions or behavior of the individual organism is concerned* and relations obtaining among objects prior to *or* independent of the self-interests of the perceiver in the perceived—this is never thematized, never disengaged as such as an explicit component of a categorial scheme. Yet, prior to such a thematization, in all our direct experiences of objects, the objects are given in an apparently unified way which in fact conceals the profound differences between an object as a thing in its own right and an object as an element of experience being accounted for by the perceiver in terms entirely born of its own needs and desires.

Thus, all objects of direct experience, from an independent viewpoint, are known to be an at best imperfectly discriminated amalgam of what is, in terms of cognition-independent being, being and nonbeing, that is, cognition-independent and cognition-dependent interwoven networks of objectified relations.

The discrimination of relation as such, as a mode of being distinct from and superordinate to related subjects, seems to take place only upon a comparative analysis—not always self-conscious and transparent to itself, be it said—which is also able, in principle at least, to further distinguish among relations so discriminated between those whose entire actuality is the work of the perceiving organisms (whether idiosyncratically, by custom, or by social institution) and those which obtain physically as well as through our experience. This relative discrimination of cognition-dependent elements in the objective structures of experience and (in further refinements) beyond the experimentally given—never wholly secure, to be sure, because never exhaustive (caught as we are in time which throws up new structures in direct apperception faster than we can reflexively disengage their pure elements)—is what underlies the possibility of a system of signs containing irreducibly stipulated components demonstrably understood as such by the controlled flexibility human beings display in imaginative discourse and, perhaps especially, fairy tales.

This peculiar capacity for thematizing and critically reassessing under various circumstances the line between reality and unreality, exhibited in the partially controllable indifference of our discourse to what is and what is not the case, is found nowhere else in the animal kingdom, certainly not in the recent "sentences" constructed by our neighbors in evolution, the chimpanzees. It is an activity unique to and in some ways definitive of human understanding. (See Deely 1975; and Notes following.)

5. In 1632, Poinsot, in his *Tractatus de signis* (642a24–29; 301a1–306b45; esp. 304b11–306a5; 747a33–b2), expressly regarded such an approach as an essential propaedeutic to the doctrine of signs. Among contemporary authors, only Jacques Maritain (1957:87–91), a student of Poinsot's thought, has made any development of what is involved here, and that only in the brief passages which I cite:

"The birth of ideas and thus of intellectual life in us seems bound up with the discovery of the signifying value of signs. Animals make use of signs without perceiving the relation of signification. To perceive the relation of signification is to have an *idea* . . . .

"For the first stirring of an idea as distinct from images, the intervention of a sensible sign is necessary. Normally in the development of a child it is necessary that the idea be 'enacted' by the senses and lived through before it is born as an idea; it is necessary that the relationship of signification should first be actively *exercised* in a gesture, a cry, in a sensory sign bound up with the desire that is to be expressed. *Knowing* this relationship of signification will come later, and this will be to have the *idea*, even if it is merely implicit, of that which is signified. Animals and children make use

of this signification; they do not perceive it. When the child begins to perceive it (then he exploits it, he toys with it, even in the absence of the real
need to which it corresponds)—at that moment the idea has emerged."

"The discovery of language, then, coincides with the discovery of the
relation of signification, and this would explain why, as a matter of fact,
the invention of language and the birth of ideas, the first release of the intellect's power, probably took place at the same time.

"It is conceivable, I think, that a genuine language of *natural* sensory
signs may have preceded language strictly so called (made up of conventional sensory signs), and that the latter may have developed out of the
former. The 'miracle' would have happened at the moment when man,
beyond the fact of using natural gestures to express hunger, anger, or fear,
would also have grasped the notion that this gesture was possessed of the
virtue of signifying. By the same stroke a field of infinite possibilities would
have opened. Then, once the relation of signification was discovered, the
process of arbitrarily selecting or inventing other gestures and of using them
as *conventional* signs no doubt developed quite rapidly."

". . . as a philosopher I wish to . . . emphasize that what defines language
is not precisely the use of words, or even of conventional signs; it is the use
of any sign whatsoever *as involving the knowledge or awareness of the relation of signification,* and therefore a potential infinity; it is the use of signs
*in so far as it manifests that the mind has grasped and brought out the rela-
tion of signification.*" (Maritain's italics.)

". . . In any case, the invention of those particular conventional signs
which are words, the creation of a system of signs made up of 'phonemes'
and 'morphemes' was in itself a second 'miracle,' a further discovery of human intelligence, no less characteristic of man, but less essential than, and
by nature not prior to, the discovery of the relation of signification.

"So far we have spoken of genuine language. Let us point out that the
word 'language,' when referring to animals, is equivocal. Animals possess a
variety of means of communication but no genuine language. I have observed that animals use signs. But, as I also pointed out, no animal knows the
relation of signification or uses signs as involving and manifesting an awareness of this relation.

"The full import of this is best realized in connection with the use of
conventional signs by animals"—e.g., in the case of bees (von Frisch 1950),
or the more indirect but no less intriguing case of the balloon flies (Kessel 1955).

Non-linguistic animals "use signs—and they do not know that there are
signs."

The prospects of such an analysis suggest that the famous "deuxième
article" of the *Statuts* of the Société de Linguistique de Paris, approved in
March of 1866 (*Mémoires* . . . , 1868:3: "La Société n'admet aucune communication concernant . . . l'origine du langage . . . ."), may be principally

an admission of the radical inadequacy of presemiotic approaches to the semiotic phenomenon *par excellence*, human discourse.

6. If one considers the difference between the post-linguistic and the pre-linguistic systems, and the fact that the post-linguistic structures, when they acquire a semiotic dimension, as they invariably do (if indeed they do not have it from the outset), can be understood in the way that is essential to them *as* post-linguistic *only by linguistic animals*, then it is also clear that as they redescend below the linguistic interface, as they are experienced by the non-linguistic animals, signs designating them function in a completely different way. The post-linguistic meaning never survives as common to the two levels. The *materially same* sign designating a post-linguistic structure in those of its elements that are accessible in pure perception pre-linguistically is *formally diverse* from its designating what is actually proper to those elements *as* post-linguistic.

Take the case of civil government. Consider the notion of a president—the President of this country. If I were the Premacks, I would teach my chimpanzee each time, say, Richard Nixon walked into the room, to put on the board plastic symbols indicating "Here comes the President." Now, if I were the Premacks, I would forthwith claim that I had taught Sarah or Washoe or whichever chimp the meaning of the word "president." But the fact of the matter is that the monkey doesn't see a *president*. Indeed, a president, *as such*, never appears *to the eyes*. The monkey doesn't have clue one as to what is referred to by the term "president," as it designates something distinct and distinguishable from the given concrete individual. When the chimp associates the word "president" with Richard M. Nixon, and when a human being says, "Richard M. Nixon was the President of the United States," the materially same sound or symbolic marker for "president" is functioning in a completely different sense, once above the linguistic interface as well as below it, the other time below it only. To stipulate the meaning of a word, to teach it to a chimpanzee by standard associative techniques, and then to assert that the word is functioning in the chimpanzee's sign system in precisely the stipulated sense is a particular version of "clever Hans" that I would call the fallacy of linguistic anthropomorphism.

7. This would suggest that the complete reduction of culture to social system, as characteristic of British anthropology and of American anthropology since the time of Radcliffe-Brown, is an oversimplification. Earlier American anthropology, with its concept of culture system as "superorganic" and wholly transcendent to social system, went too far in assigning autonomy to the cultural vis-à-vis the social. But the opposite view, that culture is nothing but the uniquely complex forms of social organization proper to man, also goes too far, as a result of an inadequate understanding of semiosis as it occurs in specifically human language. It is true that the unreal relational components of human experience only exist through the cognitive functioning of living individuals, and in this sense the cultural system does

have actuality only in and from social interaction. But this "unreal" dimension of experience recognizable as such, and as providing "a substitute for experience which can be passed on [through language] *ad infinitum* in time and space" precisely because it is *cognitively separable* from this or that specific concrete individual or group of individuals with whose activity it is here and now—or was there and then—de facto identified, is in itself something distinct from even though immanent within social interaction and social system, and is the ground of the cumulative transmission of learning that makes human society as enculturated different in kind from the animal societies that cannot jump the links of individuals connecting the generations. This is one of the points of view, I would suggest, that reveals most sharply the revolutionary importance of semiotics for anthropology and for clarifying the foundations of the social sciences generally.

REFERENCES

Crystal, D. 1974. Paralinguistics. In *Current Trends in Linguistics, vol. 12: Linguistics and adjacent arts and sciences*, T. A. Sebeok, ed., 265–95. The Hague: Mouton.

Deely, J. N. 1975. Modern logic, animal psychology, and human discourse. *Revue de l'université d'Ottawa* 45:80–100.

———. 1978. Toward the origin of semiotic. In *Sight, sound, and sense*, T. A. Sebeok, ed., 1–30. Bloomington: Indiana University Press.

Huxley, J. S. 1942. *Evolution: the modern synthesis*. London: George Allen & Unwin.

Kessel, E. L. 1955. The mating activities of balloon flies. *Systematic Zoology* 4:96–104.

Lotman, J. M. 1977a. Primary and secondary communication-modeling systems. In *Soviet semiotics: an anthology*, D. P. Lucid, trans. and ed., 95–98. Baltimore: Johns Hopkins University Press.

———. 1977b. *The structure of the artistic text*, R. Vroon, trans. Ann Arbor: University of Michigan Press.

Lucid, D. P. 1977. Introduction. In *Soviet semiotics: an anthology*, D. P. Lucid, ed., 1–23. Baltimore: Johns Hopkins University Press.

Maritain, J. 1957. Language and the theory of sign. In *Language: an enquiry into its meaning and function*, R. N. Anshen, ed., 86–101. New York: Harper & Brothers.

Mémoires de la Société de Linguistique de Paris 1868, vol. 1. Paris: Librairie A. Franck.

Morris, C. 1971. *Writings on the general theory of signs*. The Hague: Mouton.

Poinsot, J. 1632. Tractatus de signis. In J. Poinsot, *Ars logica*, B. Reiser, ed. Turin: Marietti, 1930.

Price, H. H. 1950. *Perception*. 2d ed. London: Methuen.

Sebeok, T. A. 1978. "Talking" with animals: zoosemiotics explained. *Animals*, December 1978, pp. 20–23, 36.

————. 1979. Looking in the destination for what should have been sought in the source. In *The sign and its masters*, T. A. Sebeok, ed., 85–106. Austin: The University of Texas Press.

Sebeok, T. A.; Hayes, A. S.; and Bateson, M. C., eds. 1964. *Approaches to semiotics.* Transactions of the 1962 Indiana Conference on Paralinguistics and Kinesics. The Hague: Mouton.

von Frisch, K. 1950. *Bees, their vision, chemical senses, and language.* Ithaca, N.Y.: Cornell University Press.

Language and
the Genetic Code

ROBERT B. LEES

Molecular biologists frequently refer to certain features of the cellular nucleus using linguistic terms; they distinguish between familiar physical, chemical, and biological properties on the one hand, and, on the other, linguistic structure or behavior. Some have called attention to similarities between languages and the so-called genetic code. Are these references mere nonce allusions or trivial metaphors, parallel to, for example, the language of flowers?

A few studies have emphasized significant differences between the superficial structure of languages and that of the genetic code. Nevertheless, I shall argue that despite these obvious contrasts, there is after all a deep connection between them—a very abstract and distant connection, the study of which may eventually elucidate fundamental characters not only of our linguistic faculties but even of the mind itself, its origin, and its evolution.

To appreciate the nature of the analogy between language and the genetic code, or more properly, between the mind and the cell, we must extract the relevant details from the better understood of the two, the biological case. I shall begin, therefore, with a whirlwind sketch of the current favorite view of the origin and the evolution of life. I suggest that the mind arose and evolved in parallel fashion, aided by the invention of an internal representation system, language, in much the same way that biological evolution was aided by the invention of the genetic code.

The first significant insight into the nature of life occurred when the Moravian abbot Gregor Mendel, in the 1850s, developed a convincing explanation for certain remarkable cases of inheritance in which the proportion of individuals in a population of progeny bearing a certain trait inherited from their parents is expressible by a fraction with very small integral numerator and denominator. Perhaps Mendel's most noted case is the one involving a crop of field peas, where each plant is a hybrid cross between a purebred yellow parent and a purebred green

218

parent; all these children are yellow, but when they in turn are hy-
bridized to yield a field of grandchildren peas, ¼ of these descendants
are green while ¾ are yellow. Mendel explained the appearance of elementary arithmetic in otherwise quite unintelligent peas by postulating
that individuals do not inherit their color directly; rather, they inherit
abstract "factors" from their parents, one from each. The yellow-pea
factor (Y), he explained, is, moreover, "dominant," and the green-pea
factor (g) is "recessive." Thus, since each hybrid child bears a Y
and a g, it is yellow; and since random matings among gY children must
yield ¼ gg, ¼ gY, ¼ Yg, and ¼ YY grandchildren, only ¼ of the
grandchildren will be green (gg).

This brilliant insight, though simple to us and actually applicable
to only a few cases of inheritance, analyzed biological descent into
deep structures (factors) and surface structures (traits), or in more
modern terms, *genes* and *traits*, the so-called *genotype* and its reflected
phenotype. Mendel's identification of genes (he did not actually use
that term) introduced the possibility of conceiving and representing inheritance in terms of concrete chemical entities in a germ cell, passed
on from generation to generation.

Later, A. R. Wallace and Charles Darwin each painstakingly contributed to the development of the other cornerstone of biology, an
explanation of the evolution of traits; and they did this without benefit
of a viable theory of inheritance, for neither had heard of Mendel's
success. Charles Darwin explained the appearance of new species simply
by noting that (1) if traits are, by and large, inherited by progeny,
(2) if in every generation there are always (for whatever reason) individuals of various types, of greater or lesser degree of diversity, (3)
if some types (for whatever reason) leave behind more progeny than
others, and (4) if environmental conditions affect the reproductive success of a type, then, inevitably, as environmental conditions change slowly
over geologic time, new types will emerge, their concentration in the
population will increase at the expense of other reproductively less successful types, and some types which formerly interbred will no longer
do so and hence will comprise new species. (Incidentally, to the extent
that more complex and less complex types can coexist in slightly different habitats or niches, the more complex types must eventually appear; this, then, solves the puzzle of why evolution has produced increasingly complex organisms, as though it were preprogrammed or
directed by an outside agency.)

Nearly everyone has by now heard of the 1953 discovery by J. D.
Watson and F. H. C. Crick in London of the stereochemical structure
of DNA (deoxyribonucleic acid), for which they received the Nobel
Prize in 1962. Most of our children learn in school of the fundamental

importance of DNA. Although it was first isolated among the various nucleic acids by Miescher in 1858, it was not until the middle of our century that it became clear to most biologists that DNA bears the secret of inheritance.

There was a very good reason for scientists' reluctance to acknowledge DNA's paramount role: it had to prove itself capable of unbelievably delicate discrimination. The operation of the immune system, by which every organism distinguishes between its own proteins and those of others, is an example that clearly illustrates how any substance that is responsible for specifying the constituency of biological types must itself bear a very high degree of specificity. Until recently, proteins were the only substances known to exist in such a profusion of subvarieties in a living organism that they might be the locus of this required specificity. Few researchers, if any, suspected that a substance as simple in gross structure as a nucleic acid could encode such a high degree of biological individuality.

Like proteins, DNA and the closely related RNA (ribonucleic acid), are large polymers, like starch, rubber, and plastics. A polymer is any substance whose molecule is an indefinitely long chain of monomers, each of which is a small molecule capable of attaching at one end to another monomer in a fixed way and at the opposite end to a third monomer in a fixed way. When the monomers are of more than a single species, the chain is a copolymer; when the linear order of the monomers in a mixed chain is not predictable by any fixed rule, the chain is irregular copolymer. DNA is an irregular copolymer of four different monomers, each of which is one of four organic bases attached each to a deoxyribose sugar ring that is itself attached to a phosphoric acid molecule. The bases are adenine (A), thymine (T), cytosine (C), and guanine (G). RNA differs from DNA only in having a molecule of ribose in each monomer as its sugar and in having uracyl (U) as one of its bases in place of T.

What Watson and Crick discovered is that DNA normally consists of two of these long strands intertwined helically, with the phosphates on the outside, the bases stacked along the inside of the tube, and the two helices attached to one another by hydrogen bonds from each of the bases on the one strand to a corresponding base on the other. The monomer bases are so matched in size and in structure as to form two invariant pairs: A and T can easily fit together across the space between the two strands, and C can match G. This is critical for the two functions performed by the DNA (or RNA) in every cell.

The individuality of the DNA borne by a given individual or type inheres in the particular choice and sequence of its bases along either strand. In human DNA, there may be a million bases along a strand.

Thus, there are, for all practical purposes, infinitely many different varieties of DNA available to specify an individual—expressed exponentially, at least $4^{1000000}$, or 10^{600000}!

Because of the rigid pairing of the bases (A-T and C-G), the two strands of the double helix are exact complements. This is the basis of the surprisingly simple mechanism which underlies self-reproduction. At mitosis, an enzyme-catalyzed chemical reaction unzips the helix, and each of the strands picks up a complement mate from the surrounding soup of component parts and builds a new double helix of its own, each element identical to the original, barring accidental errors (one of the sources of mutation).

The second function of DNA and RNA in the cell is to preside over the synthesis of proteins. An organism consists mainly of proteins; differences among organisms are mainly the result of differences in the proteins that compose them.

A protein is an irregular copolymer of twenty different monomers, each an amino acid linked to the next in the chain by a peptide bond. For an organism to acquire the amino acids for the assembly of its proteins, it must either synthesize them itself or eat another organism that already contains them. Proteins taken in from another organism must usually be restructured by the ingesting organism to ensure that only its own proteins appear. Its cells consult their DNA to determine which strings of amino acids to put together.

This assembly process occurs on organelles in the extranuclear cytoplasm (ribosomes). Therefore, the precious information from the DNA must be transcribed and conveyed out of the nucleus to the ribosomes as needed. That task is performed by short, single strands of RNA. This messenger-RNA (^{m}RNA), reads a relevant section of DNA by complementation, A-U or C-G, passes outside to a ribosome, and picks up, again by complementation, small pieces of transfer-RNA (^{t}RNA), each of which carries a particular amino acid; then the ribosome assembles, monomer by monomer, a chain of these accordingly.

We can now define the genetic code as the translation schema for determining in each case which of the twenty amino acids is selected by the information that the ^{m}RNA has transcribed from the nuclear DNA strand. Since there are only four different bases used for encoding, but twenty different amino acids, clearly the code must involve some combinatory schema with at least three bases per translated acid (two bases can distinguish only $4^2 = 16$; three can separate $4^3 = 64$). Despite several ingenious theories designed to match sixty-four to twenty, clever experiments eventually determined that each translation is indeed specified by a triplet of DNA monomers, and the code is therefore quite degenerate, although the resulting redundancy is, of course, a welcome antinoise resource. Three amino acids are each encoded by six different triplets, five by four triplets each, one by three triplets, nine by two triplets each, and two amino acids by a single triplet each. That makes sixty-one triplets for twenty amino acids; the extra three triplets serve as full-stop punctuation marks!

This superficial linguistic analogy can be carried still a bit further. A triplet of successive nucleotides (DNA monomers) on the DNA strand plays a role like that of a word. Each is one of a finite set of minimal functional units that bears a symbolic significance: a word (in most cases) has a meaning, a triplet specifies a particular amino acid. Thus, a nucleotide is analogous to a phoneme. The stretch of DNA transcribed by ^{m}RNA at any one reading is translated into a protein and is the analog of a sentence; there are an infinite number of them, and it requires higher-order information not connected to the transcription and translation mechanisms to determine which stretch is to be read. A sentence is chosen because of the function of its meaning in a setting, and a stretch of DNA is read because of the function of its protein in the cell. A triplet is called a *codon;* the stretch of DNA that is read is called a *cistron.* For a sizable family of cases, a cistron is an appropriate interpretation for a gene or for one of Mendel's factors. Finally, the punctuation mark which flags the point along the DNA strand where a cistron begins functions like the capital letter that starts a sentence.

Recent research reveals that reading is initiated and terminated in a much more complicated manner than is implied by the simplicity of the local mechanisms. The complicated gene-expression system that determines when a certain gene is read is not itself a simple matter of reading off a message; rather, it involves the whole complex chemical control system of the cell and all of its external environmental influences. Similarly, the choice of a certain sentence, or even of a certain word, is hardly ever grammatically specified, but instead involves the whole mental life of the speaker.

It has also been known for some time that traits are, for the most part, not determined by single genes, just as the expression of a certain idea may require the formulation of several different sentences. It can even happen in some cases that a given stretch of nucleotides functions in the transcription of parts of two different genes. Analogously, a word or a string of words may be structurally ambiguous, that is, capable of functioning in two different constructions or sentence types. For example, in one reading of the sentence "He left out the back," the word *out* is in the direction adverb, as in "He left by the back door" (departed thence); in a second reading, the word *out* is in the verb, as in "He left out one word" (omitted it). Thus, we have crude analogs of syntax, ambiguity, and homophony, all normal features of any linear encoding of information which functions in a complex system of higher order.

The genetic code is universal. Except for a few minor variants, every living creature on earth employs the code described above—not merely the overall schema, but even the translations of individual codons in the code book. So far as we can tell at present, the translations are largely unmotivated from a chemical, physical, or biological point of view, in exactly the sense that words are largely arbitrary from a semantic point of view; that is, one could have made oneself just as clear in English had the verb *buy* meant 'sell' and *sell* 'buy', but so too could our genetic code have fulfilled its function had the codons AAU and AAC translated each to the amino acid glutamine, while CAA and CAG translated each to asparagine, instead of the other way round. This remarkable fact bears witness unimpeachably to our kinship with every other type of organism on this planet.

The boundaries between life and death have become much clearer in this light; in fact, that puzzle no longer torments us as it once did, for nothing of great importance hangs any longer on our choice of exactly where to draw the boundary, except for the legal problem of death in humans. A virus is best viewed as a nonliving piece of genetic-message DNA (or RNA) with some associated proteins that requires a living-cell environment for self-reproduction. This requirement highlights the significant fact that the living cell, and hence every living creature, is a strictly self-referent system: the genetic message which specifies the constituency of a certain cell is read and translated only within that cell itself (though it could in principle, of course, be read and translated within any living cell).

A cell, then, is a bag of chemicals, mostly structural and control proteins. These are organized into various organelles and structures which interact with one another in an immensely complex way to absorb available nutrients and energy and to grow to the point of splitting into two daughter cells. The various reactions are, for the most part, mediated by control proteins, or enzymes, whose concentrations in different places wax and wane.

Enzymes are proteins, or polypeptides, seen from the point of view of their remarkable catalytic function. An enzyme is synthesized as a long strand of linearly linked amino acids; once it is synthesized, it forthwith coils up almost like a ball of string. The cross-links which fold it into its quasi-spherical shape are specific to each protein, and that protein folds in the same way on every occasion. The resulting ball has special regions on its surface, complex cavities among the twisted and intertwined strands, where certain smaller molecules can fit. Chemical reactions among these molecules are activated by the electrochemical effects of the surrounding coils of the enzyme substrate.

The strands of DNA in a cell are also accompanied by a certain protein cover, mainly histones, which, together with the more mobile enzymes, comprise a control system that opens up and closes down certain cistrons, or genes, at various times.

Thus, the cell is a *complex control system* of interacting elements, a dynamic microcosm of chemical structures. When these are interacting, we say the cell is alive (or, more obscurely, we attribute to the cell the reification 'life'), just as we refer to an automobile engine as on or off. By obstructing a critical reaction, or a sufficiently large number of noncritical ones, we may bring the process to a halt; for cell or engine we may say that we have killed it, that it has died.

Of course, there is an interesting difference between cells and engines, but it has nothing to do with the character of life itself. Engines do not reproduce themselves. However, there is no good reason why engines could not be constructed so that they could propel automobiles and also occasionally assemble new engines from spare parts; the technological problem is indeed formidable, but it is not in principle unsolvable. At present, however, each engine must be assembled by a man or a factory, while cells are born of parent cells (i.e., assembled from raw materials by a parent of a sort).

This fact often confuses one into supposing that the first cell must have had its life inspirited by a prime blower. This misconception arises from several failures in judgment. First, it is not the cell now before us whose spontaneous assembly must be explained, but rather the quite primitive Ur-cell of long ago. Second, the nondegenerating assembly that became the Ur-cell arose by chance, the survivor of a billion or so years of chemical recombination in sterile seas. The cell we see today is the offspring of literally countless subsequent evolutionary interactions.

Third, there is an important difference between intelligence of self-consciousness in complex animals and life in cells. The elements of a higher nervous system are themselves cells, already very smart; the elements of a cell are chemical molecules, by comparison quite stupid. Cells are very well understood in principle, no matter how complicated an actual cell may be. The operation of the complex nervous control system that underlies self-consciousness or creativity in primates is barely understood at all. The role played by the genetic code in organizing and maintaining the integrity of a cell and its genetic line is well understood; the role played by the mind's representational systems in organizing and maintaining the integrity of the personality or of an intellect is barely understood at all.

Yet the analogy between these two levels is unmistakable. On at least two separate occasions in the history of our corner of the universe, a new kind of complex control system of interacting elements arose spontaneously to generate a self-contained, homeostatic, evolving organism. The first, the biological world of life, arose on a substrate of chemical interactions, and in time it invented a genetic code. The second, the mental world of the intellect, arose on a substrate of nervous interactions in the brains of higher species, and in time it invented a linguistic code.

Others than myself have entertained such an analogy, notably the eminent contemporary philosopher Sir Karl R. Popper. He considered the traditional mind-body problem and, at least for the time being, accepted a trialist view of three hierarchically interconnected but, in a sense, independent worlds: first, the physical universe of molecules, cells, and brains; and parasitic on it a second domain of mental events—thoughts, intentions, and emotions; and generated from this, in turn, a third world of the products of the mind—the world of theorems, proofs, sciences, philosophies, and religions.

It is not implausible that mental events are just physical events, albeit complex ones, in the nervous system. Such a resolution of the traditional mind-body problem is not a simple-minded physicalist reduction of mental events to physical objects. An event in the nervous system may be a very much more sophisticated and abstract notion than that of an object or a substance; and it may be quite some time before we can specify or predict the nature or occurrence of such complex interactions among countless numbers of axons, synapses, or neural nets; but it no longer seems mysterious to us that a higher organism experiences mental events when, for example, one part of its brain scans activities in another, just as a sense organ scans some external input of auditory or visual or tactual signals.

However, the independent world of products of the mind specified by Popper, if it is a viable notion, does seem quite puzzling. In the sense of the foregoing paragraph, it is not at all clear how we should conceptualize the relation between physical objects or mental events and the content of a thought. Once an idea has been formulated, and maybe also represented, it can be rendered free from its creator and developed, or used as the basis of deductions, or incorporated into a theory, or refuted, and so on. In any case, it seems incongruous to view an idea as a mental event, even if it happened to originate in a mental event, or even if every idea must originate in mental events.

It is not difficult now to see a language as a device for representing ideas. It differs from other representation schemata used by men and animals just by the fact that it permits the representation of propositions, and it is to these propositions that truth-values may be attached and from these that arguments and proofs may be constructed. Primitive instances of argument may be possible for a linguistically innocent organism, just as primitive arithmetic conceptualization is exhibited by creatures who possess no numerals, but the advantages of sharing ideas can be achieved only with propositions represented concretely, either auditorily or visually, in a common mode. Moreover, linguistic encoding of meanings serve as, perhaps, an indispensable memory aid. Complex meanings are compressed into single words, succinct compounds or short phrases, and these can be stored not only semantically, but also phonologically or visually, and thus also permanently.

Let me summarize briefly here. Life arose spontaneously when certain chemical control systems crossed some boundary of complexity to become nondegenerating; organisms then further improved their ability to survive changes in the environment by inventing a finely tuned evolution system using simple self-reproduction and growth mechanisms which were based, in part, on a genetic code. An individual is delicate, and can be instructed by its environment to change only within narrow limits; but a species is rugged, and changes over long periods of time not by instruction, but by selection among independently occurring variants.

I advocate that linguistic competence be viewed analogously to the genetic code as a mechanism invented by minds to serve as a scratch pad for logic and a repository of ideas. Each mind dies with its substrate brain, but ideas, once shared or recorded, live on and evolve to nourish future minds. We should seek to formulate the basic principles that govern the appearance and evolution of complex control systems such as cells and central nervous systems; we may yet uncover the origin of and the motivations for language.

Facial Signals

PAUL EKMAN

INTRODUCTION

Most of this report will be about two different but related types of facial activity: emotional expressions and conversational signals. To discuss either, we must have an accurate way to describe and to distinguish among the great variety of facial movements that occur in humans. Terms such as *grimace, frown, sneer,* or *smile* can each cover too many different actions, concealing differences that may have import. Some of the disagreements that characterize past discussions of emotional expressions may have arisen from such imprecise descriptions. I will begin by discussing our recently developed method for describing facial movement, which offers more precision than has been previously available.

DESCRIBING FACIAL MOVEMENT

A number of different systems have been proposed for describing facial actions: one from a linguistic approach to social behavior (Birdwhistell 1970); most others from ethological approaches (e.g., Blurton Jones 1971; Brannigan and Humphries 1972; Grant 1969; Young and Decarie 1977). Each has been incomplete, without an explanation of what has been left out or why it was omitted. The units or items of description have at times specified a signal action ("nostril flare" [Brannigan and Humphries 1972]), and have sometimes included complex actions due to a number of muscles ("grimace" [Brannigan and Humphries 1972]). Descriptions have often been contaminated with inferences about meaning (e.g., "sad frown" [Grant 1969]) so that it is not possible to use the descriptions to test whether the meanings are actually associated in such a manner. The specification of units has sometimes been so vague that investigators could not know if they were cataloguing the same actions. Descriptions of actions have occasionally been anatomically incorrect. And, these systems have not dealt

227

with the ways in which individual or age-related differences in physiognomy may confuse the recognition of certain actions. (See Ekman and Friesen 1976 for a review of facial measurement systems.)

We hoped to avoid these problems by developing a facial description system based on the anatomy of facial action. We were disappointed to find that most anatomists had not distinguished among the facial muscles on the basis of how they distinctively change appearance or on their capability for independent action. Instead, muscles were named and distinguished by their appearance when the skin was removed. Exceptions were Duchenne (1862), Hjorstjo (1970), and Lightoller (1925). Building on their findings, and incorporating information scattered throughout many anatomy texts, we learned how to move our own facial muscles. Using a mirror and videotapes, we studied how single muscle actions and combinations of muscle actions would change our appearance. There were a few instances where there was ambiguity of whether we had succeeded in contracting a particular muscle. In those cases, we electrically stimulated a muscle to observe the resultant change in appearance. We also studied the spontaneous facial actions shown by hundreds of people from a number of cultures in our film and videotape library to verify that the system we were developing would allow description of any observed movement.

Learning how the equipment works—how both single muscles and combinations of muscles change facial appearance—provided only part of the basis for developing our facial measurement system. It was also necessary to take into account the variations in facial performance that observers can distinguish; otherwise the descriptive system would be unreliable. We taught a group of people our descriptive system and then had them score a variety of facial movements. Only the discriminations they could reliably make were incorporated into the final system. The Facial Action Coding System (FACS) (Ekman and Friesen 1978) includes a self-instructional manual, illustrative photographs and cinema, practice materials, and a final test for proficiency and reliability. People who have studied these materials have been successful in learning to reliably describe facial action, without any direct contact with us.[1]

The descriptive units in FACS are called "Action Units" rather than muscle units. They are the product of what the muscular equipment can do and what the perceiver can distinguish. Most of the units have a one-to-one correspondence with the muscles distinguished by anatomists. Occasionally, however, more than one Action Unit is provided for what anatomists describe as a single muscle: this was necessary when we found that a single muscle could produce visibly different actions. In one instance, we have combined three muscles into one Action Unit, since those three muscles rarely operate independently and observers could not distinguish their separate appearance. There are forty-four Action Units in FACS; each has a distinctive appearance, and each can combine with other Action Units to produce complex appearance changes. Figures 1 and 2 give an example of how complex facial expressions can be analyzed in terms of the elemental Action Units which combined to produce them.

Developing FACS taught us a few rudimentary pieces of information about facial activity. We learned that there is a much larger capability for action in the lower areas of the face (cheeks, mouth, chin) than in other facial areas. The brows and forehead contain only three Action Units, which can combine to produce four complex movements. By comparison, the lower face has thirty-one Action Units, which can combine to produce thousands of different appearances. There are eight Action Units which change the appearance of the eyelids and the skin immediately adjacent to the lids, although the Action Units in the brows and some of those in the lower face also change the appearance around the eyes.

There are some Action Units which appear to function as a signal when they occur alone, without any other facial action, and there are some Action Units which appear to function as a signal only in com-

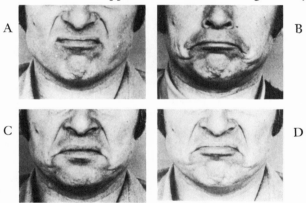

Fig. 1. Expressions A through D.   These four lower face expressions are similar but different. The lip corners are lower than the center of the lip in each, but they differ: some have a wrinkled chin; some have bags or pouches below the lip corners; some have a marked wrinkle running up from the lip corner to the nostril wings. These are complex expressions involving two or three elemental Action Units. Once the elemental Action Units have been learned, it is easy to describe the complex expressions and to show exactly how and why they differ. Examine the simple three Action Units below, which are the bases of the complex expressions.

SOURCE: *Facial Action Coding System Manual,* © Consulting Psychologists' Press, 1978.

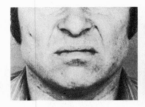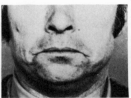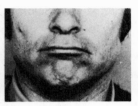

Fig. 2. Action Units 10, 15, and 17. A few moments' study of these single Action Units should allow you to score the complex expressions as you would using FACS. Expression A is the combination of 10 and 17; B is 15 and 17; C is 10 and 15; and D is 10, 15, and 17. This example illustrates the logic of FACS, whereby any facial expression can be described in terms of the particular Action Units which produced it. Note, however, that although FACS can be used to describe still photographs, it was designed to measure facial movement recorded on videotape or film.

SOURCE: *Facial Action Coding System Manual,* © Consulting Psychologists' Press, 1978.

bination with other Action Units. It is hypothetically possible for as many as eighteen of the forty-four Action Units to act simultaneously, but we have never seen that happen. The typical facial movement that we have observed involves two to five Action Units acting in concert. Let me turn now to the emotional facial expressions.

EMOTIONAL EXPRESSIONS

There is by now a large body of evidence that specific patterns of Action Units universally signify particular emotions. Quantitative studies have provided evidence in more than thirteen literate cultures and in two visually isolated preliterate cultures. Qualitative studies support this evidence in a great number of visually isolated cultures. The studies include the work of anthropologists, ethologists, pediatricians, psychologists, and sociologists. The people studied include infants, children, and adults, most of whom were sighted but some of whom were blind. Naturalistic observations as well as laboratory experiments have been conducted. Spontaneous and contrived facial expressions have been measured in various contexts, and the interpretations of faces by members of different cultures have been compared (see Ekman 1973 for a review of this work).

Despite such evidence, some still argue that there are no universals in facial expressions of emotion (Birdwhistell 1970; LaBarre 1947; Leach 1972; Mead 1975). Elsewhere (Ekman 1977) I have attempted to explain the basis for the disagreement between those who argue from a linguistic analogy and those who argue an evolutionary view, offering a theoretical framework which attempts to embrace both, to reconcile the disagreement. Here I will only mention some of the relevant issues.

One major source of disagreement has been the failure by many of the universalists to explain what they mean by emotion terms such as *anger, fear, surprise,* and *sadness.* Emotion terms imply a complex variety of quite different but interrelated components: emotion elicitors, immediate facial and other physiological responses, appraisal processes, rules for controlling appearance, memories, images, expectations, and so on. There is both universality and cultural variation in regard to each of these components of emotion; commonalities and variability in different respects and to a different extent depending upon which aspect of emotion is considered. Emotional expression is neither culture specific nor universal; it is both. The issue is to explain how and in which respects (see Ekman 1977 for an attempt to do so).

Another major source of confusion and contradiction about emotional expressions is the issue of whether facial expression is voluntary or involuntary. The accounts of the cultural relativists have suggested or implied that facial expressions are: deliberate; feigned; chosen; employed as masks; unreliable indicators of feelings; the product of social conventions about appropriate feelings to be displayed in specific contexts. Some of those arguing for the universalist position have implied that facial expressions: are involuntary; occur without awareness or choice; are difficult to control; may reveal information the person is trying to inhibit. Both views are partially right, but neither offers a satisfactory account (see Ekman 1979).

The observations by cultural relativists of variations in facial actions associated with emotion may be the consequence of their observing social occasions where different rules about controlling appearance (what we have termed *display rules*) were operative, or where the same display rule was followed in the cultures compared. The universal facial expression of anger (or any other emotion) will not invariably signify that the person observed is angry. It may just as well mean that he wants to be viewed as angry. And the failure to observe a facial expression of anger does not necessarily mean that the person is not angry. The system is not that simple.

A number of major questions remain about emotional facial expressions. How many emotions have a universal facial expression?

Currently there is evidence for five emotions, but there may be more. For any emotion that appears universally, such as anger, how many different facial expressions are universal? How often do people in natural situations show the distinctive, universal patterns of facial expression? These and other questions are discussed in a review of research on facial expression in Ekman and Oster (1979).

CONVERSATIONAL FACIAL SIGNALS

Compared to the emotional expressions, relatively little is known about conversational signals. We do not know of any quantitative studies of these actions. There have only been scattered qualitative observations, which are unsubstantiated by careful description and are without systematic cross-cultural comparisons. We have begun to observe conversational signals only within the last few years, and have started systematic study only last year; therefore, what I report must be considered tentative.

Efron (1941) proposed the term *baton* for hand movements that appear to accent a particular word as it is spoken. We have noted that batons appear to coincide with primary voice stress, or, more simply, with a word that is spoken more loudly. When we have asked people to place voice stress on one word and put the baton on another word, they cannot do so. The voice emphasis shifts to the locus of the baton. The neural mechanisms responsible for emphasis apparently send impulses to both voice and skeletal (or facial) muscles simultaneously when both modalities are employed. We expect this relationship between baton and voice emphasis to be maintained across languages and cultures, but have no data as yet.

Birdwhistell (1970) and Eibl-Eibesfeldt (1971) have commented that facial actions can emphasize speech. Birdwhistell does not specify any particular facial emphasis action; Eibl-Eibesfeldt mentions only what we call a *brow raise* (both inner and outer corners of the brow). Almost any facial action could be employed as a baton, but few are. The upper eyelid raise is sometimes used, as is nose wrinkling, although the latter is more typical of females than males. The most common facial actions employed in the baton (and in many other conversational signals) are: (1) the brow raise and (2) the *brow lower and draw together*.[2]

Most people show both brow raise and brow lower, more of the former than the latter, but some of each. We (Ekman, Friesen, and Camras in prep.) are completing a study which supports our hypothesis that, when brow lower is employed as the baton, there is some evidence in the emphasized words of uncertainty or difficulty of some kind. Not that this will always be so, but sufficiently to reject the notion that the occurrence of brow lower versus brow raise is random.

Another conversational signal is a facial action which appears to function as a *comma*. When a person describes a series of events, a variety of facial actions can be inserted after each event in the series, much as a comma would be if the speech was written. Lip pressing, pushing up of the chin, and brow raise or brow lower are the most common actions used as commas.

Birdwhistell (1970), Blurton Jones (1967), Darwin (1872), and Eibl-Eibesfeldt (1971) have all commented on the use of brow raises to indicate a *question*. Linda Camras, during a post-doctoral research fellowship at our laboratory, examined eyebrow actions in the course of conversations between mothers and their five-year-old children. Her preliminary findings suggest that both brow raise and brow lower are used in question statements, although raise is more common than lower. Her findings support our prediction that (as with batons) there is a difference in the contexts in which brow raise or brow lower occur. If the mother is less certain about the answer to her question, more in doubt or perplexed, then brow lower is more likely to occur than brow raise. When observers were allowed to listen to and to watch the context which immediately preceded the use of either brow raise or brow lower in a question, they were able to do better than chance in guessing which eyebrow action subsequently occurred, although often they could not explain their guess.

Camras also has preliminary evidence that may indicate when a brow action is most likely to be recruited to signal a question mark. A brow raise is more likely to occur in a question when the words do not provide a clue that a question is being asked. For example, if the statement does not begin with *what, where, who, when,* or *which,* a brow raise is more likely than in a statement that has such a verbal or syntactic indication of questioning.

The brow lower movement is often used when an individual is engaged in a *word search* during speech. This may be shown during a filled pause (when a person says, "ah" or "uh") or an unfilled pause. Certain hand movements (e.g., finger snapping, or movements which seem to be trying to pluck the word from space) occur in the same location during speech, instead of or in addition to the brow lower facial action. These movements may indicate to the other participants in a conversation that a word search is occurring, that the speaker has not given up his turn. Another common facial action during word search is a brow raise with the eyes looking up, as if the word was to be found on the ceiling. Apart from the brow action, during word searches it is typical for the gaze to be directed at an immobile spot, reducing visual input. This visual inattention may increase the risk of losing the floor, and the brow actions may serve to signal the listener not to interrupt and not to take over the speaker's turn.

We have so far only described *speaker* conversational signals (and only some of them), actions shown by the person who is talking. There are also a series of facial conversational signals emitted by the person listening to the speaker, what Dittmann (1972) called *listener responses*. Dittman described how the listener provides head nods, smiles, and "um-humms" during conversation. He found that these actions occur at specific locations in relation to the structure of the speaker's words. In classroom exercises, we found that students find it hard to withhold listener responses, doing so only as long as they concentrate on this task. When they succeed, the speaker usually inquires whether something is wrong or whether they are listening, etc.

What Dittman described can be termed *agreement responses*, which indicate not only that the listener is attending, but that he understands and does not disagree with what is being said. The brow raise together with either a smile, a head nod, or an agreement word also functions as an agreement listener response.

Eyebrow actions also function as *calls for information*. The brow lower may show that the listener does not understand what the speaker has said. Or this action may be a metaphorical comment that the listener finds what the speaker has said to be figuratively, not literally, incomprehensible. Another call for information is the question mark brow raise shown by the listener in the same manner as it is performed by the speaker. As does the brow lower, this brow raise may indicate that the listener does not understand, or it may metaphorically signal incredulity at what the speaker has said. If the latter is the signal, it will be more explicit when joined by other facial actions used for the disbelief message, described below.

Some people make movements around the mouth which seem preparatory to speaking. Such movements conceivably might also signal to the speaker when the listener wants his turn to speak. There are probably other facial listener responses but we have not focused as much on these in our research.

So far, we have considered only facial actions which occur during conversation by speaker or listener. These actions are usually ambiguous outside of the context of talk in which they occur. Their role is known by examining what is being said: intonations, pauses, turns, and so on.

Now consider facial actions which can occur when there is no talk, yet communication is intended. We have used Efron's (1941) term *emblem* to refer to such actions with specific semantic meaning; most of our previous work on emblems has focused on hand movements (Ekman 1976).

Eibl-Eibesfeldt's (1971) account of what he calls an eyebrow *flash* emphasizes a repeated brow raise as a greeting signal. He mentions that an upward tilt of the head, a smile, and the upper eyelid raise also may be included. Our own observations in New Guinea suggest that the flash typically involves one or another of these actions in addition to the brow raise. We disagree with Eibl-Eibesfeldt's claim that the flash is a universal greeting signal. It is definitely widespread across cultures, but our own studies of symbolic gestures, as well as studies by our students (see Ekman 1976 for a review), suggest that it is not employed as a greeting in a number of cultures.

Eibl-Eibesfeldt may have come to the conclusion that the flash is a universal greeting signal because he did not distinguish the various functions of the brow raise. This movement is a frequent action occurring in many different conversational signals—emphasis, yes/no, question mark, exclamation mark, etc. The brow raise can also be part of a surprise emotional expression. It would not be uncommon for people to be surprised or to show mock-surprise when first seeing another person. Nor would it be uncommon that a person might show a question mark or an exclamation mark upon first seeing another unexpected person arrive. It would be necessary to rule out these other uses of the brow raise in order to be certain that all appearances of the brow raise during initial encounter are truly greetings.

Another facial emblem, shown by Americans (and probably, therefore, by people in at least some European countries), is for *disbelief* or incredulousness. The brow raise in this case is joined by pulling the corners of the lips down, relaxing the upper eyelid, pushing up the lower lip, raising the upper lip, and rocking the head from side to side. The performance for the *mock astonishment* emblem is quite different, and involves the brow raise accompanied by: raised upper eyelid; dropped open jaw; and an exaggerated element to the performance, created by an abrupt onset followed by a longer duration than occurs for actual surprise. Often the head will be tilted to the side and the eyes will sharply point away.

Darwin (1872) described an *affirmation* signal among Abyssinians, in which the head is thrown back and the eyebrows are raised for an instant. Eibl-Eibesfeldt commented also on this signal, particularly among Samoans; but he noted that among Greeks the brow raise makes the statement "no." Our observations in Turkey, where it also signals *negation*, show that it involves eyelid movement, sharp upward movement of the head, and raising of the chin. Darwin also noted that the Dyaks of Borneo show affirmation with brow raise, and negation with the lowering and drawing together of the brows "with a peculiar look from the eyes" (1872 [1955]:274).

There are other facial emblems, but these are the ones which have been most discussed by others. Note that an emblem differs from a speaker or listener conversational signal in that the emblem can be used without spoken conversation, yet can clearly communicate a very specific message. Emblems, of course, can be embedded within speech to replace, repeat, contradict, or qualify a verbal message.

Let us inquire why the brow raise and the brow lower, rather than any of the other facial actions, occur in so many conversational signals. First, we suggest that brow actions, compared to lower face actions, are often recruited to be conversational signals because they are physically available for use, not ever needed for speech articulation. This explanation does not, however, tell us why the two brow actions—raise and lower—occur so much more often than the other five brow actions that are possible. The two actions represent the extremes in how the brows can be moved, and while research on this point has not been done, we expect studies would show that they are the most visually contrasting and most easily distinguishable of the brow actions. The brow raise and brow lower also are the easiest to perform. We (Ekman, Roper, and Hager 1980) found that children as young as six years of age have no difficulty voluntarily performing these movements, while they do have difficulty with other brow actions.

It is tempting to suggest that brow raise and brow lower are recruited to be conversational signals, in part, because they are the easiest to perform. (Of course, the data do not prove that.) They might be the easiest to perform simply because they are prevalent social signals. We believe that differences in ease of performance could be shown to predate the use of these eyebrow actions in conversational signals, but there is no evidence, as yet, to suggest that we are correct in attributing such differences to the neural basis of facial actions, rather than to social learning. Even if such evidence existed, we would only be able to say that the eyebrow actions which are most often employed as conversational signals are the easiest to do and the most visually contrasting. These factors would not explain why one action rather than the other is deployed in a particular social signal: for example, why is brow lower not commonly used in greetings, while brow raise is? Why does there appear to be some negative implication in conversational context when brow lower is used, rather than brow raise, as a baton or a question mark?

Let us examine briefly some of the theoretical possibilities for explaining these phenomena. (Ekman 1979 considers the issue in detail.) The role of these actions in conversational signals may be based on their biological function of increasing or decreasing the scope of what is visually perceived. Raising the brows increases the superior visual field, letting the person see slightly more of what is above. Lowering the brows does just the opposite, decreasing the superior portion of the visual field. The extent of this influence depends, of course, on the prominence of the eyebrow ridge, how deeply set the eyes are, and the amount of eyebrow hair. The role of the two eyebrow actions in conversational signals may be analogous to the biological function. It seems consistent for a movement which increases vision to be employed in greetings, exclamations, and question marks, and for a movement which decreases vision to be employed in calls-for-information, and in emphasis marks and question marks where there is some uncertainty or difficulty.

Alternatively, it might be that the role of these actions in particular conversational signals is based on their role in emotional expression. The raised brow, as a part of surprise (which entails sudden events and orientation towards source), is a more sensible candidate for a greeting than brow lower, which is seen as part of the anger, fear, and distress expression. The connotations of a brow raise would certainly be less disruptive of greeting than would be the connotations of a brow lower. The use of brow raise and brow lower as batons might be similarly explained. Brow lower, which is employed in a variety of negative emotions, would carry an implication of something negative, whereas brow raise would be more likely to suggest surprise or interest.

Of course, the question can then be raised of why the brows are raised, not lowered, in surprise, and lowered, not raised, in anger. No definitive answer can be given, although many have attempted to answer this type of question. Ekman 1979 discusses some of the problems in the various explanations which have been offered, and points to the type of research which might illuminate these matters. Even the issues regarding the origin of facial expressions point to the necessity to distinguish emotional from conversational signals. There is no necessary reason why origins must be the same. How the brows customarily came to be raised with one type of question and lowered with another may or may not be related to how the brows came to be raised in certain emotions and lowered in others. Confusion can best be avoided by recognizing the variety of facial signals and their potential independence.

NOTES

The research I report and many of the speculations presented here are the product of collaboration over the last thirteen years with Wallace V. Friesen. This research has been supported by a grant, MH 11976, and a Research Scientist Award, MH 06092, from the National Institute of Mental Health and a grant from the Harry Frank Guggenheim Foundation. Most of what is reported here was first presented at the Human Ethology Conference in Bad Hamburg, Federal Republic of Germany, 1977, and is described in greater detail in the chapter, "About Brows: Emotional and Conversational Signals," in the book, *Human Ethology*, edited by M. von Cranach, K. Foppa, W. Lepenies, and D. Ploog (Cambridge: At the University Press, 1979).

1. FACS is now being used by a number of investigators to study normal adults, psychiatric patients, stutterers, deaf users of American Sign Language, normal children, retarded children, children with craniofacial abnormalities, and premature infants and neonates.

2. I will hereafter refer to the brow lower and draw together just as the brow lower, although typically the inner corners of the brows are also drawn together. For anyone familiar with our FACS system, the brow lower is AU 4, the brow raise is AU's 1 + 2.

REFERENCES

Birdwhistell, R. L. 1970. *Kinesics and Context*. Philadelphia: University of Pennsylvania Press.

Blurton Jones, N. 1967. An ethological study of some aspects of social behavior of children in nursery school. In *Primate Ethology*, D. Morris, ed., 347–68. Chicago: Aldine.

———. 1971. Criteria for use in describing facial expressions in children. *Human Biology* 41:365–413.

Brannigan, C. R., and Humphries, D. A. 1972. Human non-verbal behaviour, a means of communication. In *Ethological Studies of Child Behavior*, N. G. Blurton Jones, ed. Cambridge: At the University Press.

Darwin, C. 1872. *The expression of the emotions in man and animals*. New York: Philosophical Library, 1955.

Dittmann, A. T. 1972. Developmental factors in conversational behavior. *Journal of Communication* 22:404–23.

Duchenne, B. 1862. *Mécanisme de la physionomie humaine où analyse électrophysiologique de l'expression des passions.* Paris: Bailliere.

Efron, D. 1941. *Gesture and Environment.* New York: King's Crown. (Current edition as *Gesture, Race and Culture* [The Hague: Mouton, 1972].)

Eibl-Eibesfeldt, I. 1971. Similarities and differences between cultures in expressive movements. In *Nonverbal Communication*, R. A. Hinde, ed., 297–311. Cambridge: At the University Press.

Ekman, P. 1973. Cross cultural studies of facial expression. In *Darwin and Facial Expression: A Century of Research in Review*, P. Ekman, ed., 169–222. New York: Academic Press.

———. 1976. Movements with precise meaning. *Journal of Communication* 26(3):14–26.

———. 1977. Biological and cultural contributions to body and facial movement. In *Anthropology of the Body*, J. Blacking, ed., 39–84. London: Academic Press.

———. 1979. About brows: emotional and conversational signals. In *Human Ethology*, M. von Cranach, K. Foppa, W. Lepenies, and E. Ploog, eds., 169–202. Cambridge: At the University Press.

Ekman, P., and Friesen, Wallace V. 1976. Measuring facial movement. *Environmental Psychology and Nonverbal Behavior* 1(1):56–75.

———. 1978. *The facial action coding system.* Palo Alto, Calif.: Consulting Psychologists' Press.

Ekman, P.; Friesen, W. V.; and Camras, L. In preparation. Facial emphasis movements. Manuscript.

Ekman, P., and Oster, H. 1979. Facial expressions of emotion. *Annual Review of Psychology*, vol. 30, 527–54. Palo Alto, Calif: Annual Reviews.

Ekman, P., Roper, G., and Hager, J. C. 1980. Deliberate facial movement. *Child Development* 51:267–71.

Grant, N. G. 1969. Human facial expression. *Man* 4:525–36.

Hjorstjo, C. H. 1970. *Mans face and mimic language.* Lund: Studentlitteratur.

LaBarre, W. 1947. The cultural basis of emotions and gestures. *Journal of Personality* 16:49–68.

Leach, E. 1972. The influence of cultural context on nonverbal communication in man. In *Nonverbal Communication*, R. Hinde, ed. Cambridge: At the University Press.

Lightoller, G. H. S. 1925. Facial muscles: The modiolus and muscles surrounding the rima oris with some remarks about the panniculus adiposus. *Journal of Anatomy* 60, Part 1:1–84.

Mead, M. 1975. Review of *Darwin and Facial Expression*, ed. by P. Ekman. *Journal of Communication* 25(1):209–13.

Young, G., and Decarie, T. G. 1977. An ethology-based catalogue of facial/vocal behaviour in infancy. *Animal Behaviour* 25:95–107.

Iconic Relationships between
Language and Motor Action

DAVID McNEILL

Language and motor action are not usually regarded as closely related. The theoretical arguments and the evidence presented in this paper, however, support the claim that language and motor action are intimately connected—ontogenetically, perhaps phylogenetically, and in the continuous daily use of language by adults. The connection is close and apparently pervasive, enough to suggest that linguists must consider the extent to which the form (i.e., universal grammar) of language itself has been adapted to the relationship of language to motor action.

THEORY OF THE PLACE OF
MOTOR ACTION IN LANGUAGE

THE SYNTAGMA

In terms of psychological function, the syntagma is a better unit than such familiar linguistic units (actually levels) as the sentence, clause, sentoid, and phrase. The latter are structural and static, whereas the syntagma is functional and dynamic. It is thus easier to see the connection of language to motor action, which itself is dynamic, when language is viewed in terms of functional syntagmas.

A syntagma (but not a linguistic level) can be defined as the smallest unit of language that has all the properties of a whole (Vygotsky 1962). Kozhevnikov and Chistovich (1965) define it as a meaning unit pronounced in one action, as a single output. As a unit, a syntagma includes both content and action. Alteration of one implies alteration of the other. Action and meaning fuse within a syntagma. To recognize a syntagma requires knowing both how an utterance was pronounced on a given occasion and what its meaning was. For example, the same

Preparation of this paper and the research reported in it have been supported by USPHS grant MHS26541-04 and by the University of Chicago.

sentence (structure) can be produced as at least six different syntagmas in four patterns:

event		I táke that one	
person + event	|Í	take that one|
event + entity	|I táke	thát one|
person + event + entity	|Í	táke	thát one|

The stress peaks and vertical bars indicate single outputs—phonemic clauses, most likely—that have some kind of conceptual unity, as suggested by the terms event, person and entity. Phonemic clauses that disrupt conceptual unity (such as |táke that | one|) cannot be called syntagmas. In fact, phonemic clauses without conceptual unity are rare in discourse (McNeill 1979).

Each syntagma corresponds to a unit of activity in producing or comprehending speech. The activity units have the semantic and phonological properties of speech-thought wholes. For example, *I take*, though structurally incomplete (a transitive verb without its object), is a single concept of event articulated as a single phonological pattern. Thus, according to the examples, different speakers may engage in one, two, or three distinct actions in producing the same sentence.

BASIS OF SYNTAGMAS IN MOTOR ACTIONS

To see the connection clearly, it is convenient to move back to the very beginnings of speech in children. Here, at the source, a connection of speech to motor action is more obvious. The inner organization of psychological functions is revealed by observing developmental changes, and we will see how motor action alters in form but persists in its connection to speech; in fact, in its altered form, action is the foundation on which subsequent speech development is constructed.

The earliest speech for which one can say that meaning accrues occurs at about seven or eight months of age. At this point, motor action and vocalization seem to be coparts of the same activity. The child reaches for something and vocalizes [m] as a single act, for example (Carter 1975). At this stage, according to Piaget (1952), there is a very imperfect separation of the child's conception of objects from his activity of reaching for or manipulating objects. The world is represented in terms of sensory-motor action schemas. In one of Piaget's demonstrations, for example, a child watched while an object, which she had just previously found in one place, was hidden in a different spot; but in searching for it a moment later, she still looked for the object where she had last found it. The object, represented as an existent, included previous actions of retrieval. Speech, a copart of the same kinds of motor actions, is already a part of the child's sensory-motor representation of the world.

The fusion of speech with motor action and sensory-motor meaning can be viewed as a type of indexical sign (in the sense of Peirce 1931–58). Speech is an index of the concurrent action and, taking into account the sensory-motor character of meaning at this stage, of meaning as well. The indexical relationship, in which speech seems to be part of meaning, is most obvious when, at this stage, representation is still imperfectly differentiated from overt action. However, the indexical relationship remains a constant in the syntagma, although its character is forced to change with the child's continuing intellectual development.

The predominant line of development during the first two years of life is what many observers have called the interiorization of sensory-motor action schemas. Gradually, actions are reconstructed internally (Vygotsky 1978), until the child becomes able to represent actions exclusively as mental schemas (Piaget 1952). The internally reconstructed sensory-motor schemas retain their epistemological function, and at the same time are a crucial new step in the child's cognitive and linguistic development. The indexical relationship of speech to action turns inward. It becomes possible to say that speech now denotes internal sensory-motor representations. For the first time, speech implies inner thought. There is a qualitative change between a child's use of [m] when actually reaching for some object and its use of *my* or *more* in descriptive statements (*that's* $\left\{ {more \atop my} \right\}$ *N*) (Carter 1975). The new development of speech grows naturally out of the gradual internal reconstruction of motor actions; creates the conditions for all further speech development; and now brings into being the kind of syntagma that older speakers employ, in which there is external speech and internal representation of meaning.

The indexical relationship of speech to meaning was well known to Vygotsky (1962), who told the story of the rustic who could very well see how astronomers with all their instruments were able to discover how far away the stars are but who could not understand how they learned their names. Vygotsky investigated this relationship with children: children could not completely accept exchanges of names between objects; for example, calling dogs *cows;* and, when asked if cows had horns, children as old as five or six years would insist that these cows must have at least small ones.

SEMIOTIC EXTENSION OF SENSORY-MOTOR SCHEMAS

The indexical fusion of sound and meaning within syntagmas is possible only at a sensory-motor level. Sensory-motor schemas are uniquely part of both the realm of meaning and the realm of action. No other level of representation appears with this dual citizenship. Speech output, also a type of motor action, is easily assimilated into the child's concurrent manipulative actions on objects in the world; and the same manipulative actions, together with speech from an early stage of development, are the basis of the construction of the sensory-motor schemas of representation (Piaget 1952).

Syntagmas must connect with other meanings organized at higher levels of representation—in Piagetian terms, meanings at the representational and operational levels (cf. Inhelder and Piaget 1958). In the case of such higher meanings (often the literal meanings of adults), there is not a direct fusion of meaning with sound as at the sensory-motor level; but there is still a connection of meaning with sound, supported by a sensory-motor fusion that gives the impression of necessity to particular sound-meaning combinations (hence such comic figures as the rustic described by Vygotsky; but more sophisticated speakers also can feel indexicality beneath their feet). The relationship of non-sensory-motor meanings to speech can be called *semiotic extension*. According to this process, the syntagma, involving interiorized sensory-motor schemas, is extended to other meanings that are organized at higher representational levels. This step, too, can be viewed in terms of signs. Semiotic extension in fact is a kind of meaning relationship that makes possible the connection of abstract thought and intentions to speech by way of concrete sensory-motor models.

Semiotic extension, in effect, makes sensory-motor schemas into signs of other non-sensory-motor meanings. Thus, every utterance contains a sensory-motor component of meaning where action and meaning fuse. It is for this reason that abstract utterances seem to contain concrete ideas, like event, location, or state. For example, *the story came to an end* seems to include the idea of an event. This concrete idea reflects the fusion of action with meaning. Semiotic extension works by taking such sensory-motor schemas, which are themselves the *objects* of indexical signs (speech indexes sensory-motor schemas), and viewing them simultaneously as the *sign vehicles* of iconic and symbolic signs. The latter two types of sign refer to abstract meanings. Semiotic extension thus relies on an interlocking of symbolic, iconic, and indexical signs within syntagmas.

One kind of iconic sign can be brought out when speakers describe their own actions. Consider, for example, a situation in which two actions are performed in a sequence: lifting up a bottle and then filling it. This can be described in alternative ways: *I lift the bottle before I fill it, before I fill the bottle I lift it, I fill the bottle after I lift it,* and *after I lift the bottle I fill it.* These are symbolically equivalent in the sense that all describe the same sequence of actions. If, as is usually assumed, speech has indexical and symbolic values only, one would expect that all these sentences should be correlated with action in the same way; for example (actions written in capital letters):

LIFT   FILL
I fill the bottle after I lift it
I lift the bottle before I fill it
before I fill the bottle I lift it
after I lift the bottle I fill it

However, if there is an iconic component of sentence meaning, different relationships should appear in the way in which speech is correlated with action, as is suggested in the following:

LIFT   FILL
I lift the bottle before I fill it

LIFT FILL
before I fill the bottle I lift it

LIFT   FILL
I fill the bottle after I lift it

LIFT   FILL
after I lift the bottle I fill it

In each case, lifting precedes filling (as is required symbolically), but the differing temporal relationships of the action to the sentence iconically depict the same meaning that is coded symbolically; specifically: when the adverb is "before A," the production of the clause with the adverb is in fact before the performance of A; and when the adverb is "after A," the production of the clause with the adverb is in fact after the performance of A. This particular correlation of action with speech is an iconic depiction of the same information coded symbolically by the adverbs. The indexical relation (the link between the production of speech output and the internal representation of the syntagma) interlocks with the iconic relation (the representation of the syntagma and the performance of the action) to reflect the sequence of actions.

EMPIRICAL STUDIES OF THE PLACE OF MOTOR ACTION IN LANGUAGE

The following studies examine the way in which speakers temporally correlate their speech with actions. In the first study, the actions involve manipulations of real objects, and in the second they involve manipulations of virtual objects (i.e., the actions are gestures). Occurrences of the adverbs *before* and *after* are too infrequent to provide a good data base, but the same type of iconic relationship is predictable for the dimension of aspect. Aspect has the advantage of being obligatorily marked in English speech, so that every sentence potentially offers an observation of interest. In practice, I have limited my observations to actions that are described by verbs in the present tense.

A basic aspectual contrast is between actions regarded as either imperfective or perfective (Kuryłowicz 1964), along what may be called the perfectivity dimension:

Any uninterrupted action necessarily passes through phases *a*, *b*, and *c* and point *x*, but the speaker has the freedom of regarding or emphasizing the action as being in any one of these phases or at point *x*. If the action is thought of as: in phase *b*, an imperfect meaning is involved (*I'm pressing the button*); at exactly point *x*, a perfective meaning is involved (*I've pressed the button*); in phase *a*, a future meaning is involved (*I'll press the button*); in phase *c*, a past or stative meaning is involved (*I pressed the button, the button is pressed*). The action that the verb describes may be performed at any time relative to the speaker's uttering the verb, but if there is an iconic component of the meaning of the sentence, a verb marked for imperfective aspect should be produced at a later point during the performance of the action than a verb marked for perfective aspect. That is, we would predict something like the following:

> PRESS BUTTON
> I'm pressing the button

> PRESS BUTTON
> I've pressed the button

In the first example the verb is uttered during phase *a* of the action, and in the second it is uttered at or near point *x*.

SPEECH AND ACTION

Figure 1 shows the duration and the relative positioning of the described actions and the verbs used in statements describing the actions. The actions represented in this figure occurred during the performance of simple tasks such as assembling a small table-top aquarium, tying a bow knot, tying a necktie, and the like. The subjects (staff and students at the University of Chicago) were given these tasks one at a time, and were told to describe the movements they made as they

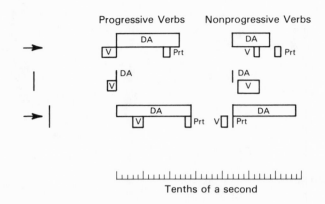

Tenths of a second

Fig. 1

performed them. The form in which the subjects were to combine speech and action was unspecified. The entire session was recorded on videotape and then analyzed frame by frame.

In this situation, a large number of present progressive verbs, but no present perfect verbs, appeared. A small number of present non-progressive verbs appeared; these are also represented in figure 1. There were a few future tense verbs, but no past tense verbs. The future tense verbs are not shown in figure 1.

In addition to progressive and nonprogressive tenses, figure 1 shows three types of action. These differ in how the actions described by the verbs were performed. Actions of the → type are homogeneously extended in time; for example, pressing on a surface or pushing something across a table. Although such actions have beginnings and ends, these points are not described by the verbs *press on* and *push across*. Actions of the | type are not extended in time. They consist of nothing else besides beginnings and ends, which coincide; for example, letting go of or releasing something. Although each action has preliminary and recovery movements, the phases are not described by the verbs *let go of* or *release*. Finally, actions of the →| type have both extended and momentary phases; for example, putting down on or grasping something. The verb *put down on* describes both a homogeneously extended movement (the hand moving to a surface) and the moment of contacting the surface. Omitting either phase results in a "different" action, described by some other verb: for example, *touch* or *lower*.

Several points can be observed in figure 1. First, → and →| actions are of longer duration when described by progressive verbs than when described by nonprogressive verbs. Extension of the duration of an → or →| action prolongs phase *b* (i.e., the imperfective phase), coinciding with the use of the progressive tense.

Second, actions described by progressive → and | verbs usually start only after the end of the verb, whereas actions described by non-progressive → and | verbs begin well before the start of the verb. The imperfective meaning, with progressive verbs, of this combination with the described action is quite clear. The opposite pattern with nonprogressive verbs suggests that in a significant number of cases, at least, the neutral present nonprogressive verb form was used by the speakers in a contrasting sense, in places where the present perfect would also have been appropriate, that is, to refer to a perfective meaning.

The following two examples show nonprogressive and progressive verbs, respectively, combined with actions that jointly embody two appropriate points on the perfectivity dimension (phase *b* and point *x*):

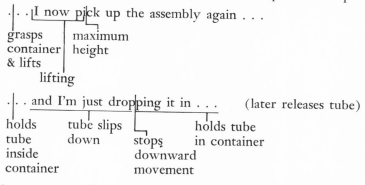

In the nonprogressive example, the action of picking up starts before the verb is uttered and is completed coincident with the production of the verb; the speaker seems to have regarded the action as complete, but not past (this impression is reinforced by the adverbial *now*). In the progressive example, the action of dropping is clearly not completed (in fact, the speaker deliberately interrupts it) until after the verb is uttered. In both examples, there seems to be an iconic relationship between the action and the utterance of the verb with respect to the perfectivity dimension.

Third, progressive verbs of the →| type are produced early in the described action, which clearly embodies an imperfective meaning (a late occurrence would have been incompatible). The occurrence of nonprogressive verbs before →| actions, however, cannot be due to a perfective meaning. Recent experiments by Levy and McNeill show that if one instructs subjects to regard →| actions as complete (perfective), nonprogressive verbs appear near or after the end of the action. This result supports the conclusion that a perfective meaning for some reason was absent with nonprogressive →| verbs in figure 1.

Fourth, verb particles coincide with ends or beginnings of →| actions, but are uncoordinated with → actions (no | verbs with particles appeared). It is possible that verb particles are not part of the embodiment of perfectivity in action and in speech. Rather, they seem to have a deictic relationship to the action, indicating the start or the end of the action. This is possible only if the verb (including the particle) describes an →| action with a definite end point.

Fifth, in a certain number of cases (not included in figure 1), the speaker completed the action before starting a progressive verb. This sequence at first appears to contradict the progressive verb pattern in figure 1. However, looking at these cases separately, we discover that the speaker has symbolically *extended the action in time* with a gesture; this gesture ends after the verb has been uttered. The embodiment of perfectivity has been shifted to a gesture. The following is an example

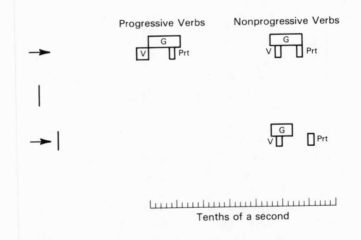

Fig. 2

of an extension in which a container (already picked up) is rocked back and forth while the speaker says "picking":

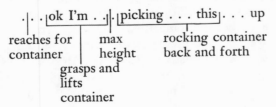

In such cases, the correlation of speech with action and the iconic representation of imperfectivity seems dramatically clear; extensions are not, even remotely, counterexamples.

To summarize, when speakers are asked to perform and to describe actions concurrently, they combine speech and action in a way that iconically represents the meaning of imperfective (and possibly perfective) actions. This combination is an iconic sign of perfectivity that appears with different kinds of actions and engenders gestural extensions of actions when the coordination threatens to break down. Verb particles do not seem to be part of this reconstitution of perfectivity. Rather, they appear to indicate deictically the beginnings or ends of actions, when the described action has a definite end point. In respect to both perfectivity and this deixis, speech and action appear to be generated coparts of a single activity by the speaker. The theory of the syntagma presented previously provides a basis for explaining this fusion of speech with action at a meaningful level.

SPEECH AND GESTURES

The gestures to be considered were induced by having subjects imagine and describe performing various actions. For example, the subjects imagined and described: tying a necktie (this was before the actual activity); the movements of a multiply hinged tong ✕✕✕✕✕✕✕✕✕ ;

how one could tell whether 🔗 is a knot; folding a two-dimensional cutout, presented in a drawing, into an imagined three-dimensional figure (cf. Shepard and Feng 1972). The speakers were not informed that their gestures were under investigation, and gestures were not mentioned at all. Gestures, nonetheless, appeared spontaneously in large numbers.

The gestures in this situation were generally of the type that Efron (1941) classified as *physiographic*, that is, concrete and iconic. Abstract gestures (what Efron called *ideographic*) were rare. The subjects were recorded on videotape, and their performance was analyzed frame by frame.

Figure 2 shows the duration and the relative placement of progressive and nonprogressive verbs and accompanying gestures. There are no examples of | verbs and only nonprogressive examples of →| verbs. The comparisons below, therefore, are generally limited to → verbs. Figure 2, representing gestures, can be compared with figure 1, representing genuine actions. The same distinctions between types of action have been drawn insofar as possible. For example, *push across* is considered to be →, and any accompanying gesture is placed into this category; the other types are treated similarly.

For → verbs, figure 2 is, in fact, remarkably similar to figure 1. Subjects seem to view imagined → actions as imperfective or perfective, and their accompanying gestures, together with speech, iconically embody these meanings. There are several observations to note in figure 2 that point to this conclusion.

First, the duration of gestures is longer for progressive than for nonprogressive → verbs, which is also true in figure 1. This can be explained if the activity of which the gesture and speech are coparts is prolonged when it is regarded as imperfective (extending phase *b*).

Second, progressive verbs end before the gesture starts, whereas nonprogressive verbs begin after the gesture starts (scarcely after, in the case of →| verbs). The imperfective meaning of this correlation of action with speech is quite clear with progressive verbs, and perhaps we can infer a perfective meaning with nonprogressive verbs also.

In addition to such evidence of an iconic depiction of the perfectivity dimension in gestures, gestures also iconically depict the movements conveyed by verb particles; for example: gestures involving upward movement accompanied *bend over, fold upwards, lift up, pick up,* and *turn up;* downward movement accompanied *go down, pull down, put in, stuff in,* and *push down;* movement of hands or fingers toward or away from each other accompanied *become smaller, bring together, come together, flatten out, go in a continuum, go in little jerks, make a loop, pull inwards, pull out, put together,* and *straighten out* (not all are particles, truly speaking); and so forth. Although a deictic function does not link particles to gestures, there is still a close semantic connection between the movements spontaneously made by the speaker and the descriptive content of particles and verbs used by the speaker.

CONCLUSION

Motor actions and language are connected in several ways: (1) the earliest speech of children appears as an integral part of ongoing motor actions; (2) the child's basis for the representation of meaning is a schematic representation of actions performed on the world; (3) the syntagma arises when the resulting sensory-motor schemas are internalized by the child; (4) speech output is an indexical sign of syntagmas. These connections of language to action describe the early stages of language development. But language is connected to motor action in adults as well. We see this in the ability to extend syntagmas to form iconic relationships with actions, and in the generation of gestures. We draw from this evidence two important conclusions: first, the linkage of language and action in adults is close enough to capture abstract concepts, such as aspect; and second, within language, we are not limited to symbolic and indexical signs, for there are iconic signs as well.

In fact, iconic signs become important just where abstract meaning is connected to action via the mediation of language. A chief source of linguistic creativity is using language in ways that establish new models, or icons, of abstract meanings. The addition of aspectual meaning to the temporal flow of speech is only one example. The very act of creating speech is a diagram of thought.

REFERENCES

Carter, A. 1975. The transformation of sensorimotor morphemes into words: A case study of the development of "more" and "mine." *Journal of Child Language* 2:233–50.

Efron, D. 1941. *Gesture and environment.* New York: King's Crown.

Inhelder, B., and Piaget, J. 1958. *The growth of logical thinking from childhood to adolescence.* New York: Basic Books.

Kozhevnikov, V. A., and Chistovich, L. A. 1965. *Speech: Articulation and perception.* Washington: U.S. Department of Commerce Joint Publications Research Service (30, 543).

Kuryłowicz, J. 1964. *The inflectional categories of Indo-European.* Heidelberg: Winter.

McNeill, D. 1979. *The conceptual basis of language.* Hillsdale, N.J.: Erlbaum.

Peirce, C. S. 1931–58. *Collected works of Charles Sanders Peirce.* Vols. 1–6, C. Hartshorne and P. Weiss, eds.; vols. 7–8, A. W. Burks, ed. Cambridge: Harvard University Press.

Piaget, J. 1952. *The origins of intelligence in children.* New York: Norton.

Shepard, R., and Feng, C. 1972. A chronometric study of mental paper folding. *Cognitive Psychology* 3:228–43.

Vygotsky, L. S. 1962. *Thought and language.* Cambridge: MIT Press.

———. 1978. *Mind in society.* Cambridge: Harvard University Press.

Abduction and Semiotics

DAVID SAVAN

In the stimulating and innovative paper, "Abductive and Deductive Change," Henning Andersen (1973) uses Peirce's theories of abduction, induction, and deduction—but especially his theory of abduction—as models to explain certain types of language change. This paper considers how the abductive model of linguistic change proposed by Andersen may be joined with a semeiotic[1] analysis. It will first summarize Andersen's use of the abductive model, and then go on to reinterpret his analysis on the model of Peirce's semeiotic.

The dialect of Old Czech which Andersen names Teták evolved in the fourteenth century. It differed from the surrounding dialects by a striking peculiarity exemplified in the word for *five*—'pet' in the surrounding dialects and 'tet' in Teták. Hence the names given to these dialects by Andersen, Peták and Teták. In Teták, for a small number of common lexemes, apico-alveolar consonants /t d n/ replaced the corresponding bilabial consonants /*p *b *m/. In the nineteenth century, this peculiarity disappeared. How can these two changes—first the substitution of dentals for labials, and later the substitution of labials for dentals—be explained?

Andersen finds that Peirce's analysis of scientific method, and, in particular, of the role of abduction within that method, provides the needed explicative model. What is an abductive inference? Andersen follows Peirce's earlier syllogistic formulation, in terms of rule, result, and case. An abductive inference begins with a situation that is ambiguous and puzzling. For example, Andersen suggests that "a learner observes the verbal activity of his elders, construes it as a 'result'—as the output of a grammar—and guesses at what that grammar might be" (1973:776). He is guided by the linguistic laws which he shares with all members of his species and which govern the relation between a grammar and its output. These laws, then, are his major premise, the rule. His conclusion, the case, is the underlying grammar which he formulates. Having formulated it, he deduces a verbal output and

252

tests this output inductively. If case or conclusion is inductively disconfirmed, the learner then attempts a new abduction.

Another formulation of abduction, also given by Peirce and more familiar today, goes as follows. We begin once more with an ambiguous and puzzling situation, *q*. To explain and clarify *q*, we form the hypothesis that if *p* were true, then there is a law such that *q* is derivable from *p* under that law. We conclude that *p*.

It is a well-known fallacy to suppose that *p* follows with necessity from such premises. It is also a fallacy, Peirce points out, to assign any quantifiable probability to the inference of *p*. It is characteristic of abduction that the conclusion is plausible only, and that its likelihood increases as more consequents are confirmed.

There is another salient feature of abduction which recommends it to Andersen as a model for his analysis of linguistic change. Unlike those introduced by induction and deduction, the hypotheses introduced by abduction may be new ideas and conjectured facts hitherto unobserved—perhaps unobservable. Abduction is "the only kind of reasoning that supplies new ideas" (*CP* 2.777).[2] It "supposes something of a different kind from what we have directly observed, and frequently something which it would be impossible for us to observe directly" (*CP* 2.640)—quarks, for example, or other minds, or past events, or underlying grammars.

Andersen now distinguishes three types of phonological change. Two of these, which he calls *evolutive* and *adaptive* change, are abductive, he argues. The third, which he adumbrates briefly, is deductive. This paper is confined to consideration of the two forms of abductive change. The origin of Teták is explained as an evolutive change, and its disappearance as an adaptive change.

The Teták dialect evolved because the acoustic manifestation of tonality syntagmas is ambiguous. The acoustic dimension of frequency is a continuum that the language learner must bisect to discriminate correctly the phonemes of his language. Assume that some children, as they learn a language like Old Czech (which includes the phonemic feature *sharped vs. plain*), perceive the sharped labial consonants as dentals. The speech of such children would then be characterized by dentals corresponding to the sharped labials of their elders.[3] As they grow older, such children become or are made aware of their deviant pronunciation and try to correct it. Some children—and these are the carriers of the evolutive change—adapt their pronunciation to the norm, without giving up their underlying dentals. They do this by formulating an *adaptive rule* (A-rule), roughly of the form [t] → [p], applicable only to certain lexical items and to the output of certain morphophonemic rules. These children grow up with an underlying dental stop that, because of the adaptive rule, is realized as sharped labials. It is important to note that Andersen maintains that both the underlying deviant bisection and the A-rules by which it is adapted to the received pronunciation are abductive in form.

The second stage in the evolutive change is the evaluation by the first generation of children of the same deviant bisection in the next generation of children. Speakers with underlying dentals and A-rules evaluate the childish dentals as a natural simplification and are more tolerant of them. The children of the second generation (1) respond to this tolerance by continuing for a longer time to produce dentals instead of labials, and (2) associate the A-rule with such extralinguistic factors as age or status difference. The A-rule is treated as a stylistic rule, used in some speech situations, but suspended in others. Such an optional rule tends to be eliminated, and the number of lexemes to which it applies tends to be reduced. The final stage of this process, then, is a homogeneous linguistic community, in which all sharped labials are replaced by dentals, except, perhaps, when used on certain formal occasions.

Andersen argues that the disappearance of the Teták peculiarity in the nineteenth century is also an abductive change, but is of a distinctly different form, which he calls adaptive change. Here the initiating factor is the increase in geographical and, perhaps, social mobility which results in increasing contacts between Teták speakers and outsiders. The outsiders evaluate the Teták peculiarity as a symbol of social inferiority; the Teták speakers accept the outsiders' evaluation, and come to regard their peculiarity as something best suppressed. They then adapt their speech to the newly internalized norm by means of a new A-rule. The next generation of children finds little ambiguity in the new norms, and formulates its phonology with underlying labials (instead of dentals) and an optional A-rule to derive dentals (instead of labials). Once these abductive steps are taken, the old Teták peculiarity quickly declines.

The foregoing is an outline of only the portion of Andersen's paper that deals with abductive change; his outline of deductive change has been omitted, because substantive linguistics is not the focus of this paper. From this point, I will, first, show that the abduction-induction-deduction model is, in fact, embedded in a comprehensive and articulated semeiotic structure; and, second, suggest that this larger semeiotic structure raises some questions which the abduction-induction-deduction model overlooks.

Peirce sees logic, and the general assessment of scientific method, as part of semeiotic. He does so, for the following reason. All knowledge, from the most tentative guess to the most demonstrative certainty, is grounded on evidence; it is supported by data, credentials, warrants, and premises. The data are not themselves evidence for that to which they attest; they must be interpreted to be evidence, to give some credibility to what they support. In short, the data are a sign of what they are interpreted to stand for. Everything and anything may be interpreted as a sign or a complex of signs. Peirce mentions music and the arts, social institutions, animal and plant behavior, human behavior, and sensation, emotion, perception, and attention. Semeiotic includes logic, but also much more. Logic studies chiefly the formal elements, structures, and evaluation of evidence, so far as they are formulated in language or in agreed symbols.

Nevertheless, the three forms of inference do express three basic principles of semeiosis. Let us call them simply "First Principle," "Second Principle," and "Third Principle." The three combine in a complex variety of ways in every semeiotic function, but they may be treated separately for purposes of analysis and description. It must be remembered, however, that in every concrete case all three are involved, in different relations of subordination and superordination. Peirce moves toward a theory of semeiotic change in accordance with his three principles (notably in "Evolutionary Love" [*CP* 6.287–317], but also in other papers). He outlines three major types of semeiotic change, calling them *tychastic*, *anancastic*, and *agapastic*.

The First Principle of semeiosis grounds and initiates the whole process by introducing the idea of a sign or a representation into whatever is present. It does this by identifying some qualitative feature and taking that feature as the respect in virtue of which something may be a sign. The feature must be general, that is, it must be potentially repeatable in indefinitely many instances, so that each instantiation may thereby be a sign of other instances embodying the same or a similar feature. Further, the feature must be determinate enough to serve as a diacritical mark, distinguishing its instances from noninstances. The significant feature may be a simple quality, like tone or color (Qualisign); or it may be the singularity of a spatiotemporal occurrence (Sinsign); or it may be the regularity of a law (Legisign). In any case, the generality and repeatability of the feature cannot be given in what is present. It must be taken to be a sign. To take something as a sign introduces something new, by which the indeterminate situation may be determined. It is this originative aspect of the First Principle which underlies Peirce's theory of abduction, and it is one of the chief reasons he calls it the first, or Firstness. The First Principle might be formulated, then, as follows: an indeterminate situation may be rendered more determinate by an originative transformation of some feature into a sign that is repeatable and distinguishable from other features.

It is clear, then, that Andersen's Teták language learners act in accordance with the First Principle when they select dentals as a significant feature in the acoustic continuum. However, to analyze the learning of a phonology, two other principles must be brought to the process. The language learners must encounter the sign in some actual instantiation as dynamically related to an existent object, and for this to be explained, the Second Principle must be brought in. Further, a language is learned through interpretants of the sign, and it is the Third Principle that introduces the interpretant.

By the same token, the First Principle does not give us an abduction, but only an ancestor of an abduction. An abductive inference, as Peirce understands it, concludes to a singular object, existing at some time, and it reaches this conclusion through an interpretant rule or law. The notions of the object and the interpretant of a sign require the Second and Third Principles. The First Principle gives us the sign only as a possibility, without instantiation or interpretation.

Turning to the Second Principle, we might formulate it thus: a sign is actually instantiated (or embodied) if it is spatially or temporally related to some existent object that is independent of the sign and is dynamically active upon the sign instance in such a way as to produce some semeiotic effect within the sign. Such an object, essential to the actual occurrence of any sign in some particular context, is called by Peirce the *dynamic* or *real object* or *utterer* of the sign. Its actual semeiotic effect within the sign serves as a clue or sample of the dynamic object. Peirce calls it the *immediate object*. The relation between the dynamic object and the sign may be any one of the familiar triad: iconic, indexical, or symbolic.

It should be clear that when Peirce writes that a sign "stands for" its object, he means something more than that it *refers, designates,* or *indicates.* The major difference is that reference and its congeners are ways in which signs are interpreted to select an object. Peirce, on the other hand, maintains that a sign stands for the object that acts in such a manner as to instantiate or realize the sign. It is the action of the object on the sign, and the trace or clue which it leaves within the sign, that may later be used by the interpretant to determine the reference of the sign. In Andersen's example of evolutive change, it is the established speakers of Old Czech who are the dynamic objects or utterers of the sign, and it is the sounds as actually heard by the new language learners that are the immediate object within the sign. The relation between the utterers and the heard sounds is predominantly indexical, although there are subordinate iconic and symbolic relations as well.

The Second Principle is one of asymmetrical duality—the agency of the dynamic object contrasts with the evidence of that agency in the immediate object of the sign. This is one of the reasons Peirce speaks here of Secondness. The asymmetric duality is not induction, but it is the semeiotic ancestor of induction. The immediate object is the presence of part of the dynamic object within the sign, and the distribution of features in the immediate object may be inductively interpreted as a sample of the distribution of those features in the collective object of which it is a sampled part.

The Third Principle characterizes the *interpretant*, and is formulated thus: every actually occurring sign must itself be the object of another sign, its interpretant, which (*a*) represents that the grounding sign is the sign of some object or other, (*b*) includes within it an immediate object dynamically produced by an utterer or dynamic object, and (*c*) represents a rule or law, of which the interpretant is itself an instance, in accordance with which its dynamic object is identified with the object of the original interpreted sign. Since the interpretant instantiates a law, each interpretant sign is a member of a potentially infinite series of interpretants, each instantiating the same law. In assigning its own dynamic object to the interpreted sign, the interpretant assesses the assurance or reliability of the sign as evidence of that object. The law provides a general formula for assessing the validity and weight of the sign in its relation to the object.

The Third Principle can be illustrated by applying it to Andersen's example of evolutive change. Suppose we take the feature in respect of which the physical sound waves are a sign to be the acoustic continuum as it might be heard. This is instantiated in actual speech contexts, and the sounds as actually heard are the immediate object, the utterers are the dynamic object, and the productive relation between them is indexical. Within the area of ambiguity of the heard sounds, the language learners spontaneously, directly, and immediately (Andersen says, "naturally") envisage the possibility of a bisection which would put heightened low tonality together with simply high tonality; that is, sharped labials would be classed as dentals. They then interpret the immediate object—the immediately heard speech—accordingly, and ascribe the production of dentals to the utterers.

This is the *immediate* interpretant, and the Peircean semeiotic thus far is in accord with Andersen's analysis. Notice two things: first, the immediate interpretant interprets itself as an instance of a law; that is, it is an incipient habit, a propensity to replicate the same interpretation in further circumstances of a like kind. Second, the immediate interpretant is not critical, articulated, premeditated, or intellectual. Peirce characterizes it variously as primitive, sensory, perceptual, emotional, and as an interpretant which is felt, not reasoned.

In "Evolutionary Love" (*CP* 6.302–11) Peirce argues that changes which originate in this way are tychastic; that is, they arise gradually, through a succession of small steps, and the direction of this succession is a matter of chance. However, as he was well aware, changes in cultural matters are almost never purely or merely tychastic.

Language learners who have immediately interpreted certain phonological terms as dentals will then produce these dentals in their speech. Their speech is an interpretant, but unlike the immediate interpretant, speech is a public act requiring the exercise of muscular energy. Such energetic and public interpretants Peirce calls *dynamic* interpretants. The childish dentals are then dynamic interpretants, and they are related to the immediate interpretants of the sign by suggestion.

At some point, the childish dentals encounter an obstacle. The learners are corrected, or in some other way come to conflict with the older speech community. Following Andersen, we can suppose that some of the children will not abandon their immediate interpretants, the underlying dentals,[4] but will formulate an adaptive rule (A-rule), which they will apply only to certain lexical items in certain contexts to produce a labial stop. Andersen's view is that the formulation of the adaptive rules is an abductive step (Andersen 1973:781). At this point, a semeiotic analysis diverges from Andersen, and the difference has some importance, since it alters the analysis of the second kind of change considered by Andersen—what he calls adaptive change. The semeiotic approach suggests that adaptive rules are formed inductively, or, rather, proto-inductively, since they are not deliberate and critically drawn inductions.

There are four reasons against classifying the formulation of adaptive rules under the abductive model. First, the weakest argument: according to Peirce, abductive change proceeds by small and almost insensible steps, but the formulation of an A-rule in Andersen's scheme is not a small step, and, since it involves a publicly ascertainable speech act, it is not insensible. Second, abductive change introduces novelty and is consequently unpredictable. Peirce calls it tychastic. The adaptive rules, on the other hand, produce conformity to a previously given labial stop. Third, an abductive act has a certain spontaneity or freedom. The adaptive rules, however, are formed under some compulsion from the larger linguistic community, and they prescribe imperatives for the production of certain dynamic interpretants under specific conditions. This anancastic factor, as Peirce calls it, is characteristic of the way brute fact and hard experience force us to change. Induction is a sampling of such hard facts.

Fourth, we turn to abduction only when induction fails us, and in this case induction can adequately account for the A-rules. We may suppose that the learner interprets the distribution of phonemic feature values in the teachers' speech in certain situations as samples of a similar distribution in similar situations in the larger community. The inductive generalization follows: probably, all members of the speech community in such contexts produce labials. But Andersen's hypothesis, which seems correct here, is that the learners retain the earlier immediate interpretant: underlying dentals are a sign of the same speech community. From these two premises, one inductive, the other abductive, the learner can deduce the conclusion that underlying dentals will, in certain situations, produce public labials. (In some of his early work in logic, Peirce calls an argument of this form *analogical, CP* 2.513, 733.) The A-rule translates this conclusion into an imperative (Peirce's term, in contrast to the earlier mentioned suggestive relation) for the production of labials from underlying dentals in certain contexts.

There is a fifth reason for doubting the classification of A-rules under abduction; namely, the role of norms and values in the formulation of A-rules. (That point will be discussed below.) We can conclude here by saying that a semeiotic analysis takes the formulation of A-rules to be an inductively (proto-inductively) formed imperative relation between immediate and dynamic interpretants.

One problem remains, however, with evolutive change. How can we account for the gradual elimination of the A-rule in Teták, which completes its evolution? Andersen's suggestion is that such a rule would be eliminated for two reasons: (1) the rule would be applicable only in certain speech situations, and would even then not be obligatory; and (2) "since its domain would be defined in terms of individual lexemes specifically marked as subject to it, the number of lexemes to which it applied would tend to be reduced" (Andersen 1973:774).

Peirce's semeiotic suggests a different hypothesis, which is consistent with Andersen's, and which includes it as a subcase. The semeiotic account relies on the third type of interpretant distinguished by Peirce, the *final* interpretant. (He also uses the modifiers *normal* and *destinate.*) The word *final* should suggest Aristotelian final causation, and with it the concepts of goal and norm. Peirce's position is briefly this: successive dynamic interpretants exhibit a regularity or law, the final intepretant. Like all interpretants, the final interpretant brings a case under the First Principle (in our example, underlying dentals as immediate interpretants) into harmony with cases under the Second Principle (the utterances which are dynamic interpretants). Since interpretants are semeiotic and not mechanical phenomena, the law appears in its instances as a norm, or goal-directed propensity that is not necessarily conscious. (In fairness to Andersen, we must note that he emphasizes the goal-directed character of adaptive rules and adaptive change.) Such a norm, Peirce says, acts on its instances not by compulsion but by attraction—agapastically, he says. Telic causation by attraction is not exact, and allows for numerous deviations, but over the course of its action, these deviations tend gradually to diminish in amplitude and in frequency, unless additional factors are introduced *ab extra*. Furthermore, if the law under consideration is subordinate to a superior governing law, the subordinate law will conform increasingly to its governing law.

Let me now return to the A-rule and discuss the role of the norm. It is not sufficient that the learners encounter the labial stops of their teachers. They must also view positively taking their teachers' pronunciation as a norm or goal. In Peirce's terms, they must adopt the labial stop as a final interpretant. But our hypothesis is that they do so only in a special class of cases under special conditions; in short, that this is a law which is subordinate to some superordinate final interpretant, and which will tend increasingly to conform to its governing final interpretant. The A-rule will then eventually disappear. As mentioned earlier, this semeiotic account is quite consistent with Andersen's, but it puts his scheme in a broader semeiotic context.

Finally, and briefly, let us turn to the second type of linguistic change distinguished by Andersen, what he calls adaptive change. He considers that this, too, falls under the abductive model, but in a markedly different and more complex way than evolutive change. His example is the decline and fall of Teták, brought about in all likelihood by more frequent encounters with a wider language community, and by the adoption by Teták speakers of the outsiders' low evaluation of the Teták peculiarity. The hypothetical reconstruction of the course of events is as follows. First stage: Teták speakers encounter a language community which has labials where Teták has dentals, and which jeers at the Teták peculiarity. Second stage: Teták speakers accept the outsiders' evaluation and abductively (according to Andersen's interpretation) formulate an A-rule to produce the more highly valued labials. Third stage: Teták speakers notice that doublets with labials are always acceptable to their models, and abduct a new phonology with underlying labials to replace the old phonology with underlying dentals. They formulate another, and optional, A-rule to produce dentals. Fourth stage: rapid disappearance of the Teták peculiarity. Andersen points out that adaptive change is more complex than evolutive change in two ways: first, it involves the introduction of two sets of A-rules; second, it begins by departing from an established phonological structure.

The divergence between the semiotic approach and Andersen's approach should be clear by now. The process of adaptive change begins at the interpretant level. The encounter with the outsiders' phonemes is, at first, simply an irruption of an external fact. The outsiders' speech might be accepted by the Teták listeners as samples drawn from a larger population; but in that event, the effect upon Teták speech would be mechanical and, in Peirce's terms, anancastic. Before the outsiders can stimulate Teták speakers to produce labials in the proper contexts, they must be accepted by Teták speakers as models or goals—in brief, as final interpretants.

Nevertheless, according to Andersen, the labial norm, taken as a final interpretant, governs only a special and exceptional set of cases. The special cases may then be interpreted by the Teták speakers only as changing the composition of the sample of phonemes produced by a speaker. The A-rule by which a Teták speaker first produces a labial in place of a dental would then be a procedural rule within an inductive process. Peirce writes that induction "is founded upon a classification of facts, not according to their characters, but according to the manner of obtaining them" (*CP* 2.692).

These A-rules would lapse, as they did in the earlier case of evolutive change, were it not for one major difference. The final interpretant, that is, the acceptance of labials as norms, stimulates the formation of a new and innovative immediate interpretant—a phonological structure with underlying labials. The governing law in this change is not abduction, nor is it yet induction. It is the final interpretant acting agapastically, by attraction, to bring an abductive immediate interpretant into harmony with an inductive dynamic interpretant.

To summarize: comparison of Andersen's linguistic example and Peirce's semeiotic approach reveals that the relations among abduction, induction, and deduction are richer and more subtle than Andersen's models suggest at first. It also shows that it might be fruitful to add a model of induction to our models of abduction and deduction, and that Peirce's conception of the final interpretant might repay detailed study as a theoretical instrument.

NOTES

1. Peirce followed John Locke (*Essay Concerning Human Understanding*, IV.21) in adhering to the Greek spelling of the term. I accept the sug-

gestion of Professors Max Fisch and Kenneth Ketner that, when referring to Peirce's distinctive theory of signs, we write 'semeiotic' rather than 'semiotic'.

2. References to Peirce are to the *Collected Papers of Charles S. Peirce*, edited by C. Hartshorne and P. Weiss, and refer to volume and paragraph numbers.

3. "It is indeed a provocative thought that in early child language velar consonants tend to develop last and that dentals frequently substitute for labials or velars . . ." (Rauch 1973:262).

4. I follow Andersen in speaking of underlying dentals. Some may question the concept of an underlying phonology. A semeiotic analysis would speak of an immediate interpretant as an incipient habit interpreting the sign as issuing from utterers who usually produce dentals in certain kinds of contexts.

REFERENCES

Andersen, H. 1973. Abductive and deductive change. *Language* 49:765–93.

Peirce, C. S. 1931–58. *Collected Papers of Charles S. Peirce*. Vols. 1–6, C. Hartshorne and P. Weiss, eds.; vols. 7–8, A. W. Burks, ed. Cambridge: Harvard University Press.

Rauch, I. 1973. Some North-West Germanic dental conditioners and Laryngeal Effect. In *Husbanding the Golden Grain: Studies in Honor of Henry W. Nordmeyer*, L. T. Frank and E. E. George, eds., 255–64. Ann Arbor: University of Michigan, Department of Germanic Languages and Literatures.

Language and the
Semiotics of Perception

RAIMO ANTTILA

EMPIRICAL DEFENSE OF FIRSTNESS
AND SECONDNESS IN LANGUAGE
FACULTY AND USE[1]

Cognition is becoming a key word in current linguistic theorizing, and the focus on cognitive processes somehow tends to replace the Chomskyan innateness revival without necessarily providing any practical effects to the contrary. Many of those who now talk about cognition easily forget that it encompasses perceiving, remembering, imagining, conceiving, judging, and reasoning; in short, it deals with the essential aspects of conscious life. Furthermore, consciousness itself has been a tabu word in American linguistics. The concepts of perception and memory have been dealt with arbitrarily and inaccurately, which has led mainstream linguistics (transformational-generative grammar) to a basically antisemiotic stance. It is true that this stance has concentrated on the rhema (universal concept) and the dicisign (proposition with truth value), but no semiotic coherence was reached, because of various inconsistencies and the neglect of context and use, in particular.[2]

It is not surprising, considering the state of brain physiology at Peirce's time, that he interpreted the nonexistence of a central cell as evidence that the unity of consciousness is a metaphysical notion without physiological origin (CP 6.229). But we are today in a very different position from Peirce, because there is growing evidence that the highest level of cognitive functioning takes place in the brain stem and not in the cerebral cortex, and that the brain stem has a symmetric functional relationship with both hemispheres. This one mind (through holistic interaction) is matched by holistic memory storage. This point is crucial; memory does not operate via feature analyzers and piecemeal storage. Penfield, in particular, has provided clear evidence for a permanent holistic record of the stream of consciousness, which can be retrieved like a sound movie through electric stimulation or epileptic fit (Penfield and Jasper 1954:142–43):

> The hallucination thus produced may be auditory or visual, or both, but it is neither a single sound nor a frozen picture. These are psychical hallucinations of an order quite different from the sensory experiences of vision or hearing produced by stimulation in auditory or visual areas of the cortex.
>
> It may be remembered experience. It may be the reproduction of a song that he has heard. If so, he "hears" it from beginning to end, not all at once. The experience may seem to the patient to be a dream, rather than an accurate memory. But it is a dream in which familiar places are seen and well-known people speak and act. Such hallucinations, or memories, or dreams continue to unfold slowly while the electrode is held in place. They are terminated suddenly when the electrode is withdrawn.
>
> This is a startling discovery. It brings psychical phenomena into the field of physiology. It should have profound significance also in the field of psychology provided we can interpret the facts properly.
>
> . . . Viewed in retrospect, memories do not appear to us as the hemianoptic pictures that might have been photographed by the visual apparatus upon the cortex of one hemisphere. They are not limited to material from one sense alone—far from it.
>
> *Recollection* of previous experience brings back material that is derived from various sensory systems—the visual stimuli that reached both hemispheres and the sounds and bodily sensations all fused into a whole. More than that, recollection may carry with it the emotion that the individual "felt" at the time of the original experience and the deductions, true or false, that he made concerning the experience.
>
> The same is true of memories produced by stimulation. Although there are doubtless many, many ganglionic patterns in the temporal cortex, only one pattern is activated by the stimulus and only one recollection is presented to consciousness. But the record is not that of an event alone. With it is stored a record of the substance of the individual's thinking concerning that experience and the attendant emotion (of fear) that may have accompanied it.

More of this evidence is available in literature, but let me remind you that neurophysiological research does provide us with evidence for a central metaorganizing system in the brain stem. Its immediate importance for semiotics and language structure is physiological support for supersigns.[3]

The concepts of holistic memory storage and of perception are complementary, making it possible for us to see the total sign as *mental* (objects are brought by the sign into the heads of observers) (Russell 1927[1960]:292):

> I take it that, when we have a percept, just what we perceive (if we avoid avoidable sources of error) is an event occupying part of the

region which, for physics, is occupied by the brain. In fact, perception gives us the most concrete knowledge we possess as to the stuff of the physical world, but what we perceive is part of the stuff of our brains. not part of the stuff of tables and chairs, sun, moon, and stars. Suppose we are looking at a leaf, and we see a green patch. This patch is not "out there" where the leaf is, but is an event occupying a certain volume in our brains during the time that we see the leaf. Seeing the leaf consists of the existence, in the region occupied by our brain, of a green patch causally connected with the leaf, or rather with a series of events emanating from the place in physical space where physics places the leaf. The percept is one of this series of events, differing from the others in its effects owing to the peculiarities of the region in which it occurs—or perhaps it would be more correct to say that the different effects *are* the peculiarities of the region.

There is thus a certain isomorphism between the laws of our conscious experience and the relevant aspects of the external world.[4]

The isomorphism hypothesis is one of the central tenets of Gestalt psychology. One hears now and then that modern cognitive psychology has superseded the findings of Gestalt psychology (that ultimately the same laws of field dynamics that underlie the organization of perception underlie the organization of thought). This is simply false. *Gestalt psychology is cognitive psychology at its best*, and there is no reason to change the name. Furthermore, Gestalt psychology properly emphasizes the primacy of perception (Firstness) for thought (Thirdness). Witness Peirce on this matter:

> . . . every general element of every hypothesis, however wild or sophisticated it may be [is] given somewhere in perception, . . . every general *form* of putting concepts together is, in its elements, given in perception. [*CP* 5.186; cf. Reilly 1970:52]

For Peirce, "there is no meaning, no understanding of the universe, except what can be derived in some way from experience" (Reilly 1970:53). Perception and experience go together like Firstness and Secondness (similarity and contiguity), which underlie the dynamics of thought and memory and the formation of perceptual units. But Peirce says that "by experience must be understood the entire mental product . . . hallucinations, delusions, superstitions, imaginations and fallacies of all kinds" (*CP* 6.492), that is, anything that is cognitive. The power of similarity and contiguity in affecting spontaneous unification in sensory fields is a well known psychological phenomenon (e.g., the stroboscopic movement of neon signs). (Cf. Anttila 1976 for a discussion of allomorphy).

One of the gestalt laws must be singled out for further consideration: closure. Gestalt completion phenomena provide the basis for the functional interaction of memory and perception; the holistic memory process becomes completely unified with an incomplete percept for which memory supplied the missing part. This is hardly surprising, because the above implies that the field processes underlying memory and perception are of the same nature. As Slagle points out (1975), concepts can now be considered rules that unify memory processes and similar perceptual processes, with similarity as the key factor (see also Slagle and Anttila forthcoming). Similarity itself is a property of the relations among fields, rather than of isolated entities; in other words, the context allows the determination of similarity. "Therefore it is also never possible to *define* what is meant with similarity" (Cornelius 1897:42); one does not start with the abstract concept of similarity, but with the concrete presence of a fact that we learn to designate as similarity after the formation of the abstract concept has taken place (Cornelius 1911:244; cf. Anttila 1977a:48–49). As Ransdell has pointed out (herein), likeness must be there, even if only through convention.[5] Note that *the criteria for classification are all sensory*, a concept which is crucial for a theory of meaning. The criteria are not, of course, capable of being experienced contemporaneously. Memory allows the temporal spread of the experiential correlates to be unified according to similarity. Thus, concepts such as 'justice', 'liberty', and other legal fictions are based on real constraints of systematic behavior which can be perceived in a spatiotemporal frame. These constraints of behavior are holistically stored with the symbols used in language. Thus the basis for classifying tokens into concepts is also the ostensive definition. It is utterly misguided to maintain that concepts like 'dog' are acquired through the senses, whereas prepositions like *from* necessitate the innateness hypothesis (Jackendoff 1976). Relations are also given in the spatiotemporal sensory frame (cf. Marty 1910:68); the syntax of perception determines the syntax of language. The concrete situation of use provides the basis of concepts (signs); this fits well with the pragmatic requirements of the current philosophical side of the argument, but linguists should remember that it has all been well explicated in the long and solid philological tradition.

From the philological tradition, the investigation of lexical fields (*Wortfeldforschung*) (now conveniently available in Schmidt 1973), particularly Porzig's *wesenhafte Bedeutungsbeziehungen* Schmidt 1973: 78–103, originally from 1934) is important for this argument. Certain collocations are given in the perceptual experience (e.g., *go* and *feet*, *hear* and *ear*, etc.; or Posner herein: *mow* and *grass*, *cut* and *hair*) and are stored together, and generally are brought to consciousness together. The primacy of the field is important, and if that aspect is added to the notion of *use*, a fuller frame results (Posner herein mentions the complementarity of particle and wave). In recent times, the situational motivation of language has been elegantly expressed by Maher (1977), who generally argues for meaning minimization (to use Posner's term). He shows how full semantic investiture of words takes place in the total context. If we translate this into semiotic terms and combine it with what Ransdell (herein) and Posner (herein) say, we can make the statement that since symbolic meaning is supposition, strong indexical ties to other signs and to the context are necessary for interpretation, that is, for semantic investiture. Because symbols are unutterable fictional rules, indexes have to replicate them (Ransdell herein), and if agreement in interpretation constitutes symbolic meaning, agreement can only be enhanced with maximal indexical mooring. These indexes provide the footholds for the iconic interpretation of the conceptual field in question. I think that Ransdell is right: this is characteristically a gestalt tendency, a gestalt completion of all the relevant information at hand.

But let us return to Maher's linguistic and semantic explication. He does not accept the prevalent arbitrary and artificial dichotomy between lexical and grammatical meaning, or concrete and abstract meaning, because every phenomenon can be accompanied by an epiphenomenon (Maher 1976:232):

> Consider expressions like *pitch-black*, which in certain cultural situations is clearly motivated. Someone who at one time wanted to emphasize the blackness of an object picked for a referent a noun which is by nature black, pitch. By phenomenon, then, I mean this, that there is a straightforward mapping between lexemes and referents in the context of situation. But the human brain never stops here. Every phenomenon is attended also by an epiphenomenon. *Pitch-black* means not only "black as pitch," it also means epiphenomenally, "very black." Children who grow up in an urban setting do not know what pitch is, and so they correctly infer that *pitch-black* means "very black." Thus on leaving Frankfurt Airport once five years ago, my then six-year old son looked down at the clouds once we had broken through the cover and said, "Those clouds are pitch-white." Now this experience is quite common. It is in the nature of things that we experience phenomena and generalize from them.

In cases like this, we see quite clearly that the total field guides interpretation, because lexical contradiction (*pitch-white*) is no problem on the higher level. In fact, literal meaning is the problem (Posner), because it is a necessary fiction. In the real world, speakers strive to make sense according to their experiences. Hörmann's notion of *sense constancy* expresses that reality; for example, *Not all women are female* can be interpreted by changing the meaning of a constituent (1976:279). Another example is provided by Maher: in the Latin phrase *festina lente* 'hurry slowly', the apparent contradiction in the speed words indicates that speed is not the primary concern, hence the meaning 'strive at your goal with determination'.[6]

Maher's student, Stephan Langhoff, has studied the semantic under-specificity of infinitives (1977, 1979), particularly from the point of view of modality. Modal meaning is added in the context of use; for example, *a paper to read* can be paraphrased as a paper that *can* be read, *should* be read, or *must* be read. This instance shows clearly that the prevalent either-or treatment of possible readings (in the deep structure, or the like) is inadequate. No deep structure will work. Instead, we must adopt a framework of as-well-as readings, guided by the total situation. Modality is, of course, a grammatical meaning, but it cannot really be separated from lexical signs. We have a gestalt switch between a grammatical and a lexical *haben* in *Haben Sie etwas zu verzollen?* 'Have you got to declare anything?' or 'Have you got anything to declare?'. Consider the following anecdote. A visitor to Warsaw is shown various buildings and other monuments donated by the Russians, until he comments: "You must love the Russians for all these wonderful things!" The answer is: "Yes, we must." The modern either-or stance (e.g., transformational-generative grammar) would explain this with *must*$_1$ and *must*$_2$, thereby destroying the actual meaning altogether.[7]

A short digression is now in order, as a conclusion to this section. The position delineated above maintains that observation is the basis of human knowledge. In other words, we need an empirical frame for linguistics. The above refutes again the traditional arguments against empirical theories of mind (see Slagle 1975) that are based on the assumptions that there is a difference between the structure of memory and the structure of perception, and that one cannot explain the rules that concepts represent in terms of sensory factors. In discussion, Robert Lees has expressed the opinion that there is no hope for scholarly communication across school boundaries (i.e., between empiricists and the transformational-generative position), but more particularly, that there is no hope for empiricists; that one should just let their line die out. Nothing could be more typical of the old transformational-generative arbitrary orthodoxy than this denial of the only viable position.

REALISTIC DEFENSE OF THE ICONIC AND INDEXICAL ELEMENTS OF LINGUISTIC SIGNS

The first section of this paper is called "empirical defense" for convenience. It shows many lines of compatibility with about half the papers presented at the conference, from biological considerations to treatment of the pragmatic component. In particular, my discussion of Firstness and Secondness complements Wells's discussion of Thirdness; and, in addition, I support Ransdell's position. This section repeats my argument from a different angle; it consists of a "realistic defense." I structure this defense loosely with an emphasis from icon to index to symbol (thus roughly the reverse of Ransdell's emphasis).[8]

"*Nihil est in intellectu quod non prius fuerit in sensu* . . . comes to mean that there is no meaning except what originates in the perceptual judgement" (Reilly 1970:49). This refers to the well-known Peircean sequence from percept to perceptual judgment, and to the way in which perceptual judgments are preabductive inferences (Reilly 1970; Buchler 1939:20–44; and Savan herein). Meaning derives from perception, through abduction, the only truly *ampliative* inference.

> Whereas perception is abductive, attention or the abstracting process of thought is held by Peirce to be inductive, attention bearing the same relation to sensation as induction, inferentially considered, to abduction. [Buchler 1939:38]

Buchler's reminder warns linguists that terms like perception, abduction, induction, and abstraction are not transformational or post-transformational achievements. The situation has been confused by relying on deduction as the only valid mode of inference. Deduction, even if augmented by the innateness hypothesis, does not lead to new knowledge.

> Attention or abstraction, Peirce believes, "is roused when the same phenomenon presents itself repeatedly on different occasions, or the same predicate in different subjects. We see that A has a certain character, that B has the same, C has the same; and this excites our attention, so that we say, '*These* have this character'. Thus attention is an act of induction; but it is an induction which does not increase our knowledge, because our 'these' covers nothing but the instances experienced. It is, in short, an argument from enumeration" (5.296). . . . The inductive character of attention is seen if we consider, analogously to the case of perception, the effects of attention on the nervous system. The formation of a habit is for Peirce an induction. [Buchler 1939:44].[9]

The semiotic cycle that leads to habit has been admirably explicated by Michael Shapiro (1976, ch.1: see particularly figure 3 on page 25, in which habit in the pragmatic component reflects back to reality in the perceptual component). Habit arises from the interpretant in the evaluative component, which itself has a two-way link with the conceptual component (sign). Shapiro's figure shows in one glance how current linguistic pragmatism lacks a semiotic foundation.

The interplay of attention and abduction leads us naturally to abstraction, another notion that has been mistreated by linguists. To quote Feibleman (1946[1970]:135):

> Abstraction, in the logical "sense in which an abstract noun marks an abstraction," (4.235) has been confused with "that operation of the mind by which we pay attention to one feature of a percept to the disregard of others. The two things are entirely disconnected." Logic is concerned only with the former, which Peirce termed "*hypostatic* abstraction, the abstraction which transforms 'it is light' into 'there is light here'." It is by means of symbols that we make abstractions. (4.531)

Since all linguistic signs are symbols, a certain degree of abstraction is always involved, but note that the abstraction stems from Firstness and perceptual reality; it is not given from above. Abstraction is thus the process behind linguistic fictions or general concepts (rhemas). In linguistics, this state of affairs has long been understood (Leibniz, Bentham, Brentano, Vaihinger), but by few mainstream practitioners (although Marty 1910 and Ogden and Richards 1923 deserve particular mention). The position of this tradition is, roughly, that abstract nouns are *fictitious*, though *natural;* hypostatization is an indispensable convenience, and the very essence of language.[10] Vaihinger is the best known philosopher of fictions (*as if*), but Peirce's realistic position is superior to Vaihinger's espousal of nominalism, as is amply shown by the growth of signs from icons to symbols and the interpretation of symbols in real experience.[11]

The most important exponent of the as-if approach to language is Fritz Mauthner (see Weiler 1970). He notes that language and thought do not follow the logic of logicians. Instead, they follow analogy; hence language is, in one sense, illogical. Yet it is the illogical kind of inference which is the basis for concept formation, that is, observation of similarities (Weiler 1970:70, 250–52). This is a rather explicit plea for abduction as ampliative inference. Furthermore, Mauthner believes that induction and abstraction are the same process (Weiler 1970:290), which is a position very close to that of Peirce, described above. Mauthner gives preference to adjectives, because they inform us of qualities that our senses record (this is the sensationalism of Locke and Mach) (Weiler 1970:150). Once qualities are temporally interrelated, we have the verbal mode or the world of becoming (Weiler 1970:283). Thus verbs and adjectives both portray reality, but do so with stylistic differences.[12] The border between the two categories is, of course, not clear-cut, and the noun cannot be neatly separated from either of the two (Weiler 1970:154). The noun is a serious defect.

Of course, language uses not only adjectives. In describing reality we rely primarily on thing-words or substantives. Mauthner regards this as the main shortcoming, philosophically speaking, of human language. For the assumption underlying the use of substantives contradicts the sensualist premises of his whole philosophy. A thing, such as an apple, is but the sum-total of observed qualities: 'What it can be beyond these adjectives (everything which we know of it *qua* chemists or botanists can equally well be expressed in adjectives) is a metaphysical question. For us it is a group of adjectives, out of which corporeality is constructed; what the apple is in itself we do not know.' [Weiler 1970: 150–51]

Words are short-hand means of referring to clusters of qualities, and there are no actual experiences of abstract general ideas (Weiler 1970: 151–52).[13]

Aaron (1952) has in fact delineated a position that matches quite well my argument from the semiotics of perception. He points out that common nouns need not entail exact combinations of qualities, because, for example, in everyday experience the class of houses is quite vague but works perfectly in communication. Note this important gestalt argument:

> A more promising suggestion is that the use of such words rests on a familiarity with an undifferentiated whole met with frequently in experience, a pattern or *Gestalt* whose parts have not been analysed. When I do discriminate between the various parts I find that these objects differ more from one another than I had at first thought. But at first I do not differentiate, but fall into the habit of grouping together objects which roughly resemble one another and associating a name with the group. I hear the word 'houses' used sometimes in the presence and sometimes in the absence of houses and I come to understand from the context what the word 'houses' means. I do not remember consciously grouping the *Gestalten* together, I do not remember learning how to use the word. But I find myself now possessed of certain habits, habits of expectation, habits of behaviour and of speech. Such habits or dispositions are gained by me not by my observing the recurrence of precise qualities identical with one another or closely resembling one another, but as a consequence of a long familiarity with recurring *Gestalten* between whose detailed features I do not differentiate. As the result of these experiences I know how to use the word 'house' successfully and I am also ready to recognize an instance of a house when I see one and to deny that something wrongly called a 'house' is in fact a house. [Aaron 1952:167–68]

We have already seen Langhoff's application of gestalt principles, but the high point of the gestalt argument in language was reached by

Slagle, who says that "disembodied actions and qualities are not to be found in immediate experience", rather:

actions and qualities are found only as differentiating aspects of 'things'. Thus, for example, one will never encounter a 'dancing' as an entity with a segregated givenness in sensory experience, although one might well see a bear dancing. Nor would one ever encounter a 'tall', but rather tall things or people. Consequently, since the denotata of adjectives and verbs occur only as differentiating aspects of entities with segregated givenness, and since entities with a segregated givenness are generally denoted by nouns, then it is clear that the restrictions in regard to which nouns can co-occur with which adjectives and which verbs, are ultimately based on whether the segregated entities denoted by the nouns can manifest the 'actions' or attributes denoted by the given verbs and adjectives. Although it might seem that only spatial entities can have a segregated givenness, this is not the case. Figure-ground differentiation is perhaps the most ubiquitous mode of perceptual organization, for some form of figure-ground differentiation is possible in all sensory modalities. As Walter Ehrenstein 1965 astutely pointed out, by focusing our attention on a given aspect of sensory experience, we can achieve a much greater degree of awareness of that particular aspect, with this aspect becoming the focal point of our consciousness, and thus being set off from the rest of the given perceptual field which then constitutes the ground. Consequently, we can focus on any aspect of our sensory consciousness in such a way as to experience it as a segregated entity. This applies, of course, to the attributes and actions, aspects which normally do not have a segregated givenness in experience. Thus, phenomena which would normally belong to either the verbal or adjectival domain of reference can be focused on in such a way as to become the focal point of our awareness and thus achieve a segregated givenness in terms of figure-ground differentiation and consequently belong to the nominal domain of reference. From the foregoing, it is obvious that we believe Roger Brown (1957:3) was correct in suggesting that the part-of-speech membership of a word operates as a perceptual filter guiding our attention toward the relevant aspects of the phenomena being classified. Indeed, within this framework one can easily explain the meaning of the part-of-speech membership of words. For once one realizes the importance of figure-ground differentiation in this context, nouns constitute no problem—nouns characteristically denote phenomena with a segregated givenness in sensory experience. And verbs can be considered as characteristically denoting those temporal aspects of segregated phenomena which manifest qualitative or spatial change (or absence of change) in time; while adjectives characteristically denote attributes without regard to whether or not they are manifesting some sort of change in the process of time. Shifts in form class, as we have already indicated in our discussion of nouns, can easily be explained in terms of shifts in the sensory criteria required to correctly use a term. Needless to say, the classification of form class meaning given here is meant to be merely illustrative and not in any way exhaustive. [Slagle 1975:188–89]

Finally, a few words must be said about the question of universals as a continuation of this theme. Universals represent another catchword of contemporary linguistics that is deficiently understood, because it is common in linguistics to take universals as a replacement of underlying things, that is, as some kind of god-given *ante-res res* (*substantes*). This is utterly unworkable. The truth is again simple: universals rest on Firstness and Secondness, that is, on similarities and recurrences.[14] "Similarities and universals are not the same. But they are first cousins" (Buchler 1966:179).[15] Or, as Aaron explicates in more detail:

The recurrence of these similarities is as useful a basis for classification as is the recurrence of identical qualities and relations. Here too are universals. Perhaps it is not so easy to pinpoint them in this case as in the case of ultramarine. They are recurring likenesses. But these likenesses too are observable, so that our classification, using these as principles of grouping, is empirically based. Hence recurring similarities as well as identities are universals, and we consciously use them to classify and order our experience, and are thus able to use a further set of general words successfully.

To hold that the recurring similarity is a universal, along with the recurring identical quality or identical relation, is to go beyond Aristotelian realism. [1952:235]

Aaron goes on to point out that nominalism is ruled out when grouping is based on observed similarity, and that, as was mentioned above, similarity is the only way to deal with the various aspects of cognition. Aaron defines universals as, "in the first place, recurrences found in the natural world" (232), and he ends with the position that universals are both natural recurrences and principles of grouping and classifying.

We come back to the same conclusion we reached earlier in this paper, when we examined the neurophysiological evidence: all the relevant roads lead to similarity (see also excerpt from Buchler in Note 15).

Classes are now recognized as symbolic fictions, and logisticians will only be logical when they admit that universals are an analogous convenience. The World of Pure Being will then be definitely denuded of its quondam denizens, for which the theory of Universals was an attempted explanation. It should be noted that our symbolic machinery (similarity, etc.), becomes both more valuable and more comprehensible when these desiccated archetypes have faded away. [Ogden and Richards 1923:95]

Since Wittgenstein was mentioned a few times at the conference, there is reason at this point to discuss his use of family resemblances as a tool to overcome the defects of nominalism and realism. But at this juncture I consider my argument strong enough to leave out this well-known support to my position. A final quotation from Wittgenstein's forerunner, Mauthner, does seem to be in order, however.

> Making an aesthetic judgement is therefore always a case of *seeing* a particular object as something or other. To use a well-known example, the duck-rabbit, which Wittgenstein borrowed from Jastrow, can be seen either *as* a rabbit or *as* a duck; it can be subsumed under the general concept *rabbit*, or under that of *duck*. The drawing itself does not determine our choice of general concept.
>
> There is here, what both Kant and Mauthner claim there must be, viz. an ability to observe similarities and dissimilarities. Mauthner's argument, then, is that all concept formation is basically of this kind; it consists in seeing something *as* this rather than *as* that. In other words, the kind of comparing activity which underlies all our concepts is a creative comparing in the sense that we focus our attention selectively on some characteristics of a thing. Those characteristics we single out will form the basis of comparison. The resulting comparison may seem witty or it may not but it will always be an effect of the exercise of wit in Kant's sense.[16] [Weiler 1970:160]

SEMIOTIC DEFENSE OF SOUND CHANGE

After defending the empirical, physiological, philological, and realistic underpinnings of semiotics, and thus also of linguistics, I now turn to phonology and sound change. These issues are important to our discussion because phonology has a rather precarious rating as a sign-system, and because sound change is generally considered to be a useless disturbance. If semiotics does not help us explicate or understand this domain of language, we must abandon the combination of semiotics with linguistics. Sound change is a traditional testing ground of linguistic theories. We can say that phonemes are Firsts and syllables Seconds; therefore, we can explicate Firstness and Secondness with linguistic signs, and in this case, we will do so particularly as they pertain to perception.

The question of the semiotic nature of synchronic phonology has in principle been answered by Roman Jakobson, Henning Andersen (1966, 1974), and Michael Shapiro (1974a, 1974b, 1976). As normally understood by linguists, phonemes do not have meaning. However, the categories for classifying phonemes are similarity and difference. Similarity keeps one phoneme together, and difference separates it from other phonemes. The function of the phoneme on the morphemic level is to keep morphemes apart, and this trait immediately points toward Secondness and indexicality. We have a door to the semiotic appreciation of phonemes.

First, let us establish a perceptual appreciation of phonemes, focusing on the similarity factor that keeps phonemes together. Similarity in perception establishes the crucial, basic meaning of the phoneme: otherness. This seeming paradox translates into the diacritic denotation that keeps morphemes apart. The phoneme is, after all, a symbol for that meaning. The problem appears to be allophonic variation. Why would such a disturbing agent be the rule in the languages of the world? The answer lies in the very essence of perception, described by Vernon:

> Thus although we expect the world around us to retain its constant identity, and the objects within it to remain relatively unchanged, the perceptual system is geared to understand and respond appropriately to frequent change. Recent experimental investigation has shown that change and variation of stimulation are essential to maintain the efficiency of perception, and of the cognitive processes associated with it. If people are exposed to artificial conditions in which stimulation remains homogeneous and unvarying over a period of time, perception may even cease to function. Or with reduction in the natural variation there may be a decrease of alertness and of attention to certain features of the environment. Contrasted with this are the rapid perception of and response to sudden change, and to novel and unfamiliar objects. Indeed, it has been established that certain physiological processes in the brain have the special function of arousing and alerting the individual to the variations in his environment. [1971:16–17]

The same has been said also by Dörner:

> Es gibt augenscheinlich ein gewisses Bedürfnis nach Unordnung, nach Unbestimmtheit, welche durch den Einsatz entsprechender geistiger Werkzeuge in Ordnung und Bestimmbarkeit umgewandelt werden kann. Die Effekte "sensorischer Deprivation" zeigen dies deutlich. Wenn man Personen durch geeignete Massnahmen gänzlich oder fast vollkommen von der Reizzufuhr abschneidet, so ereignen sich nach einer gewissen Zeitspanne dramatische Dinge. Die Versuchspersonen berichten von Parästhesien, Halluzination und insgesamt schwerwiegenden Beeinträchtigungen ihres psychischen Zustandes. Offenbar beginnt das wache, von der Unbestimmtheitzufuhr abgeschnittene Nervensystem die fehlende Unbestimmtheit dadurch zu ersetzen, dass es selbst Information erzeugt. Die weniger dramatischen Effekte schlichter Langweile deuten gleichfalls darauf hin, dass das wache Nervensystem eine gewisse Zufuhr an Unbestimmtheit braucht, die es bearbeiten und vermindern kann—durch Prozesse der Superzeichenbildung und der Superzeichensuche. [1977:77–78]

The phonetic variation is not left to lie idle; it is used for all kinds of indexical signaling, which we must call symbolic connotation (cf. diacritic denotation, above), that is, *con*-notation. Through this variation, phonemes absorb signals of individuals, emotional states, geographical regions, and social strata. The two main items on the list are quite well known through theatrical mimicry and dialect geography, even if they are not always noticed in everyday life. The meaning portrayed in those instances is, of course, symbolic with considerable iconic substance, although the indexical element clearly dominates.

One of the discoveries of those scholars who have been working with the semiotic conception of sound systems has been that phonological rules have a structural coherence, on the one hand, while they furnish us with clues about the descriptive aspect of phonologies, on the other. For example, the traditional assumption about Japanese and English obstruents has rested on the features voiced vs. voiceless. Assimilation rules work by referring to formal semiotic entities (and not to physical factors), and can be explained by the semiotic evaluation through which speech is filtered (Shapiro 1974b: 104). In general, Shapiro tests the coherence of the phonological structure and interprets the fact that Japanese vowels show voiceless realization between tenues consonants (e.g., *kEsu* 'extinguish') as a diagrammatic index of the distinctive features tense vs. lax, because the marked vocalic value (voiceless) has assimilated to the marked tense value of the obstruent. Similarly, Andersen (1974) interprets the distribution of English short vowels before "voiceless" stops and long vowels before "voiced" stops as bearing witness to a tense vs. lax distinction. Actually, this line of research, with an impetus from Jakobson, rests totally on the work of Andersen since 1966 and Shapiro (in rich simultaneous output exploring largely different aspects), and it could be termed the semiotic explication of the diagrammatic aspects of phonology.

Phonological implementation rules build diagrams of the distinctive feature hierarchies, through neutralization and variation. The resulting wave effects (in the morphemic minifields) portray the feature make-up of the units. The structural composition of the phoneme is thus thoroughly semiotic (iconic in particular), and this complements the indexical aspect that is dominant on the higher levels of functional perspectives. The variation, shown above to be perceptually and realistically *necessary*, thus carries the essential phonetic implementation of the sound units. But the phoneme is a clear supersign in its synthetic aspect (Anttila in preparation), since it is a combination or hierarchy of distinctive features. It is the unit that is given in immediate experience (another Secondness aspect). Problems of partial overlapping and the like disappear, once we realize the supremacy of the (mini)field (words or utterances). In other words, what we are dealing with are, in semiotic terms, supersign schemata (Dörner 1977), or, in perceptual terms, relations within fields. If a phoneme is a supersign, it has a certain gestalt structure carrying slots for components (cf. Dörner 1977:76), which get filled so that the relation between the components remains; in other words, the transposition of gestalts is observed. This is well known from phonemic analysis, except for the field component, which has been neglected. Dörner (1977:73) comments that most states of affairs are supersigns both through complex formation and through abstraction. This certainly fits the concept of phonemes as bundles of distinctive features and as abstractions through discarding redundant phonetic features. Dörner points out further (77) that supersigns in the sense delineated here are not perhaps full signs in terms of Bühler's theory, because they seem to lack the symbolic function. There is considerable truth in this, for the phonemes are predominantly iconic and indexical signs, although we have seen that they are, finally, also symbols.

Typically, though, the phoneme is taken as a qualisign, that is, as a quality (like color). Anttila deals with various aspects of Firstness among linguistic signs, but particularly with onomatopoeic words in Finnish, of the structure displayed below (1977b:28).

kihistä	'hiss, FIZZ'
kuhista	'murmur, whisper, SWARM'
köhistä	'rattle, RASP, RÂLE'
kohista	'murmur, swish, rumble, ROAR (water, river)'
kähistä	'wheeze'
kahista	'rustle'

Since all words are symbols, we could perhaps leave it at that; but if we ignore the symbolic aspect, we get a revealing semiotic analysis. The roots of the words end in *h* (the rest are suffixes: *-is-* 'continuous sound', *-ta* 'infinitive') and display the common element *k-h-*. This is essentially a rhematic-iconic legisign, in other words, a general diagram like Peirce's typical fever curve of a sickness (35). The diagram *k-h-* represents 'a kind of hissing/rustling noise'. To get an actual reading of the diagram, a rhematic-iconic sinsign, we have to insert a vowel as a sign of the exact quality (color, tone), which then quasi-asserts an indexical (quasi-truth) value (36). The vowels here are *images* embedded in *diagrams*, and we have, in a way, double iconicity.

The alternation between phonemes in language structure (morphophonemics) is a different matter, but is no problem for semiotic analysis. Shapiro (1974a, 1976) in particular has shown how morphophonemics is a semiotic. Morphophonemic alternation provides the material basis for markedness, or the material *Unbestimmtheitsfaktor* (cf. Dörner

1977:77–78) that serves as the trigger for the reaction that leads to the evaluative component. Again there is a wave phenomenon, but this time within morphology. Anttila (1976) discusses the gestalt aspects of allomorphs, and the results presented there agree also with Dörner's *Unbestimmtheitsreduktion*. Closure establishes the proper morpheme in the proper environment, and allomorphs show in fact the submission of the part to the total word, and thereby enhance the lexical entries, that is, supersigns through complex formation (cf. Dörner).

This lengthy, synchronic introduction to our discussion of sound change has established the following fact: phonology is a sign system in which iconic and indexical factors predominate. Signs change through use, and since sound units are complex signs, one expects them also to change. And indeed, we do know that sounds change as long as the language is spoken. Furthermore, iconicity and indexicality are the main forces of change (Anttila 1972), and if these factors are the prime constituents in phonology, one has further grounds for expecting change to be the normal modality.

Physical variation in sound production provides the basis for change, when variation is given direction. The same situation obtains for evolution in general (Anttila 1978). Recent sociolinguistics has made it completely clear that sound change results when variation is socially encoded, that is, when a particular pronunciation feature is assigned social meaning. The sound then becomes a social index (a pragmatic index, pertaining to the speakers) of a class or a region, and its fate is tied to the vicissitudes of that class or region, The linguistic facts of the situation are extremely well known and need not be discussed further.

One thing must be stressed here: sound change typically produces the allomorphy hinted at above. (Anttila 1975, 1977a, and 1978 discuss this point.) This is the so-called disturbing effect of sound change—it pulls unified paradigms apart, apparently without rhyme or reason. The facts are again well known, their semiotic explanation is not. First, the result is a service to the *gewisses Bedürfnis nach Unordnung* (see Dörner above), thereby supplying the basis for active perception and the necessary prerequisite for the esthetic satisfaction of interpretation (another aspect of Firstness) (cf. Dörner 1977:78). Second, as already indicated, sound change has a blurring effect on morpheme boundaries, thereby enhancing the unity of the total word (supersigns through complex formation).

The sound that takes on the blurring effect becomes a *syntactic index* that refers beyond itself and leaks information about the phonetic make-up of the following morpheme. Even if the information leakage is not perfect, it is selection nonetheless, and is therefore a semiotic process. The allophonic origin of such an index inheres in Korhonen's definition of a *quasiphoneme* (1969:335) (cf. the indexical quasitruths and quasiassertions above): a unit which is an allophone according to its distribution, but which bears phonemic indexical function in the linear order of morphemes (see Anttila forthc. for quotation). We see here the field effects of the total word or other, larger signs. The sound units find their best symmetry distribution by leaking features, normally between adjacent units. The physiological and acoustic basis of the process is quite well understood; the process itself has been called *assimilation*. Assimilation can be taken as adaptation iconicity, in that a sound adapts to a neighboring one. The result is an increase in continuity. Note that it is indexical contiguity that releases iconic assimilation, and the result is a new index for syntactic cohesion. A typical example occurs in pre-English: the plural of **mūs* was **mys-i* 'mouse'. The fronted allophone [y] of /ū/ was an index to a following front vowel, and its information value was thus considerable. In fact, the **-i* could be dropped without any loss of information, whereby the allophonic variation becomes morphophonemic alternation of phonemes in Old English *mūs/mys*. This process is known as secondary split, and it points to the fact that quasiphonemes typically snap into autonomous phonemes; in other words, the diacritic function finds its optimal distribution of field forces in the autonomous phoneme (Anttila forthc.). But this snapping into phonemes does not delete any of the connotative functions, which are usually retained.

The syntactic index as developed here is a grammatical sign that increases symmetry within words and thereby emphasizes contrasts between other words in the same paradigm. (This is clear evidence against the underlying invariant forms of generative phonology.) The index often also becomes a categorical index for parts-of-speech membership (cf. Slagle 1975:188–89, quoted above; and see Anttila 1978), for example, *safe/save, belief/believe*. It is true that this normally happens via the syntactic index; but, in principle, straight grammatical conditioning cannot be ruled out, if one accepts that grammatical categories correspond to reality. I claim that they do have a correspondence to reality (see again Slagle quoted above). But now we have come back to the question of abstraction and fictions, and can stop here, noting that sound change does have an important semiotic, sign producing function. It constantly provides new possibilities for abductive inference.

The triple defense of Firstness and Secondness (perception and experience, icons and indexes, abduction and induction) in connection with linguistic signs that has been presented here is intended to show the usefulness and necessity of these categories. There is growing criticism of this type of argument that will have to be answered; but the criticism will not be able to weaken the basic foundation of the semiotic approach to perception. And as for language, the strong evidence of the deep semiotic justification of sound change remains (cf. Savan herein).[17]

NOTES

1. Here I consider a few issues from the border between familiarity and neglect, that is, notions that are quite well known to linguists, but which are often inadequately or wrongly interpreted in the theoretical or semiotic frame. I defend such neglected aspects in a general way, and thus I provide only minimal bibliographical apparatus, either pertaining to semiotics in general or to the philosophical and psychological implications of gestalt theory or similarity. (For example, such relevant issues as those presented in Holenstein [1972] are not discussed.) My references to the other contributions to this volume are based on my understanding of the oral presentations at the conference, not their final written versions. References to Peirce are to the *Collected Papers of Charles S. Peirce*, edited by C. Hartshorne and P. Weiss (Cambridge: Harvard University Press, 1960), and refer to volume and paragraph number.

2. There may be objection here by linguists who would point out, quite accurately, that pragmatic considerations have been gaining ground over the past few years. In this volume the pragmatic component is most strongly represented in those contributions that concentrate on language rather than on semiotics. Pragmatics is in fact summoned to aid in the interpretation of linguistic forms; it is not taken at face value as *experience*, to use a term from the title of the conference on which this volume is based. When one uses pragmatics as an appendix to various formal accounts of linguistic structure, one approaches experience from the wrong viewpoint, from above (from Thirdness to Secondness); whereas, for a full account, one must approach it from below (Firstness). Cognition is misused by linguists in the same way: perception is derived from it. For these reasons, this reminder of the primacy of Firstness might complement some of the other papers in the volume.

3. This is a very important point, but its full appreciation would lead us far afield from our present concern. Courtesy of Roland Posner, I was able to acquaint myself with *Zeichenprozesse* (Posner and Reinecke 1977) at this conference. That volume, like this paper, begins its story with brain research ("Neurobiologische Grundlagen der Zeichenerkennung" by Otto-Joachim Grüsser); and the book goes on to have a section on supersign formation. I leave the issue here at this hint, but I will single out Dörner's article on the theme below.

4. I repeat the warning given in Note 1 on the limits of the bibliography provided at the end of this paper. Very little is listed from the extensive philosophical literature on the topic. I have omitted Husserl (but see Holenstein 1972) as well as many works supporting the primacy of perception (but see Merleau-Ponty 1964).

5. Eco (1972, 1976) goes too much in this direction, it seems.

6. Epiphenomenal readings lead, of course, to transferred meanings and to metaphor.

7. It is still common practice for current literature to give examples such as finding *to bear children* and *to bear a burden* to be accidental homophony (*bear*$_1$ and *bear*$_2$). Such inadequate analysis results from denying the perceptual basis of grammatical theory.

8. This is convenient for the issue of language acquisition and sound change, and it also agrees with the structure of perception.

9. This can be taken as part of an explication of the synthetic unity of apperception.

10. Note again how transformational-generative grammar obfuscates the situation by resorting to underlying forms.

11. The necessary realism must be *in rebus* and *inter res*, not merely *ante res*.

12. Cf. Peirce's statement (*CP* 5.293) that a feeling is accompanied by movement.

13. Mauthner's position contrasts interestingly with Bentham's, who, toward the end of his life, actually preferred to use nouns.

14. On a higher level, one can say that both aspects reflect symmetry dynamics.

15. The paragraph continues and ends the following way:

> The vexatious problem of universals derives from puzzlement over the "reference" of universal terms, and the same problem arises with respect to classes, kinds, or forms. To say that universals are "nothing but terms," verbal devices used to manipulate particulars (to identify, classify, compare them), rests on the opinion that these particulars "in reality" have nothing in common and are absolutely particular. Absolute particulars would have to be absolutely unique. Since the notion of absolute uniqueness, as there is small need to repeat, implies disconnectedness and unrelatedness to anything else, each particular would have to inhabit an inaccessible domain of its own. But whether these particulars are "in the mind" and invested with similarity (including common involvement in a relation) to cover their unintelligible nakedness, or in the world and utterly alone "in themselves," the notions of similarity and difference are inevitable and indispensable. [Buchler 1966:179]

16. Peirce recognized the importance of the gestalt switch for a theory of perception (*CP* 5.183) (see Reilly 1970:50).

17. There are linguists who do not like the term 'semiotic'. For them I suggest that my *semiotic defense* be translated to *theoretical defense*.

REFERENCES

Aaron, R. I. 1952. *The theory of universals*. Oxford: At the University Press.

Andersen, H. 1966. Tenues and mediae in the Slavic languages: a historical investigation. Ph.D. dissertation, Harvard University.

———. 1974. Phonology as semiotic. In *A semiotic landscape: Proceedings of the first congress of the International Association for Semiotic Studies*, S. Chatman et al., ed., pp. 377–81. The Hague: Mouton, 1979.

Anttila, R. 1972. *An introduction to historical and comparative linguistics*. New York: Macmillan.

———. 1975. *The indexical element in morphology*. Innsbrucker Beiträge zur Sprachwissenschaft, Reihe Vorträge 12.

———. 1976. The metamorphosis of allomorphs. In *The second LACUS forum 1975*, P. Reich, ed., 238–48. Columbia, S.C.: Hornbeam Press.

———. 1977a. *Analogy*. Trends in Linguistics; State-of-the-Art Reports 10. The Hague: Mouton.

———. 1977b. Toward a semiotic analysis of expressive vocabulary. *Semiosis* 5:27–40.

———. 1978. The acceptance of sound change by linguistic structure. In *Recent developments in historical phonology*, J. Fisiak, ed., 43–56. The Hague: Mouton.

———. In preparation. Totality, relation, and the autonomous phoneme.

Buchler, J. 1939. *Charles Peirce's empiricism*. London: Kegan Paul.

———. 1966. *Metaphysics of natural complexes*. New York: Columbia University Press.

Cornelius, H. 1897. *Psychologie als Erfahrungswissenschaft*. Leipzig: Teubner.

———. 1911. *Einleitung in die Philosophie*. Leipzig: Teubner.

Dörner, D. 1977. Superzeichen und kognitive Prozesse. In *Zeichenprozesse: Semiotische Forschung in den Einzelwissenschaften*, R. Posner and H.-P. Reineke, eds., 73–82. Weisbaden: Athenaion.

Eco, U. 1972. Introduction to a semiotics of iconic signs. *Versus* 2(1):1–15.

———. 1976. *A theory of semiotics*. Bloomington: Indiana University Press.

Feibleman, J. K. 1946. *An introduction to the philosophy of Charles S. Peirce*. Cambridge: MIT Press, 1970.

Holenstein, E. 1972. *Phänomenologie der Assoziation*. The Hague: Nijhoff.

Hörmann, H. 1976. The concept of sense constancy. *Lingua* 39:269–80.

Jackendoff, R. 1976. Toward a cognitively viable semantics. In *Semantics: theory and application*, C. Rameh, ed., 59–80. GURT. Washington: Georgetown University Press.

Korhonen, M. 1969. Die Entwicklung der morphologischen Methode im Lappischen. *Finnish-Ugrische Forschungen* 37:203–362.

Langhoff, S. 1977. Underspecified modality in *have to/be to*: a contrastive study on semantic investiture. Unpublished manuscript.

———. 1979. Gestaltlinguistik: Eine ganzeinheitliche Beschreibung syntaktischsemantischer Sprachfunktionen am Beispiel modaler Infinitivkonstruktionen des Deutschen und Englischen. Ph.D. dissertation, University of Hamburg.

Maher, J. P. 1976. Discussion on Anttila. In *Current progress in historical linguistics*, W. M. Christie, ed. 231–32. Amsterdam: North-Holland.

———. 1977. *Papers on language theory and history I*. Amsterdam: John Benjamins.

Marty, A. 1910. *Zur Sprachphilosophie. Die "logische", "lokalistische" und andere Kasustheorien*. Halle a.S.: Max Niemeyer.

Merleau-Ponty, M. 1964. *The primacy of perception*, J. M. Edie, ed. Evanston, Ill.: Northwestern University Press.

Ogden, C. K., and Richards, I. A. 1923. *The meaning of meaning*. London: Kegan Paul.

Penfield, W., and Jasper, H. 1954. *Epilepsy and the functional anatomy of the human brain*. Boston: Little, Brown.

Posner, R., and Reinecke, H.-P., eds. 1977. *Zeichenprozesse: Semiotische Forschung in den Einzelwissenschaften*. Wiesbaden: Athenaion.

Reilly, F. E. 1970. *Charles Peirce's theory of scientific method*. New York: Fordham University Press.

Russell, B. 1927. *An outline of philosophy*. New York: Meridian Books, 1960.

Schmidt, L. 1973. *Wortfeldforschung. Zur Geschichte und Theorie des sprachlichen Feldes*. Wege der Forschung CCL. Darmstadt: Wissenschaftliche Buchgesellschaft.

Shapiro, M. 1974a. Morphophonemics as semiotic. *Acta Linguistica Hafniensia* 15:29–49.

———. 1974b. Tenues and mediae in Japanese: a reinterpretation. *Lingua* 33:101–14.

———. 1976. *Asymmetry*. Amsterdam: North-Holland.

Slagle, U. 1975. A viable alternative to Chomskyan rationalism. *The first LACUS forum 1974*, A. and V. B. Makkai, eds., 177–93. Columbia, S.C.: Hornbeam Press.

Slagle, U., and Anttila, R., Forthcoming. Field theory and constant systematization in language. In *Papers from the third international conference on historical linguistics*, J. P. Maher, ed. Amsterdam: John Benjamins.

Vernon, M. D. 1971. *The psychology of perception*. Harmondsworth: Penguin Books.

Weiler, G. 1970. *Mauthner's critique of language*. Cambridge: At the University Press.

Between Linguistics and Semiotics: Paralanguage

IRMENGARD RAUCH

I

If language is the many children of several disciplines, then para-language is also; but paralinguistics is to linguistics, unfortunately, a neglected stepchild at most. George Trager's admonition, over twenty years ago, to the linguist that "communication is more than language" (1958:1) and that in using language we are ultimately dealing with and dependent on what he terms the "voice set", ". . . the physiological and physical peculiarities resulting in the patterned identification of individuals as members of a societal group and as persons of a certain sex, age, state of health, body build, rhythm state, position in a group, mood, bodily condition, location" (4), expresses a viewpoint with appeal to a growing number of contemporary scholars. One would certainly expect to find a receptive audience for it in today's pragmatic linguistics; however, David Crystal, in his recent overview of paralinguistics, reports: "Most linguists were—and are—of the opinion that paralanguage is at best of marginal significance to linguistics, and equally well or more appropriately studied by other disciplines" (1974:267).

This is surprising, in view of the fact that Crystal's study shows that linguists as a group do not appear to know what paralanguage is, what, precisely, it encompasses. In part, the responsibility for this ignorance resides with the twentieth century progenitors of paralanguage. On the one hand, Sievers' postulation of the physiognomic curves (1924); or Jakobson's recognition that, "In addition to the multiform intentional information, our talk carries inalienable and unalterable characteristics which are generated chiefly in the inferior part of the speech apparatus, from the abdomen-diaphragmal area to the pharynx" (1971:682); as well as Trager's conviction (quoted above) act as certain fulcrums in the linguistic inquiry of paralanguage. On the other hand, such certainty is by far outbalanced by a range of attitudes including complete rejection for linguistics, qualified inclusion, and equivocal assignment. Thus, for example, Trager's attitude is somewhat Janus-like in that it relegates paralanguage to metalinguistics and consequently to the periphery of language proper. Sapir, whose influence pervades the entire century, believed that: "All that part of speech which falls out of the rigid articulatory framework is not speech in idea, but is merely a superadded, more or less instinctively determined vocal complication, inseparable from speech in practice. All the individual colour of speech—personal emphasis, speed, personal cadence, personal pitch—is non-linguistic fact . . ." (1921:47). And finally, Archibald Hill, the creator of the term paralanguage, held kinesics and paralanguage to be one and the same field of communication activity (1958). In short, the seeds for obscuring the domain of paralanguage were inherent in its twentieth century rebirth for linguists by linguists.

And yet, Trager's "first approximation" of a paralanguage system still represents in essence all that the linguist has. Furthermore, it remains not without attraction for the linguist, because Trager employs the usable and familiar binary feature framework in (1) identifying *voice qualities* of pitch range, vocal lip control, glottis control, pitch control, articulation control, rhythm control, resonance, and tempo, and (2) isolating *vocalizations* consisting of (*a*) vocal characterizers such as laughing, crying, yelling, whispering, moaning, groaning, whining, breaking, belching, yawning, (*b*) vocal qualifiers such as intensity, pitch height, and extent, and (*c*) vocal segregates such as the onomatopoeic sequence in English *uh - uh* for negation or the hushing hiss *shhh*.

Crystal wrestles with alternatives such as human and nonhuman vocalization, vocal and nonvocal human communication, segmental and nonsegmental features or suprasegmental features alone, in an attempt to delineate the boundaries of paralanguage. He proposes for linguistic analysis "a *scale* of linguisticness" to approach the nonsegmental sound system. One of the distinguishing characteristics of his approach is the constraint that "Vocal effects lacking any semantic force would . . . be considered nonlinguistic . . ." (1974:281). It seems, however, that the determination of "semantic force" recycles the problem, since the field of linguistic semantics has an analogous problem of delimitation. A more fruitful enterprise, for the time being at least, would be to free ourselves of the compulsion to contain the field, and to seek simply the identification of paraphonological features on the basis of their necessary interdigitation with hard linguistic features. In the second part of this paper a data-based case is considered, in an effort to use cofeatures to determine a paralanguage feature. The case offers several added challenges, not the least of which is that it deals with a language void of live data, and thus brings to the immature field of linguistic paralanguage the further insight that the field is able to identify and to isolate a paralanguage feature setting the basis of articulation in a historical language.

II

The language chosen for the demonstration of paralanguage in a dead language is Old Saxon, once spoken in the northern part of the present primarily German speech area, and attested most fully in the two major ninth and tenth century manuscripts of the *Heliand*, an epic work of approximately six thousand lines. Old Saxon, among the historical German dialects, shares with Gothic the puzzling position of being extended in time without immediate predecessors or descendants. Preceding Old Saxon is only a reconstructed proto language, West Germanic, and succeeding is Middle Low German, not attested until some four hundred years after the *Heliand* data. That the provenience (date, place, author) of the *Heliand* manuscripts is unknown, on the one hand, stimulates linguistic investigation in search of philological answers and, on the other hand, leads to degeneration into circular argument, whereby the data are considered impossible to interpret because they have neither locational nor temporal identification.

The manuscript data are popularly held to be ambiguous due to the preponderance of orthographic variation. This has stimulated the development of many theories, which range from those that hold Old Saxon to be an indigenous koiné, albeit hybrid (e.g., Wolff's [1934] double-faced, original English–German character of Old Saxon), to those theories which advocate Old Saxon as a lingua franca or pidgin language, used for literary purposes in the case of the *Heliand*, for example, Mitzka's (1948/50) supradialectal business language.

Among the many debated Old Saxon linguistic data, the key vocalic issue is the determination of the sounds represented by the digraphs <uo>, <ie> and their variations, primarily the monographs <u>, <e>, respectively. *Heliand* manuscript M (ninth century Monacensis in Munich) exhibits approximately 1460 <o> spellings as opposed to 34 <uo> graphs, while *Heliand* manuscript C (tenth century Cottonianus in London) attests to some 1750 <uo> graphs against 119 <o> spellings. Assorted scattered spellings include <o, u, v, ó, oo, ou>. (The data for the <ie, e> distribution are parallel to those for the <uo, o> tabulation.) Obviously, the graphic evidence in these two major manuscripts is in direct conflict. In generative studies such as Voyles (1971), an optional diphthongization rule is posited, which may occur under primary stress, as in *guod* 'good,' or under secondary stress, as in the derivative suffix *-duom* in *kuningduom* 'kingdom'. The optionality designation thus completely sidesteps accountability for the fact that manuscript C tends to use digraphs, whereas manuscript M uses monographs. Voyles posits this optional diphthongization rule without any manuscript or dialect constraint. In so doing, he follows those Old Saxonists who exploit the manuscript material in continuous search of a common Old Saxon, that is, archetypal forms (e.g., Rooth 1956), even though it appears that he is interested in synchronics while the others are generally aiming at reconstructed language. The two generative dissertations, Barnes (1971) and Woods (1975), disappointingly contribute no insight into the diphthongization problem. Barnes dismisses the orthographic evidence by writing: "The actual phonetic value [of ie, uo, e, o] is not important as far as this dissertation is concerned" (52). Woods chooses to study the language of manuscript M only, for the reasons of text length, availability, and authenticity. The first two reasons are unfounded, if not erroneous; the third reason is a moot question, precisely the sort of question which a solution to the diphthongization problem could help answer. By studying M exclusively, Woods too, then, can avoid concern with digraphs for Germanic *$\hat{o}$, of which there are only thirty-four in manuscript M, and consequently with a possible diphthongization in Old Saxon.

Taxonomic studies such as Moulton (1961) serve to reinforce the dominant theory regarding the <uo> and <ie> graphs in Old Saxon scholarship of the past quarter to half century, namely, that the digraphs are prestigious orthographic borrowings from Old High German. Thus, Moulton's statement that <ie> and <uo> are ". . . nur als fränkische Orthographie für phonemisches [<ê, ô>] zu beurteilen" (1961:18) is reminiscent of Rooth's conviction that "Als Sachse sprach [der Heliand-dichter] *ô*, und die *uo*-Schreibungen müssen als solche, Schreibungen, gedeutet werden, die unter dem modischen Einfluss des Fränkischen standen" (1956[1973]:211–12).

It would seem that evidence such as the appearance of supposed High German orthography in manuscript M in a word such as *gilîk* 'like' (adverb), which occurs as *gilih* and *gilîch*, but its complete absence with High German Sound Shift spellings in manuscript C, should already weaken the researcher's faith in the orthographic borrowing theory. However, by and large, Old Saxon scholarship has been so mesmerized by the seemingly enigmatic orthographic data that attention has not been paid to phonological maneuvers within the total system, a failing which is rather surprising in view of the fact that linguistic structuralism was coterminous with the rise of Old Saxon studies in the nineteenth century. Van Ginneken (1956:576) posits as one of Jakobson's "sworn-comrades" rules that of "the tendency towards diphthongization of the main syllable and that towards apocope of the accompanying syllable." If we look at the end syllables in the digraph-producing manuscript C, we are stunned by the fact that their weakly stressed vowels are far better preserved than those of the monograph-producing manuscript M—a fact which has long been disputed and judged incongruous by researchers working with Old Saxon umlaut phenomena. In effect, we find in manuscript C a correlation in which glided vowels, if not full diphthongs, are compatible with full vowels, which then requires a rule that is the *converse* of the Jakobson–van Ginneken rule (van Ginneken 1956). The converse rule is possible if it is paralinguistically conditioned by the Tragerian vocal qualifier feature of *extent*, which opposes *drawl* to *clipping*. The drawl conditioner finds its substantiation not only in the preservation of weakly stressed vowels and diphthongs, but also in the cofeature of vowel epenthesis in the neighborhood of resonants (e.g., *burug* 'city'), which abound in manuscript C compared to manuscript M. Obviously, this view is not meant to disparage the orthographic data; that would be a false impression, since its premises rely heavily on orthographic evidence. What is rejected here is the outright simulation of foreign orthography, what we might call the parasite view, which should have been challenged all along, if for no other reason than that the *Heliand* manuscript C does not, in fact, mimic the Old High German diphthongization orthography. Consider, for example, manuscript C *nuon* 'none, the ninth hour', which reads *non* in manuscript M as well as in Old High German. Consider further that Old Saxon *hie* 'he' and *thie* 'that, who' (demonstrative, relative pronoun, masculine, nominative singular), with the digraph spelling <ie>, are words foreign to Old High German; and therefore, Old High German absolutely could not serve as a model for these Old Saxon words.

As can be expected, the implications of the converse Old Saxon diphthongization rule with its paralanguage conditioner drawl are many and stimulating. Within Old Saxon, the language specific social function of the paralanguage feature is of interest, while the transcultural mapping of a northern-southern isogloss may be suggested. A cursory examination yields indications of corroborating evidence from such Old Saxon allied languages as Middle Low German, Dutch, English, and High German, which could serve as a point of departure. This, in turn, certainly argues for a further search for possible northern-southern drawl or drawl-like isoglosses beyond the languages immediately involved here.

In a sense, the introduction of the paralanguage feature *drawl* into the Old Saxon phonological system represents a missing link in the breaking of the Old Saxon code. But, beyond this, it bespeaks the richness of linguistic paralanguage, the twilight zone between semiotics and linguistics, that awaits our investigation.

REFERENCES

Barnes, M. 1971. Phonological and morphological rules in Old Saxon. Ph.D. dissertation, University of California, Los Angeles.

Crystal, D. 1974. Paralinguistics. In *Current trends in linguistics, vol. 12: Linguistics and the adjacent arts and sciences*, T. A. Sebeok, ed., 265–95. The Hague: Mouton.

Hill, A. A. 1958. *Introduction to linguistic structures*. New York: Harcourt, Brace and World.

Jakobson, R. 1971. Linguistics in relation to other sciences. In *Roman Jakobson: selected writings II*. The Hague: Mouton.

Mitzka, W. 1948/50. Die Sprache des Heliand und die altsächsische Stammesverfassung. *Niederdeutches Jahrbuch* 71/73:32–91.

Moulton, W. G. 1961. Zur Geschichte des deutschen Vokalsystems. *Beiträge zur Geschichte der deutschen Sprache und Literatur* (Tübingen) 83:1–35.

Rooth, E. 1956. Über die Heliandsprache. In *Fragen und Forschungen im Bereich und Umkreis der germanischen Philologie* (Veröffentlichungen des Instituts für Deutsche Sprache und Literatur 8), 40–79. Berlin: Akademie-Verlag. (Reprinted in *Der Heliand*, J. Eichhoff and I. Rauch, eds., 200–46. Darmstadt: Wissenschaftliche Buchgesellschaft, 1973).

Sapir, E. 1921. *Language*. New York: Harcourt Brace.

Sievers, E. 1924. Ziele und Wege der Schallanalyse. In *Stand und Aufgaben der Sprachwissenschaft* (Wilhelm Streitberg Festschrift), 65–111. Heidelberg: Carl Winter.

Trager, G. 1958. Paralanguage: a first approximation. *Studies in linguistics* 13:1–12.

van Ginneken, J. 1956. Roman Jakobson, pioneer of diachronic phonology. In *For Roman Jakobson*, M. Halle et al., eds., 574–81. The Hague: Mouton.

Voyles, J. 1971. The phonology of Old Saxon(2). *Glossa* 5:3–30.

Wolff, L. 1934. Die Stellung des Altsächsischen. *Zeitschrift für Deutsches Altertum* 71:129–54.

Woods, J. D. 1975. A synchronic phonology of the Old Saxon of Heliand-M. Ph.D. dissertation, University of Massachusetts.